WOMEN IN ROMAN LAW AND SOCIETY

The legal situation of the women of ancient Rome was extremely complex, and – since there was no sharp distinction between free woman, freedwoman and slave – the definition of their legal position is often hard. Basing her lively analysis on detailed study of literary and epigraphic material, Jane F. Gardner explores the provisions of the Roman laws as they related to women.

Dr Gardner describes the ways in which the laws affected women throughout their lives – in families, as daughters, wives and parents; as heiresses and testators; as owners and controllers of property; and as workers. She looks with particular attention at the ways in which the strict letter of the law came to be modified, softened, circumvented, and even changed, pointing out that the laws themselves tell us much about the economic situation of women and the range of opportunities available to them outside the home. Dr Gardner concludes her study by considering to what degree Roman women in fact achieved 'emancipation'.

WOMEN IN ROMAN LAW & SOCIETY

Jane F. Gardner

INDIANA UNIVERSITY PRESS
Bloomington and Indianapolis

First Midland Book Edition 1991

Manufactured in Great Britain

Library of Congress Cataloging-in-Publication Data

Gardner, Jane F.
  Women in Roman law and society.
  Bibliography: p.
  Includes index.
  1. Women—legal status, laws, etc. (Roman law)—
history. I. Title.
LAW   346.45′6320134   86-45173
                344.563206134

2 3 4 5 6   95 94 93 92 91

ISBN 0–253–36609–7 cloth
ISBN 0–253–20635–9 paperback

Contents

Preface

1 Introduction   1

2 The Guardianship of Women   5

3 Marriage   31

4 Some Effects of Marriage   67

5 Divorce   81

6 Dowry   97

7 Sexual Offences   117

8 Children   137

9 Inheritance and Bequest   163

10 Slaves and Freedwomen   205

11 Women at Work   233

12 The Emancipation of Roman Women   257

Bibliography   267

Index   277

Preface

Source references and citations (on the Harvard system) of modern works are given in the notes to allow those interested to pursue matters in greater detail than was possible in the compass of this book. Periodical titles are abbreviated following the conventions of *l'Année Philologique*. Since it is hoped that others besides those with a conventional training in classical languages will be attracted by the subject, I have translated or explained Latin words and phrases, at least on their first occurrence, and also transliterated the occasional Greek one. Some guidance is given on the dating of persons and events; however, a basic familiarity with the outlines of Roman history is assumed.

I am grateful for helpful discussion and advice to Dr Edward Champlin, Professor John Crook and Mr David Noy; they are not to be held responsible if I have erred thereafter. Special gratitude is owed to Mrs Sybil Lowery for her patient preparation of a sometimes crabbed text.

Pietas (which I shall not attempt to translate) requires particular thanks to the Glasgow branch of the Scottish Classical Association and especially to the late Henry Chalk; it was a letter from him as their Secretary, inviting me to speak, that first set me thinking on the subject of Roman women.

Jane F. Gardner
University of Reading

1   Introduction

'You know nothing about law.' So my fellow undergraduates and I were told by an Oxford don, advising us on preparation for the dreaded General Paper in Ancient History in our final examinations. He was quite right. There has been less excuse for ignorance since the publication of the highly readable *Law and Life of Rome* (Crook 1967a). That admirable work set out to encompass a much wider subject than the present book, no less than the entire range of Roman law, expounding its principles and setting them in their social context. Women were mentioned where appropriate, although there was not space to examine in depth the relevant aspects of the law.

Hitherto, there has been no detailed study of Roman law relating to women. Women's studies made a relatively belated appearance among the concerns of ancient historians and classicists, and references to law, if made at all, tended to be confined mainly to marriage, *tutela* (guardianship) and divorce, not straying much further afield. The changes that occurred in those areas of the law have tended to be presented in terms of increasing independence for women, rather than of the possible purposes of the (male) makers of the law. What these purposes were is one of the themes that will be found threaded through this book.

An early tendency in Roman women's studies (to use a convenient phrase) was to rely mainly on literary evidence, restricted in period mostly to the last century of the Republic and the first of the Principate, and in subject matter to the upper classes and what Crook (1967a: 104) has called 'the antics of Roman "night-club" society'. This produced some rather over-dramatic accounts of Roman society and an exaggerated estimate of the self-assertiveness and independence of Roman women. Some late blooms of that crop are still appearing. A statement of the legal facts seemed desirable.

Attention to non-literary evidence such as papyri and inscriptions, on the other hand, has unearthed more information about the working and even the domestic lives of more ordinary women, both slave and free. This valuable material needs a historical frame of

1

reference if it is to be of use in shedding light on the nature of the society which produced it, and in that frame the rules of law are an important part. They are highly relevant, for example, to matters such as the economic situation of women and the range of opportunities available for them outside the home.

Many detailed studies of Roman law exist, written by and for lawyers. They follow a regular pattern of arrangement of topics, often exclusively from civil law, and concentrate on the setting out of all the legal rules in all their ramifications. They use the technical language of the subject, making few if any concessions to lay terminology or to the liking of ordinary people — ancient historians included — for the occasional relief of being told a story. Most are unreadable and most are unread, save under stress of necessity, by historians. A few more specific studies attempt to pull together the materials relating to a particular area of human concern or a particular section of society. Of those in English, Corbett (1930), *The Roman Law of Marriage,* is of the former type, and Buckland (1908), *The Roman Law of Slavery,* the latter, though both, especially Buckland, are still rather arid fare. The numerous monographs of Alan Watson are more palatable, and have rather more to say than either of the others about the historical and social background, but are restricted in scope.

The chapters which follow will study in detail the legal position of Roman women. Using non-legal as well as legal texts, they will attempt to show the ways in which in practice the law affected women in various aspects of their lives — in families, as daughters, wives and parents; as heiresses and testators; as owners and controllers of property; as workers. Slaves and freedwomen will be included, since in Roman society, unlike Greek, there was no sharp discontinuity between slave or freed on one hand and citizen on the other, and much of the Roman citizen population was ultimately of servile descent. On sexual offences, it may be instructive to compare emphases placed by the Romans and by contemporary societies.

Since, in many ways, an examination of the legal situation is as much an account of restrictions upon Roman women as of their rights, it will be important to give some attention to ways in which the strict letter of the law came to be modified, circumvented or softened, and the reasons for these. Particular attention must also be given to changes and development in certain areas of the laws themselves, and the question considered whether in fact, and how soon, Roman women achieved any significant degree of 'emancipation'.

In the course of our examination, something may also be discovered about the principles underlying the legal system, the nature of Roman society as the Romans themselves perceived it, and the changes in that society which in turn brought forth changes in the law. The views of individuals, jurists or emperors, may sometimes be observed, on how society was — or rather ought to be; for law, as I shall have occasion to say again, is about what people may or may not do, not what they actually do. Law is created for a number of purposes, but, in general, it is meant to serve what a given society conceives as its interests, by proscribing or prescribing particular actions. These interests tend to be those of the wealthier members of society, and so most of the legal system (and this is especially true of the Roman) is concerned directly or indirectly with the ownership of property.

The period under consideration will be roughly the last two centuries B.C. and the first three of our era, that is, the great classical period of Roman law. Before that, there is little usable evidence, though some mention will be made of the main changes thought to have occurred previously. After that, Roman law, like Roman society itself, underwent a number of striking changes, in part at least due to the Christianising of government. The legal position of women in later Roman society would more appropriately be the subject of a separate study.

2 The Guardianship of Women

With a few exceptions, all Roman women were for their entire lives subject to some degree of limitation on their capacity for independent legal action. Authority to act must either be obtained from, or was vested in, a man —father, husband or guardian *(tutor)*. Until the time of Augustus, the only exceptions were the six Vestal Virgins; after Augustus, freeborn women who had borne three children, or freedwomen who had borne four, and who were *sui iuris* ('independent', in the sense of being subject to the control neither of a father nor of a husband), were able to dispense with tutors. In the absence of statistics on the birthrate and the longevity of Roman men, we cannot determine what proportion of women benefited from this concession.

However, as we shall see, women were not necessarily so gravely disadvantaged in comparison with men as this bald statement might make it appear. Paternal authority over male and female children was almost equally comprehensive, successive modifications to the law relating to tutorship made it little more than a routine inconvenience and *manus*-marriage virtually passed out of use. Moreover, though control could be exercised harshly and oppressively, that does not entail that it usually was. What the law says people *may* do, as we must constantly remind ourselves, is not necessarily the same as what they actually do.

Daughters and *Patria Potestas*

A legitimate child was, from birth, subject to the control *(potestas)* of the father,[1] either as *filiusfamilias* (son) or *filiafamilias* (daughter). The father *(pater)* was head of the *familia,* the basic Roman social and property-owning unit. The *familia* under his control consisted of his children, whether living with him or not; his sons' children, if any; his wife, if married with *manus* (see p.11); and his slaves. The *pater,* therefore, could be the grandfather or even great-grandfather of some of the persons in his *potestas;* nevertheless, for convenience,

5

'pater' and 'father' will be used interchangeably. The *familia,* obviously, could include several nuclear families, living apart (those of the married sons), as well as daughters married and living in families belonging to other *familiae.* At the death of the *pater,* the children (and wife) ceased to be *alieni iuris* (subject to another's control) and became *sui iuris* (independent). Each adult son became a *paterfamilias;* no woman ever did — *materfamilias* in Latin was merely the term used to designate the wife, or strictly the wife in *manus,* of a *paterfamilias.* [2] A woman's children, if legitimate, belonged to the *familia* of their father; if illegitimate, they were *sui iuris.*

The powers of the *pater* were extensive,[3] and they lasted over his sons and their children as long as he lived, and over his daughters likewise, unless they previously had passed into the *manus* of a husband. Some of these powers, originating in a very primitive stage of Roman society when protection of the group rested on self-help rather than the rule of law, had become in their extreme form rather an embarrassment by the classical period. This applies particularly to the power of life and death (*ius vitae necisque*) and the powers of sale or surrender.

It was the father's right to refuse to rear the newborn child, and the mother had no legal power to prevent this. Child exposure was practised, and was not made illegal until A.D. 374, although the evidence does not allow us to determine whether there was any discrimination against girl babies. The father had also the right, as mentioned in the Twelve Tables and in the formula of adoption by *adrogatio,* to punish his children up to and including the infliction of the death penalty.[4] This was finally abolished in the reign of Valentinian and Valens. The authority of the *pater* over his children remained almost intact throughout the classical period. Although the authorities from time to time intervened to check abuses of disciplinary powers, and although the *pater* was expected to consult a council of family or friends before exercising severe discipline, no legal restrictions were introduced until later imperial times.[5]

Women condemned by the judgment of the state were sometimes handed over to their families for private punishment, as, for example, those condemned in the suppression of the Bacchanalia in 186 B.C. In A.D. 57 the Senate referred Pomponia Graecina, accused of 'foreign superstition', to her husband's judgment. He took the advice of relatives, who acquitted her. In 154 B.C., when Publilia and Licinia, the wives of two consulars, were accused of poisoning their husbands, their relatives took matters into their own hands. Giving bail to the praetor, they judged and condemned the women and carried out their execution by strangulation. Some of these women may have been *sui iuris*. In any case, what these examples reveal is the state's recognition of the continuing separate identity and authority of the family, in the wide sense. Men, once they were independent, were subject to the state's justice; sons *in potestate* and women were regarded as being still to some extent the responsibility of the family.[6]

Recorded instances of fathers actually putting their sons and daughters to death are few. In the case of daughters, unchastity was typically the offence felt to merit the penalty. Valerius Maximus reports two instances. Pontius Aufidianus killed both his daughter, who had lost her virtue to her *paedagogus* Fannius Saturninus, and also her seducer, 'so as not to have to celebrate her shameful nuptials'. A certain Atilius, himself a prostitute in his youth, killed his daughter because she had fouled herself with *stuprum* (sexual immorality). The daughter of P. Maenius, who was merely guilty of kissing her father's freedman, got off more lightly. Her father punished the freedman, as a warning to her to save herself for a husband.[7]

Augustus' *lex Julia de adulteriis* (18 B.C.) specifically allowed a father to impose summary justice on a daughter caught in the act of adultery in his or his son-in-law's house; but, as it must be imposed immediately and as he was obliged to kill the adulterer as well and must not kill either without the other, this in effect constituted a restriction on the *ius vitae necisque,* and it is possible that the intention was in practice to discourage such killing.[8]

Included in the power over the child's person was the right of sale or surrender. Originally this included the right to sell a child into actual slavery, but this was obsolete by the end of the Republic, except for noxal surrender. The *paterfamilias* was legally liable for the actions of his children, both male and female, as well as his slaves, and if one of these committed a delict, the *pater* must either make himself responsible in court for the damages, or surrender the guilty person. In order to terminate *potestas,* the surrender had to be accompanied by the formal procedure of mancipation, which took the form of a notional sale, repeated three times in the case of a son, while once sufficed for a slave. There was originally no distinction of the sexes in noxal surrender, though the classical jurists use the masculine, and it is assumed by some moderns that surrender of daughters had become obsolete before the end of the

Republic. Justinian, formally abolishing noxal surrender except for slaves, says:

> The ancients permitted this also both for male and female children in the *familia*. Modern society, however, has considered that such harshness is rightly to be rejected and this has passed out of common usage. For who allows his son and especially his daughter to undergo noxal surrender to another, so that the father is almost at personal risk, rather than the son, while in the case of daughters due regard for modesty rightly excludes this?

The implication is that surrender had in practice been abandoned earlier for both sexes.[9]

Notional sale was used classically in certain situations where it was desired to terminate or create *potestas* — that is, emancipation, adoption and the various applications of *coemptio* (see pp.12 and 17). Only men could adopt, since only men could have *potestas*. *Adoptio* in the strict sense, i.e., of someone in the *potestas* of another, involved the abolition of the *potestas* by a notional sale, which had to be performed three times for a son, but only once for a daughter. The adopter then claimed the child as his. The other form of adoption, *adrogatio,* was used only in the case of persons already *sui iuris*. In form, it was a legislative act, carried out by thirty magisterial lictors, representing the curiate assembly of the Roman people and summoned by the Pontifex Maximus. The formula used is preserved by Gellius. It was accepted that women could not be adopted by this method; there would have been little point, indeed, as the procedure, involving as it did the destruction of one *familia* or potential *familia* (that headed by the *sui iuris*)was not lightly to be undertaken, and was intended for use when it was urgently needed in order to save a *familia* and also its domestic worship (*sacra*) by providing an heir. Women could have no direct legal heirs, in this sense, and could not found a *familia*.[10]

There is some evidence suggesting that ex-slave married couples sometimes secured the enfranchisement of children born to them in slavery. Whether they adopted them is unknown — in inscriptions, such children would not necessarily be differentiated in designation from freeborn children. If the parents did wish to adopt them, however, *adrogatio* was probably the only available method, since it is uncertain whether adoption of slaves was permitted. The ineligibility of women for adrogation meant, then, that the slave-born daughters of such couples probably could not be adopted into their natural families. However, adoption conferred little legal gain. The father's patron (former owner) had a claim against adoptive children of up to half the estate on intestacy, and until A.D. 178 intestate succession to a woman's estate did not go in the first instance to children, and after that, both legitimate and illegitimate children had a claim (by the *senatusconsultum Orphitianum*).[11]

The fictitious sale was also used to emancipate the son or daughter from *potestas*. Again, a son was 'sold' three times, a daughter once. One purpose of emancipation was to allow the making of a will, which was not possible for someone under *potestas*. Another common reason was to fulfil the conditions of an inheritance left to the child. Persons *alieni iuris* had no legal ownership over property, and so any bequests to them would simply be absorbed in the father's property. Sometimes a testator specified that this was not to happen. Pliny describes an instance. Domitia, the daughter of Domitius Lucanus, had been made the heiress of her maternal grandfather, Curtilius Mancia, on condition that her father emancipated her. Mancia evidently disliked and distrusted his son-in-law and wanted to prevent his taking over the inheritance. However, Mancia's wishes were initially frustrated, for the child was promptly adopted by her father's brother Tullus, an elderly and childless man, and since the brothers were operating the family property jointly, the girl's inheritance came under Lucanus' control after all and only subsequently into her possession when she became Tullus' heir.[12]

Persons *in potestate* could own no property. Anything given or bequeathed to them belonged to the *pater*. The principle, despite its manifest inconveniences, and indeed absurdities, remained valid throughout the classical period. A son might be a grown man, with an active commercial or professional career, active in public life, even a leading magistrate, married and with children, and yet legally own nothing. A daughter might be married and a mother — even, like Cicero's daughter Tullia, who predeceased him, have had several marriages. Ways round the difficulty were devised. The son was, like the slave entrusted with business as his master's agent, given control over a sum of money or some property, a *peculium*.[13] Soldiers were even, from Augustan times, given testamentary rights over it. Probably as a result of the existence of *peculium*, sons and slaves were allowed to undertake contractual obligations. Daughters were not. Does this mean that they had no *peculium*? Ulpian interprets the masculine gender as covering both sexes, in a passage of the praetorian edict granting actions *de peculio*. Pomponius speaks of a situation in which a woman draws upon her *peculium* to provide herself with a dowry. Gaius says the action is granted 'especially when the woman (whether daughter or slave) is *sarcinatrix* (clothes-maker or clothes-mender) or weaver or engaged in any common trade.'[14]

This, the sort of work that dependent women might do to help the family income, could perhaps involve the need of some capital for materials and stock, if the women were working separately and not as part of a family enterprise. However, the Egyptian and Pompeian evidence for weavers shows employment, mostly, though not entirely, of slaves, in a 'factory' situation, with the worker supplying only the labour.[15] As we shall see later, for the most part the evidence for working women seems to concern family firms, or freedwomen, who are *sui iuris,* or the provision of labour and services. In other words, the situation of the dependent daughter or female slave operating a business and needing a *peculium* would be much less common than that of the son or male slave. A married son would also need access to some income for running his house-hold; the married daughter, on the other hand, would normally be equipped with a dowry, which had its own set of legal regulations.

Real life is never so tidy as the law, and in most households, even if no specific grant of *peculium* was made, there must have been a certain amount of hard cash handed over by the father for the women's personal purchases, as well as an accepted treating of various items and commodities as common household property. This sort of situation is reflected, for married life, in the detailed discussion of lawyers as to what did or did not count as a gift between husband and wife.[16]

The *pater*'s consent was necessary to the marriage of sons or daughters. In early law, *their* consent may not have been needed, but in the classical period it seems that a father could not force his son to marry. The daughter's situation is less clear. Ulpian[17] indi-cates that non-objection on her part is taken as consent, but goes on to limit her right of refusal apparently to cases where the groom is morally undesirable. Since the legal minimum age for the marriage of girls was twelve and betrothal could happen even earlier, their consent, for a first marriage at any rate, may often have been formal. It is clear nevertheless both from legal and non-legal texts that in practice older sons and daughters often took the initiative in matrimonial matters — Cicero's daughter Tullia is perhaps the best-known instance. From the time of Augustus, they could appeal to a magistrate if their father refused to permit the marriage.[18]

Sons and daughters in 'free' marriage, remained subject to the father's *potestas* after marriage.[19] Until the time of Marcus Aurelius, a father could dissolve his children's marriages even against their will. Thereafter, he was prohibited from breaking up a happy marriage (*bene concordans matrimonium*).[20]

The situations of sons and daughters wishing to divorce were not symmetrical. A son married in free marriage could probably divorce irrespective of his father's wishes. If he had married with *manus*, his wife was technically in his father's *potestas* and the latter must be involved. A daughter married with *manus* was out of her father's control. One married in free marriage could, at least until late in the classical period, divorce only through the *pater*.[21]

The father's death terminated *potestas*. Both sons and daughters had equal rights of intestate succession. Both became *sui iuris* at his death, but whereas the adult son now became fully capable of independent legal action, including the right of testamentary disposition, and acquired the powers of a *paterfamilias*, a woman had no *familia*, or, rather, 'she is both the source and the end of her own *familia*',[22] since she had no *potestas* over her children. Her legal capacity was limited by the requirement of having a tutor, whose authorisation was necessary for a wide range of legal transactions. Furthermore, until the time of Hadrian, in order to make a will she must also go through a form of *coemptio* (see below).

Wives and *Manus*

Manus (literally 'hand') meant a relationship in which the wife stood in the power of the husband. She was regarded as being *filiae loco*, in the situation of a daughter, in relation to her husband. She had the same rights of intestate succession as her husband's children. His power over her, though, was more restricted than that over his children. He did not have the right of life and death over her, nor of noxal surrender or sale (other than the fictitious one in a fiduciary *coemptio*). She could possess no property of her own; everything was vested in her husband or in the latter's father, while he lived, and anything accruing to her by gift or bequest or in any other way during the marriage was absorbed into her husband's property.

However, once widowed, the wife married *cum manu* had two

important advantages; it was possible, at least by 186 B.C., for a husband to give his wife in his will the right to choose her own tutor;[23] and as by entering into *manus* she had undergone *capitis deminutio*, a change of status,[24] she could make a will without the need of a further *coemptio*. These advantages might be regarded as offset by the likelihood that, husbands being generally younger than fathers,[25] she would have to wait longer to enter into independence than a woman married without *manus*. She would also be unable to invoke the protection of her *pater*, as she had passed out of his *familia*, nor, of course, did she retain any rights of intestate succession in her family of origin.

Manus could come into existence in three ways, of which two, *confarreatio* and *coemptio*, were procedures usually gone through at the time of marrying, while the third, *usus*, became effective only after a year.[26]

Confarreatio[27] took its name, we are told, from the use of a cake made of spelt (*far*) in a sacrifice made to Jupiter. Its survival into the Empire was ensured by the fact that it was essential for the maintenance of the state religion, since the principal *flamines* and the *rex sacrorum* had to be born of parents so married and the priesthood must themselves marry in this way. It may have been confined to patricians.

In A.D.23, because of a shortage of candidates for the office of *flamen Dialis*, a law was passed, based on a *senatusconsultum* of 11 B.C., to the effect that the wife of the *flamen* should come under her husband's *manus* only so far as religious rites were concerned; in all else, she was to have the status of a woman in free marriage.[28] Tacitus cites as reasons for the unpopularity of this form of marriage distaste for the difficulties of the ceremonial and the 'negligence' (*incuria*) of both men and women. This probably refers to their lack of interest in the maintenance of the priesthood. Further reasons he mentions are not only that it involved the wife's entering into *manus* but also that the *flamen* himself was removed from paternal jurisdiction. We should not be justified, therefore, in supposing that the apathy or antipathy lay mainly among women.

Coemptio[29] for matrimonial purposes (to be distinguished from *coemptio fiduciae causa*)[30] was a form of notional sale of the woman. If she were *sui iuris*, the consent of 'all her tutors' was needed, since all her property would pass with her; responsibility for her existing debts, however, remained with her.[31] Two instances of *coemptio* in one family in the first century B.C. are known from the so-called

Laudatio Turiae.[32] One of these, between the parents of 'Turia', was apparently contracted some considerable time after the marriage. Gaius, in the second century A.D., speaks of it as a living institution, but it is likely to have been rare even then. Paul speaks of *conventio in manum* in relation to Augustus' laws on adultery; Ulpian mentions it in relation to a pronouncement of Antoninus and Commodus; for Servius in the fourth century it is already a practice of the past.[33].

Usus involved no ceremony. After one year of marriage, a wife passed into the *manus* of her husband, unless, as provided in the Twelve Tables, she stayed away for three nights, repeating the manoeuvre every year. This method of creating *manus* was already obsolete by Gaius' time; known to Cicero, it was possibly no longer automatic in his day. It was abolished by statute, possibly under Augustus.[34]

Watson (1967: 21–23) suggests that the three-nights' rule finally disappeared around the end of the first century B.C., being replaced by a requirement (based perhaps on an interpretation of another clause in the Twelve Tables about the usucaption of a woman's property) for the authority of the *tutor legitimus* to be given for *usus,* and that this requirement was then extended to *all* tutors and to *patres* as well. In other words, instead of contracting out of *manus* deriving from *usus,* it would be necessary to contract in.

The avoidance of *manus,* then, is attested from the time of the Twelve Tables — too early for it to be attributed to a 'humanistic' trend in Roman family law, still less to feminine rebellion.[35] Like so much family law, both in Rome and in other ancient societies, it has to do with the transmission of property — in this case, probably with a desire to try to keep the property of the *familia* as intact as possible.[36] Dowry was probably not recoverable at the time of the Twelve Tables,[37] whether a marriage ended in death or divorce, nor was any legacy bequeathed to a wife *in manu.* Even if left *sui iuris* by her husband's death, she would be unable to make a will without the consent of her tutor, probably a close relative of her husband. In free marriage, however, even if dowry was not yet, at the time of the Twelve Tables, returnable, the wife's *pater* assumed any property accruing to her during his lifetime, and after his death, though retaining her rights of intestate succession in her family of origin, and henceforth possessing property in her own right and independently of her husband, she was in the tutorship of her agnates (unless her father had made a will and provided otherwise) and unable without their consent to make a will which might bequeath her property away from her family of origin (e.g., to her children).[38]

The ascription of motives, however, in anything to do with the transmission of property through Roman women is always dangerous, because, private sentiments apart, the interests of the man as father tended to conflict with those he had as husband. To have a wife *in manu* would secure him more property for the *familia;* to have a daughter in free marriage would tend to prevent property going out of the *familia*, at least in the early state of Roman law. As we shall see later, sentiment gradually gained ground, though never entirely ousting the claims of the *familia*.

Women and Tutors

All children with no *pater* were required to have a guardian, *tutor impuberis*. For boys, this tutelage ended at the age of fourteen, and they became legally independent. For girls, the *tutela impuberis* ended at the age of twelve, only to be replaced by the *tutela mulieris*. An adult woman (*mulier*) who became independent on the death of her father or husband was also required to have a tutor.[39]

Tutors were appointed in a number of ways, the three principal being the intestacy of the father or husband, by will and by magistrate's appointment. The oldest type attested, and the most significant as an indication of the original purpose of the institution, was the *tutor legitimus*. Where the father or husband had made no provision in his will, the *tutela* was assigned to the male agnates, either all or the one nearest. For the daughter, this would usually be her brother or paternal uncle, or even her cousin in the paternal line. If she had been married with *manus,* the most likely would be her husband's brother, or even her own son. Attested in the Twelve Tables, this rule was not abrogated until the reign of the emperor Claudius.[40] If there were no agnates, the *gens* could claim the *tutela,* and did as late as the middle of the first century B.C. The woman commemorated in the *Laudatio Turiae* had resisted a fraudulent claim of this sort.[41]

A freedwoman had no agnates, as she had no *pater,* but on manumission her patron (former owner) became her *tutor legitimus.* A woman emancipated by her *pater* could have him as her tutor. Strictly, he was her *tutor fiduciarius* (see below), but as the 'manumitting parent' (*parens manumissor*)[42] he was regarded by the jurists as having *tutela legitima,* similar to that of a patron, with the difference that the patron's male descendants inherited a *tutela legitima,* while that of the *parens manumissor* became fiduciary in the next generation. Otherwise, the *tutor legitimus* normally appeared only in cases of intestacy.

A *tutor testamentarius,* or *dativus,* was one appointed by the will of the father or husband. The latter (though apparently not the former) could allow the woman to choose her own tutor, a right first attested for the year 186 B.C. This option could be limited or unlimited — i.e., the woman could, according to Gaius, unless specifically limited, change tutors as often as she wished.[43] 'Obviously,' says Schulz, 'a woman chose only a person whom she could rely on to raise no difficulties about giving his *auctoritas.*'[44] The question must be asked: why, in that case, should Roman men be willing to allow such unfettered control and disposal of property to women married with *manus* while withholding it from daughters, married or unmarried, who had been in their fathers' *potestas,* and from freedwomen? Were all women in the latter categories regarded as less sensible and responsible than *manus*-widows? In any case, with the progressive decline in *manus*-marriages, the women able to benefit, even supposing that *all* husbands in that category gave them the choice, would become a diminishing, and ultimately negligible, proportion of the whole, and so even the unlimited possibility of changing tutors, mentioned by Gaius, would represent no very substantial accession to the 'emancipation' of women in general.

The original motivation of the provision that a widow might be allowed choice of tutor (bearing in mind that we do not know how long before 186 B.C. it had been available) may be connected, like the decline of *manus,* with the preservation of the property of the *familia.* A woman *in manu* acquired no property — it was absorbed in that of her husband — and, except for certain rights over her dowry, what she received by his will depended on his generosity. A remedy for nearest relatives who felt unjustly treated in a will, the *querela inofficiosi testamenti* ('complaint of unduteous will')[45] was available to her, but this, though established by the time of Trajan, may not have originated until almost the end of the Republic. So, in a sense, the husband's *familia* stood to lose only what he had decided he was willing to spare. As to the risk of the woman choosing a pliable tutor, one should not overlook the ties of affection with her family of origin, or the possible pressures exerted by it, or, indeed, the likelihood that, for many widows, specially the younger ones, the men best known to them would be those of their own original families (and not of their husbands'). The choice of tutor, then, might often fall on one of the woman's natural relatives. As husband, the Roman took a limited risk of the *familia* losing; but as father, brother, uncle, etc., he probably expected it to gain, especially as the woman could now acquire further property in her own right and since if he as tutor consented to her making a will he might avoid the property's all going back eventually to the husband's family.

A decree of the Senate passed in the time of Marcus Aurelius and Commodus (A.D.175–180) prohibited marriage between a female ward and her tutor or his male descendants, to prevent any conceal-ment of mishandling of the property. An exception was made where the girl's father had betrothed her to her guardian or expressed a desire for the match in his will. Whether, conversely, a husband was banned from being tutor to his wife, except as appointed in the father's will, is not known. Examples of husbands as tutors are found in Roman Egypt, both before and after the date of the decree, but these may have been influenced by Greek practice.[46]

If a tutor had been appointed in neither of the above ways, the *lex Atilia* (c.210 B.C.) provided for appointment at Rome by the urban praetor and a majority of the tribunes of the plebs. A freedwoman with a woman patron had a tutor appointed in this way. From the time of Claudius, the consul also could appoint, and later emperors extended the function to other magistrates in Italian towns and Latin towns and colonies. In the provinces the governors could make appointments under the *leges Juliae et Titiae* (mid-first century B.C.). Egyptian examples indicate that the woman herself might suggest a suitable candidate: 'To Claudius Valerius Firmus, prefect of Egypt, from Aurelia Ammonarion. I ask you, lord, to give me as tutor Aurelius Plutammon, according to the Julian and Titian laws and the Senate's decree.' The prefect confirms the grant, adding 'providing that this is not to the exclusion of a just tutor' (meaning, presumably, a *tutor legitimus*).[47]

Women requiring to be assigned a tutor by this method would include those whose fathers or husbands had made no testamentary provision for a tutor and (before Claudius) who had no agnates; also freedwomen whose patron had died with no male issue;[48] and women whose tutors had died or undergone *capitis deminutio*, by captivity or in some other way.

A magistrate could also appoint a replacement tutor,[49] e.g., when a lawsuit was being brought against an existing tutor, or when the temporary absence of a tutor was impeding the transaction of legal business. Replacements were not allowed for *tutores legitimi,* e.g., for agnates (before Claudius), manumitting parents, patrons or their sons. Freedwomen would be the largest group of women affected by this ban, and they were allowed even temporary replacements only for important matters affecting their property, such as the acceptance of an inheritance or the creation of a dowry. The grounds for the ban, as for certain other exceptions in their favour, was probably that the interests of *tutores legitimi* were involved, since they had succession rights. Since no lower limit seems to have been set for the distance (and so the duration) of the absence, this magisterial replacement is usually interpreted as a mere device for change of tutor, underlining the unreality of the *tutela* in classical law.

Other methods of changing tutor were by *cessio* and by *coemptio fiduciae causa,* both of which represented a real surrender of the succession rights of *tutores legitimi. Cessio* was open only to the *tutores legitimi* of women, not to those of minors. They were allowed to make formal surrender of the tutorship to another person; on his death, or that of the original tutor, the *tutela* reverted, in the former instance, to the original tutor, in the latter to the person next in degree to the original tutor.[50] In the interim, however, the woman might have obtained the new tutor's consent to such radical action as, e.g., the making of a will.

Coemptio fiduciae causa[51] was a notional sale of the woman, with the tutor's consent, to a man of her choice, who then manumitted her and became her *tutor fiduciarius.* As we have seen, when this means was used to end *potestas,* with a slightly more involved procedure, ending up with the *pater* as tutor, he was regarded as a *tutor legitimus,* and so protected the family's rights of intestate succession. Before the time of Hadrian, it was a necessary condition, for any woman who had not otherwise undergone *capitis deminutio* (e.g., by *manus*-marriage or manumission), in order to be qualified to make a will. It was not a sufficient condition, however; the tutor's consent was still necessary for the making of the will, and could be compelled — but only if the tutor was not a *tutor legitimus.* The wider application of *coemptio fiduciae causa* was simply as a device for changing tutors.

While the duties of a minor's tutor could include the administering of the ward's property, those of an adult woman's tutor consisted of interposing his *auctoritas*, i.e., giving or withholding consent to certain of her actions. This was required if the action were of a kind that might diminish the property — alienation (including manumission of slaves), undertaking contractual obligations, promising a dowry, marrying with entry into *manus*, accepting an inheritance (since that could involve liabilities) and making a will.[52]

Authority was required for alienating only the type of property classed as *res mancipi*, namely, slaves, oxen, horses, mules, asses, land in Italy both urban and rural (which included also any buildings on the land)[53] and rustic servitudes — that is, the land itself and the power of man and animal needed to work it, which were the bases of production in the peasant economy.[54] Anything else, a woman could dispose of freely, and she was free to purchase what she could.[55] She could sell sheep, goats, poultry, jewellery, clothes, furniture, houses and land outside Italy — in short, everything that was *res nec mancipi* — and she could lend money. Faustilla, who appears several times in graffiti at Pompeii, seems to have been a pawnbroker, receiving such items as earrings and cloaks as pledges for small loans.[56]

Obviously, the well-to-do would be most affected by the need for tutor's authorisation, especially in a society in which land was the principal form of wealth. Of the landowners owning clay-yards in the Roman area in the second and third centuries of our era thirty per cent were women, of whom ten (from a total of about fifty) were members of imperial families and seven possibly of senatorial rank. As many women as men proprietors are known from the time of Antoninus Pius, and inheritance from father to daughter is common.[57] Domitia Lucilla, of whom we have already heard, inherited a clay-yard in A.D. 108 and bequeathed it in due course to her daughter, who became the mother of Marcus Aurelius.[58] In three recently published papyri from Oxyrhynchus we find three sisters, apparently sharing family estates with their brother, a local gymnasiarch and banker, and contracting with a potter to make jars in their workshops, from materials supplied by them, apparently as containers for the wine produced on their estates.[59]

The requirement of tutorial consent for marriage and for the creation of a dowry reveals the original concern of the Romans to control movement of property between *familiae*. Consent was apparently not needed for marriage without *manus* even in the early Republic, and by Cicero's time consent was needed for the establishment of *manus* both by *usus* and *coemptio*.[60].

As stated above, a valid will could not be made without a tutor's authorisation, and until the time of Hadrian it was also necessary for the woman to undergo *capitis deminutio*. The reason for the requirement of *capitis deminutio* is obvious, namely to break agnatic ties. Buckland and Kaser both derive it from the primitive *tutela* of the agnates, at the period when they necessarily inherited the property. Watson, however, points out that it can scarcely predate the introduction of the will made *per aes et libram* (again, a kind of notional sale), the only form originally open to women, and the only one of the three ancient procedures of will-making surviving into the classical period.[61] Gaius believes that the procedure *per aes et libram* was introduced later than the other two forms.[62] It is not mentioned in the Twelve Tables, and views vary on the date of its introduction, yet the agnates' monopoly of the *tutela* (of minors as well) was already broken by the time of the Twelve Tables, which provided for testamentary tutors.

The combination of a tutor from outside the group of the agnates and an available testamentary procedure would make it easier for women to leave property away from agnates. It must be remembered that, for a widow who had been married with *manus,* the agnates in question would be those acquired through her husband. Watson's view[63] has much to recommend it, that the original purpose was to allow women who had married with *manus,* at a time when this was still common, to leave property back to their natural relatives, but that, as the rule was expressed in terms of *capitis deminutio,* it was open to other women to satisfy the qualifications by *coemptio*. From a humane point of view, this would, for example, enable the wife married without *manus* to make bequests to her husband and children — and, incidentally, also to her own family, since *coemptio,* other than to her father, would have extinguished the agnatic succession.

The tutor's consent was also required for any actions tending to diminish the property. This was originally intended to restrict the movement of property away from the *familia*. By Gaius' time,[64] however, tutors, except for *tutores legitimi,* could be compelled to give their consent. The latter could not be compelled, because their interests were affected. They were the heirs on intestacy (and they had it in their power to ensure intestacy). Most of the women affected would be freedwomen; for them, the tutor's authority continued to be a real and active restraint. The law operated in the interests of patrons. Other Roman women, intestacy being the exception rather than the rule among their menfolk,[65] did not usually have *tutores legitimi,* and for them the main advance towards independence in controlling their property came, not with Claudius' abolition of the *tutela* of their agnates, but much earlier, firstly with the supersession of control by the agnates by provision for testamentary tutors and later — tantalisingly, we do not know how much later — by acquisition of the means to compel tutors' consent through application to the praetor. The principle of discouraging dispersal of family property was maintained in other ways than through the *tutela* .

Augustus' social legislation drove a coach and horses through the concept of *tutela*. By the provisions of the *lex Julia* (18 B.C.) and the *lex Papia Poppaea* (A.D.9) women were released from the necessity of having a tutor if they had three children (four, for a freedwoman). The richer and more influential could, by imperial dispensation, obtain the relief without the children.[66] Given the primitive state of medicine and postnatal care,[67] one may speculate upon whether women thought the bargain a good one, specially freedwomen, whose children born before their manumission did not count. Where the patron was also the husband, the tutorship might not be irksome, so long as the marriage went well. Daughters with a father living had to wait to be orphaned or emancipated before they could benefit from their fecundity.

Nevertheless, some women did achieve the 'privilege of children' (*ius liberorum*), and it is frequently cited in papyri from Egypt. One third-century document survives from which we gather that women claiming the right to be exempt from tutelage had to apply to the prefect's office (or, presumably, that of the appropriate official elsewhere) to have their claim placed on record.[68] Aurelia Thaisus, also known as Lolliane, says:

Women honoured with the privilege derived from children are given the right to act independently and to conduct their own affairs, in any business they transact, without a guardian, much more so women who know how to write. So I also, having the good fortune to be honoured with many children, and being literate and able to write excellently well, with complete confidence apply to your Highness through this petition, so that I may henceforth be able to conduct my affairs without any impediment.

A copy of the prefect's reply is appended: 'Your application will be placed on record'.

Obviously, illiteracy would hamper a woman in the full exercise of her right, but literacy was not a requirement for the *ius liberorum*. Aurelia is probably not boasting, so much as, nervous of officialdom and ignorant of the precise requirements of the law, anxiously including what she feels might buttress her claim.

The existence of women *sui iuris* who were not required to consult tutors made it difficult to find a justification for the continued existence of *tutela*. Gaius comments:[69] 'The early lawyers thought that women, even if they had reached majority, ought to be in *tutela* because of their lack of serious judgment (*propter animi levitatem*)', but remarks that this opinion does not correspond with observed facts. 'There appears,' he says,

> to be hardly any worthwhile argument for women of full age being in *tutela*. The common belief, that because of their instability of judgment they are often deceived and that it is only fair to have them controlled by the authority of tutors, seems more specious than true. For women of full age manage their affairs themselves, and in certain cases the tutor interposes his authority as a matter of form and often is obliged by the praetor to give his authorisation even against his will.

That, he points out, is why adult women cannot bring suit against their tutors for their conduct of the tutorship, while tutors who administer the affairs of minors are accountable.

It is not because his consent can be compelled that the tutor is not legally accountable, for *tutores legitimi* could not be obliged to give consent. Their unaccountability is grounded rather in the fact that, unlike the tutors of minors, they did not administer. Even the power of the *tutor legitimus* was essentially negative — he could prevent action. As individuals, tutors might from time to time offer women advice, but if the women chose to take it and it turned out badly, that was not the law's concern.

Women's supposed weakness of judgement or, more generally, weakness of their sex (*imbecillitas sexus*) is an idea, possibly deriving from Greek philosophy, which is repeatedly asserted in rhetorical literature from Cicero onwards.[70] It gained some colour from the ignorance of law and business practice forced on many women by their exclusion from public life, which in turn was made to justify this exclusion. It did not correspond with the observed facts that many women could and did handle their affairs competently,[71] nor with the whole trend of legislation and with legal practice. The illogicalities and absurdities of the situation arose from the contradictions between men's political and public roles and their private and personal relationships. The retention of *tutela* meant the retention of the appearance at least of men's control over the disposal of property. It is as well to remind ourselves, however, of the difference between what is permitted and what is done. That a tutor's consent *could* be compelled does not entail that it usually *had* to be; that the assent of a *tutor legitimus* could not be compelled does not prove that it was normally withheld.

The silence in literary sources about the tutor's part in the property dealings of women such as Cicero's apparently efficient wife Terentia[72] indicates that in such a case it was a matter of form. However, the tale of the inexperienced and trusting Caesennia is instructive. She has a tutor from her own family, who eventually becomes heir to her first husband's estates on the death of their son, and who, Cicero assumes, must have given his consent to her 'buying' land from her husband, since this is a manoeuvre involving her dowry. When, however, she subsequently buys another estate, although she takes the advice of friends and relatives beforehand, her tutor apparently is not involved at all. Caesennia commissions an outsider, a certain Aebutius, to handle the actual negotiations for the purchase. She is prepared to believe that she needs a man to handle her financial affairs, even handing over her account books to Aebutius. After her death, he is found to have cheated her of the estate.[73]

Women outside the Family: Vestal Virgins

The legal status of the priestesses in charge of the cult of Vesta was anomalous in a number of ways.[74] Girls of citizen birth of all ranks were eligible to be Vestals, including, from A.D. 5, the daughters of freedmen.[75] They must be between the ages of six and ten at entry and must not merely have both parents living, but that parenthood must be unblemished. So, neither the girl herself nor her father must previously have been emancipated, since that would make her technically orphan. In A.D. 19, when two girls were offered to fill a vacancy, one was rejected because her parents were divorced.[76]

Tacitus' words (*in eodem coniugio manebat*) seem to indicate that the other's mother was *univira* — this had been her one and only marriage.

On becoming a Vestal, the girl passed out of *potestas*. She did this, however, without undergoing *capitis deminutio* and without emancipation. Although she had passed out of her father's *potestas*, she was not fully independent, since she was subject to discipline by the Pontifex Maximus.[77] However, he does not appear to have stood to her in the relation of a *pater* (or of a husband in a *manus*-marriage). He could inflict corporal punishment, but had not the *ius vitae necisque*. Vestals who broke the rule of virginity and were condemned *incesti* could be put to death, but only after an investigation by the whole pontifical college.[78] This was not the equivalent of a domestic council, since the entire college seems to have borne joint responsibility.[79] The punishment (entombment alive) does not correspond to the usual treatment of *stuprum* or adultery or 'incest', in the narrower sense. The Pontifex Maximus was not a tutor either; Vestals were exempt from *tutela*.

The Vestal lost her rights of intestate succession in her family of origin, as normally happened on emancipation (even though she had not been emancipated), and if she died intestate no one had rights of intestate succession. Her property went to the public treasury. Labeo comments: 'What legal principle is involved is uncertain.' Moyle finds the explanation in the Vestal's relationship to the gods: 'Her life had been devoted to their service, and it was only consistent that, on her dying without disposing of her property by will, it should go to the treasury for sacrificial purposes.'[80] This is unsatisfactory. In the first place, although the Vestal was involved in a number of the state's religious rituals, connected with the worship of various gods, she was in the service, strictly, only of Vesta. In the second place, we are nowhere told that the escheated property was earmarked for sacrificial purposes. Moyle is drawn to this rather desperate suggestion because he finds the Roman jurist's puzzlement inexplicable if the solution were simply that she had no agnates, having lost her agnatic family, and that as a woman she could have no direct heirs on intestacy. Much more likely is the suggestion of Guizzi,[81] who draws attention to the fact that the remark comes from Labeo's commentary on the laws of the Twelve Tables. Labeo may have been puzzled to find this provision about the Vestal's estate apparently at so early a period, when escheat of vacant estates to the treasury was a much later development in Roman law.

There were other anomalies. Without *capitis deminutio* or *coemptio*, the Vestal had nevertheless acquired the right to make a will. She had property to dispose of: besides any gifts or inheritances that might come her way, she received a sum from the state on entering the order, and was paid a stipend.[82] The money from the state should perhaps be regarded as a kind of *peculium*, to compensate for the loss of her patrimony. The sum on entrance is not to be compared with a dowry; there is no real warrant for the view that the Vestal was the 'bride' of the Pontifex, like the queen of the sacral king in early Rome.[83] By the time of Augustus, candidates were in short supply. Fathers were reluctant to offer their daughters. Augustus tackled the difficulty by extending eligibility to the daughters of freedmen and, later, by giving Vestals the *ius liberorum*, and Tiberius raised the sum on entry to two million sesterces.[84] The benefit derived from the *ius liberorum* was not exemption from *tutela*, which they already had, but freedom from the restrictions on inheritance which Augustus' legislation had imposed on the unmarried and childless.

The Vestal could manage and dispose of her property as she liked, being free from *tutela*.[85] The function of tutors was essentially to protect not the person but the property, in the interests of the *familia*. Since the Vestal's *familia* no longer had any rights to her estate, the tutor's function was gone.

Beard's suggestion (1980: 17) that the Vestal's sexual status was ambivalent, that they were, in part, classified as male and that this is shown by their being given certain privileges almost exclusively associated with men, does not really fit the facts.[86] A man, on emancipation, became fully independent and head of a new *familia*, losing his inheritance rights in his family of origin. The *flamen Dialis* who, like the Vestal, passed out of *potestas* without emancipation or *capitis deminutio*, became a *paterfamilias* in his own right and founded a *familia;* however, he did not lose his inheritance rights. The Vestal did not become fully independent; as a woman, she could not found a family; and, in contrast to the *flamen*, her loss of succession rights is specifically attested. She had no tutor; but she had left her family in her father's lifetime, without emancipation or passing into another family. No one, therefore, *could* stand to her in the relation of a tutor, whether *legitimus*, testamentary or of any other sort. Also, like other women, she had no direct heirs on intestacy. The oddities of her position seem rather to arise from her position as one in charge of a worship central to the whole state and not belonging to any one family in the state. She was taken out of her family, with certain legal consequences, but she did not cease to be a woman.

After thirty years, the Vestal was free to leave the order and marry, if she wished. It is said that few did, and that they came to an unhappy end and regretted their choice.[87] Tradition has preserved the names of a few Vestals who served a great deal more than thirty years but, disappointingly, no details of the ill fate that befell the brides. Perhaps it was nothing less commonplace than that likely to befall a virgin, by then relatively elderly and infertile, attracting a husband by money rather than by youthful looks and the prospect of children. Possibly also their way of life, a mixture of public receipt of respect and deference and exercise of a measure of power with private subjection to discipline and meticulous observance of ritual, left them ill-suited to ordinary domestic matrimony.

The juridical consequences of a return to private life can, in the absence of direct evidence, only be guessed at. It has been suggested that a return into *potestas* was possible,[88] the Vestal having, in the interval, been notionally in the *potestas* of the goddess, possibly in a position juridically comparable to that of a prisoner of war. Captivity, whether of father or of child, removed *potestas* but did not destroy it, merely holding it in suspense, as it were. On the end of the captivity, all anterior rights were restored.[89] In the procedure at the Vestal's entry into the college, unique to Vestals among the Roman priesthood, she was 'taken'. 'As if taken in war' is, however, only Gellius' own interpretation, and although he also says that the law was that the Pontiff should take the girl 'and she should become Vesta's (*eaque Vestae fiat*)', these words are not found in the formula of the *captio*, which he quotes from Fabius Pictor's *History* (early second century B.C.)[90] The parallel is, in any case, very limited in application. A prisoner had *no* rights; the Vestal, as we have seen, had extensive privileges.

Certainly, the Vestal had not changed status by emancipation or *coemptio* or any other legal process. If leaving the order merely restored her to her former status, she would either come once again under her father's *potestas* or, in the more likely event of his being already dead, be required to have a tutor for her property dealings and be unable to make a will without tutor's consent and *coemptio*. That is, she would lose her special independence. Such a consequence might well carry weight in a Vestal's decision to remain in the order (though it could be an inducement to relatives to encourage her to leave). Problems could arise, however. If a father had died, without including in his will a clause of disinherison, the ex-Vestal, on recovering her rights of inheritance, could attack his will on these grounds, or more generally as 'unduteous' — not very logically, perhaps, since he had had no legal duty to include or specifically exclude one who, at the time, was no longer one of his direct heirs, but certainly legally. No test case is recorded, and no such claim has left any ripples in the legal tradition. However, it was open to fathers to bequeath legacies (within the limits of the law) to their Vestal daughters, and that might have sufficed.

The argument from silence cannot really help us here in determining the character of the Vestal's status while a Vestal or the juridical consequences of her ceasing to be a Vestal. The sources are detailed and specific on the privileges attendant upon membership of the order. On the situation of those who left we hear only that they were unhappy and unfortunate.

Notes

1. On *patria potestas* in general, see RE XXII. 1040 ff.; Buckland (1966) 101–4; Kaser (1971) 60–65, 345–350; Watson (1977) 23–30.
2. Cic. *Top.* III. 14; for the wider sense D. 50.16.46.
3. But for their gradual 'humanising' see Schulz (1936) 166 ff.
4. XII T.4.2; Gell. *N.A.* 5.19.9
5. Mommsen (1899) 18–26; Schulz (1936) 165–168, 198–9; Kaser (1971) 60 ff., 341–345; Rabello (1979) 144 ff.
6. Livy 39.18.6; Tac. *Ann.* 13.32; Livy, *Per.* 48; Val. Max. 6.3.8; Mommsen (1899) *l.c.*, especially p.19; Kunkel (1966), especially pp. 238 ff. Note, however, that two of the cases cited are concerned with religion, rather than solely matters provided for under the criminal law. In the third, the poisoning, although a criminal offence, occurred within the family.
7. Val. Max 6.1.3 and 6.
8. *Coll.* 4.8.; D. 48.5.21,23,24; Corbett (1930) 137–9; Raditsa (1980) 313; Richlin (1981) 399 n.5. For the view that this provision of the *lex Julia* applied also to the daughter married *cum manu* and constituted a power separate and distinct from the *ius vitae necisque*, see Rabello (1979) 215–224.
9. G. IV. 74, 79; *Inst.* IV. 8.7; D. 9.4.2 and 32 ff.; Buckland (1966) 104, 603; Watson (1967) 99.
10. XII T. 4.2.; Cic. *leg.agr.* 2.12.31; G.II. 101, 104; Gell. *N.A.* 5.19.9.
11. On the enfranchisement of children, see Fabre (1981) 198–9. Adoption of slaves: Watson (1967) 90–98. Inheritance to freedmen: see especially G.III. 40–41. *Sctum Orphitianum:* Meinhart (1967).
12. G. I. 132 ff.; Pliny, *Ep.* 8.18
13. Crook (1967c) 119–120.

14. G.III. 104; (Ulpian) D.15.1.1.2–3; (Pomponius) D.23.3.24; (Gaius) D.15.1.27.pr.

15. D'Avino (1967) 14–21; Moeller (1969) 561–6; Hengstl (1972) 87 ff. Occasional references in literary sources to independent workers suggest that they made a meagre living: Kampen (1981) 121–3.

16. D.24.1 *passim.*

17. D.23.1.12.

18. Cic. *ad. Att.* 6.6.1, *ad Fam.* 3.12.2; D.23.2.19; Corbett (1930) 4; Watson (1967) 45.

19. As Lewis (1970) shows, this was one of the areas in which, in Egypt, lay minds were confused by the variation in rules between Roman and non-Roman codes; see also Taubenschlag (1955) 130–149.

20. Paul. *Sent.* 5.6.15.

21. Corbett (1930) 242 argues against this that numerous texts of the Digest presuppose that she had this liberty. It does not seem, however, that the texts he cites establish his point.

22. D.50.16.195.5.

23. Livy 39.19.5; G.I.150–4; Watson (1967) 148; Kaser (1971) 368.

24. Ulp. *Reg.* 11.13.

25. Though there are instances of relatively old men eventually being married to young wives; Cicero and the younger Pliny are examples.

26. G.I. 108–15, 136; Ulp. *Reg.* 9; Boethius *in* Cic. *Top.*3.14; Serv. *ad. Georg.* 1.31 ff; Gaudemet (1953) 323–53; Kaser (1971) 76–81; Watson (1975) 9–19. Although they are sometimes described as having been originally forms of marriage (e.g. Corbett (1930) chapter III; Watson (1967) chapter 3), it is now generally accepted that *manus* and marriage were separate and distinct from the earliest times and that the performance of *manus*-ceremonial was not essential to constitute legal matrimony. (Volterra (1940) 2–29; (1948) 675 ff.; Schulz (1951) 115; Huber (1977) 121 n. 1).

27. Corbett (1930) 71–8; Kaser (1971) 76–8.

28. G.I.136; Tac. *Ann.* 4.16.

29. Corbett (1930) 78–85; Watson (1967) 24–5.

30. G.I. 114–5, 136–7; in neither type was the woman reduced to servile status (*ib.* 123). MacCormack (1978) 179–197 attacks the view that *coemptio* is evidence for primitive marriage by purchase (cf. Volterra (1948) 686).

31. Cic. *pro Flacco* 84; G.III. 84,IV. 38.

32. FIRA III no. 69; Durry (1950); Horsfall (1983).

33. G.I. 136; *Coll.*4.2.3.; Ulp. *Reg.* 26.7; Servius *l.c.*note 26 above; Meinhart (1967) 67.

34. G. I.111; Gell.*N.A.* 3.2.13 ff.; Wolff (1939b) 145–83; Watson (1967) 21–3. Villers (1950) suggests that it was still operating as late as A.D.57.

35. Schulz (1936) 189 ff.; (1951) 103 ff.; Balsdon (1962) 179. However, the early establishment of separate property of husband and wife has important consequences for the social and economic independence of women. Gratwick (1984) 46–49 suggests possible social, financial and political considerations influencing fathers, at least in the late Republic, to avoid *manus*-marriage for daughters.

36. Wolff (1939b: 178–9) suggests that an additional motive, after the legalisation of marriages between patricians and plebeians by the *lex Canuleia* (c.444 B.C.) may have been to avoid putting a patrician bride in the *manus* of her social inferior.

37. Watson (1965b: 38 ff.; 1971: 67; 1975: 39).

38. Watson (1967: 152 ff.; 1971: 22 ff.).

39. On *tutela* in general, including that of women, see G.I. 142–96; D.26 *passim;* R.E. VII A. 2.1497 ff.; Schulz (1951) chapter V; Zulueta (1953) II. 42–52; Buckland (1966) chapter 4; Watson (1967) chapters 9–12; Kaser (1971) 85–90, 352–69.

40. G.I. 155, 157, 164, 171. Of course, even after Claudius, agnates could

still be appointed as tutors in other ways; for examples from Roman Egypt, see Taubenschlag (1955) 172 n. 9.

41. FIRA III no. 69 vv. 18–24. Details are lacking, but the *gentiles* seem to have argued that *coemptio* (of the mother) had broken the father's will, made earlier (Watson (1967) 25 and 121–2). This could have been because either the mother, now one of his *sui heredes* (direct heirs) would need to be instituted heir, or a disinherison clause put in the will.

42. G.I. 166, 172, 175, 192; II. 122.

43. XII T.5.6; Livy 39.19.7; G.I.151–3.

44. Schulz (1951) 185–6; in the case of a tutor for a single transaction, he says, she would get him to promise his consent in advance.

45. *Ibid.* 275 ff.

46. Corbett (1930) 44–6; Taubenschlag (1955) 175.

47. G.I.185, 195; Kaser (1971) 357–9. On the dates of the laws see Kaser, *l.c.*, p. 357, nn. 42 and 47 and, on the *leges Juliae et Titiae*, Taubenschlag (1955) 32 and RE XII 2391–2. For the formulae used, see Cavenaile (1958) 307–10; Modrzejewski (1971); FIRA III, nos.24 (quoted above) and 25. In the latter, a man makes the request on a woman's behalf.

48. First attested in 186 B.C.: Livy 39.9.7.

49. G.I. 173–83.

50. G.I. 168–72.

51. G.I. 114–5; Buckland (1966) 119–20; Watson (1967) 152 ff.; Kaser (1971) 324.

52. Cic. *pro Flacco* 84; G.I. 178, II. 118, III. 176: Ulp. *Reg.* 1.17; *Frag. Vat.* 45; *Inst.* I.21.

53. *Inst.* II.1.29.

54. G.II 14–19, 80–4; Buckland (1966) 239; Diósdi (1970) 56–58.

55. Pliny's friend Corellia, for example, buys land of his valued at 900,000 sesterces (*Ep. 7. 11 and 14*).

56. Lending money: G.II.81. Faustilla: *CIL* IV. 4528, 8203, 8204; Andreau (1974) 119 ff.

57. Helen (1975) 112–3; Setälä (1977) 210–11, 232–40.

58. Setälä *l.c.,* 209; for the family tree, Syme (1968) 72–105.

59. *P. Oxy.* L. 3595–7; Cockle (1981). In 3595, the girls being still minors, a guardian (*epitropos*) acts for them.

60. Watson (1967) 149.

61. References in note 51 above.

62. G. II. 102.

63. Watson (1971) 11 ff.

64. G. I. 190–192, II. 122, III. 43; Schulz (1951) 188–9; Zulueta (1953) II. 51–2.

65. Crook (1973) 38–44.

66. Dio 55.2; G.I. 145 and 194; Paul *Sent.* 4.9. Pliny (*Ep.* 10.94) petitioned Trajan successfully on behalf of his friend Suetonius. Further benefits conferred by the right were accelerated careers in public life (for men) and relief from the disabilities Augustus had imposed on the childless in regard to the receipt of bequests.

67. See Celsus' *Medicina,* especially II. 7.16, 8.14, 30 (danger of diarrhoea to pregnant women) and the 'pharmaceutical' books of the elder Pliny, *N.H.* XX–XXXII. Tombstones — admittedly evidence of doubtful statistical reliability — seem to show high mortality in women between the ages of fifteen and twenty-nine (Durand 1959–60; Hopkins 1966). For the consequences for a woman's health of repeated pregnancies, inadequate medical care and, especially for poorer women, lack of rest after confinement, see Rice (1939) chapter III and appendix 3.

68. *P. Oxy.* XII 1467 — FIRA III no.27; Taubenschlag (1955) 177. On literacy in Egypt, Calderini (1950) 14–41, Lewis (1983) 59–64. Literacy was not a requirement

in Roman law for exemption from *tutela*. From a total of 110 women acting without tutor known from papyri from Roman Egypt, 36 give some indication of their literacy, and of these 29 are *agrammatoi*, i.e., illiterate (Sijpesteijn 1982: 158–71).

69. G. I. 144, 190–1.

70. Cic. *pro Murena* 27 and references in Schulz (1951) 181–2.

71. Huchthausen (1974) observes that about a quarter of the imperial rescripts addressed to private persons between A.D. 117 and 305 were addressed to women. Although the proportion rises sharply under Diocletian, women still account for almost a fifth in the period from Hadrian to Alexander Severus.

72. Terentia: RE V A 714 ff.

73. Cic. *pro Caecina*, esp. 11–18; discussed in Rantz (1982).

74. On Vestals in general: RE VIII A 1732 ff.; Guizzi (1968).

75. Dio 55.22.5.

76. Tac. *Ann.* 2.86.2.

77. Plut. *Num.* 10.

78. Cornell (1978) 31.

79. Livy, *Per.* 63; Cornell (1978) *l.c.*

80. Labeo, quoted in Gell. *N.A.* 1.12.18; Moyle (1912) 183.

81. Guizzi (1968) 166–7.

82. Will: Plut. Num. 10, Gell *N.A.* 7.7.2: G.I. 145. Money from the state: Livy I. 20; Tac. *Ann.* 4.16.

83. Mommsen (1887) II. 53; RE VIII A 1740 ff.; Beard (1980) 15.

84. Suet. *Aug.* 31; Tac. *Ann.* 4.16; Dio 55.22.5., 56.10.2.

85. Plut. *Num.* 10; G.I. 145.

86. Of the other examples she cites, the privilege of having a lictor, not exclusively male, as she admits, since it is shared by the wife of the *flamen Dialis,* is an honour attaching to the public function of the Vestal. On giving evidence see, as well as Gell *N.A.* 7.7.1, *ib.*10.15 and Guizzi (1968) 174–5.

87. Plut. *Num.* 10.4; Dion. Hal. 2.67.

88. Denied by Düll (1953) 380 ff.; Guizzi (1968) 196 is more inclined to entertain the possibility.

89. Guizzi (1968) 66.

90. Gell. *N.A.* 1.12.11, 13–14; G.I. 130; Ulp. *Reg.* 10.5; Guizzi (1968) chapter 2, especially 35–45.

3 Marriage

In a society with an advanced level of agriculture, an economy capable of producing, at certain levels, a significant surplus, and a clearly defined hierarchical social order, one should expect to find that the arrangements for marriage, as for transmission of property by inheritance, show a concern to maintain the status of the family as a whole by maintaining the status of the sons and daughters in each generation. Certain features are to be expected, such as selection by the family of suitable partners (arranged marriages), monogamy (to avoid too much dispersal of property) and dowry provision.[1] More will be said about dowry later; meanwhile, it is interesting to note that the younger Pliny on one occasion (*Ep.* 6.32) contributes to the dowry of a friend's daughter in order to enable her to keep up appearances appropriate to her husband's position. In all three respects, then, Roman marriage arrangements conform to the pattern.

The Legal Requirements for Marriage

Certain conditions must have been fulfilled for a marriage to be legally valid (*iustum matrimonium*).[2] Otherwise, a cohabiting couple were not married. The conditions were three: legal capacity — *conubium*; age — puberty; and consent of the relevant parties. The nonfulfilment of any of these conditions meant that no legal marriage existed.

Capacity — conubium

There was legal capacity if both parties were free and citizen. Slaves had no *conubium*, and although inscriptions from large slave households may apply the terminology of marriage to continuing relationships between members of the household, these had no legal status as marriages and no juridical effects.[3] There was no *conubium* between Roman citizens and foreigners.

This seems a simple doctrine. In practice, it was qualified in

31

relation to numerous categories of persons. Latins and foreigners (*peregrini*) might be given *conubium* by special grant. Gaius' account (to be discussed more fully later) shows that the main concern is with the status of children born of the union.[4] *Potestas* existed only over children born of a *iustum matrimonium*, or, in other words, only such children could be admitted to an existing *familia*. So, the *lex Aelia Sentia* (A.D. 4) gave informally manumitted slaves, known as *Latini Juniani*, the incentive to show themselves solid members of society, by providing that, through marriage and production of a child who survived to one year of age, they could obtain citizenship, and, for the father, *potestas* over the child, i.e., in effect, the father could become a *paterfamilias* (and, incidentally, ward off his patron's claim on his estate).[5]

Much more numerous, however, were the categories of persons between whom, although of citizen status, there was no *conubium*. Marriage between patricians and plebeians, still invalid at the time of the Twelve Tables, was legalised soon after by the *lex Canuleia* of 445 B.C., although it is possible that, at least as late as 186 B.C., it was regarded as quite reasonable and justified for a tutor to refuse consent for a rich woman to marry with *manus* outside her own *gens* ('clan-group').[6]

Marriage between freeborn and freed was probably valid throughout the Republican period, although ill-regarded socially, at least in the higher ranks of society.[7] Evidence on this is scanty. What is clear is that by Augustus' legislation on marriage of 18 B.C. senators and, from the time of Marcus Aurelius at least, their male and female descendants for three generations were banned from marrying several categories of person: freedmen and freedwomen, actors and actresses and their children, prostitutes, procurers, procuresses and their ex-slaves, convicted adulterers and persons convicted in a public prosecution. With the exception of the freed, all these were regarded as *probrosi* — morally reprehensible. Actors and actresses were regarded as no better than prostitutes (and no doubt often were), and a similar assumption was made about barmaids and waitresses. A *senatusconsultum* from the early years of Tiberius forbade senators, *equites* and their families to work as actors or gladiators. That the marriage ban was concerned with upholding the dignity and status of the upper classes is clear from Paul's commentary on Augustus' *lex Julia* on adultery: a senator's daughter, he says, who has been a prostitute or an actress or been condemned in a criminal court *can* marry a freedman, because she has forfeited her rank. Marriage of a senator with a respectable freedwoman could scarcely be condemned on moral grounds, but Augustus' marriage legislation (*lex Julia et Papia*) elevated to a legal prohibition what had previously been expressed only in social disapproval.[8]

Freeborn men of humbler rank could and did marry freedwomen, sometimes their own.[9] In a sample of 198 couples of whom one partner was freed, there were 174 freedwomen, of whom 30 were married to freeborn (or probably freeborn) men, and 13 of these men were their patrons. On the other hand, only 11 of the 159 freedmen were married to certainly or probably freeborn women. This may reflect a relatively greater social disapproval of the latter type of union.[10] Attitudes seem to have hardened by the time of Septimius Severus at least. A constitution of that emperor banned a freedman from marrying not only his own patroness, but the widow or female descendant of his patron. It was made a punishable offence, with condemnation to the mines as penalty, though Ulpian expressed the opinion that it might as well be overlooked when the patroness herself was of such lowly status 'that even marriage to a freedman would be honourable for her.'[11] It seems then that, while slaves of both sexes, at least in the towns, might reasonably aspire to freedom and marriage with their former co-slaves or other ex-slaves, slave women, except in the imperial household (Weaver 1972: 175–6), had better prospects of social mobility. The reason for the sex differential may be to do with inheritance. A freeborn grand-father might not welcome the prospect of some of his patrimony passing to the children of a freed son-in-law; a freedwoman, how-ever, could not affect the transmission of her father-in-law's estate.

Some functions or offices created a ban on marriage. Tutors, as we have already seen, were banned from marrying their wards save in specified circumstances. By imperial mandate, provincial officials might not, during the course of their term of duty, marry a woman of the province, except in their native province. Both prohibitions were presumably intended to guard against the exercise of undue influence by the man. If they cohabited, this was not in itself penalised. Some later jurists held that the woman (but not the man) ought to be allowed to receive under her partner's will; in other words, their relationship should not be regarded as *stuprum*.[12]

Soldiers, probably from the time of Augustus, at least, were forbidden marriage during their time of service, and marriages previously contracted were dissolved on entry into military service.

One such case is probably illustrated in a papyrus from the second century A.D., a document witnessed by seven Roman citizens. Demetria, daughter of Lucius, acting through her tutor, declares that she has made some sort of arrangement (the text is unclear at this point) with Gaius Valerius Gemellus, serving with the ship *Draco* of the imperial fleet at Alexandria, 'to whom she was previously married and from which marriage she bore sons, Justus aged 14 and Gemellus aged ten, and to whom she specified a dowry.' Valerius Gemellus acknowledges receipt of the dowry. This document is incomplete and has been variously interpreted. The most probable explanation is not that it represents an arrangement for return of dowry upon dissolution of the marriage, but rather that, the marriage having been annulled by the husband's enlistment, he and Demetria are making sworn declarations that a marriage *had* existed, the purpose being to attest the legitimacy of the sons and protect their inheritance rights, and also to identify and secure the dowry property to Demetria in the event of Valerius' death.[13]

Despite the ban on marriage, soldiers could and did contract unofficial liaisons during their period of service. Under the empire some attempts were made, possibly in the interests of maintaining recruitment, to mitigate the effects of the ban by allowing the men to enjoy the inheritance rights under Augustan laws of married men, and by protecting the inheritance of their illegitimate children.[14] Their women's interests, however, were less well catered for. If the soldier lived until discharge, he had *conubium* and he and his 'wife' and children all had or were given citizenship, and a regular marriage could be contracted.[15] If he died in service, she might be left high and dry. While he lived, she could, unlike a wife, receive valid gifts from him, and she had the dubious advantage of being unable to be prosecuted for adultery. On the other hand, she could not at his death or the end of their relationship for some other reason reclaim anything she might have given him as a dowry. In A.D. 117, the prefect Lupus in Egypt refused a woman's claim to some money deposited with a soldier, now deceased, on the grounds that it could not constitute a dowry, since soldiers were not able to marry.[16]

Even if made a beneficiary under a soldier's will, a woman might have difficulty in establishing her right to inherit. An enactment of Domitian had banned from receiving inheritances women of known immoral life. Hadrian had confirmed in a rescript that this applied to bequests in soldiers' wills, and this was taken to apply also to 'good-time girl' camp-followers.[17] A soldier's relict might find herself obliged to try to demonstrate the essential respectability of her character and of her association with the deceased. Demetria was probably trying to forestall such problems by preparing documentary evidence well in advance.

There was no *conubium* between persons related in certain degrees. Broadly speaking, marriage between ascendant and descendant was forbidden at all times, even if the relationship was contracted by adoption, and even if the adoption was subsequently cancelled by emancipation. In the early Republic, until about the end of the third century B.C., there was apparently no *conubium* between cognates up to the seventh degree, that is, second cousins. This rule (and probably also the restriction of ascendant–descendant relationships) derived from custom, not law, and it was first broken, we learn from a fragment of Livy, Book 20, by a patrician. Such exogamy doubtless made sense in a primitive stage of society, as security against the potential hostility of other territorially based clan-groups. In classical Rome, however, there is by the second century B.C. an observable tendency to endogamy within or between certain aristocratic *gentes*, and by the first century B.C. marriage between first cousins was permitted.[18]

In the senatorial class, the political aspects of such marriage alliances are too well attested to need comment; and both there and at lower levels of society a degree of endogamy could be a strategy, along with the encouragement of marriage without *manus*, for trying to restrict the dispersal of family property. Few, however, are likely to have carried it so far as the egregious collection of people featured in Cicero's *pro Cluentio*. To be fair, though, the tangle of intermarriages described in that speech between the families of the Aurii, the Cluentii and the Oppianici, are mainly engineered by the acquisitive pair Oppianicus and Sassia. They end up married to each other, having brought off also a match between his son by a previous marriage and her daughter by a previous marriage (her second) to a man who, apart from being her nephew by marriage, had been married to her daughter by her first marriage. Cicero is duly shocked, but does not say the matches were actually illegal in his day. The precedent of the emperor Claudius made it possible for a woman to be married to her paternal uncle; however, maternal uncles and aunts on either side were excluded by imperial constitutions, and in the course of the early empire the rules seem to have been explicitly formulated and laid down.[19]

In short, by the time of Gaius, a woman was banned, on grounds of relationship, from marrying any ascendant or descendant, a collateral within the third degree (except her paternal uncle) and certain in-laws. She could marry her sister's former husband or her former husband's brother, but not her father-in-law or son-in-law. She could not marry her stepfather, but could marry his son by a different mother. (Adoption was no bar to collaterals, once either party had been emancipated.) In contrast to classical Athens, where sons excluded daughters from inheriting, Roman daughters had equal inheritance rights with sons, and so there was no institution corresponding to the Athenian epiclerate.[20]

Roman practice was not universal within the Roman world. Notoriously, in Egypt full brothers and sisters married. Found occasionally in Pharaonic royal families, more often in Ptolemaic, the practice is frequently attested among commoners in Roman Egypt. Though it was illegal for Roman citizens, some nevertheless followed local custom. The *constitutio Antoniniana* of A.D. 212, conferring citizenship on the free inhabitants of the empire, made such unions illegal for all the population of Egypt and created embarrassments and some attempts at concealment.[21]

Elsewhere in the Roman empire, also, there seems to have ensued upon the wholesale acquisition of Roman citizenship a lengthy period in which people, possibly through genuine ignorance, persisted in habits which had been legal under their own systems of law. Eventually, Diocletian and Maximian in A.D. 295 issued a ferocious-sounding edict[22] against the behaviour of those who 'rushed into illicit unions in the promiscuous manner of farm animals or wild beasts, driven by execrable lust, with no regard for decency or righteousness'. Their conduct, arising, say the emperors, from inexperience or ignorance of the law, deserves the most severe punishment. They ought to think themselves lucky to get away with their lives. Anyone breaking the rules after December 30, 295, will be punished with appropriate severity (the decree is dated May 1, 295), and no one need expect clemency. Nevertheless, despite all this huffing and puffing, what the edict amounts to is a complete amnesty for illicit unions to date, though it is pointed out that the children of these unions are not legitimate. For the future, there is no mention of any additional penalty.

A union outside the permitted degrees was 'incestuous' (*incestum*). The word, meaning also 'unchaste' is used of sexual relations with a Vestal Virgin, and also of 'incest' in the narrower sense, as in English, i.e., sexual relations between close relatives. Since there was no *conubium* within the specified degrees, these unions would come under the penalties for extramarital sexual relations which were established by Augustus' law on adultery, the *lex Julia de adulteriis coercendis* (18 B.C.), which created a range of sexual offences punishable by the state. Despite its title, the law was concerned with *stuprum* in general, of which adultery and *incestum* were types.[23]

All forms of union outside marriage and concubinage were treated by the *lex Julia* as delicts. The usual punishment was banishment and, where both adultery and *incestum* were involved, deportation to an island.[24] Jurists, however, were disposed at times to regard the woman's fault as less grave than the man's. From the mid-second century A.D. imperial jurisdiction *extra ordinem* tended to the remission of penalty for the woman, and even for both, so long as the liaison was given up, in cases which deserved special consideration. Marcus Aurelius and Verus gave a reply to a certain Flavia Tertulla:

> We are influenced by the length of time during which, in ignorance of the law, you have been in matrimony with your uncle, and by the fact that you were placed in that state by your grandmother, and by the number of your children. In view of all these contributing factors, therefore, we confirm the status of the children you had of this union, which was formed 40 years ago, just as if they had been legitimately conceived.

It is clear from the tenor of this reply that Tertulla is being given a special concession, and that this decision is not meant to constitute a precedent. We do not know where she lived. Presumably, the uncle was on her mother's side. Whether he is still living is not clear, nor why Tertulla should be anxious about the children's right to inherit.[25]

Incidentally, under the Augustan law sexual relations between unmarried couples, whether they were betrothed or not, were *stuprum* and therefore constituted an offence. Cohabitation without evidence of sexual relations was apparently not an offence.[26] English society has grown accustomed in recent years to acceptance of premarital sex and of the practice of couples living together for some time before the marriage ceremony. In Roman society, as we shall see, marriage dated not from the performance of a specific formal ceremony but from the wife's entry to the husband's home. Luckily, in the eyes of the law, children could be born anything from six to ten months after conception,[27] a fact which gave time for shotgun weddings and avoidance of the consequences of a conviction for *stuprum*, should any ill-wisher choose to prosecute.

Marriageable Age

A legal marriage existed only if both partners had reached puberty. For boys, it was still disputed in Gaius' time whether this should be determined by examination of physical development or simply fixed at the age of 14.[28] Even proponents of the former view accepted that age should be the criterion in the case of a *spado* (one naturally impotent). This was important, since for a boy entry into manhood meant release from *tutela* and the assumption of political and legal rights and responsibilities, from which impotence alone would not be held to disqualify him. Impotence was not a disqualification for marriage either, though castration was.[29]

For girls, puberty was deemed in law, from at least the time of Augustus, to have been reached at the age of twelve, and a girl was therefore marriageable at that age.[30] The actual onset of menstruation probably occurred later for most girls. Medical opinions placed it as occurring in the fourteenth year, and modern research concurs.[31] Girls, therefore, could legally be married before they had in fact reached puberty. Various questions arise. Were some girls in fact married as young as twelve years of age? Were such marriages in fact consummated fairly early on, even before the girl reached puberty?[32] Did some girls cohabit before the age of twelve?

The evidence, literary, epigraphic and legal, seems to point towards an affirmative answer to all three questions, though it does not enable us to state with any degree of confidence what proportion of relationships this represents.

Literary sources give several examples of girls in upper-class circles who were married young. Cicero's daughter Tullia was relatively mature — engaged at twelve, married at 16 and a widow at 22. The emperor Claudius' daughter Octavia was married at 13, and Agrippina, Nero's mother, at twelve. Several other women of the imperial house married at between 13 and 15 years of age.[33]

Some funerary inscriptions enable a calculation of age at marriage, e.g., by giving age at death and length of marriage. Such evidence is biased in several ways. There is a class bias; only those who could afford it would commemorate their dear ones. There is likely also to be an age bias; women who predeceased their husbands were perhaps more likely to be commemorated by them than widows were by their relatives. Census declarations from Egypt also have some bias. Nevertheless, both types of record show a substantial proportion of early marriages.[34] Out of 171 inscriptions in Harkness (1896), 67 recorded women married before the age of 15 and 127 before the age of 19. Some were apparently 'married' even before the age of twelve; in the sample in Hopkins (1965b), eight per cent were married at ten or eleven. Of 155 married women in the Egyptian census declarations, 51 were married before the age of 20, and 16 before the age of 15; to these should probably be added others who had not had children before the age of 20. Hajnal points out that these figures show a different marriage-pattern from that of post-mediaeval Europe, which was characterised typically by high age at marriage and a high proportion who never married.[35]

Legal evidence also indicates that marriage at twelve was not unknown. Several texts are concerned with the juridical status of a relationship where a girl less than twelve years old was already cohabiting with a man. Pomponius says: 'A girl wed (*nuptam*) before the age of twelve will become a lawful wife when she has attained the age of twelve while still cohabiting'. Ulpian, citing Labeo, and Papinian both speak in this context of the girl being *deducta* (led, as at marriage) to the man's home. Ulpian considers the question of whether, when someone takes his betrothed to wife when this is not allowed by law, gifts between them are valid, as betrothal gifts, and not gifts in marriage. 'Julian', he says, 'deals with this question in the case where a girl under twelve has been *deducta* to the home of her quasi-husband, when under age; he says she is a fiancée (*sponsa*), even if not a wife.' Girls under twelve would not have free disposal of their persons, and so the reasons for these early matches are likely to be those of the menfolk. Some can be guessed at: politics and family alliances in the upper social reaches, help with the domestic economy, and a dowry, in the lower. Julian thought that a father should be assumed to be acting from excess of affection rather than from any fraudulent motive.[36]

Clearly, some girls were living with men even before the age of twelve, and so, *a fortiori*, at the age of twelve. Whether such relationships were consummated is, in the nature of things, much harder to ascertain, and there has been some emotional resistance in modern times to believing that this was so.[37]

Twelve was up to two years before the average age of menarche. Nevertheless, Roman lawyers use both calendar age and the language of physical maturity (*viripotens*: 'capable of receiving a man') to define juridical capacity for marriage.[38] Literary evidence shows a similar tenor. Plutarch and Soranus, both Greeks, express some concern.[39] According to Plutarch, Lycurgus, the (unhistorical) fashioner of the Spartan way of life, postponed marriage in that society until girls should be physically ready, and so emotionally disposed to love their husbands and physically strong enough to endure the strain of conception and childbearing. The Romans, on the other hand, wanted to ensure that their brides would be pure and undefiled in body and mind when their husbands took them; and he conjures up horrid images by suggesting that the Greek system would produce 'a kindly love, instead of the timorous hate that follows unnatural compulsion'.

However, Soranus, a medical man, recognised that some girls, if not properly brought up, felt sexual desire early. He argued that defloration ought not to occur before menarche; the implication is that it did frequently enough to be taken notice of, and that girls were often married and sexually active from the start of puberty.

This would have consequences for their health. Even allowing for the phenomenon of subfertility in the first year or so after menarche, girls could and would be exposed to the possibility of pregnancy from an early age, before their bodies had reached full growth and maturity. Abortion carried its own risks. Contraception was used, but amulets, sympathetic magic and potions crowd the relatively few prescriptions in the texts for pessaries, or similar preparations for vaginal use, which might have been effective, and the use of the 'safe period' was not understood.[40] One might expect miscarriages to be frequent. A few instances, of women in high society, are mentioned in the literary sources. The 'technical literature' (e.g., the elder Pliny, Celsus, and Soranus) has quite a lot of advice on bringing away the placenta and treating various complications attendant on miscarriage, prolapse and other female disorders. One would expect a high rate of death in childbirth or from its consequences. Epigraphic evidence seems to confirm this (though with the reservations already mentioned), showing a 'bulge' in mortality of women between the ages of 15 and 29; however, the *average* life-span for both men and women was under 30, and one recent study would put it as low as 21.11 years.[41] Early sexual intercourse carried its own risk, apart from pregnancy; there is recent evidence to suggest that it increases the risk of cervical cancer.[42]

Garcia Garrido (1957: 85), while accepting the evidence for cohabitation before the age of twelve, suggests that a *mariage blanc* may have been maintained until the age of twelve was reached. He bases his conclusion partly on the jurists' use of *viripotens*, apparently interchangeably with the age of twelve, as a requirement for the existence of legal marriage, and partly on the law relating to *stuprum*, which was defined as all sexual relations with free unmarried women.[43] No marriage could exist until the girl was twelve; any premarital sexual relations with her would be unlawful and probably constitute a delict.

The law may prohibit; but that of itself does not guarantee abstention, especially in domestic privacy. The question must remain open.

Consent to Marriage

The third requirement for a valid marriage was the consent of the relevant parties. In classical law, these were defined as the marriage partners, if they were *sui iuris*, or their parents, if they were suject to *potestas* (so Ulpian; Paul says the marrying couple *and* their parents), though Ulpian thought that the daughter's consent could be withheld only if the father had selected someone morally undesirable.[44]

The father's consent was apparently necessary in law at all times. In the Republic, he could prevent a marriage. When Pompey, recently widowed, proposed that he would marry a daughter (or, in another version, niece) of Cato Minor, and his son another, the women of Cato's household were keen, but Cato refused the match and, being on the spot in Rome, was able to enforce his wishes.[45]

On the other hand, Cicero's wife and his daughter Tullia between them arranged and carried through Tullia's marriage to Dolabella while Cicero, in Cilicia, was unaware of the fact. Caelius had informed Cicero from Rome early in the year (50 B.C.) that Dolabella's previous marriage had broken up. However, since Cicero and Dolabella were about to be on opposite sides in a forthcoming trial, Caelius advised Cicero not to commit himself openly for the moment. Meanwhile, Cicero was approached in Cilicia by an eligible young man, Tiberius Nero, and sent word to Terentia and Tullia about him. The womenfolk in the meantime had gone ahead and concluded the betrothal with Dolabella. Cicero could have used his paternal authority to stop the match; but he chose to acquiesce, and wrote philosophically to Atticus: 'I hope this will turn out for the better; certainly the women are delighted with the young man.'[46]

Whatever the law said, children in real life were able to take the initiative as Tullia did in choosing a marriage partner. From time to time they even presented their parents with a *fait accompli*. Paul gives it as his opinion that 'The marriages of persons in the father's *potestas* cannot legally be contracted without his consent, but once they are contracted they should not be dissolved. The public good should take priority over private convenience.' By the latter statement he appears to mean that the stability of a marriage is to be preferred to a father's wishes, a viewpoint similar to that of Marcus Aurelius on a father's interference in a *bene concordans matrimonium*.[47]

Augustus passed a law allowing consuls and provincial magistrates to compel a father to consent to the marriage of a child, if his opposition was judged to be unjustified (*iniuria*).[48] This degree of legal interference with the *patria potestas* was possible in a period when *manus*-marriage had become uncommon and the daughter, as always the son, remained in her father's *potestas* after marriage. It would surely have been unthinkable that a father should be compelled to give up *potestas* over his daughter for a *manus*-marriage.

It seems likely that in strict law, at all times, the *pater* could compel his children to marry, though the jurists felt that he ought not to do so, since they insist upon the consent of the couple themselves. Possibly a daughter was easier to compel than a son.[49] However, one must not be led astray into accepting the law's version of society, where the *pater* compels, as a picture of what usually happened. We ought to do Roman fathers, even in the heyday of *manus*-marriage, the justice of assuming that most of them had *some* feelings of affection for their sons and daughters and were not actuated only by financial considerations in arranging their marriages, to the extent of regularly overriding any personal feelings their children might have.

The arranged marriage should not be regarded merely as a bogey, in some sense a violation of personal liberties. It was a sensible strategy, still used in some societies (but becoming less appropriate as other economic and cultural influences pervade them) to maintain the economic and social security and welfare of the next generation. Neither the young Roman girl in a wealthy family, nor indeed her brother, is likely to have been in a position, at least for the first marriage, to have much acquaintance with young persons of the opposite sex outside the family, other than those included in their parents' social circle. That in itself helped to ensure that anyone on whom their fancy was likely to fall would be socially acceptable, though there could perhaps be (although less likely with the very young) the occasional threat of a *mésalliance*, with the equivalent of a chorus-girl or a servant, such as appears in literary and legal sources. For the most part, adult Romans on their second or subsequent marriages probably gravitated to persons of their own status. The poorer child, in an urban setting, may have had a wider experience before marriage of society outside the household; but, again, we are not really justified in imagining a plethora of thwarted juvenile romances.

It is salutary to remember that Dolabella was the choice of Tullia herself and her mother, and he turned out a thoroughly unsatisfactory husband. And there was always divorce, and that much more easily than in modern Britain; but that must be dealt with later.

The glimpses that we do have of Roman life (albeit mainly of the upper classes) show the women of the family taking a lively, and sometimes even a directing, interest in the arranging of their children's marriages. Cato and Cicero had their women to contend with. The story of the betrothal of the elder Tiberius Gracchus has some fictional qualities; still, it was repeated by a Roman writer in the time of Augustus, and has therefore some evidential value for what might be considered credible wifely behaviour then. In 187 B.C., says Livy, members of the Senate, dining on the Capitol, begged Scipio to betroth his daughter to Gracchus. He did so publicly, there and then (in the daughter's absence, be it noted). On his return home he told his wife, who, 'annoyed as a woman would be that he had not consulted her', said that the girl's mother *ought* to have been consulted, even if the proposed husband was Tiberius Gracchus. Scipio rejoiced (as well he might) that their views coincided.[50]

A much more factual impression of the workings of arranged marriages can be gleaned from the letters of the younger Pliny; from these, it can be gathered what qualities he and his social equals found desirable in a husband. Good family, good character and scholarship are desirable in Pliny's eyes; official position is a recommendation too, and he helps a friend with his daughter's dowry so that she can marry a public man. Ample means are important, since posterity must be provided for. Pliny comments on the looks of one prospective groom and the charm of another. The niece of Pliny's friend Junius Mauricus is *sui iuris*, her father being dead, but is apparently very young (she is a virgin), and her uncle's greater experience of the world is being used to find her a husband. He is probably her tutor.[51]

The Formal Procedures of Marriage

Marriages were not celebrated on certain days and at certain times of the year. The ban was not legal, but rather religious and customary. The unpopularity of the month of May and the early part of June probably originally lay as much in the fact that it was a busy time of year for farming, as in any other reason. The three days a year when the *mundus* or door to Hades was opened at Rome and ghosts walked were avoided, and the eight days of the festival of the dead in February. It was not good to have a wedding on the fixed days of each month (Kalends, Nones and Ides) because the days following were 'black' days and therefore unlucky for starting anything new, according to Varro. Macrobius elaborates. *First* marriages should not be celebrated on Kalends and Ides, because they involved 'an onslaught on virginity'. But, he says, Varro reports that a famous expert in pontifical law, Verrius Flaccus, was in the habit of saying that the reason was that it was permissible to clear out old ditches on those days but not to make new ones; therefore they were more suitable for marrying widows than virgins. One is inclined to suspect Varro (or Verrius) of trying to make a joke.[52]

Usually, as nowadays, a marriage was accompanied with a celebration of some sort, a wedding, the culmination and central part of which was the torchlit procession, with musicians and ribald jesting, that escorted the bride to her married home. That did not of itself constitute a valid marriage, any more than the cake-cutting, facetious speeches and pelting with confetti at a modern wedding.[53] However, the Romans seem to have attached importance to having such celebrations, and their features are often referred to in literature,[54] and to be able to adduce witnesses to such a celebration would create a strong presumption that there had been marital intent.

Although in the eyes of the law the existence of a marriage was not dependent upon the performance of any specific ceremony, there were certain procedures and arrangements usually attendant upon a marriage. In particular, the intention to marry might be signalled by a formal betrothal (*sponsalia*).

Betrothal[55]

In the early Republic, when *manus*-marriage was still common, the participating parties were the groom or his *pater* on one side and the bride's *pater* or tutor on the other. The parties gave promises (*sponsa*), which amounted to making a verbal contract, *stipulatio*. Whether *stipulatio* was made by both sides, or only on the bride's side, and whether it was actionable are disputed questions. In Latium, betrothal seems to have involved double actionable stipulations until the absorption of the Latins into the Roman citizen body. In Roman law, also, there was probaby originally a *stipulatio* on both sides, which was actionable. The bridegroom's side promised to take the girl in marriage (whether or not bride-price was also involved in early Rome need not concern us); the bride's side promised to deliver her into the *manus* of the bridegroom's family, and perhaps also stipulated a dowry. By the first century B.C. *stipulatio* had ceased to be used in betrothal, and arrangements for dowry were made separately. The plays of Plautus include several scenes concerning betrothal and use the vocabulary of stipulation. Whether it is fair to conclude, as Watson (1967: 14–15) does, that, because the comic writer in one place omits half the formula, this represents current usage and the promises were no longer actionable by the beginning of the second century B.C., is doubtful, and presses the evidence too hard.[56]

Marriage without *manus* was freely terminable by the wife or her *pater* (as marriage with or without *manus* was on the husband's side), and as this type of marriage became more common, there would be less point in maintaining a binding contract for entry into marriage. Betrothal developed into a matter of simple consent. The elements of binding contract which sometimes accompanied it (marriage 'contracts', penalty clauses, etc.) were not strictly part of the betrothal itself.

In betrothal by simple consent, there was no action for breach of promise. Betrothals could be, and were, broken off without penalty. The practice grew up of making a stipulation at the time of betrothal that a penalty should be paid if the marriage did not take place. Paul took the view that marriage ought not to be subject to such constraint.[57]

There was no legal minimum age for betrothal, though there was for marriage. Augustus (then Octavian) betrothed his daughter Julia to a son of Mark Antony when she was about two years old. Later, as part of his legislation to encourage marriage, betrothed men were exempted from the penalties attaching to *caelibes* (bachelors). Because many were abusing the privilege by betrothing themselves to infants, he ordered that no betrothal should be valid unless the man married within two years. This meant, in practice, that, although betrothals might be made with younger girls, they would not earn the men exemption until the girls were ten years old. Modestinus, two hundred years later, says: 'In making betrothals, there is no age specified for the contracting parties, as there is for marriage. Therefore betrothals may be made from early childhood.' The passage continues: 'so long as both parties understand what is being done, that is, if they are not less than seven years old.' This latter section was probably added by the compilers of Justinian's *Digest* and does not represent classical practice.[58]

The *pater* or tutor would act for children *in potestate* or under age. A man *sui iuris* could act for himself; so, apparently, could a woman, unless contracting a marriage with *manus*.

Although betrothal by informal agreement could not be legally enforced, it did have certain consequences. A person who formed a second engagement, or married someone else, without breaking off the first engagement, was liable to praetorian *infamia*. The penalties incurred by being declared *infamis* were mainly certain disabilities in litigation. Women were subject to most of these disabilities anyway, because of their sex, and so the main effect was probably to prevent them from appointing *cognitores* (representatives) in lawsuits.[59]

Betrothal also brought the parent or child of the other party within the prohibited degrees for marriage.[60]

Severus and Caracalla issued a rescript allowing a man to prosecute his unfaithful fiancée, not just for the general offence of *stuprum*, but specifically for adultery, by the right of third parties (since he was not actually a husband).[61] He himself was not required to be faithful, however. So long as he abstained from married women and unmarried citizen women (other than prostitutes, actresses and the like), the law was not interested.

Betrothed persons were treated as near relatives for the purposes of exemption from certain limitations on gifts and legacies under the *lex Cincia* (204 B.C.) and the *lex Furia Testamentaria*. The purpose of these laws was to prevent excessive depletion of the property of a *familia* by generosity to outsiders. With the development of free marriage, husband and wife were regarded as 'outsiders' in customary law, as far as gifts were concerned, but engaged couples apparently remained exempt from the Cincian law. Legal evidence on such gifts (*donationes ante nuptias*) in the classical period is scanty, but it looks as though in some cases the gifts were in effect used to constitute part of the dowry, and this may be the reason for the continuing exemption. In post-classical law, such gifts were brought under a hard and fast set of rules for marital and financial settlements.[62]

A fiancé was regarded as part of the family, in that the Augustan law providing that close relatives and in-laws could not be compelled to give testimony against each other was held to apply to him and his future father-in-law.[63] On the other hand, if he murdered or was murdered by the bride's father or brother or sister, this counted as parricide; the same applied if she treated his family in this way. Not all families are happy ones. (Presumably, in those circumstances, the engagement was usually broken off.)[64]

Proofs of Marriage

No specific ceremony was legally required for the creation of a marriage. Jurists, in attempting to define marriage, tend to stress the mutual agreement of the parties, and the fact that they live together. 'Marriage', says Modestinus, 'is the *coniunctio*, the joining together of a man and woman and the sharing of their entire life, the joint participation in rights human and divine.'[65]

Living together was not in itself enough to distinguish marriage from *concubinage*. There must be *affectus maritalis*, that is, the couple must regard each other as man and wife and behave accordingly.[66] A mental condition is something whose existence is not easy to prove, especially if either party had died or refused to acknowledge the marriage. One other circumstance which must occur was that the wife should be *in domum deducta*, that is, she should take up residence in the husband's home. Jurists considered that the inception of a marriage could be held to date from that point. A woman, therefore, could not marry in absence or by proxy, although a man could. Her presence was essential, so that she could formally enter the marital home.[67] In itself, though, cohabitation was not enough to constitute marriage.

In practice, there were usually various other attendant circumstances, of no legal significance in themselves, but which could be pointed to as presumptive proof of existence of a marriage. A rescript survives, issued by the emperor Probus (A.D. 276–282) to a man named Fortunatus:

> If, with the knowledge of neighbours or others, you had a wife at home for the purpose of procreating children (*liberorum procreandorum causa*) and a daughter was acknowledged from that marriage, then, even although no marriage documents (*tabulae nuptiales*) were drawn up, nor any relevant documents concerning your daughter, none the less the truth about your marriage or the daughter you acknowledged is valid.[68]

Fortunatus was clearly a poor man. His wife's dowry must either have been nonexistent or too humble to be put on record formally; otherwise, the existence of such a marriage settlement would have characterised the intention of the relationship sufficiently for the purpose of the law. He had apparently not registered the child's birth, either; there was, indeed, no legal compulsion on him to do so. However, he might have heard enough of the law to know that such documents could be useful in establishing one's status as a married man and father, and therefore one's right to exemption from the disabilities Augustus' legislation had placed on the unmarried and childless.

Where *manus* had been created by *confarreatio* or *coemptio*, evidence of the performance of the necessary procedure could be produced to show that a marriage relationship existed. This was lacking, of course, in 'free' marriage. It has been suggested that in the Republic when the census was taken the censors required an oath, from men married in free marriage, that they had a wife for the purpose of procreation, and that this distinguished their relationship from mere cohabitation.[69] The evidence for such an oath is scanty.

In 231 B.C., a certain Spurius Carvilius Ruga divorced his wife on grounds of barrenness. This divorce was a milestone in Roman history, not, as mistakenly asserted by Dionysius of Halicarnassus, as the first Roman divorce, but because it led to the introduction of a legal process for recovery of dowry upon divorce. Ruga swore to the censors that he had a wife for the procreation of children. Gellius appears to make his having sworn this oath his ground for divorcing her, since he could not fulfil it. On the other hand, Dionysius describes the oath *after* the divorce, and his account could bear the meaning that Ruga was taken to task by the censors for divorcing his wife other than for one of the causes acceptable in the early Republic (see Plut. *Rom.* 22), and the oath was part of his self-exculpation before them, rather than a regular part of the census.

Dionysius, describing the census process as instituted by Servius Tullius, says that citizens were required to give the following information: names, monetary valuation of property, names of fathers, age, names of wives and children. The only oath mentioned is to the truth and good faith of the declaration. However, names of wives and children are listed among the information given. Wives and children are not mentioned in the procedure as outlined in the *Tabula Heracleensis*, an inscription preserving the census procedure as it operated in the first half of the first century B.C., but it is likely that both were included, even if not by name. Widows and orphans were listed separately. The other piece of evidence is a story told by Gellius and Cicero about an ill-timed joke made by a man in reply to the censor, who, administering 'the usual oath regarding wives', asked: 'Have you, to the best of your knowledge and belief, a wife?' It is likely, then, that men made a census declaration of their married status (though without the addition about the purpose of procreation). It does not seem, from what we know of the census, that this would have proved very useful in enabling a woman to prove the existence of a marriage. Though in theory obligatory upon citizens, with penalties for nonregistration, the census could be avoided. In any case, it took place only every five years at best and only spasmodically in the last century of the Republic. After the Flavians, no census was held in Italy.[70]

Augustus' legislation on manumission and on marriage gave an incentive to Romans to register the birth of legitimate children with the praetor or provincial governor, and this could serve as presumptive proof of the mother's status as wife. Registration was not compulsory, however (our man Fortunatus had not registered his daughter), and, obviously, childless women could not appeal to this type of evidence.[71]

Probably the piece of documentary evidence most commonly available would be the record of arrangements for dowry, since this could involve the conveyancing to the husband of rights over money, land or other property.

In various parts of the Roman empire, from the first century A.D. on, there developed the practice of having signed and witnessed marriage contracts (*tabulae nuptiales*). These were not 'marriage certificates' in our sense, since they did not testify to the performance of any legally required ceremony, nor were they subscribed by an authorised public official. In essence, they were agreements of a financial character, and were not themselves constitutive of marriage, unlike the *syngraphai* of Greek law. The wealthy widow whom Apuleius eventually married had previously, under pressure, made *tabulae nuptiales* with Sicinius Clarus, but had managed on various pretexts to avoid marriage. The oldest known example we have of one of these agreements is on a papyrus from Roman Egypt and dates from around A.D. 100. Like another, similar, example, also written in Latin, it begins with a statement by the bride's father that he has given her in marriage in accordance with the *lex Julia de maritandis ordinibus* for the procreation of children. It continues with a list of the property which he has promised to the groom as dowry — land, jewellery, clothing, household utensils and a slave girl. The text breaks off soon after the beginning of the statement by the husband of the property he has contributed (presumably as a *donatio ante nuptias*). The document is signed on the outside by witnesses and sealed.[72]

The difference between the Roman purely financial settlement and the Greek marriage contract is shown by a group of documents from Alexandria, from the time of Augustus.[73] Some are between the groom and the bride's parents, some between the couple themselves. As well as the statement that a marriage is being formed, and dowry details, the documents contain clauses regulating behaviour in marriage. In a typical example, it is specified that if the husband ill-treats the wife, or brings another woman into the house, he is to pay back one and a half times the dowry. She, in turn, has to do her wifely duties, and have nothing to do with another man, on penalty of loss of the amount of the dowry. Since in Greek law a wife came under the guardianship of her husband, a written contract could afford her some measure of protection against bad behaviour on his part. In Roman law, such matters would not depend on a private contract; they would form part of a suit for retention or recovery of dowry after divorce.

Widows and Remarriage

In classical Rome, the woman who had married only once, *univira*, was approved of, and was regarded as attaining some ideal of marriage. The conduct of certain religious rituals was reserved exclusively to such women. Although divorce and re-marriage were frequent, divorcées were not entirely approved of; widows, however, although lacking ritual purity and therefore not suitable for inclusion in the celebration of certain cults, seem to have attracted no disapproval in society at large by re-marrying, in contrast to the attitude that developed in the Christian empire.[74]

Nevertheless, the right of widows to remarry was subject to certain restrictions. A widow was expected to allow a certain period for mourning before remarriage.[75] In the archaic period, there seems to have been a concern with religious purity. In the classical period, the main concern seems to have been the evidence of possible uncertainty about the paternity of posthumous children. Ovid makes the connection:

> *Quod satis est, utero matris dum prodeat infans,*
> *hoc anno statuit temporis esse satis,*
> *per totidem menses a funere coniugis uxor*
> *sustinet in vidua tristia signa domo.*

He (Romulus) judged that the length of time a child takes to emerge from its mother's womb was sufficient for a year. For so many months a wife, after her husband's funeral, maintains the signs of mourning in her widowed home.

There was a tradition at Rome that their original calendar, devised by Romulus, had a ten-month year; Ovid's explanation of this is that that was the time taken by gestation.[76]

According to Paul, different lengths of mourning were expected for parents and children (twelve months), near cognates (eight months) and husbands (ten months). Clearly, the first two categories could be mourned by either sex; the last only by women. Men were not required to observe mourning for their wives. Women need not mourn their fiancés. Widows could become betrothed while in mourning and could, by imperial dispensation, marry without penalty within the mourning period. There was no penalty for marrying while mourning a parent or child, but the penalty for remarrying within the mourning period for a husband was *infamia*, even if the husband had been too bad a character to deserve mourning.[77]

The reason for the restriction, some legal opinion had it, was to avoid *turbatio sanguinis*, 'confusion of the blood'[78]; for that reason, a widow could remarry, even within the ten months, immediately after giving birth.

There is something odd here. The law apparently was not in the least concerned about the possibility of *turbatio sanguinis* when there was a divorce. Augustus' *lex Julia* expected divorced women to remarry within six months, and it was not until the *lex Papia* that the period before penalties started to operate was extended to 18 months.[79] If the divorced parties wished to assert or reject a claim regarding the paternity of a child born after the divorce, recourse was had to the praetor's judgment. It seems, according to the jurists, that children were recognised as legitimate if they could have been conceived during the duration of a *iustum matrimonium*,[80] and the 'normal' period of pregnancy, as we have seen, was reckoned to be anything between six and ten months. There was no hard and fast rule; it was up to the praetor to decide whether a posthumous child had a claim on its putative father's estate.[81]

The rules were tightened by additions to the praetorian edict in about A.D. 130. Regular procedures of inspection and monitoring of the pregnancy were prescribed, and these had to be instituted within a month of divorce or widowhood. In the case of a claim by an ex-wife, the husband could be penalised, if he failed to follow procedure, by being obliged to recognise the child as his. A widow had to notify her dead husband's relations, or anyone else with an interest in the estate, who might if they chose require her to follow the procedure.[82] As well as the pregnancy being monitored, the confinement itself had to take place with a number of witnesses present, and people on guard outside, to stop and search anyone entering, in case an infant should be smuggled in. Even the entrances to the room, save one, had to be boarded up, and there had to be at least three lights in the room 'for darkness is better adapted for the substitution of a child'. All the women present had to be searched, in case one of them might be pregnant. Even after the confinement, the precautions against a possible substitution continued. After the child's birth, failing other instructions from the father, the magistrate appointed someone (the masculine is used) in whose home the child was to be reared; this guardian had to produce the child for inspection at specified intervals until it was old enough to speak. Whether the mother was allowed to remain with her child is not stated; perhaps that depended on the choice of guardian.

The details seem so bizarre that one might suppose this to be an instance of the law making elaborate provision for something that never actually occurred. However, at least one case is known. In A.D. 147, a recently widowed Roman woman, Petronilla, wrote to the *iuridicus*, Calvisius Patrophilos. From the surviving portions of her letter we learn that she had been instructed to go and see a certain woman who, together with a midwife, had examined her and reported that she was pregnant. The woman mentioned would not be able to have Petronilla in her house for her confinement, but undertook to monitor the course of the pregnancy, to ascertain that Petronilla continued to carry the child to term and that no harm came to her through her own fault. Another fragment of the archive, published recently, shows that Petronilla was threatened with a charge of *notheia* ('illegitimacy'), which in context means having a child of whom her late husband was not the father, by some relatives 'in the female line', probably acting for her mother-in-law.[83]

Given Roman assumptions about gestation, confusion about paternity would presumably be recognised only when a child was born more than six months after the start of a later marriage, but less than ten months after the death of the previous husband, that is, if the widow had remarried within three or four months of her husband's death. Why then, expect her to wait *ten* months?

It is unlikely that it was feared that the child already conceived might somehow take on some of the genetic material of a subsequent sexual partner. Belief in the possibility of superfetation in humans did exist in the classical world,[84] but was apparently thought to result either in two live births, or in rejection of the second foetus, rather than 'confusion of the blood' in the sense of one offspring somehow having dual paternity.

It is more likely that the explanation in terms of *turbatio sanguinis* was produced at a late stage by jurists to account for the ten-months' proscription, which originally was not concerned with biological facts so much as, in the first instance, with ritual purity, and later with a sense of the moral proprieties of what a loving widow *ought* to feel.

In the archaic period, a widow who remarried within ten months was expected to sacrifice a cow in calf. The ten months of the proscription was the original length of the Roman year. That it had to do with ritual impurity is suggested by the fact that the mourning period was on occasion waived or reduced when (as, e.g., after the national disaster of Cannae) there were so many matrons in mourning that not enough were available to carry out the state's religious ceremonies.[85]

Both the 'moral' and the 'biological' view can be found in the classical period. Arising from the 'moral' view are the following:

(i) marriage within the mourning period incurred *infamia*, but the marriage itself was valid;

(ii) Augustus' laws on marriage gave widows a longer period of grace than divorcées (one year, later raised to two, as against only six months, raised to eighteen) before they became liable to the penalties laid on the unmarried;

(iii) Ulpian cites Cinna for the opinion that the time of mourning should be respected, even if the marriage had never been consummated;

(iv) a rescript of Gordian (A.D. 239) said that although widows need not maintain the outward signs of mourning once their grief had abated, nevertheless a widow who remarried within the customary period incurred by the praetor's edict a blemish on her reputation (*labem pudoris contrahit*) — in other words, *infamia* — and so did a man who knowingly married her; Ulpian also mentioned the man's liability under the edict.[86]

For the 'biological' view can be adduced the following:

(i) men were exempt from this restriction;

(ii) Caligula refused to allow reduction of the mourning period for pregnant widows;

(iii) Labeo took the view that mourning should be held to date not from the receipt of news of the husband's death but from the actual date of death, even in the case where this might mean that the widow donned and abandoned mourning on the same day;

(iv) even an undeserving husband should be mourned, because of *turbatio sanguinis*;

(v) Pomponius gave the opinion that a widow could remarry immediately after giving birth.[87]

Sometimes, probably in the interests of children of the marriage, a husband would try to dissuade his widow from remarrying by leaving a legacy to her on condition that she did not remarry. This created a logical difficulty, in that the widow could not be seen to have qualified for the legacy until she herself died unmarried. A solution was devised, in the latter part of the second century B.C. by Q. Mucius Scaevola, the so-called *cautio Muciana*. The widow, on giving a guarantee (*cautio*) not to break the condition, was given the legacy, but forfeited it if she did remarry.[88]

The husband's concern was probably for the interests of their children, which might suffer if the widow remarried and then dis-

posed elsewhere of the inheritance she had received from her previous husband. In a funerary inscription from the first century A.D.,
the son of her first marriage records his thanks to his mother,
Murdia, because not only did she make her sons by both marriages
equal heirs to her estate (the daughter got a partitionary legacy,
perhaps to avoid the restrictions of the *lex Voconia*), but she also
left to the elder son a *praelegatum*, that is, a legacy chargeable on
the estate, 'not', says the son, 'to show preference to me and so
slight my brothers, but because, mindful of my father's generosity,
she thought she ought to return to my ownership what she had, by
her husband's wishes, received from my patrimony and kept in her
use.' 'Use' here is surely a technical term (*usus*); the widow had
behaved *as though* her husband had merely bequeathed her the
usufruct of his estate. The bequest of usufruct to the widow was a
way of avoiding diminishing the children's patrimony. It became
important with the increase of marriage without *manus*, since in
those circumstances the wife had in the eyes of the law no claim to
rank alongside the children as one of the direct heirs of her husband,
and it was a way for the husband to provide for the maintenance
of her standard of living. Later, examples in the legal texts of
usufructs specified for a fixed term of years, or until the children
reached puberty, suggest that the children's welfare had become a
prime concern and that it was expected that the widow would
remarry. The usufruct could then take on the character of a 'maintenance allowance' for the children, and it was sometimes specified that
it should last only while the mother kept the children with her.[89]

The *querela inofficiosi testamenti* was some protection for the
children who found themselves disinherited at the death of a parent,
of either sex, who had remarried. Pliny spoke in the centumviral
court on behalf of a woman who had been disinherited in favour of
a stepmother by her eighty-year-old father who had fallen in love
and remarried, succumbing, to the effects perhaps, only ten days
later; the case attracted great public interest. Augustus, according
to Valerius Maximus, annulled by decree the will of a mother who
made her second husband her heir and passed over her children.
Apuleius, courting the widow Pudentilla, encountered hostility from
her children, who were afraid that they might be disinherited in his
favour 'as often happens'.[90]

However, it was not until the Christian empire that remarriage
by widows was actively discouraged by a series of enactments

limiting the widow's power, in that case, to benefit from the property of her late husband.[91]

Statistics are lacking on the incidence of remarriage, but the young or youngish widow who never remarried, like the woman who never married at all, was probably a relatively rare phenomenon in Roman society, which appears to have suffered from the chronic shortage of marriageable women. Whether the incidence of unattached women was higher at the lower levels of society, as Penta (1980: 345) suggests, is doubtful. The social importance of marriage was not, as she appears to think, merely a matter of political affiliations and amassing of fortunes among the aristocracy. Moreover, marriage seems to have been the commonest ground for the manumission of female slaves, and the nature of their servile employment was not often such as to enable them to be economically independent. Eventually, of course, some women would reach an age at which remarriage was unlikely and die as widows.[92]

Concubines

A concubine was a free woman who was cohabiting with a man, without being his wife; it was not thought permissible for a man to have both a concubine and a wife simultaneously.[93] The fact of their living together would suffice to distinguish the relationship from a casual affair but, if the two parties had *conubium*, not from marriage. As we have seen, various external circumstances could be adduced to establish their matrimonial intent, such as the constitution of a dowry. A character in Plautus' *Trinummus* is worried because, as he says, he is badly off (*inops*) and likely to be badly thought of (*infamis*) as well, because if he betrothes his sister without a dowry, people will think he is giving her into concubinage, rather than marriage.[94]

Cicero claimed to have heard of an incident in the past when a married Roman left his wife pregnant in Spain, came to Rome and, without sending her notice of divorce, married another woman.[95] Both women produced sons, and when the man died without leaving a will, this created legal problems. Were both boys conceived in wedlock and so legitimate? Did the second marriage in itself constitute a divorce from the first wife, even without formal notice of divorce? If not, then the second 'wife' was a concubine, with effects on the status of both mother and child. (Cicero expresses himself loosely here; as citizenship is not in question, he may mean membership of both in the father's *familia*, if the mother had 'married' with *manus*.) There could also (though Cicero does not say so) be the question of whether the child of the second union had inheritance rights.

Under the empire for a number of reasons, particularly the social legislation of Augustus, relationships of concubinage probably became more commonplace. Augustan legislation on sexual offences also made it important to distinguish concubinage, not merely from marriage, but from other sexual relationships.

Freedwomen in particular were affected. It could sometimes positively be an advantage to a freedwoman to be judged to be in a state of concubinage rather than matrimony. A freedwoman who had been freed by her patron in order to marry him was not allowed by the law to divorce him and marry another without his consent (unless she had been manumitted under a *fideicommissum* — a testamentary instruction). Since someone insane could not be held to consent, Paul thought that, if the patron became insane, it would be more humane to regard the freedwoman as his concubine, so that she could leave him. Ulpian, on the other hand, did not think freedwomen concubines should be at liberty to desert their patrons; he recommended that they should be penalised by loss of *conubium*, *quippe cum honestius sit patrono libertam concubinam quam matrem familias habere*, which ought to mean 'since it is more honourable for a patron to have a freedwoman as his concubine than as a *materfamilias* (i.e., a legal wife)'. The logic is doubtful. Since the patron is (on this view of Ulpian's meaning) acquiring more honour for himself by *not* marrying her, *she* is penalised for taking advantage of this; if he sacrifices some honour and marries her, she is the loser, if the marriage is unhappy; yet it is unlikely that Ulpian meant that it was more honourable for a freedwoman to be her patron's concubine than his wife. As a concubine, also, the freedwoman was (although it is not certain how early this rule was introduced) exempted, like a wife, from the obligation of services to her former owner.[96]

Augustus' legislation on marriage and on adultery had created several categories of women who were themselves free and of citizen status, but had either no *conubium* at all, or no *conubium* with certain categories of citizen. Women convicted of adultery could not remarry, or both they and their husbands would be penalised. As we saw, senators and, later, their children, were forbidden to marry freedmen and freedwomen and various categories of people classed as *probrosi*. From the time of Septimius Severus, patronesses could not marry their freedmen. Soldiers could not marry while in service, nor provincial officials, while in office, women of their province (unless it was their natal province). At least three emperors, Vespasian, Marcus Aurelius and Antoninus Pius, chose to live with concubines after they became widowers.[97]

The niceties of social distinctions are well illustrated by an inscription, from about the beginning of the first century B.C.[98] P. Quinctius the copyist commemorates himself and his wife, *uxsor* (*sic*), Quinctia, both freed by the same former owner, and subsequently married; he also commemorates Quinctia Agate, his own former slave, whom he had freed and had as his concubine, *concubina* (presumably after his wife's death). It may be remembered that it was regarded as more honourable for a man to have his own freedwoman as concubine than as wife.

There were some ambiguities inherent in concubinage. An unfaithful concubine could, Ulpian thought, be prosecuted by her partner for adultery, not, of course, by the right of a husband, since she was not his wife, but as an 'outsider' (*iure extranei*); however, the 'other man' was not guilty of adultery. Sexual relations with one's concubine might be regarded as *stuprum*, unless the woman belonged to one of the specified categories of *probrosae*, with whom, by definition, *stuprum* did not occur. Ulpian thought it safer to avoid the possibility of prosecution for *stuprum* by having only women of that sort as concubines; Marcian included any woman of lowly status.[99]

These comments, like so much of the Roman law, seem to have been made with the upper classes in mind. Epigraphic evidence suggests that concubinage and other *de facto* marriages occurred more frequently among persons of freed and slave status than among the freeborn, and with a tendency for men to be of higher social status than women, with a noticeable number of freeborn men.[100]

As well as the free couples who lived together because the law denied them *conubium* permanently, there were those who lived together because they did not yet have *conubium*. This situation is reflected by the use of the word *contubernalis* (literally 'tent-companion', a word of army origin) in inscriptions from the city of Rome. It is likely that at least one partner in the union had, at some time in their association, been a slave. Some of these unions started as stable 'marriages' between slaves in large city households; if the union persisted after both were free, it would become valid marriage, even though the term *contubernalis* is still used in the commemorative inscription.[101] The tendency to continue using the terminology appropriate to the early stages of the relationship is shown in the following example.

> To the shades of Claudia Stepte, who lived 72 years, this was set up by Ti. Claudius Nymphodotus, freedman of Augustus, her patron and *contubernalis*, to his dearest wife, who deserved well of him, with whom he lived 46 years.[102]

Both Nymphodotus and Stepte had been slaves in the imperial household and had begun a *de facto* relationship there. He was freed; he then purchased and freed her, and she became his wife.

In one particular social group, *contubernium* between a slave man and a free woman is frequently attested, namely among the male slaves of the imperial household, from Claudius to Alexander Severus. Other examples of such unions come mainly from the upper classes. Few of the women are explicitly attested as freeborn.[103] The *senatusconsultum Claudianum* (A.D. 52) penalised women who formed such unions without the owner's consent with loss of liberty; even if he consented, a freeborn woman was reduced to freedwoman status. However, as we shall see later, the aim of the measure was probably not so much to discourage such unions as to regulate the status of the children in the master's interest.[104]

For a free man, particularly a freeborn man, however, to have a lasting relationship with a slave woman was regarded as improper, and there was the added discouragement that the children of such an association would themselves be slaves.[105] To the possible examples cited by Treggiari (1981a) from Rome we may add the following from Fiumicino, of interest also for the incidental revelations about the personal relations of the people involved:

> L. Mindius Dius made (this monument) for himself and Genucia Tryphaena his wife (*coniugi*) with whom he lived 24 years, three months, and Lucia Januaria, married (sc. to him: *maritae*) and Annia Laveria, his most blessed companion (*sanctissimae contubernali*).[106]

If the distinction between *coniunx* and *marita* here is meaningful, and not made merely for literary variety, the second marriage may have been not only considerably shorter but also less happy than the first. Lucia has no word of commendation, while both Genucia and Annia do. Annia may have ended as a wife, but the use of *contubernalis* indicates that she began as a concubine, and a slave-concubine at that. Mindius himself may be a freedman, but if the inscription is in chronological order he was already free at the start of his relationship with Annia. Another possibility, however, perhaps made more likely by the specification of the precise duration of his marriage with Genucia, is that the inscription is in reverse order. Mindius' relationship with Annia may have begun when both were slaves, and she was his first love, not his last.

Notes

1. Goody (1976a) especially pp. 104–11.
2. Ulp. *Reg.* V. 2–6. The notion of a *matrimonium non iustum* or *iniustum*, valid save that the children were not in the father's *potestas* (Corbett (1930) 30–39; Watson (1967) 27) has been shown to be mistaken (Volterra 1972).
3. Treggiari (1981a) and references there.
4. Ulpian, *l.c.* note 2 above; G.I. 56–92; Corbett (1930) 24–30; Watson (1967) 32–40. Relationships with foreigners might be regarded as marriages in foreign law, but not in Roman. Such liaisons appear to have been common in Roman Egypt; examples in Taubenschlag (1955) 106–8, who incorrectly calls them *iniusta matrimonia*.
5. *Tab. Herc.* LXXXIX: L. Venidius Ennychus and Livia Acte declare they have a daughter one year old; G.I. 29; Ulp. *Reg.* 3.3; Kaser (1971) 280. Corbett (1930: 27) takes this as a 'retroactive' grant of *conubium*.
6. T. XII. 11.1: Cic. *de re publ.* 2.37.63; Watson (1974) 333–41.
7. Corbett (1930) 31–34; Astolfi (1965) 26–7; Watson (1967) 32–7; Treggiari (1969) 81–6.
8. D. 23.2.16, 44, 47; 54.17.56.7; Ulp. *Reg*, 13.16.2; Astolfi (1965). Barmaids as prostitutes: see, e.g., AE 1978.216; Paul *Sent.* 2.26.11; D. 23.2.43; Kleberg (1957) 89–91; D'Avino (1967) 41–59; Hermansen (1981) 96–8; Kampen (1981) 110–12. Senatorial actors: AE 1978.145; Tac. *Ann.* 2.88; Suet. *Tib.* 35; D. 23.2.47, 48.5.11.2; Levick (1983). Corbett (1930: 38–9) argues from *Frag. Vat.* 168 that the law did not invalidate such marriages nor make the children illegitimate; but there is no certainty that the *lex Julia et Papia* is referred to.
9. Despite Mommsen (1887) III. 429–43. See references in note 7 above.
10. Fabre (1981) 166 ff., specially 168 n. 34. In the imperial household, however, the situation was reversed; male *servi Caesaris* had more social mobility than female (Weaver 1972: 175–6).
11. Paul *Sent.* 2.19.9; D. 23.2.13, 62.1; C. 5.4.3. Some thought it permissible if the patroness had been the man's fellow-slave and he had been made over to her: D. 40.2.14.

12. D. 23.2.38, 65 pr.; 24.1.3.1. On wills: D. 23.2.63, 30.128, 34.9.2.1–2; Gaudemet (1949) 341.

13. Corbett (1930) 39–44; Garnsey (1970a); Campbell (1978). The view that Septimius Severus abolished the ban is not securely established by the texts. Dissolution of previous marriages: D. 24.1.60.1, 61, 62. References to 'wives' and 'marriage' in contexts involving soldiers are susceptible of other explanations; see Corbett *l.c.* and Jung (1982). However, to postulate, as Jung does, the continuance of a *iustum matrimonium* of which the children, nevertheless, were illegitimate, is surely bad law. Demetria: P. Mich. VII. 442 (= FIRA III 20; Cavenaile no. 210); Fink (1941 and 1966).

14. Campbell, *l.c.*, especially 154 ff; FIRA I no. 78.

15. Granted by Vespasian: Girard (1923) 124–7; these and other privileges were also granted by decree of Domitian: FIRA I no. 76.

16. FIRA III no. 19a.

17. Suet. *Dom.* 8; D. 29.1.41.1, 34.9.14; Meyer (1895) 97–100; Astolfi (1965) 42–4.

18. G.I. 58–64; Ulp. *Reg.* 5.6; D. 23.2.39–40, 53 ff.; RE XIV 2.2266; Corbett (1930) 47–51; Watson (1967) 38–9; Kaser (1971) 75 n. 22, 316. The degrees are set out fully in D. 38.10 and *Inst.* III.6. For a simple summary, see Goody (1983) 136 and 138 fig. 2. On the breach of rule attested in Livy, see Kruger (1870); Watson (1975) 24. This provoked a political riot, raised by a plebeian, who claimed that he was being bereft of his (or 'a') betrothed; the argument apparently was that patrician exclusiveness would make it difficult for plebeians to secure rich(?) wives. Marriage of first cousins is first attested Livy 42.34.3 (171 B.C.); for the first century B.C., Cicero *pro Cluentio* 11, *Phil.* 2.99; Plutarch *Brutus* 13, *Antony* 9. Aristocratic endogamy: Thomas (1980) 353 ff.

19. Cicero, *pro Cluentio* 11–28; Tac. *Ann.* 12.6; Gaius I. 62.

20. Schaps (1979) 25–42.

21. Hombert and Préaux (1952) 151 ff.; Taubenschlag (1955) 111–12. Middleton (1962) 603–11 favours the explanation that it was intended as a means of keeping family property intact, but Hopkins (1980) 327 points out that the relevant social and economic factors occur also in other societies, where sibling marriage is not found. Effects of the *Const. Ant.*: Montevecchi (1979) 137–44.

22. *Coll.* 6.4.1.

23. Guarino (1943) 175 ff., especially 214 ff.; Thomas (1961) 65 ff. Adultery and *stuprum* are discussed below.

24. Tiberius, though, is said to have punished an incestuous father, and possibly his daughter as well, by precipitation from the Tarpeian rock; the sources hint at both mercenary and lustful interest on Tiberius' part: Tac. *Ann.* 6.19; Dio 58.22.

25. D. 48.5.12.1; 39(38).1–2, 4–7. Flavia Tertulla: D. 23.2.57a; though the word *matrimonium* is used, clearly the union was not legally a marriage.

26. Guarino (1943) 214 ff.; Garcia Garrido (1957) 82; D. 25.7.3, 48.5.35(34); *Inst.* IV .18.1. Cohabitation solely (apparently) D. 23.2.4.

27. RE XXII. 1070; D. 1.5.12, 28.2.29 pr., 38.16.3.11, 12. Eleven months not accepted: Gell. *N.A.* 3.16.12 and D. 38.16.3.11. However, L. Papirius as praetor allowed the claim as heir even of a child whose mother said the pregnancy had lasted 13 months (Pliny *N.H.* 7.39), because, he said, there seemed to be no fixed period for pregnancy. Also, precise dating of conception was made difficult by ignorance of the relationship of the menstrual cycle to fertility: Soranus *Gynaec.* 1.36.

28. Ulp. *Reg.* 5.2; G.I. 196; Corbett (1930) 51–3.

29. D. 23.3.39.1; Dalla (1978) 233–46. Whether Augustus' *lex Julia et Papia* changed this is disputed: Dalla, *l.c.* 257 nn. 79 and 80.

30. Dio 54.16.7; D. 23.1.9. On the whole question of the legal minimum age of

marriage for girls and the age at which they actually married, see Bang (1922), Garcia Garrido (1957) 76 ff.; Hopkins (1965b), Durry (1970), Ruggiero (1981).

31. Soranus *Gynaec*. I. 20; Hopkins (1965b) 310; Amundsen and Diers (1969).

32. Durry (1970) gives an affirmative answer to both questions. The counter-argument of Ruggiero (1981) 63 ff. seems founded on a misconception that Durry failed to distinguish between *de facto* physical cohabitation and consummation and the juridical status of marriage. Brunt (1971) 136–8, arguing against early marriage, seems to contradict himself on p. 138, where he says firstly, 'The poor man, moreover, needed a helpmate . . . he should therefore have looked first for a fully grown, physically active woman', and, further on, 'child labour was an asset to the poor household'. The 'poor man' of the first statement is surely thought of as a *paterfamilias*; the newlywed peasant need not have been, and his young bride could be as useful in the *familia* of his *pater* as in her own. In Roman Egypt, husbands apparently married at a markedly later age than wives: Hombert and Préaux (1952) 160 ff.

33. Tullia: RE VII A.2, 1329–36. Imperial ladies: Bang (1922), 134–5.

34. Inscriptional evidence analysed in Harkness (1896), Bang (1922), Durand (1959–60), Hajnal (1965) and Hopkins (1965b). On bias of various kinds, see Durand, *l.c.* 369–70; Hopkins (1965b) 321–6, (1966) 245–64. Egyptian census: Hombert and Préaux (1952) 160 ff.

35. Harkness (1896) 35–51; Hopkins (1965b) 321; Hajnal (1965) 120–2. See also Goody (1983) 8–9, though the evidence for delay in Egypt is less conclusive than his reference to Hopkins (1980) 333 suggests.

36. D. 23.1.9., 2.4, 3.68; 24.1.32.27. For the father's participation, D. 27.6.11.2.

37. Reinach (1956) 268 ff.; Garcia Garrido (1957) 76 ff.

38. E.g., Ulp. *Reg*. 5.2; D. 24.1.65, 35.10.101 pr., 36.2.30.

39. Plutarch, *comp. Lyc. et Numa* 4; Soranus, *Gynaec*. I. 33. Macrobius, *comm. in Somn. Scip*. 1.71, may be taking the same view, if his phrase *propter votorum festinationem* means that it is the impatience of the *girls'* desires (not that of the men) that is to be satisified by the earlier legal age of marriage. Septimius Severus and Caracalla gave a rescript (D. 48.5.14(13).8) to the effect that a man could not exercise a husband's right to prosecute his wife for unfaithfulness during their cohabitation before she reached the age of twelve, but could prosecute her as though betrothed (*quasi sponsa*). This probably means that Servus allowed the fiancé the general third-party right to prosecute her as though for adultery and not merely *stuprum*: Thomas (1961:70–71). Some twelve-year old girls are sexually eager; intercourse with three youths in one day, at her invitation, was recently achieved by a girl in Reading: report in *Reading Chronicle*, May 4, 1984.

40. Soranus, *Gynaec*. I. 36; Hopkins (1965a); Noonan (1966) 10–29.

41. Frier (1982). Skeletal remains in Greece from the Roman period have been alleged to show an average life-span for women of six years less than for men (Angel 1972), but the evidence is of doubtful validity: Samuel *et al.* (1971) 11–14.

42. Report in *The Times*, April 7, 1978; see also Tannahill (1981) 119.

43. D. 47.10.25, 48.5.6.1., 48.9.38.3, 50.16.101; Guarino (1943) 185. Concubines and women with whom there was no *conubium* were excluded. See also notes 26 and 38 above.

44. Ulp. *Reg*. 5.2; Paul, D. 23.2.2; texts in Corbett (1930) 55 n. 1; for the daughter's right of refusal, D. 23.1.12 (Ulpian). On the subject of consent, see Corbett, *l.c.* 53–67; Watson (1967) 41–7, (1975) 25–8; Kaser (1971) 314–5; Huber (1977). There is an extensive modern literature concerned not primarily with consent as a prerequisite for establishing marriage but with its function as a concept in maintaining the legal existence of a marriage: see Huber (1977) and bibliography there and the criticism of Huber by Longo (1977).

45. Plutarch, *Cato min.* 30, *Pompey* 44; Cato would presumably be tutor to his nieces.

46. Cicero, *ad Fam.* 8.6.2; *ad Att.* 6.6.1.
47. Paul, *Sent.* 2.19.2; 5.6.15; see also the sample case cited in *Frag. Vat.* 102.
48. D. 23.2.19.
49. Corbett (1930) 55 n. 1, 57.
50. Livy 38.57.5-8.
51. Pliny, *Ep.* 1.10; 1.14; 6.26; 6.32.
52. Varro *L.L.* 6.29; Macrobius 1.15.21; other references in Scullard (1981) index *s.v.* 'marriage'; Michels (1967) 63-5.
53. In A.D. 48, Claudius' wife Messalina celebrated a wedding with her lover Silius, but without sending Claudius formal notice of divorce: Tac. *Ann.* 11.26-38. Despite Narcissus' outburst (c. 30), explicable by the political significance of Silius' behaviour, Tacitus' account does not appear to assume either that Messalina's marriage to Claudius had been terminated *ipso facto* or that another valid marriage had been contracted; this is borne out also by Suet. *Cl.* 29 and Dio *Epit.* 60(61)31.
54. Catullus 61; Williams (1958) 16-18; Humbert (1972) 3-19.
55. Corbett (1930) 1-23; Watson (1967) 11-18; Kaser (1971) 75-6, 312-4.
56. Corbett (1930) 9-15; Watson (1965a) 1-9, (1967) 11-18.
57. D. 45.1.134 pr.; cf. C. 8.38.2 (Alexander Severus, A.D. 223). Not surprisingly, when the concept of indissoluble marriage returned, with greater force, in the Christian empire, a penalty was imposed by law; both parties put up a sum, *arra*, which was liable to forfeit if the match was broken off without good cause (C. 5.1.5, 5.3.15; C. Th. 3.6.1).
58. Suet. *Aug.* 63.2; Dio 48.54.4. For other examples, see Bang (1922) 133. Modestinus: D. 23.1.14; Corbett (1930) 4.
59. For the consequences of *infamia* see the summary in Buckland (1966) 91-2; for its application to women, Greenidge (1894) 170-6. Women were in any case unable to bring a lawsuit (*postulare*) on behalf of another person, nor could they prosecute in certain criminal cases, save for the murder of certain specified close relatives, nor could they hold public office: D. 3.1.1.5; 5.1.12.2; 48.2.1.
60. D. 23.2.12.1-2; 23.2.14.4.
61. D. 48.5.14.3 and 8, and see note 39 above.
62. Corbett (1930) 16, 92-3, 114-15, 204-10. On the *lex Furia*: G. II. 225, IV. 23; *Frag. Vat.* 302; Wesel (1964) 308-16; Watson (1971) 163-7. On the *lex Cincia*: Casavola (1960) 54-104.
63. D. 22.5.4. and 5.
64. D. 48.9.3 and 4.
65. D. 23.2.1.
66. D. 25.7.4 (Paul): concubinage is distinguished from marriage by the *animi destinatio*, the intention of the parties. D. 24.1.32.13 (Ulpian): even if the parties for some reason live apart for a lengthy period, this does not put an end to the marriage, *non enim coitus matrimonium facit, sed maritalis affectio* — marriage is made not by sexual relations but by the intent of the parties.
67. Paul *Sent.* 2.19.8; D. 23.2.5; Corbett (1930) 92-4.
68. C. 5.4.9; Watson (1973-4) 1123-4. Watson is surely right in interpreting the wording of the reply as indicating that Fortunatus was concerned about the validity of the marriage, not merely, as Wolff (1939a: 87) says, about the possibility of proving it. Verbal acknowledgement sufficed: D. 20.1.4; 22.4.4; Karabélias (1984).
69. Williams (1968) 382.
70. Ruga: Gell. *N.A.* 4.3; Dion. Hal. 2.25.7; Corbett (1930) 218; Watson (1965b). The census procedure: Dion. Hal. 4.15.6; *Tab. Herc.* (FIRA I no. 13) lines 142 ff.; Nicolet (1980) chapter II. Joke: Cicero *de or.* 2.260; Gell. *N.A.* 4.20. Avoidance of census: (?) Cicero, *Verr.* 2.1.41.104.
71. Schulz (1942-3).
72. Apuleius, *Apologia* 68.5; P. Mich. VII. 434 (= FIRA III no. 17, Cavenaile

208–9), and see also PSI 730 (= Cavenaile 207); Sanders (1938); Wolff (1939a), especially chapters 2 and 4; Taubenschlag (1955) 117–8.

73. BGU IV. 1050–2, 1098–1101; Wolff (1939a) 34 ff.; Lewis (1983) 55. BGU IV 1052 (= Hunt and Edgar no. 3) is cited in the text.

74. *Univira*: Lattimore (1942) 296 n. 251; Humbert (1972) 62 ff.; Lightman and Zeisel (1977). Rituals: Gagé (1963) 59–60, 120–2; Humbert, *l.c.* 51–5, 62–7.

75. RE VIII A 2099 ff.; Corbett (1930) 249 ff.; Humbert (1972) 113 ff. and references there.

76. Ovid, *Fasti* 1.33–6; Michels (1967) 119–23.

77. Paul, *Sent.* 1.21.13; *Frag. Vat.* 320–1; D. 3.2.8–11; Greenidge (1894) 44, 67, 125–7, 174; Kaser (1971) 317–8.

78. So *VIR* V. 1144.

79. Corbett (1930) 250.

80. Ulp. *Reg.* 5.10; Kaser (1971) 345–6. Tiberius' younger brother Drusus was recognised as the child of Tiberius Nero, not of Augustus: Suet. *Aug.* 62.2.

81. D. 37.9 *de ventre in possessionem mittendo*; D. 38.16.3.9 and 11. A husband could appoint an unborn child as heir in his will: D. 28.2.27. The Twelve Tables recognised the right to inherit of children born within ten months after the husband's death: T. XII. 4.4; Gell. *N.A.* 3.16.12.

82. Metro (1964) 951–7. D. 25.3 and 4; 25.4.10 deals particularly with widows.

83. Wilcken (1906); Wehrli (1982); Gardner (1984).

84. Aristotle *gen. anim.* 773a 30 ff.; Lienau (1971) and texts cited there. Some strange stories are told in Pliny *N.H.* 7.49. Two different theories on conception were current, one that man supplied all the generative elements, woman's function being merely to incubate and nourish the embryo; the other, that both sexes contributed 'semen'. For a full account of both, see Landels (1979). Neither, however, would produce 'confusion of the blood' in the sense required.

85. Sacrifice: Plut. *Numa* 12. Ceremonies: Livy 22.56.4–5.

86. Ulp. *Reg.* 14; D. 23.2.6; C. 2.11.15; 6.40.2 ff.; D. 3.2.11; Kaser (1971) 321 n. 31.

87. Sen. *Ep.* 63.13; Dio 59.7.5; D. 3.2.8, 11.

88. D. 36.1.67 pr.; Kaser (1971) 254; Watson (1971) 115.

89. FIRA III no.70; Kaser (1971) 348; Humbert (1972) 283 ff.; on usufruct, Humbert *l.c.* 233 ff.

90. Pliny *Ep.* 6.33; Val. Max. 7.7.4; Apuleius, *Apol.* 71.

91. Corbett (1930) 250–1.

92. Brunt (1971) 151 ff.; Weaver (1972) 102–4, 174–6; Treggiari (1976) 96; Penta (1980) 343–5; Fabre (1981) 166 ff.

93. Paul, *Sent.* 2.20.1; D. 25.7; Watson (1967) 1–10; Kaser (1971) 328–9; Treggiari (1981b).

94. Plaut. *Trin.* 689 ff.; Watson (1967) 2 ff.

95. Cic. *de orat.* 1.40.183. The problems seem to arise from ignorance of the husband's intention, i.e., whether or not his behaviour in Rome was to be taken as indicating the wish to terminate his marriage in Spain: Robleda (1982) 384.

96. D. 23.2.45; 24.2.10–11; 25.7.1.2; services: D. 38.1.46.

97. Dio 65.14; Suet, *Vesp.* 3, *Dom.* 12; *SHA Marcus* 29, *Ant. Pius* 8; Rawson (1974) 288; and see the case of the high-ranking Cocceius Cassianus: D. 34.9.16.

98. CIL I² 2527a (= ILLRP 795); Fabre (1981) 172.

99. D. 25.7.1.1, 3 pr., 1; 48.5.14 pr.

100. Rawson (1974); Treggiari (1981a and b).

101. D. 23.3.39 pr.; Treggiari (1981a) 58.

102. CIL VI 15598; Treggiari, *l.c.* 48–9.

103. Weaver (1967) 126–9; (1972) 114 ff.; Treggiari (1981a) 52. A similar situation had existed in the late Republic in relation to *servi publici* (Weaver, *l.c.* 127 n. 11).

104. G.I. 84, 91, 160; Crook (1967a) 62; (1967b); Weaver (1972) 164 ff.
105. Treggiari (1981a) 53–4, 57–8.
106. AE 1981.160 (*Not. d. Scavi* 1928, 139 ff).

4   Some Effects of Marriage

A woman married with *manus* was effectively in the position of an adopted daughter in relation to the *pater* of the *familia*. She had no legal independence and no independent property. A wife in a free marriage was legally independent of her husband (although possibly still under the *potestas* of her father), but her marriage did also have certain legal and social consequences.

A married woman was regarded as having taken on the social status of her husband. In a society as stratified as that of the Romans this was a matter of some importance. Already in the Republic, the senators and their families were distinguished from the *equites* and theirs, and both from the rest. Differentiation of social status could have important legal implications, particularly in the trial and punishment of offenders. Within the senatorial order, there was a social ranking according to the level of magistracies attained by the menfolk; Antony, according to Suetonius, charged Octavian, amongst other misdemeanours, with a sexual indiscretion involving a *consularis femina* (woman married to an ex-consul). Under the empire designations by office were supplemented by a range of commendatory epithets, correspondingly graded (*illustris, clarissimus, honestus*, etc.)

Ulpian, in the later second century A.D., comments on the workings of social protocol. Everyone agrees, he says, that a consular man takes precedence over a consular woman. His personal opinion is that a praetorian man also takes precedence over a consular woman, 'because there is greater *dignitas* in the male sex'. Only wives and unmarried daughters count; a woman does not become consular because her son does. A mésalliance brings a drop in status; a senator's daughter would be *clarissima* only so long as she herself was not married to anyone below that rank. Occasionally, the emperor might allow the former wife of a senator to keep her status when she married again, this time to someone of lower rank; up to the reign of Alexander Severus at least, this was very rarely allowed.[1]

Similarly, in Eastern provinces, women are found bearing the titles of magistracies and priesthoods, sometimes apparently in their own right; in some instances at least, they are so designated because their husbands are holding those offices. The offices themselves, however, had lost real executive importance and become mainly a vehicle for the bestowal of patronage and bounty in the local community.[2]

A wife was also legally regarded as domiciled in the same municipality or province as her husband or, in the case of a widow, late husband.[3]

Maintenance

A wife had no legal claim to maintenance by her husband. Usually, she brought with her into marriage a dowry which could be regarded as a contribution from her side to their joint expenses, but a dowry was not obligatory, and there does not seem to have been any legal obligation on the husband to use it for her maintenance.

In a free marriage, probably the wife's only remedy against a non-maintaining husband was divorce. This seems likely from the fact that our only evidence for a procedure to obtain maintenance concerns a situation in which divorce was, for a particular reason, excluded. 'Suppose', Ulpian says, 'a wife has gone mad and her husband does not want to dissolve the marriage.' The significance of this is that the wife, being mad, *cannot* divorce her husband (Ulpian seems to assume that her *pater* is dead). The husband is actuated by shrewdness (*calliditate*); he wants to hang on to the dowry. If he is clearly not looking after his wife, then the mad woman's keeper (*curator*) or her relatives (*cognati*) can appeal to the magistrate, to have the husband compelled to give his wife maintenance and medical treatment and all the care that it is seemly (*decet* — not, note, 'obligatory') for a husband to give his wife in proportion to the dowry.[4] The inference is that, if there was no dowry, he could not be required to provide anything; but, if there was no dowry, this neglectful husband would presumably have no motive for retaining his wife.

In practice, of course, husbands did usually maintain their wives. The lawyers shed incidental light upon domestic arrangements. Questions were bound to arise from time to time — particularly upon divorce, or the death of either partner — about the legal ownership of items of property or sums of money. Since, by customary law, gifts between husband and wife were invalid,[5] lawyers could often be called upon to advise on what should or should not be regarded as a valid gift. Even so, we find that a two-way transmission is often envisaged. Husband and wife might allow each other the use of each other's clothing or slaves, or either might live in the other's house free of charge. A husband might give his wife wool to make herself some clothes, though lawyers could not agree whether in that case the clothes belonged to him or her. She could use his slaves, *gratis*, to make up her own wool into clothes for herself; if the clothing was for him, he should pay her for the wool. The wife might have slaves or animals which were *in usu communi*, kept for common use, and the husband could not, it was thought, require his wife to refund any money he spent on their upkeep. Sometimes, cash changed hands. A husband might give his wife travelling expenses for a journey to be undertaken on his behalf, and that money was not recoverable. The implication is that — in the eyes of the law at least — any other trips would have to be made at the wife's own expense.[6]

Some husbands made their wives a yearly or monthly allowance. Ulpian thought that valid, so long as it did not exceed the revenue of the dowry. Sometimes the husband and wife would agree that she should use her dowry to maintain herself and her slaves. Husband and father-in-law might specifically agree the question of maintenance between them before the marriage.[7]

A wife who brought a large dowry might feel justified in putting pressure on her husband to keep her in a correspondingly lavish style. In Plautus' *Aulularia*, a nagging wife is represented as making her expectations clear: 'I brought you a dowry far bigger than the money you had; so it's fair that I should be given purple clothes, gold jewellery, slave-girls, mules, grooms, footmen, pages and a carriage.' On the other hand, when a (relatively) poor friend's daughter married well, Pliny seemed to think it natural that her family and friends, not her husband, should provide the means for her to be dressed and attended in the style to which her husband was accustomed.[8]

There were occasions in the year when a Roman husband liked to give his wife presents. Her birthday was one. The first day of March, the festival of the *Matronalia*, was another. Legal opinion was that only a moderate gift was permissible. However, it was all right for him to give his wife money for the general enhancement of her life-style. So, she might be given money to spend on delicacies (*in opsonio*), or perfume, or to feed her own personal slave staff, 'because she does not appear to have been made wealthier' by such a gift (though if a husband wanted to be awkward and demand payment for anything he spent on the upkeep of his wife's slaves, Pomponius thought he was entitled to do so).[9]

Gourmet foods, perfumes and personal servants were the little luxuries of life. It could normally be taken for granted that the wife could avail herself of the furnishings in the house and share in the ordinary domestic diet of the household. To maintain their ordinary standard of living, widows were often left as legacies household goods (*supellex*) and provisions (*penus*), the latter of which might be a fixed amount or an annual allowance. Jurists' comments give us an idea of their nature and extent.

Supellex included the basic furniture, pots and pans, crockery and household textiles belonging to the *pater* and intended for general household use. Paul gives a representative list which includes tables, seats, beds ('even inlaid with silver'), mattresses, covers, water-pots, basins, candelabra and lamps. He was doubtful whether coverlets should properly be classed with household goods, like pillows, or counted as clothing. Such things as clothes or books, or the chests and cupboards used to contain them, were not included (presumably because their use was personal, not general); for the same reason Alfenus excluded writing tablets and notebooks. There was some discussion on the propriety of including items made of particularly costly materials (and presumably not separately specified in a will). Paul and Papinian admit furniture partly or wholly of silver and even gold, and crystal vessels, but are doubtful about silver tableware. Modestinus reports a case where the opinion was given that anything silver among the furniture was to be included in the bequest, but not the tableware, without separate proof that the husband had intended the wife to have it. Celsus, writing in the latter part of the first century A.D., looks back to a less luxurious age:

People used to have household goods made of pottery, wood, glass or copper; now they are of ivory, tortoiseshell and silver. Nowadays they even have them made from gold and precious stones. So one has to consider the nature of the objects rather than the material of which they are made, to decide whether they are household goods, silverware or clothing.

Of course, the jurists are writing about the appurtenances of the homes of the wealthy; recourse to law over humble furnishings was less likely.[10]

Penus[11] was defined by the great Republican jurist Q. Mucius Scaevola as those things eatable or drinkable which had been procured for the use of the *pater* or his wife or children or the household; some jurists added also his friends and clients and 'those about him' (i.e., enough to allow for some entertaining) and the domestic animals. It was agreed that basic foodstuffs were included, such as grain, vegetables, oil and wine, though there was some hesitancy about honey, *garum* (fish relish) and seasonings and flavourings such as herbs and spices. Some added wood and firing (presumably for cooking) and even incense and wax candles. There was argument about perfumes and writing paper: Ulpian wanted to include only writing paper for household accounts. Containers were excluded; obviously, liquids had to come in containers, but the empties should be returned. Sometimes, apparently, the legacy might be in the form of a sum of cash, for the purchase of provisions.

However much lawyers might solemnly discuss the precise content and extent of general legacies of *penus* and *supellex*, it may be assumed that in her husband's lifetime the wife would have had the free use of all the sorts of things specified, as well as some measure of control over their management and use, in her role as housekeeper.[12]

Separate Property

A wife *in manu* had no property of her own, and anything given or bequeathed to her was absorbed in her husband's property.[13] Any property a woman (*sui iuris*) owned before entering a marriage with *manus* went to her husband, but was reckoned, Cicero tells us, as dowry, and so presumably was liable to be returned at the end of the marriage.[14] A wife *in potestate* also had no property of her own, during her father's lifetime. The father might assign the husband additional property, over and above the dowry, for his daughter's support, but apparently with the proviso that it should not, as the dowry was, be regarded as subject to possible claims for retention by the husband at the end of the marriage. A married daughter who became *sui iuris* might be bequeathed this property; even if she was not, Papinian thought she had a claim to it.[15]

Women *sui iuris* could have property of their own. Although it was entirely theirs, they sometimes chose to have the administering of some, or all, of it done by their husbands, particularly of property which they contributed for the running of the household. The arrangements might be very formal, with an inventory, and the husband required to render account. This sort of practical arrangement probably goes back to the early days of free marriage. It can be seen that it might lead to friction. Thus the elder Cato (no advocate of female independence) in his speech against the proposal of the *lex Voconia* (169 B.C.) brings it in as the crowning indignity which the husband of a wealthy wife might have to face:[16]

To begin with, the woman brought you a big dowry; next, she retains (*recipit*) a large sum of money which she does not entrust to her husband's control, but she gives it to him as a loan; lastly, when she is annoyed with him, she orders a 'reclaimable slave' (*servus recepticius*) to chase him about and pester him for it.[17]

Cato is drawing to a climax. In the first place, he assumes his audience's familiarity with the uppishness of a well-dowered wife (as Plautus also does in the passage of the *Aulularia* already quoted). In the second place, it is humiliating for a man to have to borrow money from his own wife. And the last straw is when she demands it back through one of the household servants — but one who, what is more, is technically hers, not his, and can get away with such insolent behaviour towards the master.

A more roseate view appears in the *Laudatio Turiae*.[18] The writer's wife had contributed her entire inheritance to the common fund, and anything she acquired as well. A cynic might remark that, in these circumstances, her husband could hardly object to her having supported and, apparently, even lodged, several of her relatives; however, the community of property went so far that he contributed to the dowries of members of her family. Such total sharing was perhaps unusual among the wealthy. In humbler households, specially in the countryside, where the property shared might consist mainly of basic chattels and utensils, the situation might resemble that in the house of Columella's idealised farmer of the past (contrasted with his contemporary absentee rancher): 'There was no obvious division of property in the home, nothing which husband or wife claimed by right as their own, but both conspired together for the common advantage.'[19]

Trouble would come — then as now — upon divorce, when disputes arose over ownership of the household goods. There could be problems also on the death of a husband, when there might be uncertainty about the provenance and legal ownership of some of the property in the widow's possession. To meet this difficulty, a solution was devised by Q. Mucius Scaevola, the *praesumptio Muciana*. He said that, where there was no proof as to the source from which she obtained it, it would be both truer and more honourable to assume that the woman got the property from her husband or someone in his *potestas*.[20] It is usually assumed that the original occasion for the *praesumptio* concerned a wife *in manu*, whose husband had bequeathed her a legacy in some such terms as 'whatever my wife received from me in marriage'. This is quite likely, though clearly the situation could arise also, concerning both material property and money, in relation to a wife *sui iuris*, specially if she did not always keep a strict record of her financial dealings; nor does the text actually say that the woman's husband was dead.

Pomponius commented that Mucius' purpose in giving this judgment appears to have been *evitandi turpis quaestus gratia circa uxorem*, 'to avoid shameful enquiry, with reference to a wife'.

What the *turpis quaestus* might be, one may speculate. What Pomponius (and perhaps Mucius) had in mind was probably something like the uncovering of gifts from an adulterous lover. Further light is shed on this by the story of a greedy woman, Otacilia Laterensis.[21] She was the mistress of one C. Visellius Varro. He fell seriously ill and expected to die. Wishing to leave her a legacy discreetly, he concocted with her a fake debt of 300,000 sesterces, which she was to reclaim from his heirs after his death, and Otacilia made an entry in her account books to the effect that she had paid him this sum. To her chagrin, he did not die. Throwing off the mask of affection, she sued him for the money. The case was judged by C. Aquilius (praetor 66 B.C.), in consultation with other leading Romans. If he could simultaneously have released Varro from the financial obligation and condemned his conduct he would have done so. As it was, he dismissed Otacilia's vexatious private prosecution and left the charge of adultery to be punished by a public court (says Valerius Maximus, apparently forgetting that adultery did not constitute a criminal offence until Augustus' legislation of 18 B.C.).

The whole point of the manoeuvre must have been that Otacilia expected to have to be able to account for her personal wealth in the event of the termination of her marriage. The implications are, not only that women of some wealth were in the habit of keeping account-books, but that such inquiry into a wife's or widow's affairs was not uncommon.

It would be very much in a wife's interests to record the sources of her property. The text relating to the *praesumptio Muciana* appears in the *Digest* in the section relating to gifts between husband and wife. Since such gifts were void, the effect of the *praesumptio Muciana* would be that all property which the wife could not otherwise account for would be assumed to belong to the husband.[22] If the *praesumptio* applied in the event of divorce as well as of widowhood, it would provide an unscrupulous husband with a strong motive for dishonesty.

Protection of Separate Property

The ban on gifts between husband and wife was intended to prevent their affection from causing them to 'despoil themselves'. If both parties were equally generous, of course, the *status quo* would ultimately be preserved; however, it was recognised that freedom to alienate their property to each other could produce inequality, and it could also, it was suggested, introduce an element of purchase into marriage. Dowries were overlooked in this connection, presumably because they were not normally expected to be sources of clear profit for the husband. Since, however, the ban extended also to persons in the same *potestas* as either, and to the *pater* of either, the real reason seems to have been the aim of preserving the property of the respective *familiae*.[23]

Husband and wife were not the only persons affected by the ban. Gifts between most in-laws (including the fathers on either side) were banned — but not between mother-in-law and daughter-in-law, since, in free marriage, neither belonged to the husband's *familia*.

Gifts in certain circumstances were valid. Three of the situations specified anticipate the termination of the marriage: a gift might be made which would become the legal property of the recipient upon the death or exile of the other partner or the termination of the marriage by divorce.[24] Several other circumstances are mentioned. (i) If a house owned by the wife was destroyed by fire, the husband could give her enough money to pay for rebuilding it. The reasoning behind this may be that it was felt that, whereas a husband had a certain moral obligation to provide a roof over the head of his wife (and widow), he might not want to bequeath to her the actual house they occupied together in his lifetime. (ii) A slave could be given, to be manumitted by the recipient. He did not become the property of the recipient until the manumission process began. The benefit of the gift would lie in the fact that the recipient, not the former owner, would enjoy the rights of a patron; but the property of the donor was not diminished, since the assumption was that he/she would have manumitted the slave anyway; and those gifts were valid which did not make the giver poorer and the recipient richer. (iii) On similar grounds, either husband or wife could give the other a site for a burial place or a religious shrine. It ceased to be the property of the donor only when a body was interred there, or it was consecrated, but it then became 'religious' and therefore inalienable. (iv) A constitution of the emperor Antoninus Pius allowed a wife to make a gift to her husband to enable him to enhance his status, by entry into the senatorial or equestrian order, or by the giving of games. Since a wife shared her husband's social status, obviously the gift could be held to confer a benefit on her too.[25]

Until the end of the Republic, both husband and wife were apparently able to stand surety for each other's debts. Augustus, and then Claudius, issued edicts forbidding women to intervene (*intercedere*) on behalf of their husbands. This was generalised, in the middle of the first century, by the *senatusconsultum Velleianum*, into a ban on all 'intervention' by women on behalf of anyone.[26] Although it was subsequently given a very wide application and interpreted, e.g., by Ulpian as a protection introduced because of the 'weakness of the sex', it is plain from the wording of the *senatusconsultum* as quoted in *Digest* 16.1.2, and from Paul's paraphrase of it, (i) that it was primarily concerned with sureties and pledges, and (ii) that it arose from a feeling that such matters were properly the preserve of men. Paul explains why: because giving surety put the *res familiaris* in danger. In essence, therefore, the edicts of Augustus and Claudius seem to have been similar in nature and intent to the ban on gift-giving. The wife was not to be allowed, because of undue influence on her husband's part (or her excessive affection for him) to endanger her own property, in which her family of origin or, if she were freed, her patron had an interest. *Tutela* might not in practice be exercised very effectively, but it had been there as a safeguard of those interests. The Augustan *ius liberorum* created a whole category of women free from tutelage; Claudius' abolition of agnate *tutela* removed the direct interest of many tutors.

The emperors' edicts restored some measure of protection for the interests of the *familia* against the particular danger of exploitation of women by pressure from those to whom they were most likely to be susceptible, i.e., their husbands. The *senatusconsultum* strengthened and generalised this protection. As cited by Ulpian, it included the phrase: 'it is not equitable that women should undertake the duties of men and be bound by obligations of such a kind.'

What does this mean? A man *sui iuris* was head of a *familia* or potential *familia*, and answerable to no one for his disposal of the property. A woman's *familia* consisted solely of herself, and there was usually another *familia* with a claim on the property. Her personal enjoyment of the property was one thing; but to give it away, or hazard its loss by making it a security for someone else's obligation was another, and 'inequitable' in view of the other interests involved. This asymmetry between the way in which male and female ownership of property was regarded is shown by the contrast between the ban on gifts between marriage partners and that on 'intervention'. The latter was barred by legal enactment and magisterial action; the former, which applied to both men and women, rested merely on customary law.

Although classical lawyers described a wife *in manu* as ranking as a daughter in her husband's *familia*,[27] his power over her was, as we have seen, limited in classical times by absence of the right of life and death and the right of noxal sale or surrender. Over a wife in free marriage he had no *potestas* at all. Nevertheless, the law regarded any assault upon the wife, whether *in manu* or not, as entitling the husband to bring a suit, *actio iniuriarum*. If she was still *in potestate*, both her father and her husband could bring actions and be compensated. The father could be compensated at the rate at which an assault on a widow was compensated; the husband, at the rate appropriate to a woman *sui iuris*. A woman *sui iuris* could herself also bring a suit. If the offender was the woman's patron, she could not sue; her husband could, but only if he was not also a freedman of the same patron.[28]

The reasoning is that the offender, if he knew that the woman was married or *in potestate*, intended to insult the father or husband. The relevant passage of the *Digest* does not set matters out very clearly, but it looks as though a plea of ignorance by the defendant could bar a suit by the husband. The provision allowing the husband to sue probably goes back to a time when most wives were *in manu* and therefore not legal persons in their own right. Its persistence in the age of free marriage reflects rather the fact that a woman, even if legally independent, socially and politically had no function in Roman society in the way that a man, as actual or potential head of a *familia*, did. Her *familia* consisted of herself alone; she was, as it were, an honorary member of her husband's.

Husbands and wives were expected not to bring penal or defaming actions against each other. These were not totally excluded, but a lesser penalty might be awarded.[29]

Husbands could not be compelled to give evidence against their in-laws; whether the same was true of husbands and wives is uncertain.[30]

If either stole property from the other, a suit should be brought not for theft, since that was an action bringing *infamia*, but for removal of goods (*rerum amotarum*). However, this action could be brought only after divorce. Otherwise, use was to be made of the quasi-contractual procedure of *condictio*, in which the owner expressed the right to be given his/her own property — a legal illogicality, noted by Gaius. Only the husband is mentioned, but no doubt this action was available also to the wife. An accomplice, however, would be liable for an action for theft. Since the dowry property was technically the husband's, in full legal ownership, it was he, and not the wife or the father, who had the right to prosecute for theft of such property.[31]

Augustus' Legislation

The laws of 18 B.C. and A.D. 9 (*lex Julia et Papia*) did not so much reward marriage as penalise celibacy. Marriage could remove some, but not all, of the disability; the production of legitimate children completed the process, and, as we have seen, fertility could also bring rewards.[32] Those chiefly affected by the penalties imposed on the unmarried were the well-to-do. Clearly, one at least of the aims of the original legislation (though not the only one) was to 'stabilise the transmission of property and consequently of status' among the Roman upper classes.[33]

Unmarried women between the ages of 20 and 50, including widows who had not remarried within a year (later two years) and divorcées not remarried within six months (later 18) were affected. The rules underwent modifications and additions over the years, aimed at stopping up loopholes; at the same time, exemptions could be bestowed by the grace of emperors upon the influential and their friends. *Senatusconsulta* of the reigns of Tiberius and Claudius ruled that women who did not marry before the age of 50 should not escape the penalties on reaching that age, even if they should then marry.[34]

The principal penalty was a ban on receiving legacies under wills, except, apparently, from relatives up to the sixth degree. Leaving legacies to persons outside this circle seems to have been a habit predominantly of the wealthier classes. Most people would lose little or nothing, in that respect, by remaining single; there might even, from the family's point of view, be some advantage in their men's doing so.[35] Marriage allowed the inheritance of half the legacy, and the whole as soon as a child was born and survived. Dio says that the *lex Papia* exempted some women from the operation of the *lex Voconia*. The latter law had banned women in the highest property class from being instituted heirs or receiving more than half an estate as a legacy. The Gnomon of the Idios Logos in Egypt says that women with patrimonies of more than 50,000 sesterces, without husbands or children, could not receive inheritances; women below the age of 50 could succeed if they had three children, or four for a freedwoman (the same qualification as for exemption from *tutela*). Which of the provisions of the Gnomon stem directly from Augustan laws and which from later modifications is uncertain. There were special rules for inheritance between husband and wife, but these are not really 'effects' of marriage *per se*, any more than the Gnomon's rules (24–26) about the forfeiture of the dowry to the fiscus at the end of marriages contracted by persons outside the specified age limits.[36]

The other major penalty to be removed by marriage within the prescribed limits of age or time was taxation. Again our evidence comes from the Gnomon. Unmarried women, whether freeborn or freed, with over 20,000 sesterces were subject to a one per cent tax.[37]

Notes

1. Suet. *Aug.* 69; D. 1.9.1; 8; 12, Chastagnol (1979); Holtheide (1980); Alföldy (1981) 194–8; legal implications in Garnsey (1970b), e.g., differential treatment of adulterers of low and high rank, *l.c.* 23–4, 104, 136.

2. Magie (1950) 44, 1519–8; Pleket (1969) nos. 11, 13, 18, 21, 23 (some Roman, some Greek); Garnsey (1974) 229–52, spec. 238; Jameson (1980) 847–9; MacMullen

(1980); Merkelbach (1980) 85 ff.; van Bremen (1983). Two of the (Greek) women in Pleket, nos. 21 and 23, are specially said to have volunteered to serve.

3. D. 50. 1.22.1; 32.

4. D. 24.3.22.8

5. D. 24.1; Casavola (1960) 103; Kaser (1971) 331–2. The ban probably originated during the Republic: Watson (1968) 229 ff.

6. D. 24.1.18, 29, 31. pr. 1; on travel, D. 24.1.21 pr.

7. D. 17.1.60.3; 24.1.15; 24.1.21.1. On the husband's rights of ownership over dowry revenues, see Dumont (1943).

8. Plaut. *Aulul.* 499 ff.; Plin. *Ep.* 6.32.

9. Plaut. *M.G.* 691; Tibullus 3.1.2. ff.; 8.1; Tertullian *de idol.* 14; D. 24.1.31.8, 9,10.

10. D. 33.10; Watson (1971) 152.

11. Gell. *N.A.* 4.1; D. 33.9.

12. Women keeping the keys: XII T. 4.3 (Cic. *Phil.* 2.69); Cicero's mother: *ad Fam.* 16.26.2; Pearce (1974) 25–8.

13. Ulp. *Reg.* 19. 18–19.

14. Cic. *Top.* 4.23; Watson (1967) 64, 76; despite Corbett (1930) 110 — the reference is to previous ownership (*fuerunt*) not subsequent acquisitions.

15. D. 6.1.65.1, 23.3.9.3, 35.2.95 pr.; Corbett (1930) 203 and references there; Kaser (1971) 330.

16. ORF³ fg. 158; Gell. 17.6.8; Kaser (1971) 330. n. 7. Kornhardt (1938) and Solazzi (1939) propose an alternative, but less convincing, explanation that the money and the slave both formed part of an inheritance she *received* during marriage.

17. Similar rhetoric was used by British politicians against the Married Women's Property Bills of 1857 and 1870: Holcombe (1983) 92–3, 164, 174–5.

18. FIRA III no. 69, 37 ff.

19. Columella, *R.R.* 12, *praef.* 8.

20. D. 24.1.51; Kaser (1971) 332; Watson (1971) 153.

21. Val. Max. 8.2.2; Watson (1965a) 32–36.

22. This may have been the origin of the later doctrine of European common law, not superseded in England until the laws of 1870 and 1882, that acquisitions during marriage were the property of the husband: Schulz (1951) 131; Stetson (1982) 8–9, 54–6; Holcombe (1983) 177 ff.

23. D. 24.1.1, 2, 3.

24. D. 24.1.9–13.1, 43.

25. (i) D. 24.1.14. (ii) D. 24.1.5.8, 7.8–9.1. This may be how Livia Culicina, whose parents' owner, C. Proculeius, manumitted them but bequeathed her with the rest of his legacy to Augustus, came to be the freedwoman of Livia (CIL 6.1815 = ILS 1926). On the same grounds, a husband might reject a legacy in his wife's favour: D. 24.1.5.13. (iii) D. 24.1.5.8. (iv) D. 24.1.40–42; Ulp. *Reg.* 7.1.

26. D. 16.1; Paul *Sent.* 2.11; Solazzi (1953); Humbert (1972) 188.

27. E.g., G. I. 114, 136.

28. D. 47.10.11, 18.

29. D. 11.3.17; 25.2.2, 3.2; Kaser (1971) 323 and n. 20.

30. Kaser, *l.c.*, n. 25.

31. G. IV. 4; D. 25.2.1, 7, 25, 29; 47.2.52. pr., 1, 2. It is interesting to observe that classical texts mostly envisage only the possibility of the wife stealing from the husband.

32. There is a very large body of modern writing on the Augustan laws. For a small selection of significant recent discussions, see Astolfi (1970 and 1973); Brunt (1971) 559–66; Csillag (1976); Raditsa (1980); Wallace-Hadrill (1981).

33. Wallace-Hadrill, *l.c.*, 59.

34. Ulp. *Reg*. 16; Kaser (1971) 318–21; 724–5. Exemptions: Pliny *Ep*. 10.94 (the beneficiary is Suetonius); Csillag (1976) 123.

35. Brunt (1971) 564; Wallace-Hadrill (1981) 62–4; Hopkins (1983) 236–41.

36. Dio 56.10; *Gnomon* 28, 30 (FIRA I no. 99).

37. *Gnomon* 29; Besnier (1949) 107–8. The rules on inheritance between husband and wife are summarised by Brunt (1971) 564.

5   Divorce

Divorce in the classical period was easy.[1] As marriage was based on consent, so the will of either of the consenting parties in free marriage to renounce it sufficed. As we have seen, until Marcus Aurelius, 'consenting party' included the *pater*.

From the point of view of the man, particularly in the wealthier classes, ease of divorce, allowing for serial marriage, was one strategy for securing an heir to his property. In pre-industrial societies, the probability of a man dying without a son to survive him was high. How common a motive this was for divorce among Romans we cannot easily determine. In England, in the period between about 1670 and 1857, when full divorce permitting remarriage was obtainable only by Act of Parliament (and therefore virtually confined to the wealthier classes), only about 200 such Acts were passed, nearly all instituted by men.[2]

Roman jurists mention sterility among typical causes of divorces by consent; however, a certain asymmetry is evident. Although male sterility was recognised as a possibility, almost all our evidence relates to divorce on the grounds that the wife had not produced children. Given the state of medical knowledge and techniques in the ancient world, it was not an unnatural assumption, except where the husband was actually impotent, that the deficiency lay with the wife. In any case, the man had a more direct interest in the production of heirs. We have already seen that by the time of Hadrian the law prescribed a procedure relating to a wife pregnant at the time of divorce; though liable on default to be obliged to recognise the child, the husband had the option of denying paternity. If he wished to claim the child as his, he could insist on the pregnancy and confinement being under surveillance, to avoid the possibility of substitution or a suppositious child. A generation later, because of a test case brought before the urban praetor, the emperors Marcus Aurelius and Lucius Verus issued a rescript specifying what should be done in the opposite situation, where a husband claimed that his divorced wife was pregnant and she denied it. If the husband insisted, the wife must be examined by three reliable midwives, chosen by

81

the urban praetor, at the home of a respectable matron. However, the emperors issued a warning that, if the husband's claim turned out to be false, his reputation would suffer.[3]

Among upper-class Romans, politics, as well as finance, influenced divorce, especially in the late Republic; moralists of the early empire were inclined also to blame the *dolce vita* of high society. These factors are less likely to have weighed among the humbler people. Divorce is not easy to detect, however; inscriptions recording persons married more than once do not necessarily specify whether the earlier marriages were ended by death or divorce. From the city of Rome, 23 inscriptions have been found where a dead woman is commemorated by two living 'husbands'. Although marriage is claimed, some at least of these unions began and ended as *contubernium* or had one slave partner; the remainder accounts for about two-thirds of the total. Even these people were relatively well-off, able to afford an inscription; among the poor, the desirability of maintaining the household as a viable economic unit might have been a disincentive to divorce.[4]

'Turia', we are told, offered her husband divorce, so that he could remarry and try to obtain an heir, but he refused. One of the more sensational instances preserved in anecdotal literature concerns the orator Hortensius (114–50 B.C.) and Cato the Younger. Hortensius in the first instance asked Cato to dissolve his daughter's marriage to Bibulus, so that he could marry her and have a son by her. When this was rejected, he persuaded Cato and his father-in-law to consent to Cato's divorcing his wife Marcia, who was then married to Hortensius. As Plutarch tells the story, politics played as much part in Hortensius' calculations as progeny, since he already had a surviving son. Cato's reluctance may not have been very strong; when Hortensius died a few years later, he left Marcia a very rich widow, and Cato remarried her. Marcia's opinions are not recorded; but if she was now rich in her own right, she must by then have become *sui iuris*, and freely consented to the remarriage. She and Cato had had surviving children by the earlier marriage.[5]

Augustus' legislation, while doing little or nothing to discourage divorce, encouraged remarriage and the production of children.

Divorce was a private act and as such was subject to no limitation by law, with one exception, introduced by Augustus. A freedwoman married to her patron could not divorce him without his consent.[6] This is the exception that proves the rule. The reason for the exception lies in the patron's rights (as heir on intestacy) over his wife's property. In other words, patron–freedwoman marriage was the one type of free marriage in which there was not complete separation of property as between husband and wife. Moreover, the Augustan *ius liberorum* meant that, if a patron-husband released his wife to marry another man, he risked losing his inheritance rights over her property, to the benefit of another man's children.

Divorce in Marriage with *Manus*

We have little direct evidence for divorce in *manus*-marriage.[7] Since the wife was part of the *familia* of the husband, then steps must be taken to exclude her from the *familia*. Originally, the wife could not take the initiative and obtain release from *manus*. This meant, in effect, that a husband could divorce his wife, but she could not divorce him.[8]

Plutarch comments on the severity of this. However, from what he says, it appears that in the early Republic at least (if not actually by a 'law of Romulus') divorce was permitted to the husband only on a few specific grounds. Because of the original absence of punctuation in classical texts, these grounds could be read as 'poisoning of children, substitution (or theft) of keys, wine-drinking' or 'poisoning, substitution of children or keys, wine-drinking'. Whatever the significance of the earlier part of the list, the last two items show a concern for the safety of the household property and, perhaps, for the sexual restraint of the woman. There appears to have been a provision in the Twelve Tables about divorce, but its precise nature cannot now be recaptured. At all events, it seems that in the early Republic divorce was permitted to the husband only for a few specific causes, and he was liable to forfeit his property, paying half to his ex-wife and half to the goddess Ceres, if he divorced her for any other reason.[9]

The results, according to Dionysius of Halicarnassus (2.25.7), were excellent. There were no divorces at all for the first 520 years of Rome's existence. This takes us down approximately to the date of the divorce by Spurius Carvilius Ruga; and Dionysius is perhaps wrong.[10] Women were led to behave themselves with modesty and decorum and, having no other recourse, to conform themselves to the will of their husbands. Their rewards were to be mistress in the house to the same degree as the husband was master, and after his death to succeed to his estate as a daughter to a father (Dionysius omits to add — sharing the estate with any children by that or other marriages, and only if the husband had not provided otherwise by will).

Carvilius divorced his wife, not for any of the specified causes, but because she had failed to produce children. Watson (1965b) argues plausibly that Carvilius pleaded (successfully) against surrendering any property to his wife, and that this created a legal precedent. Henceforth, an innocent wife could be divorced and receive no financial compensation. The result was the development of pre-marital agreements to secure the return of the dowry, and also a legal procedure for its recovery, the *actio rei uxoriae*. In later Republican law, there were no fixed grounds for divorce.

Dionysius adds that marriage with *confarreatio* was totally indissoluble. That may already have ceased to be the case by the end of the Republic, since in Festus *diffarreatio* is explained as a ritual by which a man and woman may be sundered. It is unlikely to have remained indissoluble even for the *flamen Dialis* very long after Tiberius' limitation of the effects of *confarreatio*; by the time of Domitian the *flamen Dialis* could obtain a divorce, by imperial dispensation. In the historical period few outside the priesthood are likely to have been married with *confarreatio*.[11]

Divorce in *manus*-marriage would require not merely a repudiation but the breaking of *manus* by 'remancipation' of the wife. The text of Gaius is defective at a crucial point, but it looks as though by this time, doubtless under the influence of free marriage, it *was* possible for a woman or her father to take the initiative in obtaining a divorce from a *manus*-marriage. A daughter, he says, cannot compel her father, but a wife, if she has sent a *repudium* (notice of divorce), can compel her husband (*sc.* to remancipate her), just as though she had never been married to him.[12]

Procedures for Divorce

The law prescribed no fixed procedure for divorce from a free marriage. It is sometimes alleged that the Twelve Tables, as cited in Cicero *Phil.* 2.69, did lay down a fixed formula of words, at least for divorce by the husband, the only type then available. What Cicero says is: *Illam suam suas res sibi habere iussit ex XII Tabulis clavis ademit exegit.* However, the meaning changes, depending on whether one punctuates after *iussit* or after *Tabulis*: (i) 'He told his wife to keep her own belongings; in accordance with the Twelve Tables, he took away the keys and drove her out'; (ii) 'In accordance with the Twelve Tables, he told his wife to keep her own belongings; he took away the keys and drove her out'. The second version would mean that the Twelve Tables specified a formula of words, *tuas res tibi habeto*. An (unconvincing) attempt has been made to relate these words to a legal procedure for regulating the property and recovering the wife's dowry.[13]

Certainly, some such phrase seems to have been traditional. Gaius says merely that in divorces, 'that is, in the announcing of the divorce', this phrase is acceptable, and so also is *res tuas tibi agito*; he does not say that they were either essential or compulsory.[14]

The stories of the man with a wife in Spain and another in Rome, and the aftermath of Messalina's wedding to Silius (see Chapter 3, notes 53 and 95), indicate that a divorce could be held to have taken place, even without a formal declaration, if there appeared to be the *intent* to divorce. In the latter case, Tacitus specifically says that Messalina had sent no notice of divorce; however, those closest to Claudius at court treat the matter as a political crisis and assume that Silius is aiming at supplanting the emperor. Narcissus, trying to rouse the emperor to a sense of the danger, excitedly tells him that he is divorced. The former case, Cicero tells us, aroused considerable dispute among jurists. The man himself was dead and could not be questioned as to his intention. Later, we find jurists in the empire implicitly assuming the primacy of intention, when they say that if a couple divorced and then came together again this should be counted as one and the same marriage. A particular instance is mentioned, that of Maecenas and Terentia, whose on–off marriage gave lawyers food for argument about the legal validity of gifts that passed between them.[15]

Paul, in a commentary on the *lex Julia de adulteriis*, said, 'No divorce is valid unless witnessed by seven adult Roman citizens besides the freedman of the person (*qui* — masculine) divorcing.' This shows that Augustus did make this procedure a legal require-ment and is apparently confirmed by Suetonius' remark that Augustus imposed on divorce a set form (*modus*). 'Limit', another possible meaning, would not make sense here, since Augustus' legislation tended to encourage divorce, rather than the reverse.[16] All that this shows, however, is that Augustus provided for a procedure in the case, namely, the adultery of a wife, where divorce was compulsory and it was important for the husband to be able to establish the fact of divorce, on penalty of prosecution as a *leno* (pimp). It does not show that a formal procedure was instituted for divorce in general.

A formal declaration by the divorcing party to the other partner in the marriage does appear to have been usual; he or she *nuntium remisit*, 'sent notice of divorce'.[17] Although no classical text actually says so, the declaration of divorce, rather than its reception by the other party, terminated the marriage; otherwise (especially given the nature of communications in the ancient world) the power to divorce and remarry could in some circumstances have been severely limited, as for instance in the prolonged absence of a husband, whose fate was unknown. A mistaken presumption of his death could give rise to an 'Enoch Arden' situation, if there were no possibility of divorce by simple declaration.[18] However, a woman married to her patron would be in a particularly awkward position, since his consent was necessary to a divorce. Simple absence did not dissolve the marriage. Our earliest evidence for a woman being allowed to remarry comes from the reign of Constantine; it concerns the wife of a soldier (permissible by that time), who had had no news of him for four years. She is allowed to remarry if she has first applied without result to the appropriate military officer. Someone insane could not be said to have 'received' the notice, but could nevertheless be divorced.[19]

Capacity to Divorce

Persons *sui iuris* in free marriage could terminate marriage. Those *in potestate* had to have the co-operation of the *pater*;[20] the *pater* could himself intervene to end a marriage, but, as we have seen, from the time of Marcus Aurelius not if the marriage was harmonious.

Augustus' *lex Julia et Papia* forbade a freedwoman to divorce her patron against his will. Since marriage rested on consent, this ban obviously could take the form only of a *lex imperfecta*, that is, it could not prevent or penalise the act itself, it merely prevented its legal consequences from coming into effect. So, the woman would not be able to reclaim her dowry, nor would she have *conubium* with anyone else, and she would be unable to marry again.[21]

If a woman became insane, she could not divorce her husband, nor was her *curator* allowed to do so; if she were *in potestate*, of course, her father could obtain a divorce for her. Since insanity did not invalidate previous acts, but merely removed legal capacity for any further acts, a freedwoman whose patron became insane, or a daughter whose father did, was effectively deprived of the ability to obtain a divorce.[22]

Dissolution of Marriage other than by Divorce

Marriage could be terminated, other than by divorce, if either party lost *conubium* or lost *civitas*. The former occurred if men became senators when married to women in forbidden categories, or if they became soldiers.

Certain kinds of 'capital' sentence on convicted criminals involved loss of *civitas* or enslavement. Condemned persons of high rank were more likely to receive the former type of sentence, lower orders the latter.[23] The commonest form of penal slavery resulted from condemnation to work in the mines, and then only if the sentence were for life; if it was merely for a term, free status was retained, and children born of women so condemned were free. Women were usually sentenced to help the mineworkers (*ad ministerium metallorum*) rather than actually to work in the mines.[24] Citizen status was lost by a sentence *aquae et ignis interdictio* (effectively banishment) or deportation; this was a capital sentence, the condemned person being, so far as the law was concerned, dead. According to late interpolations in the Digest, deportation did not dissolve marriage, but in classical law it did. The dowry either remained with the husband of a condemned woman or could be claimed by her father (if she were still *in potestate*); but if she had been condemned of certain statutory offences, namely *maiestas* (treason), armed assault, parricide, poisoning and assassination, it was confiscated by the state.[25]

Captives in the hands of a foreign power were the slaves of the state which captured them, and were usually sold to private owners. As slaves, they had none of the rights of Roman citizens. Since captives could and did sometimes return, their rights were regarded as being suspended; should someone die in captivity, by a legal fiction he (or she) was deemed to have died at the moment of capture, so that his estate could be settled as that of a free person. If he returned, then by the principle known as *postliminium* former rights and status were restored, with one major exception — marriage.[26]

A slave could not be validly married to a Roman since there was no *conubium*, and capture therefore dissolved marriage. When the captive returned, however, marriage was not restored by *postliminium*, but it could be renewed by consent.[27] Corbett (1930: 213) takes this 'to signify merely that the effective operation of *postliminium* was subject to the condition of the other consort's consent'. This is not what the text says; *marriage* was renewed by consent. *Postliminium* normally operated automatically; the rights of the captive had merely been in suspension. This could not be done in the case of marriage, since during a marriage it was open to either partner at any time to terminate the marriage by giving notice of divorce. If one partner was taken captive, there could be no automatic retention of rights, since this would conflict with the liberty of the other partner to end the marriage at will.

There is an exception that proves the rule. Suppose husband and wife were taken captive together, and children were born to them in captivity. If *both* husband and wife subsequently returned, the children would be treated as legitimate. The reasoning here must be that, as *neither* partner had been in a position to exercise a wish to end the marriage, its continuance had not been dependent on the will of anyone other than the captives, and so *postliminium* could apply.

This ruling was given in a rescript by the emperors Severus and Caracalla. However, for the children to be regarded as legitimate, *both* parents must return; if only the mother returned with the child, it would be regarded as illegitimate. This is not discrimination against the mother; the texts, all dependent on the original rescript which was given to a provincial official, presumably in relation to an individual case, do not specify the other cases, of a child returning with the father only, or alone, but the same would doubtless apply. Since the law assumed that the dead parent died at the moment of capture, the child could not be regarded as born in wedlock.[28]

Marital Fault

English law has only recently abandoned the concept of marital offences as the grounds for divorce; the sole ground is now irretrievable breakdown of the marriage, and in the Divorce Reform Act of 1969 adultery and behaviour such 'that the petitioner cannot reasonably be expected to live with the respondent' are listed alongside separation or desertion for specified periods as 'facts' to be proved in support of a claim that the marriage has broken down. Consequently, the concept of marital fault has disappeared in the Marital Proceedings and Property Act of 1970, except for an instruction to the court to arrange matters for the parties 'so far as is practicable and, having regard to their conduct, just'.[29]

In Roman law, both pre-classical and post-classical, divorce was permissible only on the grounds of certain specified offences committed by the other partner. Divorce by consent was finally abolished by Justinian. Increasingly severe penalties were imposed in the Christian empire on persons seeking a divorce for any other reason. To loss of dowry and gifts before marriage were added temporary or permanent loss of *conubium*, deportation and, eventually, confinement for life in a monastery and forfeiture of property.[30]

In classical law, in contrast, there were no specified grounds for divorce, and the sanctions for frivolous or apparently unjustified divorce were social rather than legal. In 50 B.C., Caelius retails to Cicero among the gossip of the city that the sister of Valerius Triarius has divorced her husband, who was away on duty in a province, for no reason, just the day before his return. He adds that she is about to marry Decimus Brutus. Cicero himself divorced his wife Terentia four years later. Plutarch's account of the affair lists a whole series of complaints on Cicero's part (all denied by Terentia) ranging from serious matters, such as removal of household property and incurring of debts, which if true could have formed the basis of a series of lawsuits, to grumbles about her parsimony in supplying the travelling-expenses of his daughter Tullia when she met him after his return from exile. Plutarch comments that Cicero's real motives soon became apparent when he married the young and wealthy Publilia. He subsequently divorced her because he thought she was pleased at the death of Tullia. All this sounds like the gleanings of gossip among their social circle.[31]

Augustus, as we saw, instituted penalties for a husband who did *not* divorce his adulterous wife. The restrictions on a freedwoman's right to divorce had nothing to do with the grounds of divorce.

Nevertheless, though divorce without matrimonial offence was permitted, the concept of fault did still find expression, in two ways.

First, in classical law a wife guilty of adultery could be penalised by a praetorian action brought by the divorcing husband, the *actio de moribus*. The husband had to provide security, Gaius tells us; the reason doubtless was to discourage unfounded accusations made from dishonest motives. If successful, he could retain one-sixth of the dowry. Conversely, if the wife were suing the husband for return of dowry, he could put up a defence of *retentio propter mores*, i.e., that he had a right to retain the same amount on the grounds of her adultery. For less serious misconduct, he could keep only one-eighth. If the fault was on the husband's side, then instead of being allowed to return the dowry, as usual, in three annual instalments, he was given only six months to pay or, in the case of graver misconduct, had to pay up at once.[32]

These procedures were already available in the Republic. In 100 B.C. a certain C. Titinius of Minturnae divorced his wife Fannia, and tried to retain the dowry, alleging immoral behaviour on her part. The judge was C. Marius; when it was discovered that Titinius had known about his wife's character all along, even before he married her, Marius tried to persuade Titinius to give in and return the dowry. When he refused, Marius awarded him from the wife's dowry the derisory sum of one sesterce, saying that it was perfectly clear to him that Titinius had deliberately chosen to marry an unchaste wife because he had designs on her patrimony. Under the empire, Titinius would not have got off so lightly. As husband of an adulterous wife, who had not prosecuted her within the time prescribed by the *lex Julia*, he would not only have lost the dowry but would himself have been liable to prosecution as her pimp. The jurist Scaevola said that in such a case the husband should not be allowed to keep any of the dowry, since he himself had caused or connived at her immorality.[33] The penalties, besides divorce, imposed by the *lex Julia* on an adulterous wife will be discussed later.

Secondly, 'fault' (*culpa*) occurs in contexts where the meaning is not misbehaviour of any kind but rather 'responsibility'; it merely indicates the party who initiated the divorce. Ulpian says that the husband could retain one-sixth of the dowry in consideration of the children of the marriage (*retentio propter liberos*), up to a maximum of three children, if the divorce had been through the *culpa* of the wife or her father. Clearly, this does not mean any moral transgression on the part of the wife's father, but merely that he had sought the divorce. Cicero makes the same point but, confusingly, using *culpa* in the moral sense: 'If a divorce occurs through the fault (*culpa*) of the husband, then even though the wife sent notice of divorce nothing should be kept for the children.' If the divorce had been the woman's 'fault' as initiator, and the husband was innocent of misconduct, he could keep part of the dowry for the children; but if he was guilty of misconduct, then, irrespective of who initiated the divorce, he could not.[34]

Although there were other grounds on which a husband could base a claim to retain part of the dowry, this penalty on a wife or father who initiated a divorce applied only where there were children and was meant to make some provision for them. Otherwise, the whole dowry had to be returned. Nevertheless, Cicero himself was in a dilemma. Before he had finished paying off the instalments of Tullia's dowry, her relations with Dolabella had deteriorated to a point where Cicero was thinking of divorce. Besides, he himself would like to get back the amount of dowry already paid. In July 47 B.C. he tells Atticus: 'I think I should send notice of divorce (and you agree). Perhaps he will ask for the third instalment. Consider whether we should wait for him to raise the matter, or act first.'[35] Cicero had been dilatory in paying the first instalment of the dowry, the second had been paid over a year before, and the third was now overdue. Tullia had had a weakly seven-month baby in May 49 B.C., but no more is heard of it, and it had probably died. There were as yet no further children of the marriage, so Cicero could get back the whole dowry in the event of divorce, but that could take three years; and unless he initiated a divorce soon, he would meantime have to get together the money for the third instalment due to Dolabella. He alludes in the letter to various delinquencies of Dolabella's, apparently including infidelity. This could perhaps have been used to oblige Dolabella to return the dowry more promptly; but in the current political situation Cicero was not anxious to make an enemy of Dolabella.[36]

A year or two later, the divorce had occurred. In January 45 B.C., Cicero tells Lepta that he is trying to get Dolabella's agents to pay the first instalment of the dowry.[37] Tullia had just had a baby. A few weeks later she was dead, and the child probably did not long survive her.

Bigamy

Rome was a monogamous society. One woman could not be married to two men simultaneously, nor could one man have two wives.[38] Given the absence of any legally compulsory formality for the constitution either of marriage or, apparently, divorce, there might on occasion be difficulty in establishing whether either had taken place. Some modern writers have supposed, largely on the doubtful basis of Cicero's story about the man from Spain, that a second marriage *ipso facto* dissolved the first, so placing themselves in difficulty when they try to explain how, in that case, the Romans had any juridical conception of bigamy.[39]

To the Romans the legal position was quite clear; so long as an earlier marriage remained in existence, no other marriage could be contracted. The lawyers' problem concerning the man from Spain arose purely from this: that it had become important, for the settlement of his estate, to establish whether the first marriage had legally been terminated or not, and they lacked any proof.

That a second marriage did not of itself dissolve the first is shown, for example, by texts relating to the situation in which a woman marries again, wrongly supposing her husband to be dead. Quintilian makes this the basis of one of his *Declamations*, in which the husband, returning, kills the wife and her second husband and is himself tried for murder. His defence is that he was avenging himself on adulterers caught in the act. 'Marriage', he says,

> is dissolved in two ways, by divorcing or by death. I have not divorced my wife, and I am certainly alive. But there was a rumour of my death. She at once married someone else. What is this but the most outrageous adultery? Besides, there cannot be lawful marriage, unless the first marriage has been dissolved. So my marriage remained in existence, and that (other) marriage was not lawful.[40]

That the murdered wife, had her husband been less impetuous, had a defence, is shown by Papinian's comment on the woman in a similar case.

> This is a question of fact as well as of law. If a long time had gone by, with no evidence of immoral conduct on her part, and then on the strength of false reports, supposing herself freed from her earlier bond, she had contracted a second lawful marriage, it cannot seem that there is anything deserving punishment. But if she is shown to have pretended that her husband was dead in order to contract another marriage, this action impugns her chastity and she ought to be punished in accordance with the nature of the crime (i.e. adultery).[41]

Infamia was the only penalty for bigamy itself in the classical period, and was specified in the praetorian edict. Anyone who either independently, or as a *pater* on behalf of the man or woman in his *potestas*, contracted two marriages or betrothals at the same time, was liable. There are signs of a hardening of attitudes in a response of Diocletian (A.D. 285): 'A competent judge will not suffer a crime of this kind to go unpunished.'[42]

However, the parties to the bigamous marriage could, under the *lex Julia de adulteriis*, be charged with other crimes. As we have just seen, a wife who knowingly contracted a bigamous marriage could be prosecuted for adultery. Valerian and Gallienus in A.D. 258 gave a response in the case of a woman trapped into bigamous marriage by a married man (possibly the commoner case). They confirmed that the man who had two wives was liable to *infamia*. They added:

The man who, though he had left another *materfamilias* in the province, lured you into marriage by pretending to be a bachelor, can be accused of *stuprum* by a lawful accuser. You are not liable to the charge of *stuprum*, because you thought you were his wife. If you apply to the governor of the province, you can recover the property you lost through the marriage.

This last statement presumably refers to the dowry; the emperors go on to indicate that she is unlikely to be able to claim anything he promised her as his betrothed.[43]

Notes

1. Schulz (1951) 132–6; Kaser (1971) 81–3, 325–8. For the imposition of increasing restrictions in post-classical law see Corbett (1930) 243–8).
2. Goody (1973) 7–9; Stone (1979) 34–5; Stetson (1982) 5–7; Holcombe (1983) 96; Hopkins (1983) 69–74.
3. D. 24.1.60, 61, 62 pr.; 25.3.1; 25.4; Dalla (1978) 246 ff.
4. Kaianto (1970); Treggiari and Dorken (1981).
5. FIRA III no.69, II. 41–3; Plut. *Cato Min.* 25, 52; Gordon (1932–3).
6. D. 24.2.11 pr. Under the *lex Julia de adulteriis*, the husband of a detected adultress was *obliged* to divorce her, on penalty of prosecution as a *leno* (procurer) if he did not.
7. RE XIV. 1.1392 ff. On the ambiguity of the evidence of Plautus, Watson (1967) 48–53.
8. Corbett (1930) 222, 242; Watson (1975) 32. Social pressures, however, might have been effectively exercised by the woman's male relatives.
9. Plut. *Rom.* 22; T. XII 4.2 (Cic. *Phil.* 2.28.69);. For fanciful interpretations,

Noailles (1948) 2 ff., followed in part by Herrmann (1964) 12; more soberly, Watson (1965b) 42 ff. and (1975) 31–2; MacCormack (1975) 170–4. See also Yaron (1960).

10. For earlier datings of Carvilius' divorce, see Corbett (1930) 227. In 307 B.C. the censors expelled L. Annius from the Senate, for having divorced his wife without taking the advice of his relatives (this suggests that this divorce also broke the rules about grounds): Val. Max. 2.9.2; Kaser (1971) 82 n. 12; Humbert (1972) 132.

11. Festus, *s.v.* 'diffarreatio'; RE XIV. 1.1392; Corbett (1930) 222–3; Kaser (1971) 83.

12. G. I. 137a; RE XIV. 1.1392–3.

13. Yaron (1960), answered by Watson (1965b). Yaron (1960) recognises that in D. 48.5.44 the phrase *ex lege* should probably not be taken to mean that the Twelve Tables specified a formula, but rather that the divorce had not been for one of the recognised causes; nor is it anything to do with Augustus' law on adultery: Yaron (1964) 554–7.

14. Gaius: D. 24.2.2.1; other texts cited in Yaron (1960).

15. Chapter 3 above, notes 53 and 95; Sen. *Dial.* I. 3.10; *Ep.* 114.6; D. 23.2.33; 24.1.64; 24.2.3; RE XIV. 1.215; Yaron (1964) 533–42; Longo (1977) 470.

16. Suet. *Aug.* 34. *fin.*; D. 24.2.9; 38.11.1.1; Corbett (1930) 231–9; less aptly Yaron (1963) 59.

17. For example, Cic. *Top.* 4.19.20.

18. Yaron (1963).

19. D. 24.2.4; C. 5.17.7; Corbett (1930) 216.

20. *Pace* Corbett (1930) 242; see Chapter 2, note 21, above.

21. D. 23.2.45; 24.2.11; 38.11.1.1.

22. D. 24.2.4; 24.3.22.7, 9.

23. Corbett (1930) 210–17; Buckland (1966) 105; Garnsey (1970) Chapter 4; Kaser (1971) 325.

24. D. 48.19.2 pr., 8.8, 28.6; Buckland (1908) 403–6.

25. G. I. 128; Ulp. *Reg.* 10.3; *Inst.* 1.12.1; D. 24.3.56; 48.19.2. Interpolations D. 24.1.13.1; 28.20.5.1. Dowry: D. 48.20.1,5.

26. Buckland (1908) 291–317; (1966) 67. Against the mistaken ideas of Corbett (1930) 212–5, see Watson (1961).

27. D. 49.15.14.1; see also 24.3.10 pr. (by implication) and 49.15.12.4.

28. D. 38.17.1.3; 49.15.9, 25; C. 8.50.1; Buckland (1908) 308; Watson (1961).

29. The Divorce Reform Act 1969 (1969 c. 55) 1, 2 (1); The Matrimonial Proceedings and Property Act 1970 (1970 c. 45) 5 (1). Changes proposed in the Booth report (July 1985) have not at the time of writing been implemented.

30. Corbett (1930) 243–8.

31. Cic. *ad Fam.* 8.7.2; Plut. *Cic.* 41.

32. G. IV. 102; Ulp. *Reg.* 6.8, 9, 12; Corbett (1930) 130–3, 193; not actually attested for the Republic: Watson (1967: 73).

33. Val. Max. 8.2.3; Plut. *Mor.* 38; D. 24.3.47; 48.5.2.2, 4; Watson (1967) 68–9.

34. Cic. *Top.* 4.19; Ulp. *Reg.* 6.10; Corbett (1930) 192–3; Watson (1967) 70–2.

35. Cic. *ad Att.* 11.23.3. Watson (1967: 71) seems to misunderstand this passage. No penal retention is in question; Cicero is worried that Dolabella may press for the rest of the dowry before he himself has made up his mind to start a divorce. For his difficulties in paying the earlier instalment, see *ad Att.* 11.2.2, 3.1.

36. See Cic. *ad Fam.* 14.13 (to Terentia in July 47 B.C.) and his letters to Dolabella in the period after Tullia's death (*ad Fam.* 9. 11–14).

37. Cic. *ad Fam.* 6.18.

38. G. I. 63.

39. So, for example, Volterra (1934), Longo (1977) 469 ff.; *contra*, Corbett (1930) 224–6; Huber (1977) 53 ff; also apparently Metro (1975), though primarily concerned with a different point.

40. Quint. *Decl.* 347.

41. D. 48.5.12.12.

42. D. 3.2.1, 13.1. Diocletian: C. 5.5.2.

43. C. 9.9.18. 'Lawful accuser' refers to the fact that women could not act as accusers in public proceedings.

6 Dowry

The provision of dowry was basically a contribution, customary though not compulsory, from the wife's family to the expenses of the household of the husband. It was also one of the mechanisms by which Roman families, like those in many other pre-industrial societies, maintained their social status relative to each other,[1] and so there was a strong social if not, for most of the classical period at any rate, legal[2] obligation to provide dowries for daughters. As an indication of the importance attached to dowry, it is noteworthy that the younger Pliny on at least two occasions helped less well-to-do friends in order to secure their daughters' marriages. One was the case already mentioned of the daughter of his friend Quintilianus, who needed to have clothes and servants suited to her husband's position. The other was actually a relative. Pliny writes to the daughter, Calvina, after her father's death. She was the heir, but he had left an estate heavily burdened with debts. Pliny informs her that he personally had paid off the most pressing, so as to be left sole creditor. 'And while your father was alive I had contributed 100,000 sesterces to your dowry over and above what he had assigned you (and that also came indirectly from me, as it was payable only out of his credit with me).' Pliny is going to write off this indebtedness. Perhaps because she *is* a relative (or with an eye to subsequent publication), he then goes on at some length to explain that he is not really all that wealthy himself and has large demands on his resources, a position to keep up, etc., but with simple living he will manage.[3]

With the development of free marriage and increase in divorce it became an important concern to ensure that the dowry should return to the wife or her family at the end of a marriage, either to enhance her chances of remarriage, or to maintain the family resources, and a detailed and elaborate body of legal rules developed to secure these ends.

Dowry was the property of the husband or his *pater*. In early Rome, when marriage with *manus* was still the norm, this was inevitable, since the woman *in manu*, like one *in potestate*, was incapable of owning property. Originally, the dowry itself was irrecoverable, but, as we have seen, some protection was given to the wife by the provision that a husband had to surrender half his property to a wife divorced other than for certain grave offences against the marriage. In strict law the dowry remained the property of the husband throughout the classical period, even in free marriage; however, various means were found of enabling the wife or her family to recover the dowry at the end of the marriage, and the principle became accepted that the husband, on his part, had a duty to maintain the value of the dowry, with an eye to its eventual return, while it also came to be regarded as in a sense part of the patrimony of the wife.[4] On the other hand, the feeling that the husband ought not to be 'out of pocket' in consequence, as well as a growing acceptance of the idea that 'family', in the sense of the children of the marriage, also had a claim, led to the development of a further set of rules on which a claim could be based for the retention of at least part of the dowry at the end of the marriage.

The Constitution of Dowry (*dos*)

When a woman *sui iuris* entered a marriage with *manus*, all her property was absorbed into that of her husband or his *pater*. Cicero, *Top.* 4.23, says as much, but adds, *dotis nomine* ('under the title of dowry'). Originally, this cannot have been so. There *was* no dowry; the Roman woman so situated was in a similar position to that of English women before the Married Women's Property Act of 1882; whatever property she owned before marriage became the husband's upon marriage.[5] By Cicero's time, however, under the influence of free marriage, it had come to be accepted that such property should be counted as dowry, at least in some circumstances. Our surviving evidence relates to marriage without *manus*, but the likelihood is that where a *manus*-marriage ended in the death of either partner the normal rules of inheritance would apply (the wife would, in fact, have nothing to leave), but on divorce her property before marriage would be treated as dowry.

Usually, however, a bride, whether in free marriage or *manus*-marriage, was likely, at least when marrying for the first time, to be still *filiafamilias*, and therefore owning no property. If she was *sui iuris*, her property in free marriage stayed separate from her husband's. In all these cases, steps must be taken to constitute a dowry.

What was involved was, in effect, the conveyance of the specified dowry property into the ownership of the husband. Ulpian distinguished three methods by which this might be done: 'A dowry is given, or declared or promised'.[6] There are difficulties in trying to take these as mutually exclusive and exhaustive. The last two can be shown to refer to specific methods of contracting to give a dowry; the first is a blanket term to cover a range of methods of actual transfer of the property.

Dotis dictio (Declaring a Dowry)

This could be done only by the woman herself, her father or paternal ascendant, or a third party who was in debt to the woman. It was a verbal contract of a peculiar kind. Normally, the correct method of making a verbal contract (*stipulatio*) required that the beneficiary should ask a question: 'Do you promise X?' and the contractor was to reply: 'I promise X.' The peculiarity of *dotis dictio* lay in the fact that no previous question was required.[7]

Why this one-sided form was used is obscure. One suggestion is that it was a survival from a time before the procedure of *stipulatio* had fully developed; another, that it was one of several early forms of contract which were developed each for only one particular transaction; while a third suggestion appeals to the social awkwardness of a prospective husband, or his father, taking the initiative in asking for a dowry.[8]

Whatever its origin, *dotis dictio* constituted a contract and was actionable. How early it became actionable is not known.[9] By the time of the compilation of the *Digest*, the procedure had disappeared, and it is not distinguished there from the more general 'promise of dowry' (*dotis promissio*).

Dotis promissio

This form was open to others besides the bride and her father. The legal form used was that of the ordinary verbal contract (*stipulatio*). The husband or his *pater* asked the requisite question: 'Do you promise to give X?' and received an affirmative answer. Obviously, the actual content of the dowry proposal would have been settled previously. The agreement gave the husband a legal right to claim the dowry, from the date either of the contract or of the marriage, whichever was later. However, the wife herself and her father could be sued only up to their actual means (*beneficium competentiae*); so, unless an outsider had constituted the dowry, the husband might not be able to recover what was promised.[10]

Dotis datio

The widest in application of the three terms, *dotis datio* ('giving of dowry') covered not only actual handing over of property but also any legal actions which had the effect of improving the economic position of the husband's *familia*.

Usually, dowry did involve a transfer of actual property, whether movable (including money) or immovable. However, the punctiliousness of lawyers has preserved details of various other devices that might be used, and their legal consequences. For example, a debt owed by the husband might be cancelled (*acceptilatio*) or its payment be suspended by agreement (*pactum de non petendo*); the usufruct of property might be assigned, rather than actual property; or the bride might waive a legacy or inheritance in her husband's favour. All these, and others, could constitute the giving of a dowry. A *pater* near death might make the legacy a dowry in his will. This could create problems, both if he did not die and also in other circumstances, if, for one reason or another, the designated heirs did not wish to accept the estate and imposed obstacles to the execution of the will.[11]

A dowry in actual property was handed over to the husband or his *pater*. He immediately became owner of the property, whether or not the marriage had taken place. The appropriate legal forms of conveyance were observed, according to whether the property was *res mancipi* or not. If the marriage did not take place, an action for recovery would have to be brought.

In the absence of any special arrangements, dowry in the form of money was usually paid in three annual instalments, starting at the end of the first year. In 162 B.C., Scipio Aemilianus was left as heir to his adoptive grandmother, with instructions to pay each of his three adoptive aunts the sum of 25 talents, ostensibly as the second half of the dowry promised them by their father. If this was a genuine dowry, and not merely a device to avoid the restrictions of the *lex Voconia*, [12] clearly some special arrangement must have been made; the elder Scipio died in 184 B.C. Perhaps he had specified that some of this wealth was to remain with his widow during her lifetime for her maintenance and then be passed to their daughters, not foreseeing that she would outlive him so long.[13] Polybius, however, not appreciating the finer legal points, tells us only, as an example of Scipio's generosity, that he paid the dowry in full at once, although by Roman custom dowry should be paid in three years. Cicero's daughter Tullia married Dolabella in 50 B.C., and, as we saw, in July 47 Cicero was worrying about the third instalment becoming due.

Ulpian (*Reg.* 6.8), speaking about the return of dowry after divorce, says that property that could be weighed, measured or counted (liquid assets, in legal parlance 'fungibles') was due for return in three annual instalments. It has been suggested that the same applied to the original handing over of this type of dowry property, but there is no evidence for this. Polybius says merely that the Roman custom was that the dowry should be paid in three instalments, 'the first instalment, of the liquid assets (*epipla*), to be made in ten months'. The translation is that adopted by Walbank (1979: 508) and is surely right. The implication is that whereas the immovable dowry, such as land or houses, or transfer of various legal rights, fell due immediately, a period of grace was given for raising the part of the dowry in cash; but movables with a cash value had to be paid over earlier than the rest of the 'liquid' dowry. The very large cash dowries sometimes given among the upper classes would be hard to meet all at once from available liquid assets. When L. Aemilius Paullus (Macedonicus) died in 160 B.C., his heirs were able to raise the cash to repay their stepmother's dowry of 25 talents only by selling off some slaves, real estate and household property. Both of Cicero's two wives brought him handsome dowries, Terentia at least 400,000 sesterces cash and some urban real estate which brought in a large income, and Publilia at least 1.2 million sesterces. However, by the end of the first century A.D. writers such as Martial and Juvenal are citing one million sesterces, the qualifying income for senators, almost as a conventional round figure for an exceptionally 'rich' dowry. It has been suggested that the greater instability of marriage in the early empire is reflected in a tendency for upper-class Romans to give relatively small dowries, reserving the main part of their generosity for the inheritance bequeathed later to their daughters and grandchildren (if any). This is a possibility, although the scantiness of the evidence does not allow confidence in making quantitative statements either about the actual incidence of divorce or about the normal size of dowries.[14]

The Husband's Rights and Duties

In Roman law, unlike Greek, a dowry became the full legal property of the husband. In practice, however, regard was paid to the purpose of the dowry, to contribute to the maintenance of the wife, and also, as in time legal provision was made for the reclamation of dowry by the wife or her family in the event of dissolution of the marriage, this necessarily imposed restrictions upon the husband's liberty to dispose of the dowry during marriage.

Jurists' opinions reflect both the strictly legal and the recognised practical situation. Property given as dowry passes into the ownership of the husband. Since the husband sustains the 'burdens of matrimony', in equity any profits from the dowry should belong to him. It can also be said that a husband should display the same diligence in dealing with dotal property as in his own affairs (and can, in certain circumstances, be held liable for fraud and negligence if he does not). Ulpian considers the question of whether the husband can be called to account for maltreatment of slaves which formed part of the dowry. Elsewhere, he goes so far as to say: 'The dowry is a daughter's own patrimony.' Tryphoninus sums it up: 'Although the dowry is part of the husband's property, nevertheless it is the wife's.'[15]

By the early empire, the device of *aestimatio* was commonly used. A fixed value was set at the start on the dotal property (except, it seems, 'fungibles'), and the husband or his heir would be liable to the equivalent value at the end of marriage. Ulpian remarks that it is generally in the interest of the husband that no valuation of the dowry should be made, to avoid his being liable, and especially if he receives as dowry animals, or clothing used by the woman. 'For if the clothes are valued, and the woman wears them out, the husband will still be liable to pay the original valuation.' On the other hand, if the dowry was not appraised, the woman bore the loss (*sc.* in the event of the return of dowry at the end of the marriage), but she would gain if it had appreciated in value. Sometimes a clause would be included in the dowry agreement giving either husband or wife the right to choose whether the property itself or its value should be returned. If the property was land, and the choice had been given to the wife, then the husband could not sell it during the marriage.[16]

Fungibles were not appraised, but this, as Gaius explains (D. 23.3.42), is because they were so readily negotiable.

Property given as dowry which can be weighed, measured or counted is at the risk of the husband, because these things are given with the intention that the husband may dispose of them at his pleasure, and that when the marriage ends he or his heir shall restore others of the same kind and quality.

So, a husband in need of cash might sell the jewellery and trinkets his wife had brought, but at the end of the marriage it was not enough simply to hand over the amount of money he had received, since prices might have changed in the meantime. Presumably, though Gaius does not say so, a cash equivalent based on current valuations would have been acceptable.

Until the very end of the Republic, the husband had the power to alienate any part of the dowry as he thought fit. Unless he had had his wife's consent, however, he could be obliged on dissolution of the marriage to make repayment, if not of the property itself, then of its assessed value at the end of the marriage. In this, as in so much else, Augustus' legislation broke into the privacy of marital arrangements. A clause of the *lex Julia de adulteriis* (sometimes referred to by modern writers as the *lex Julia de fundo dotali*) forbade the alienation of any rustic or urban lands in Italy unless the wife consented (which meant effectively unless her *pater* or, in the case of a woman *sui iuris* but without the necessary number of children, her tutor, consented, such land being *res mancipi*); nor could he offer such land as security, presumably because the wife's interest meant that in a sense she would have been standing surety, and this, as we saw, was contrary to Augustan policy. In regard to dotal slaves, the *lex Julia et Papia* forbade manumission without the wife's consent. Any of the freedman's property acquired by the husband as patron was to be handed over to the wife.[17]

Even by the end of the Republic the contingencies in which a husband could be called upon to surrender all or part of the dowry at the end of the marriage were so numerous that his freedom of ownership had become rather a duty of stewardship and a right of usufruct. He was entitled to any profits he might make from the dowry; but any losses, as, for example, among livestock, must be replaced first, before the profit could be realised. The principle was established soon after 122 B.C., at the latest, that the husband, or his estate, was liable for any loss to the dotal property through fraud or negligence on his part. In the civil disturbances at the time of Gaius Gracchus' death, property belonging to the dowry of his wife Licinia was destroyed. Publius Mucius Scaevola upheld her right to restitution, giving it as his ruling that the sedition had been the fault of Gaius Gracchus.[18]

When Caesennia's first husband, a banker named Fulcinius, was having cash-flow problems, he decided to use the cash from his wife's dowry (*numerata dote*). He 'sold' Caesennia a piece of landed property for the sum in question and had the land recorded as part of the dowry. Fortunately, the acquisition of some liquid capital seems to have saved the situation, and the dowry was not threatened by claims from creditors.[19]

The necessity of conservation which was thus imposed on the husband's management of the dowry produced, in time, a whole body of case law and juristic opinion defining more closely the extent to which the husband might legitimately charge the costs of upkeep of the dotal property upon the dowry itself. These could form the basis of a claim by the husband for retention of part of the dowry *propter impensas*, 'for expenses'. A whole title in the *Digest* is devoted to this subject, which appears to have interested Ulpian and Paul in particular.[20]

Ulpian classifies the expenses as necessary, useful and for pleasure. Necessary expenses were those required to prevent deterioration of the property, e.g., repairing a collapsing building. Useful were expenditures needed not to prevent deterioration but to make the property yield more profit — for example, planting vineyards and olive-groves. The third category merely enhances one's enjoyment, for example, by the acquisition of paintings or the making of gardens. He quotes other legal opinion, to the effect that building a mill or granary or dykes counts as necessary expenditure, as does replanting ruined orchards.

Paul notes that the second category, useful expenses, should have the wife's consent, if they are to form the basis of a claim for retention. It would be unjust, he says, if a wife had to sell property in order to meet such expenses, if she could not meet them otherwise. No doubt this was meant as a protection for wives against the enthusiasms of some husbands for expensive 'improvements' which in the end did not recover the outlay. Much would depend on how experienced, or how compliant, the wife was.

Opinions differed on expenses for pleasure. Ulpian comments at some length:

The husband may claim from his wife expenses incurred for

pleasure, if she does not allow him to remove the objects of the expenditure. If she wants to keep the improvements, she should refund the money he spent. If not, she should let him remove them, that is, if they are detachable. If they are not detachable, they should be left; for a husband is to be allowed to take away an ornament he has installed only if it is going to become his own.[21]

The last part is not clearly expressed, but the implication is that the wife might find herself unable to get rid of a non-detachable decoration which she detested, but she was not to be obliged to bear the cost of it.

Clearly, as with gifts, 'expenses' gave lawyers a good deal of scope for discussion as to what did or did not consitute valid expenses, and what kind of expenses they were; and, as with gifts, the matter became the concern of lawyers at the point when the marriage had ended.

The Recovery of the Dowry

In the absence of special arrangements made on the constitution of the dowry, the fate of the dowry at the end of a marriage depended in part on the source from which it had originally come. Where agreements had been made in advance about the disposal of the dowry, it was called *dos recepticia* and was dealt with according to the terms of the agreement (*actio ex stipulatu*).

Roman law distinguished between *dos profecticia*, given by a bride's father, and *dos adventicia*, which came from the daughter herself or from some other person, or which came from the *pater*, not, however, as a direct charge on his estate but in other ways, e.g., by waiving a legacy in favour of the son-in-law, or in lieu of settlement of a debt. *Dos profecticia* was recoverable by the donor (though not by his heir) whether the marriage ended in death or divorce; a divorced daughter whose *pater* had died could also claim it. *Dos adventicia* was retained by the husband if the wife died. Otherwise it was recoverable by the wife (acting with her *pater* if she was still *in potestate*) but not by any other donor; the latter's interest in it was at an end, since he had in law made a valid gift to the husband.[22]

In all this, the importance of the concept of the *familia* and its

property is clear. At the same time, *dos profecticia* could be constituted even for a daughter who was emancipated. Ulpian attributes
this to family sentiment: 'It is not the right of *potestas*, but the title
of parent that makes a dowry *profecticia*.' Pomponius also explains
that the law returns the dowry to a bereaved father as 'solace, so
that he may not suffer the loss both of his daughter and of the
money'.[23] However, two other notices, both apparently with reference to particular cases, show legal opinion aware of the fact that
there could, in less ideally happy families, be a conflict of interest,
and that a loophole existed for removing part of the paternal estate
from the wife's *familia* or origin, to the benefit of the husband or
children of the marriage.

Ulpian says:

> If a daughter who has been emancipated gets a divorce in order
> that her husband may profit by the dowry, and defraud her
> father, who otherwise could have claimed it as *profecticia* in the
> event of her death, the law should aid the father, to prevent him
> losing the dowry.

The dowry would go to the daughter on divorce, but the husband
could claim for retentions.

In a case discussed by the late-second-century jurist Urseius Ferox
but dating back at least to the latter half of the first century A.D.,
a father complained that the husband of his daughter, who was
emancipated and was ill, divorced her, so that after her death he
could give the dowry to her heirs rather than her father. Since the
daughter was emancipated, the husband's case presumably was that
the dowry became her property on divorce, and at her death was
part of her estate, to be disposed of as she wished. Legal opinion
on the case was that the father should be allowed an equitable action
for recovery. Divorce was the loophole, and the lawyers did their
best to plug it, siding not with the husband, but with the *pater*, who
stood to lose what was originally his.[24]

Dowry upon Death of Wife

At the wife's death, the dowry, if *adventicia*, remained in the husband's possession.[25] If it was *profecticia*, the wife's *pater* could
reclaim it, as Cicero did with Tullia's, but the husband was allowed
to keep one-fifth for each child of the marriage, without limit. If the

pater was already dead, the dowry had in effect become *adventicia* and stayed with the husband.[26]

The jurists were in general agreement that the expenses of the wife's funeral should be a charge on the dowry. If the dead woman had left property, the expenses should be divided proportionately, and charged partly on the recipient of the dowry and partly on the heirs. Retentions were usually deducted from the dowry before the calculation was made. It could happen that a woman had divorced and remarried, but the entire dowry, because of retentions, had remained with the first husband; the jurist Fulcinius thought that in those circumstances the first husband should not be expected to pay for the funeral. If there was no dowry, then her *pater* or her heirs should pay. Failing either, the husband ought to pay, so as not to bear the blame for his wife's being unburied. In any case, if the dowry was due to the father, and the funeral took place before he received it, the undertaker should bill the husband, and it was up to him to settle with his father-in-law.[27]

Dowry upon Death of Husband

At the husband's death, the dowry was recoverable in entirety, and his heirs were not allowed any retentions. However, as the dowry was his property, it did not automatically revert, but had to be claimed by the *actio rei uxoriae*, either by the wife's father, if still alive, or by the wife. Her father could not act alone, but could do so only jointly with her. As the dowry was intended to help the husband sustain the 'burdens of matrimony', it was recognised that at the end of marriage it should be available, either for the maintenance of the widow, or to help to secure her another marriage. Any dotal agreements prejudicing the wife's interest in the dowry in favour of the children were void.[28]

Sometimes the husband preferred to leave the dowry to his wife as a legacy, either directly or through a *fideicommissum*. There were advantages. Immediate payment could be claimed from the estate. The dowry was not subject to the restrictions on legacies under the *lex Falcidia*. Also, if the wife was making a claim on the basis of the will, the heir could retain part of the dowry only on the plea of expenses (*propter impensas*), whereas if she were claiming under the *actio rei uxoriae* the heir could claim set-offs for gifts and for property removed by the wife.[29] A praetorian edict *de alterutro*, of unknown date, gave the wife the choice between accepting the legacy and claiming under the *actio rei uxoriae*; she could not do both.[30]

Dowry on Death of Husband's Father

The dowry at marriage went not to the husband, if he were still *in potestate*, but to his father. At the latter's death, the dowry might pass to the husband as his father's sole heir, or as a legacy on the estate. If the son was made co-heir with others, he had available to him the *actio familiae erciscundae* (suit for the division of an inheritance), under which he could claim the dowry as a charge on the estate before division. If the husband was not an heir, and had been left the dowry as a legacy, the heir could demand security for indemnification if the marriage should be dissolved, since he, and not the husband, was technically responsible to the wife for return of the dowry. Such legal niceties underline the fact that dowry was essentially a transmission of property not between individuals but between *familiae*.[31]

Sometimes the father-in-law preferred to leave the dowry directly as a legacy to his daughter-in-law. This was not a very sensible move. If the couple were already on bad terms, this might merely make them worse, since it could provoke a legal race between them. The wife could bring an action under the will to claim the legacy from the heir. The husband, however, who had an interest in getting the dowry, could bring an equitable action against the heir. In the end, of course, if matters came to a divorce, the wife would get the dowry; but in the meantime, Celsus gave it as his opinion, whichever started proceedings should be required to give security to indemnify the heir against the claims of the other.[32]

Return of Dowry during Marriage

Normally the wife or her *pater* did not expect to recover the dowry, which was technically the husband's or father-in-law's property, until the marriage ended in divorce or the husband's death. However, there could be circumstances in which there seemed to be a danger that the dowry might be lost beyond recovery, if, for instance, the husband were disinherited by his father, or if he were approaching insolvency. The wife herself, or her family, might also face some pressing need.[33]

The husband, if he were wise, would take care to have the return of the dowry specified as being for some necessary purpose. Those recognised, according to the *Digest*, were maintenance of the wife herself or of needy relations, relief to a banished father, ransom of relatives, or the purchase of an estate or payment of debts. This would make it clear that the husband's dotal obligations were being terminated; otherwise, he might seem merely to have made his wife an (invalid) gift.[34]

During the course of the marriage, dotal agreements, altering particular parts of the dowry arrangements, were made as seemed desirable or as need arose. One of the commonest was *permutatio dotis*, 'commuting of dowry'. That was, in effect, what Caesennia and her husband had done; with her consent, he had converted part of her dowry from money into land.[35]

The Dowry as Patrimony: Collation *(collatio dotis)*[36]

In Roman law, the rules of inheritance on intestacy in the praetor's edict provided for the situation where the will was upset by emancipated children appealing for a share in the estate along with the *sui heredes* (*bonorum possessio contra tabulas*) or where they claimed a share along with the *sui heredes* where there was no will (*bonorum possessio unde liberi*). By a very old provision, dating back, it was said, to the Twelve Tables, all *sui heredes* could claim equal shares of an estate, by the *actio familiae erciscundae*.[37] Since the emancipated brother or sister had been capable of possessing and acquiring property, while the others still *in potestate* had not, *collatio bonorum* was required of the former; he (or she) had to 'bring in' his property to the common amount for calculation of the division among the heirs.

This was applied to the case of the woman in free marriage. If the marriage still existed at the time of her father's death, the dowry was still the property of her husband and would not be included in her father's will. However, she might find herself passed over in her father's will, as being already provided for in marriage, and with the expectation of recovery of dowry upon divorce. She might wish to upset the will and claim a share of her father's estate on intestacy. If she had been emancipated in her father's lifetime, the general rules of *collatio bonorum* applied in relation to any other property she might have, but by the praetor's edict she also had to give the heirs an undertaking about the dowry, that if she recovered it later she would surrender an appropriate portion of it to them. The same applied if she made a claim in the case of intestacy.

If she was still *in potestate* at the time of her father's death, the edict originally did not apply. Up to the moment of her father's death, neither she nor any of the other heirs had had any independent legal capacity of owning property, and the estate was decided on that basis, ignoring the dowry. Obviously, this could lead to unfairness to the other heirs if the woman later recovered her dowry, but for a long time nothing was done about it.

The reason may have been that the heirs were originally unable to refuse estates on intestacy, and this could be a liability, if there was a heavy burden of debt. It would have been inappropriate and unjust to expect dotal property to be made to bear a share of that burden; a husband would in effect be being required to take on some of the debts of his late father-in-law. However, eventually, possibly not before the late Republic, the 'benefit of abstaining' (*beneficium abstinendi*) was introduced;[38] the praetor's edict gave heirs the power to abstain from the inheritance if they wished. If they chose not to avail themselves of this, they were said to 'meddle with the inheritance' (*bonis se immiscere*). Antoninus Pius issued a rescript[39] to the effect that a woman who did so should be required by the judge deciding the action for division of the estate among the heirs (*familiae erciscundae*) to 'bring in' her dowry. It seems that even before this the praetor had obliged her to 'bring in' the dowry in the case where there had been a will and she had actively sought to upset the will and claim a share of the intestate succession.

It is not certain whether only *dos profecticia* had to be reckoned in, or whether *dos adventicia* also came under the rules. Two texts suggest that in some circumstances it did. Ulpian says that if a dowry has been promised subject to a condition by a *pater* or an outsider the woman should give an undertaking (*cautio*) to 'bring in' the dowry once she is dowered. In A.D. 239 the emperor Gordian issued a rescript:

> Daughters are obliged to 'bring in' their dowry to the common estate only if they are succeeding on intestacy or claiming against a will; and there is no doubt that dowry, whether *profecticia* or *adventicia*, given or constituted by a father, should be 'brought in' for the benefit of those brothers who were *in potestate*; and indeed it has been determined after various opinions from learned jurists that for the benefit of those who are not in the family of the deceased only *dos profecticia* need be included.[40]

Ulpian includes dowries constituted by outsiders. Gordian limits *dos adventicia* to that constituted by fathers, and it has been suggested that 'given or constituted by a father' is a gloss. However, the discrepancy between the two may be more apparent than real, since the limitation in Gordian could have reference to the particular circumstances of the case on which he is being asked to pronounce. It seems that an emancipated son is claiming a share of the inheritance; his sister's dowry had apparently been constituted by their father, and he wants it to be counted into the reckoning of the total estate. It is not clear whether Gordian is stating the rule that already applied or making a new ruling. In any case, a distinction is made: both types of dowry are 'brought in' if daughters are sharing with brothers *in potestate*, but only *profecticia* if they are sharing with emancipated brothers; and if the daughters choose not to claim a share in the estate at all, they are not obliged to 'bring in' the dowry.

The only deduction allowed before collation was for necessary expenses. If the woman was divorced, she was liable only for as much of the dowry as she had been able to recover.

If, as well as having a dowry, a daughter had been included in her father's will, and another of his children tried to break the will, Ulpian's view was that the daughter would not be expected to contribute her dowry, so long as she accepted no more from the estate than had originally been left her in her father's will.

The cases discussed by jurists in the title of the *Digest* (37.7) devoted to this subject show that inheritance, as always. was a subject likely to promote bad feeling in families and that, whatever the technical legal ownership of dowry, brothers might be disposed to regard it as pre-emption of patrimony. Marcus Aurelius issued a rescript to settle one such family quarrel. A daughter who was one of the heirs at law (*sui heredes*) refused the estate, being content with her dowry (this presumably being to her advantage). Her brothers, on the other hand, wanted collation, to improve their shares. The dowry, it seems, had been promised, but had not yet been paid in full, and the brothers had therefore a means of bringing pressure to bear. The emperor ruled that she could not be forced to contribute her dowry and that any dowry outstanding could be collected, as it was a debt on the estate and no longer part of the estate.[41]

Return of the Dowry on Divorce

When a marriage was ended by divorce, in the absence of any special premarital contractual arrangements, an action for recovery of dowry (*actio rei uxoriae*) was available to the woman or her *pater*, if he was still alive. It was in the interest of the state that she should be dowered, and so have another chance of marriage and bearing children.[42]

If the *pater* was still alive, he, and not his daughter, must bring the action, but he could do so only with his daughter's consent. The emperor Caracalla ruled in a rescript that she should be taken as consenting if she did not actively express opposition. If she was insane, she could not express opposition and should be taken as consenting. If the *pater* was unable to act, by reason, for example, of banishment, she could act alone, so long as she gave security that he would abide by the result.[43]

By the time of Caracalla, the daughter's consent might more readily be assumed, since the ruling had already been given by Marcus Aurelius that a *pater* should not be allowed to break up a happy marriage.[44] The motive of the *pater* for doing so would presumably be greed, to recover the dowry. If the marriage was unhappy, the daughter would be more likely to be willing to end it, but at the same time the necessity for her consent to the action for recovery of dowry could help her to bring pressure on her father to be prepared to assign a similar dowry for another marriage.

Although the dowry could be reclaimed, the husband, for his part, could claim and retain some of it under various pleas. These retentions could even swallow up the bulk of the dowry, which is one reason why premarital agreements, constituting a *dos recepticia*, were sometimes preferred. The action would then be simply on the basis of the agreement (*ex stipulatu* or *in stipulatum*) with no retentions other than as specified in the agreement.[45]

Some of these retentions we have already noticed. *Retentio propter mores* allowed a husband to keep back up to a sixth of the dowry on the plea of his wife's misconduct; the corresponding penalty for his misconduct was a shortening of the time allowed for repayment.

Retentio propter liberos allowed the husband to keep up to half the dowry in consideration of the children of the marriage at the rate of one-sixth per child, but not if he himself had initiated the divorce. He, and not the mother, was responsible for the maintenance of their children, including any child born after the actual divorce, though a magistrate would decide whether the child should live with its mother.[46]

Claims for *retentio propter impensas*, on the grounds of expenses, might be harder to establish; in particular, the classification of particular expenditures, as 'necessary', 'useful' or even 'for pleasure' might give rise to argument. Necessary expenses were construed as those needed to stop the deterioration of the property, not normal running expenses; judges were advised to ignore the latter.[47] The wife's consent to the original outlay had to be proved for expenses in the other two categories. In the wealthiest families, where the dowries might consist of substantial estates, financial and other documentary records were likely to have been kept, but the likelihood is that in humbler households it did not occur to the spouses to have the wife record her consent to every item of outlay on 'her' property, just in case they should some day be divorced. If consent was established, then the wife had the option of keeping the improvements effected and recompensing the husband for them or, where practicable, allowing him to remove them. It was in her interest to agree promptly to do one or the other, because her husband had the right to retain possession until his claim was satisfied.[48]

Claims could be made under two other headings, both relating to the material effects of the couple: *propter res donatas*, where the husband claimed the value of gifts made to his wife during the marriage, which were invalid (though he could, if he wished, make a gift 'for the sake of divorce', which amounted to agreeing that ownership of the item in question should pass at the point of divorce to the wife);[49] and *propter res amotas*, under which he could claim for movables appropriated by his wife from the household, and which he claimed were his own property.[50] As we have seen, this was a way of avoiding a defaming action for theft. The wife also had a right of action against her husband on both accounts, gifts and misappropriation. Clearly, procedures of this sort would be resorted to in the event of unresolved quarrels between the couple about the ownership of specific items of household property. The modern English equivalent would be an appeal to the county court under section 17 of the Married Women's Property Act of 1882, followed, if necessary, by an application to the divorce court for transfer of the property under the Matrimonial Causes Act of 1973.

During marriage, the husband was entitled to the profits (*fructus*) derived from his management of the dowry. On divorce, these must be calculated on a yearly basis for the year or part of a year expired, the 'financial year' being calculated from the date of marriage.[51]

What remained of the dowry after all deductions were made was to be returned at once, except for 'fungibles' and money, which could be returned in three annual instalments. The husband penalised for misconduct had to return the whole lot at once or, for less serious misbehaviour, within six months. If the dowry consisted of non-fungibles, which had to be returned at once anyway, the penalty consisted in paying a sum equivalent to the revenues that the property could have earned had it remained with him for the length of time (i.e., three years) allowed for dowry of the other type.[52]

Essentially, the Roman system for financial settlement at the end of the marriage was quite simple. Apart from the dowry, the wife's property was totally separate from her husband's; indeed, if her father was still alive, she had none of her own. Her ex-husband was not liable for maintenance; that was the responsibility of her *pater*, if still alive. If he was dead, she had the remainder of her dowry, and any other property she might own in her own right.

Notes

1. Goody (1976a) 104–11. On dowry in Roman law, see especially D. 23.3–5; 24.3; RE V. 2.1580–1595; Corbett (1930) 147–204; Watson (1967) 57–76; Kaser (1971) 332–41; Humbert (1972) 264–92.

2. Kaser (1971) 335 and n. 22; Humbert (1972) 265. From D. 23.2.19 it appears that a constitution of Septimius Severus and Caracalla treated the refusal of a *pater* to give a dowry as in effect a breach of the *lex Julia* forbidding a parent to interpose unreasonable opposition to a marriage; Villers (1982) 299.

3. Pliny *Ep.* 2.4; 6.32.

4. Dumont (1943).

5. Stetson (1982) 5–7. English women from wealthy families were in a better situation after the development of the institution of marriage settlements, which allowed them at least some trust income: Cretney (1984) 630.

6. Ulp. *Reg.* 6.1–2; Kaser (1971) 335–6.

7. G. III. 95a. Why the bride's debtor is included at all is not known; see discussion in RE V. 1.390–2 (Leonhard).

8. Zulueta (1953) 156; Buckland (1966) 434; Watson (1967) 58.

9. *Pace* Watson (1967) 57–64, it is probably unwise to look for precision in use of legal terminology in the plays of Plautus and Terence.

10. Corbett (1930) 167–8 and references there.

11. Ibid. 154–63.

12. Polybius 32.13 (31.27); Pomeroy (1976) 223.

13. Walbank (1979) 507–8. The suggestion of Boyer (1950) 174–6 that the father had imposed a legacy or *fideicommissum* on his wife as heir is less probable, in view of the long lapse of time involved. One daughter certainly was, and both probably were, married by 181 B.C. For further discussion, see Dixon (1985).

14. Texts cited in Corbett (1930) 166 n.1; see Watson (1967) 65. Paullus: Polyb. 18.35; Livy *Epit.* 46. Dowry size: Shatzman (1975) 413–4; Saller (1984) 200–3. Divorce: Raepsaet-Charlier (1981–2), cited in Chapter 12 below.

15. D. 4.4.3.5; 23.3.7 pr., 17 pr., 33, 49, 75; 24. 3.24.5.

16. D. 23.3.10; 23.5.11; Corbett (1930) 172–6; Kaser (1971) 340.

17. G. II. 63; Paul *Sent.* 2.2lb; *Inst.* II.8 pr.; Corbett (1930) 180. Dotal slaves: D. 24.3.61–4; in C. 5.12.3 (A.D. 222) the wife gives directions in her will.

18. D. 23.3.10.3; 24.3.66 pr.; on the husband's duty of conservation, Dumont (1943).

19. Cic. *pro Caecina* 11; Rantz (1982) 268 ff. assumes that, as protection against creditors, the estate was handed over to Caesennia as her property, and was not the subject of a *mutatio dotis*; but, since in the event of Fulcinius' bankruptcy there would be no question of the estate being regarded as a gift *mortis* or *divortii causa*, such a transfer would surely have breached the rule against gifts within marriage.

20. Ulp. *Reg.* 6.14–17; D. 25.1

21. D. 25.1.9.

22. Ulp. *Reg.* 6.3–4; *Frag. Vat.* 116; D. 23.3.5; Corbett (1930) 183–5; Watson (1967) 66–8.

23. D. 23.3.5.11, 6 pr.

24. D. 24.2.5; 24.3.59.

25. However, Apuleius was obliged by the sons of the widow Pudentilla to make a dotal agreement promising that in the event of her death the dowry should go to them, together with any children of the later marriage (*Apol.* 91). After the *senatusconsultum Orphitianum* (A.D. 178), children could be their mother's legitimate heirs, and *patres* sometimes make dotal pacts renouncing their right of recovery of *dos profecticia* on a daughter's death in favour of her children: Humbert (1972) 283 ff.

26. Ulp. *Reg.* 6.4; *Frag. Vat.* 108.

27. D. 11.7.16–30; 35.2.6.

28. D. 23.3.2; 23.4.2; 33.4.1.1; C. 5.14.3.

29. D. 24.3.15.1; 25.3.6.3–6; 31.41.1, 48 pr.; 33.4.1, 3, 5; 35.2.57,81; Röhle (1977) 308 ff.; Ankum (1984) 31 ff.

30. D. 31.53 pr.; C. 5.13.1.3a; Corbett (1930) 189–90; Kaser (1971) 339 and nn. 20, 21.

31. D. 10.2.20.2; 51 pr.; 33.4.1.10, 13; 2; 7.2; 35.2.85; Corbett (1930) 178; Ankum (1984) 55–9.

32. D. 33.4.1.9.

33. Corbett (1930) 198.

34. D. 23.3.73.1; 24.3.20, 24 pr., 1.

35. Cic. *pro Caecina* 11; Corbett (1930) 176–7, 198–9.

36. D. 37.7; Schulz (1951) 229–32; Buckland (1966) 325–6; Kaser (1971) 732.

37. D. 10.2.

38. G. II. 158; Schulz (1951) 281–2; Buckland (1966) 305, 395; Kaser (1971) 714 ff.

39. D. 37.7.1. pr.

40. D. 37.1.7; C. 6.20.4. The matter is controversial: Kaser (1971) 732 n. 35.

41. D. 37.7.9.

42. D. 23.3.2; 24.3.1; 45.5.17.1, 18; Corbett (1930) 184–6; Kaser (1971) 336–41.

43. Ulp. *Reg.* 6.6; D. 24.3.2.1, 6.2.

44. *Frag. Vat.* 116; D. 43.30.1.5; C. 5.17.5.

45. For example, C. 5.18.5 (A.D. 259). A tablet from Herculaneum (*Tab. Herc.* 87) bears a fragmentary record of a process for recovery of dowry upon divorce which has some curious features. The wife's *pater* was apparently dead (at any rate, she was no longer *filiafamilias*), and the dowry was constituted by a woman, probably

her mother; nevertheless, the terminology of the *actio rei uxoriae* is used, and it had apparently been agreed that the terms of recovery should be as if the *pater* had still been alive, though the only specific item recoverable is that the retention for children should be one-fifth each (as on the wife's death) instead of the one-sixth allowed on divorce: Arangio-Ruiz and Pugliese Carratelli (1955) 470–7.

46. Cic. *Top.* 4.20; Ulp. *Reg.* 6.10; D. 25.3.1, 5, 8; C. 5.25.3.
47. D. 25.1.3.1; 12; 15.
48. D. 25.1.5 pr.
49. D. 24.1.11.11; 12.
50. Ulp. *Reg.* 6.8; D. 25.2.
51. D. 24.3.5–7; 11.
52. Ulp. *Reg.* 6.13.

7   Sexual Offences

Under the Republic, although some attempt was made to protect women against unwelcome sexual approaches, the law for the most part did not concern itself with the sexual activities of consenting individuals; most undesirable behaviour was dealt with, if at all, within the family. Things were very different under the empire. Augustus' social legislation interfered even between husband and wife, and prostitutes, although their activity was not criminal, were subjected to various legal disabilities.

Sexual 'Harassment'

During the Republic, several praetorian edicts were passed (and eventually, by the time of Labeo, absorbed into a 'general edict') bringing various forms of unacceptable behaviour under the concept of *iniuria*, and so making the perpetrator liable to an action for damages by the offended person or other closely interested parties.[1]

One of these was the edict *de adtemptata pudicitia* ('concerning attempts upon chastity').[2] An action for injury could be brought against anyone who addressed unmarried girls (*virgines*) or married women, or followed one of them about, or took away her attendant, whether by persuasion or by force. The assumptions are noteworthy: respectable women should not appear in public unattended, and one of the functions of an attendant was to hinder the possibility of sexual encounters.

Labeo's commentary, as cited by Ulpian, made it clear that the edict was concerned with sexual approaches, that is, when the intent of the doer was 'contrary to good morals'. 'Address' was explained as 'make an assault upon virtue by blandishing speech' and distinguished from injury by insult or foul language. Constant following about in silence was damaging to the woman's reputation. The edict did not apply where the behaviour was merely in jest or for the purpose of rendering some service honourably; so presumably the

passing wolf-whistle or the pursuit to return the dropped handker-
chief or equivalent would be exempt.

Slaves and prostitutes were relatively fair game, however. 'Anyone who addresses young girls (*virgines*), if they are dressed as
slaves, appears to commit a lesser offence, and still less if women
are dressed as prostitutes and not as respectable married women
(*matresfamiliae*).'

An action could be brought not only by the woman herself but
also by her husband or father; as we have already seen, any insult
or injury to a woman was deemed to have been directed at her
husband or father. Ulpian's opinion was that in the case of
adtemptata pudicitia a fiancé also should have a right of action. It
was particularly important to protect the chastity of a family's free
womenfolk against outsiders, because of the implications for the
paternity of children and potential heirs, but the scope of the edict
was wider. Sexual advances to persons of either sex, free or slave,
gave rise to an action, Ulpian tells us; in the latter case, the slave's
master could prosecute.[3] With regard to slaves and women, we may
suspect, Roman men were concerned not only at the affront to
dignity and repute (mentioned in D. 47.10.1.2) but at the possible
subversion of their domestic loyalty.

Rape

A criminal prosecution could be brought for rape (*per vim stuprum*:
'intercourse by force') of women or boys, under the *lex Julia de vi
publica*, introduced probably in the dictatorship of Julius Caesar.[4]
Women *sui iuris* were normally allowed to bring prosecutions in
criminal courts only for offences against themselves or their near
relations;[5] this would allow the raped woman herself to prosecute.
As with *iniuria*, prosecution would be open also to husbands and
fathers, and a rescript issued by Diocletian and Maximian informs
a man that he is entitled to bring a prosecution under the *lex Julia*
for an offence against his son's fiancée. If the woman's father did
not wish to press charges, prosecution was open to outsiders, and
there was no time-limit (unlike adultery, for which, under the *lex
Julia*, a prosecution must be brought within five years).[6]

Rape was a capital charge. The emperor Hadrian took a lenient
attitude towards people who took the law into their own hands and
killed someone attempting rape upon themselves or one of their

family; he allowed their discharge. If the woman raped was a slave, no capital charge could lie, but presumably the master would be able, as in the general case of *stuprum*, to bring an action for damages under the *lex Aquilia*.[7]

What recourse there was for rape under the Republic is not certain. A *lex Plautia de vi*, passed possibly in 70 B.C., was used against Catiline, but although it was superseded by the *lex Julia* it seems to have been concerned mainly with such offences as armed robbery rather than rape.[8] Kunkel (1962: 122–3) finds it hard to believe that there should have been no criminal process available against rapists before the *lex Julia*. He believes that capital charges could be brought for adultery and *stuprum* under the Republic and assumes that rape was subsumed under these and was then transferred to the *lex Julia de vi* (apparently regarded as Augustan) when these other offences were separately provided for under the *lex Julia de adulteriis coercendis*.

Certainly, the absence of a criminal process against men for adultery and *stuprum* is more readily understandable than its absence for rape. In the former cases, the woman had consented, and her punishment, if required, could be regarded as a matter for the *familia*, while the wronged husband had the option of divorce and a claim on the dowry. Rape was a different matter, an act of violence against a woman. A sample of the 'grand style' in a rhetorical treatise from the early part of the first century B.C. asks of an imaginary jury what fit penalty they could devise for those who planned to betray their country to the enemy. 'Our ancestors used up the most severe penalties for those who raped a male, debauched (*constuprassent*) a married woman, wounded (so Teubner text; other readings are 'violated' and 'beat') or even killed anyone; they did not bequeath a special punishment for this crime (*sc.* treason).'[9]

Treason (*perduellio*) was in fact the earliest crime prosecuted by the state, and the penalty was death. The development of criminal procedures for other types of offence was gradual, piecemeal and, until the first century B.C., largely *ad hoc*.[10] The passage above cannot really be taken as evidence for the existence in the earlier Republic of established criminal procedures with a penalty for all the various offences against the person which are listed; the speaker's concern is not with legal technicalities but with the feelings and reactions of the Romans. It must be remembered that the tradition of self-help was remarkably persistent in Roman society. *Quaestiones* (criminal courts) for several other specific crimes of violence were not set up until the legislative work of the dictator Sulla, a generation before Julius Caesar. If any legal process at all was used to seek redress for rape, it may have been that of the suit for damages, *iniuria*. Any more drastic action against a rapist could render the avenger liable to prosecution, though, as later under Hadrian, the court might be disposed to leniency.

We have no means of knowing the level of incidence of rape in the Roman world. Even in contemporary Britain and the United States, although it is commonly accepted that the number of rapes reported to the police is only a fraction of those actually occurring, attempts to estimate the size of the fraction are little better than guesses.[11] Rape has been described as 'probably the most under-reported crime'. The reasons for women's not reporting rape are numerous and include, besides personal trauma and the expectation (whether justified or not) of unsympathetic police treatment, the feeling that they are henceforth stigmatised in the eyes of men, even their nearest and dearest, and that their own innocence is regarded as suspect.[12] Given the importance attached to female chastity (at least for wives and potential wives) in the Roman world, it would not be surprising if attitudes similar to those known or anticipated among some modern men existed, perhaps to a even greater extent, among the Romans, even if not publicly acknowledged. In the later empire, the Christian emperor Constantine wanted to penalise even the girl raped against her will, on the grounds that she could have saved herself by screaming for help. However, Diocletian, towards the end of our period, states the official position thus:

> The laws punish the foul wickedness of those who prostitute their modesty to the lusts of others, but they do not attach blame to those who are compelled to *stuprum* by force, since it has, moreover, been quite properly decided that their reputations are unharmed and that they are not prohibited from marriage to others.[13]

One of the main difficulties currently encountered in England in implementing the law relating to rape is the problem of consent. The Sexual Offences (Amendment) Act of 1976 defines rape as unlawful (extramarital) intercourse with a woman who at the time of the act does not consent, when the man at that time knows that she does not consent or is reckless as to whether she does. An accused man can put up a defence on the grounds that at the time and in the circumstances he honestly believed that the woman did consent.[14] In Rome, after the passing of the Augustan laws on sexual offences, such a defence would not have helped the accused man much, and would have had its dangers for the plaintiff as well. The latter would be ill-advised to prosecute unless able positively to prove that the sexual act had occurred; otherwise, there could be an action for *calumnia* (malicious prosecution). A successful defence that the woman had consented might have released a man from the severest penalty (the maximum penalty for rape was death) but it would not have got him off scot-free. He would still have been liable to a charge of adultery (if the woman was married) or *stuprum* (if she was not) — unless, that is, he had had the forethought to rape a prostitute or a woman from one of the other categories, intercourse with whom did not constitute an offence (*in quas stuprum non committitur*).[15] Not only that, but the success of such a defence would leave the woman complainant herself liable to charges of *stuprum* or adultery, and her husband would face prosecution if he did not divorce her. The social and legal consequences of failure may have been a deterrent to bringing prosecutions for rape.

Stuprum

In general terms, *stuprum* could refer to any sort of sexual immorality, including adultery. Once the Augustan *lex Julia* constituted adultery as a separate criminal offence, *stuprum* took on in addition a more restricted meaning. Though the law sometimes used the words interchangeably (adultery being one kind of unlawful intercourse), 'adultery', we are told, should be used specifically of relations with a married woman, and *stuprum* of those with unmarried or widowed women (or indeed with boys).[16] Sexual relations with marriageable women were not to be encouraged, since they undermined that marriage and production of legitimate children on which the continuance of the *familia* depended.

However, in the Republic, it does not seem that *stuprum*, in the narrower sense at least, was something with which the law concerned itself, but rather a matter to be dealt with inside the family by paternal authority. A few examples are recorded by Valerius Maximus (cited above in Chapter 2) of fathers punishing or even killing their daughters, and in each case it seems that the girl's sexual behaviour was felt to imperil her chances of marriage. Aufidianus killed his daughter rather than be obliged to marry her to her freedman lover (the implication — since pregnancy is not mentioned — is perhaps that no one else would now marry her) and Maenius' daughter, kissing her father's freedman, is warned to save herself for a husband. Even the ex-prostitute, Atilius, fits the pattern. He killed his daughter for her *stuprum*; probably he saw his hopes collapsing that she would not follow in his footsteps but would achieve a respectable marriage.[17]

Some improving tales are also preserved for us by, for instance, the elder Pliny, of the severity of Roman husbands under the kings and in the early Republic (and presumably in *manus*-marriages) towards wifely behaviour — specifically, wine-drinking — which might have led to *stuprum*. In just one instance a magistrate is involved, and it is said that he fined the woman the amount of her dowry; almost certainly this is an example of the *actio de moribus*, brought by the husband at the time of divorce as the basis of a claim to retain the dowry.[18]

The ambiguity of the word *stuprum* makes it difficult to assess the significance of the three occasions mentioned by Livy on which magistrates (the aediles) are said to have brought citizens to trial before the people for *stuprum*.[19]

In 295 B.C., Q. Fabius Gurges, possibly curule aedile in that year,[20] brought several *matronae* to trial before the people for *stuprum*. More than 80 years later, the aediles of the plebs accused several *matronae* before the people of *probrum* (behaviour in some way 'opprobrious'), and those condemned were exiled. Much earlier, in 329 B.C., M. (or Q.) Flavius was brought to trial before the people by the aedile C. Valerius on the charge *stupratae matris familiae*, and acquitted. Valerius Maximus, who does not mention the charge at all, says that after 14 tribes had voted for condemnation, Flavius protested his innocence. The aedile's retort, that he did not care whether Flavius was innocent or guilty, so long as he was destroyed, turned the rest of the tribes in Flavius' favour, and he was acquitted. A year or so later, on the occasion of his mother's funeral, Flavius made a public distribution of meat to the populace, which some people, says Livy, interpreted as the payment of the price he owed them for his acquittal.

The language used to describe the charge against Flavius is similar to that in the rhetorical treatise cited above and could cover both sexual assault and seduction. In either case, why the aedile should be involved is not clear. Mommsen treats the case as exceptional;

particularly blatant scandal and political feuding between Flavius and the aedile are other possible explanations. Both our accounts seem to favour the latter, and weaken the case for the existence of a regular legal process at this early date.[21]

Both the other occasions of magisterial intervention involve married women, and several of them at that. Much later, around 100 B.C., the (apparently) repeated unchastity of Fannia, wife of C. Titinius, provoked, so far as we know, no action on the part of the authorities, and it is even less likely that they would have intervened in marital affairs so much earlier in Republican history. The explanation may be that the women were not simply engaging in private liaisons,[22] nor were they regular prostitutes (by which they would not actually have been breaking any law, though most prostitutes at that time were probably slaves or non-citizens), but that on both occasions there were some particular circumstances which required the aediles, the magistrates responsible for public order, to take action. What these circumstances were, we cannot say for certain; the difference in the penalties imposed indicates that the two were distinct from each other, and singular in themselves, rather than both applications of an established law. The offences in 295 B.C., punished by fines, seem to have been regarded less seriously, and may have been nothing more than disorderly and uninhibited behaviour 'under the influence' after boozy festivals such as that of Anna Perenna (March 15) or the two Vinalia, on April 23 and August 19. The last-mentioned is quite likely; one of the gods honoured on that date, according to calendars, was Venus Obsequens, and Fabius used the fines to inaugurate a temple to her near the Circus.[23]

The events of 213 B.C. were apparently more serious, and led to the exile of some women. The causes cannot be recovered; but the edgy, not to say hysterical, climate of feeling in Rome at that stage of the Hannibalic War may have had something to do with the harshness of the punishments.[24]

Augustus' *lex Julia de adulteriis* allegedly superseded several earlier laws on sexual offences, but our source for this statement belongs to the end of the second century A.D., and we have no other evidence for the number, nature and content of these earlier attempts to regulate the sexual behaviour of the Romans.[25]

After the Augustan legislation, things were different. The *lex Julia* created a *quaestio perpetua* (a special court) to deal with adultery and various other offences under the general heading of *stuprum*. Most of our evidence relates to adultery, which was essentially the same offence as *stuprum* (in the narrower sense) except that the woman was married.[26] The man's marital status was irrelevant.

Stuprum was an offence on the part of both partners. As committed by a heterosexual man, it consisted in sexual relations with a marriageable girl or woman (including widows); her marriageability seems to have been determined not only by presence or absence of *conubium*, but by social status. For this reason, some jurists advised against trying to live in concubinage, rather than marriage, with a free, respectable woman. Modestinus put it thus: 'Living with a free woman on a regular basis is to be regarded not as concubinage but as marriage, unless she has earned a living by selling her body.' Sex with a prostitute was not *stuprum*, nor indeed with an ex-prostitute if she was unmarried (*vidua*); while married, she came under the adultery law, like other women. It was acceptable to have as a concubine one's own freedwoman or a woman convicted of adultery, thought Ulpian. The latter a freeborn man could not marry; the former he could (and many did), but a certain social stigma attached to the union. Nevertheless, he seems to distinguish both these categories from the only 'safe' concubines: 'The only women one can have as concubines without fear of a charge (*sc.* of *stuprum*) are those *in quas stuprum non committitur*.' These remarks are grouped together in the same paragraph of the *Digest* as other, unconnected, observations relating to concubines, and so it may not be entirely safe to assume a connection between them. However, there does seem to be one. A man's freedwoman is not technically 'safe' as a concubine, but in practice the situation is so socially acceptable that she ought even to be penalised by loss of *conubium* (like an adultress) if she leaves against her patron's will. A convicted adultress is not 'safe', but if you marry her you are caught the other way by the *lex Julia*.

For Marcianus, social disparity makes all the difference. Freedwomen (not necessarily one's own), prostitutes and freeborn women of a humble social status can be concubines; but if the woman is of one's own class (*honestae vitae* in this context is not solely a matter of respectability), one has to marry her or at least openly declare that the relationship is a regular concubinage, or else risk prosecution for *stuprum*.[27]

However, in the absence of a regular law-enforcing police force and a Director of Public Prosecutions, a prosecution for *stuprum* would usually be brought only if some other individual had a motive for doing so. It is unlikely that this particular part of the Augustan legislation did much in practice to restrain the sexual activities of the Romans.

Sexual relations between betrothed couples would also technically be *stuprum*, but the parties most intimately concerned — i.e., the couple and the woman's father — were unlikely to prosecute. One might think that women or their fathers could use the threat of exposure and prosecution to coerce a jilting lover into marrying or making amends, but this weapon was double-edged. The woman herself would suffer loss of reputation, and run the risk of being prosecuted, and as the penalty was relegation, the risk was not to be incurred lightly.

Intercourse with a female slave did not give rise to an action for *stuprum*, but the owner might sue for damages under the *lex Aquilia*. Ulpian thought the same might apply (in addition, apparently, to a charge of *stuprum*) where the girl was free but under marriageable age. The penalty for seducing an under-age girl was by the time of Paul (late second century A.D.) either condemnation to the mines, or relegation or exile, depending on the man's social status. Although the language of physical maturity is used (*immaturam, nondum viripotentes*), the age meant is the legal minimum age for marriage.[28]

There is a contrast here with modern English law, in which the legal minimum age for marriage has no necessary connection with the legal minimum age for consent to sex, and it is the latter, rather than the former, which determines whether the sexual relations in themselves constitute an offence. Indeed, the 'age of consent' has sometimes been higher than the age of marriage. The 'age of consent' was raised in English law to 16 in 1885. The legal minimum age for marriage was twelve until 1929, when it was raised to 16.[29] In Roman law, what constituted the offence was not the girl's youth but her status as (potentially) marriageable.

Incest[30]

In modern societies it is customary, in those circles (mainly legal and anthropological) where such things are discussed, to make a distinction between incest and endogamy.[31] In English law, for example, the crime of incest is constituted by sexual relations between certain close kin, that is, a man and his daughter, granddaughter, sister or mother, or a woman and her father, grandfather, brother or son, and *a fortiori* they may not marry. The degrees of relationship within which marriage is forbidden extend in fact much wider than this, but sexual relations between these more remotely related persons do not constitute a crime.[32]

The Romans did not make this distinction explicit. *Incestum* included both sexual relations between primary kin and the contracting of marriage within the prohibited degrees of relationship, whether natural or by adoption.

Evidence is lacking for the treatment of incest during the Republic. The probability is that incest between close kin was dealt with either within the family or by the *pontifices*, as in archaic Rome. Tiberius' execution of a father and daughter may have been in accord with ancient precedent.[33] Marriages within the forbidden degrees would simply be void in law; sexual relations between the couple did not in themselves constitute an offence.

Under the empire, *incestum*, as a special type of *stuprum*, came under the operation of the *lex Julia de adulteriis*.[34] Sexual relations between 'endogamic' couples did now constitute an offence, since they were in fact unmarried, but the offence was not simply *stuprum* but, because of the kinship, *incestum*. Comments by lawyers and imperial rescripts show an awareness that the law relating to these matters was unsatisfactory. Endogamy was in practice leniently treated. A couple who had actually married (as they thought) presumably had not intended unlawful sex. If they gave up the relationship at once, that was an indication of good faith and could quash a charge of *stuprum*. If 'mistake' could be shown (presumably, ignorance of the relationship), the 'incest' could be excused. Ignorance of the law, however, might serve to excuse the woman but not the man, though his punishment might be made less severe than that for adultery. This distinction between the sexes may reflect a presumption that men, having more to do with the public world, might more reasonably be expected to know the law. A text in the *Digest* attributed to Papinian distinguishes between incest by 'the law of nations' and incest by 'our law'; a woman could be excused the latter but not the former. Incest by 'the law of nations' (*ius gentium*, i.e., moral law) probably means that between primary kin — who, even a woman would know, were not allowed to marry — whereas her ignorance about the rules on the prohibited degrees for marriage might be excused.[35]

If there was adultery as well as incest, then clearly the partners could not have intended marriage, and neither could be let off. The usual penalty for incest, as for *stuprum* generally, was relegation to an island. If there was adultery as well, the harsher penalty of *deportatio* was imposed.

Age is also mentioned as a possible ground for excusing the offence. Incest between father and child might begin before the latter had reached puberty. The imperial brothers (Marcus Aurelius and Lucius Verus), who were in general disposed to treat incest leniently, if the liaison was given up and there was no accompanying adultery, dismissed the charge of incest against a certain Claudia, on account of her age, but ordered that the unlawful union should be broken, adding, 'although otherwise adultery, committed at puberty, is not excused on grounds of age. For, as was said above, even women are not held liable for incest if mistaken as to the law, but when they commit adultery they can have no excuse.'[36] The reasoning here has been fogged by the introduction of adultery, if the charge was incest between Claudia and her father. An under-age girl was incapable of adultery, because she was legally incapable of marriage. Possibly Claudia was a very young bride, and the emperors were stretching a point.

Adultery[37]

Although the *lex Julia* embraced a number of other offences, it was commonly referred to as the law 'on (restraining) adulteries' and the sources, both legal and literary, have a great deal more to say about its operations in that area than any other. This is not surprising; adultery was the offence most likely to be pursued, since in the nature of things there would usually be at least one other person with a motive for bringing a prosecution.

Adultery now for the first time[38] became a criminal offence, but the law did not apply symmetrically to both sexes. A married woman was guilty of adultery if she had sexual relations with any man other than her husband, a man only if the woman was married, and his own marital status was irrelevant. A husband could always prosecute his unfaithful wife. A wife could not prosecute her husband, since in the eyes of the law he had committed no offence against their marriage and women could prosecute in criminal courts only for offences against themselves. She could perhaps get her father or someone else to prosecute him, but only if the 'other woman' was married, and then only if the latter's husband had failed to prosecute within the statutory time-limit. She could always divorce him, of course, and his unfaithfulness would give her grounds for recovering the dowry promptly; but unless she was feeling particularly vindictive or he was being difficult about returning the dowry, there would not perhaps seem to be much point in prosecuting him as well. Clearly, the law was intended primarily to preserve the chastity of women within marriage. That of men did not matter, so long as they kept away from other men's wives, and there were plenty of legal alternatives available.

The husband, even if he was still *in potestate*, had priority over everyone else in prosecuting his wife, and after him the woman's father. Sixty days were allowed either from discovery of the adultery or from his divorcing her, if he did divorce her. After that, outsiders were allowed to prosecute; a period of four to six months was usually granted for this. Reckoning of these times might be suspended for good cause, but in any event the charges lapsed if the prosecution was not brought within five years.

If the husband did not divorce and prosecute his wife within the priority time, he was liable to a prosecution for *lenocinium* (pandering). The seriousness with which it was intended that the offence should be regarded is shown also by the provision in the law, contrary to normal Roman practice, that the slaves of the accused could be tortured to obtain evidence against their owners. Septimius Severus, following the practice of Marcus Aurelius, tightened up the law by extending this privilege to prosecutors other than the husband or father of the woman.[39]

The woman and her alleged lover were not to be prosecuted simultaneously. Usually, it seems, prosecution was to be brought against the woman first, but if she had succeeded in remarrying before a case was brought, the man had to be prosecuted and convicted first. Papinian explains this as a protection for women against ex-husbands who might try to annul their second marriages by false charges of adultery. This might provoke a rush into remarriage by the wife. What the husband *could* do, advised Ulpian, was to give her due warning, once he had served notice of divorce, not to marry a specified man. If she did, he could prosecute her first.[40]

The penalties for convicted adulterers were severe. The woman lost half of her dowry and one-third of her property, the man half his property, and they were relegated to different islands. With the development of the system of dual penalties, persons of low status were probably sentenced to the mines, or similar hard labour.[41]

A woman condemned for adultery belonged to the category of *probrosae*, and as such she was, under the Augustan marriage laws, along with prostitutes, bawds and their freedwomen, stage-performers and women condemned by any criminal court, forbidden marriage with freeborn Roman citizens.[42] The sources do not indicate that men were subject to such a ban. Adultery did not necessarily result in divorce for the man (if already married), and unfaithfulness to his wife was not something the law concerned itself to punish.

From references in Martial and Juvenal it has sometimes been inferred that convicted adulteresses were even required, like the woman in Nathaniel Hawthorne's *The Scarlet Letter*, to advertise their guilt, by appearing in public in the style of clothing worn by prostitutes, or at least in the outer garment, the *toga*. One consequence of this, as we have already seen, would be the loss of some of the protection afforded by the edict *de adtemptata pudicitia* and greater vulnerability to pestering in the streets. Alternatively, of course, one might conjecture that convicted adulteresses commonly did, and were known to, take up a life of prostitution — which was hardly the intention of the originator of the *lex Julia*.[43]

Other penalties were *infamia* and the inability to testify in court.[44] Unmarried, *probrosae* would be unable under the marriage laws to receive inheritances; married, they were perhaps able to receive one-quarter, until Domitian took away this right.[45]

The *lex Julia* also laid down certain rules about the rights of husbands and fathers to kill those taken *in flagrante*. In the early Republic, according to a much-quoted speech by Cato, a husband could in those circumstances kill his wife. Whether this right was accepted as existing also in marriages without *manus* is unknown, and examples of its exercise are lacking; however, it seems to have survived, in theory at least, until abolished by the *lex Julia*. On the other hand, the right of the woman's *pater* to put her to death was re-affirmed but subjected to limitations. In this, as in penalising the husband who did not divorce and prosecute his wife, Augustan legislation fundamentally undermined the tradition of domestic jurisdiction.[46]

The husband was prohibited from killing his guilty wife. If, in the heat of rage, he did kill her, he was subject to the penalties for homicide, although Antoninus Pius and Marcus Aurelius were prepared to allow milder punishments. He could kill the adulterer, if the man was caught in the matrimonial home and if he belonged to certain lowly categories — slave, freedman of the family, *infamis*, convicted criminal, as well as gladiator and wild-beast fighter.[47] The woman's father could kill both her and her lover, if they were caught in his or his son's house, but he must kill both together and at once, or neither. As Papinian later pointed out, the law was giving the father an additional right (that of killing the adulterer) but was not taking away the traditional right of life and death over his daughter. In practice, though, the requirement to kill both was likely to be a deterrent to killing either, and that may have been Augustus' intention.[48]

Just as with *stuprum*, the law ruled that sexual relations with women in certain categories did not constitute adultery; obviously, they did not with prostitutes. Also exempt were concubines (though Ulpian was inclined to include them, except those living with their patrons), and women working in bars. Under Tiberius an unsuccessful attempt was made by a certain Vistilia to avoid prosecution for adultery by registering as a prostitute; she was apparently not the first to do so. Tiberius blocked this loophole by forbidding the wives, daughters and granddaughters of senators and knights to register. There was something of a fashion among the smart set at the time for taking up disreputable occupations — e.g., as gladiators, stage-players — despite an earlier ban. The purpose may have been, at least partly, to avoid the penalties placed by the Augustan legislation on their sexual activities. Tiberius took sharp action, exiling the current offenders, and forbidding them to engage in such work in future.[49]

Certain aspects of the law suggest that the marriages Augustus was mainly concerned to protect were those of the upper classes. The forfeiture of one-third of their property, loss of the right of receiving inheritances, and ban on marriage to freeborn Romans were penalties whose effect would be felt mainly at the upper levels of society. The cases recorded in literary sources are almost all heard before the senate or the emperor, and concern members of senatorial or equestrian families. Humbler people would be tried in the ordinary *quaestio* (or, later, the prefect's court).[50]

The provision of penalties for husbands caught colluding, or failing to prosecute adulterous wives, was no doubt meant to ensure that the law was implemented and the women and their lovers punished. In this, it may not have been very successful. Dio observes that he found that no fewer than 3,000 indictments had been lodged after Septimius Severus had tightened up the legislation, but that few of them were subsequently followed up, and the emperor himself gave up troubling about the matter.[51] Outsiders were likely to be in a worse position than the husband himself to obtain adequate evidence of a wife's infidelity. Some husbands may, for various reasons, have preferred a quiet divorce, even if it meant resigning a claim to part of the dowry, or acquiescence, to public scandal and perhaps the making of enemies among the friends of the accused lover. The severity of the consequences for the wife may also have been a deterrent to action.

Lenocinium

Pandering (*lenocinium*) became a criminal offence under the *lex Julia*, with penalties the same as for adultery itself. It was not a crime to be a professional *leno* or *lena*, pimping for prostitutes, though the occupation did carry with it the disabilities of *infamia*. The new crime consisted in aiding and abetting adultery.

The person primarily aimed at is the husband. He could be punished if he did not dismiss his wife and take action against her and her lover, caught in the act; if he made a deal with the adulterer, instead of prosecuting him; if he profited pecuniarily by his wife's adultery in some way. In what way is further specified. He may have received money in advance, in order to allow the adultery to take place, or after the adultery was discovered (*pro comperto stupro*), to refrain from action. However, Ulpian warned that adulterers could not expect to mitigate their offence by alleging complaisance on the husband's part.[52]

This introduction of an element of compulsion upon the husband is one of the most striking, not to say startling, aspects of the law, interfering as it did with the privacy of the marital relationship and with the husband's right to forgive his wife. In practice, however, it would not be possible to implement this part of the law unless evidence of the wife's adultery was available to outsiders. Even then, Ulpian points out, if the couple remained married, the wife could not be accused directly of adultery by an outsider; the latter would first have to prove a charge of *lenocinium* against a husband. This would discourage prosecution unless the accuser was confident of being able to prove his case, and would in effect leave open the possibility of reconciliation and survival of the marriage. Ulpian comments: 'If a wife has her husband's approval and the marriage is peaceful, another person ought not to disturb and harry it.'[53]

Another indication of the ineffectiveness of the law is perhaps to be found in the number of references in Latin literature of the first and second centuries A.D. to the complaisant cuckold, the *leno-maritus*, either acquiescing in or actively encouraging his wife's adultery. He profits from it by various means, including receiving bribes and blackmail, and reaps social as well as financial benefits.[54]

Later interpretations of the law extended its application. Anyone, man or woman, who aided and abetted by providing premises on which the adultery could take place was liable. So was anyone who received money *pro comperto stupro*, that is, a bribe to persons, other than the wronged husband, who knew about the affair, to keep silence.[55] Marcianus thought that a wife also who accepted a *praemium* (reward or recompense) from the adultery of her husband should be treated as an adulteress.[56] Presumably what he had in mind was not distinct in character from the above, being a bribe to ensure her silence, rather than a peacemaking gift to dry her tears. The latter could hardly be considered unlawful though it was invalid, unless the couple were divorcing. However, one can imagine that there might be difficulties for either side in trying to prove in court the intent behind the present.

Prostitution

Although many prostitutes, specially those in brothels, were slaves, some were freedwomen or even freeborn Romans. Like their employers, the bawds and procurers (*lenae* or *lenones*) they were probably *infames* under the Republic,[57] although prostitution was not illegal and their activities did not constitute a criminal offence. They were apparently required to register with the aediles and were sometimes subject to taxation; more will be said about their working conditions in a later chapter.

Identifying a woman as a prostitute was not always easy. If she worked in a brothel or even in a tavern, then she was openly selling herself (*palam quaestum facere*). 'Many women', remarked Ulpian, 'have women as prostitutes under the pretext of of employing them as staff in a tavern.' The woman available to all men indiscriminately (*sine dilectu*) was easily distinguished from the one engaging in an affair with one man, whether adultery or *stuprum*. Less clear-cut, however, was the status of the woman who discreetly obliged one or two lovers and received money from them — that is, women like the famous mistresses of poets and politicians. Ulpian was inclined not to stigmatise such women as *probrosae*, though not all jurists shared his views.[58]

Augustus's social legislation imposed some disabilities on prostitutes. Under the Republic, they were apparently able to marry freeborn citizens, although the latter would incur *infamia*. The *lex Julia et Papia* forbade prostitutes, as *probrosae*, to marry freeborn Romans. They could not hope to rise in society by giving up the game and marrying *ingenui*, because, Ulpian observed, the law applied to retired prostitutes as well. *Lenae*, probably themselves former prostitutes, came under the same ban, and the landlady of an inn who kept 'personnel engaged in prostitution' (*corpora quaestuaria*) was also classed as a bawd.[59]

The Augustan restrictions on receiving legacies and inheritances applied to prostitutes as to other women, and even when eligible to receive them they were restricted to one-quarter. Even this right was removed by Domitian. In one case, Hadrian refused to allow a known 'camp-follower' with the army to receive a legacy under a soldier's will.[60]

However, since sex was the prostitute's profession, she was able to engage with impunity in activities which would have rendered a 'respectable' woman liable to prosecution. Sex with an unmarried prostitute, even though she was free and a citizen, was not *stuprum*. If she was married and retired from the game, she and her husband were both liable under the adultery law. On the other hand, if she had carried on her trade after marriage, they were probably both exempt, she because she was a practising prostitute, and he because it would scarcely be appropriate to charge with *lenocinium*, in the newer sense, someone who was already, as it were, professionally engaged in *lenocinium*.[61]

The prostitute and the *lena* might be regarded as disreputable, but their activities were not illegal, and were tolerated. Prostitution was a business like any other, and rents from brothels formed part of the revenues of the estates of many respectable citizens.[62]

The ambivalence of the Roman attitude to prostitution is summed up by legal discussions concerning the action for recovery of payments made for a consideration that was immoral or unjust. The general principle was that the money could not be reclaimed where there was immorality on both sides, that of the giver and the taker — as, for example, when someone was bribed to allow *stuprum* or an adulterer or a thief paid a bribe to avoid betrayal. Money paid to a prostitute could not be reclaimed either, in the opinion of Labeo and Marcellus, but the principle on which this judgment rested was different.

> The argument is not that there is immorality on both sides, but that it exists only on the side of the giver. The woman behaves immorally, in that she is a prostitute; but it is not immoral for her to accept the money — since she is a prostitute.[63]

Notes

1. On the punishment of sexual offences in general, see Mommsen (1899) 682–704 and Kunkel (1962) 121–3; on *iniuria* Paul. *Sent.* 5.4; Mommsen (*op. cit.*) 784–808; Schulz (1951) 593–600.

2. G. III. 220; D. 47.10.15.15–26; Lenel (1956) 400.

3. D. 47.10.1.2–3; 9.4; 15.24; 18.2.

4. Mommsen (1899) 655; 664.

5. D. 48.2.1; 2 pr.; 8; 11 pr.; C. 9.1.12.

6. D. 48.5.30(29).5–7; 9; 48.6.5.2; C. 9.12.3.

7. Quint. *Inst.* 9.2.90; Paul. *Sent.* 2.26.12; 5.4.4; D. 48.6.5.2; 48.8.1.4. *Lex Aquilia*: D. 47.10.25.

8. Cic. *pro Milone* 35; Sall. *Cat.* 4; Mommsen (1899) 654 and n. 2; 664 and n. 10; Broughton (1951–2) 2.128.

9. *Rhet. ad Her.* 4.8.12.

10. Kunkel (1973) 64 ff.

11. One of the largest and most thorough studies made, the LEAA/Census Bureau survey in the United States of America in 1975, found that of a total of 27,623 attempted or completed rapes reported to the interviewers, 12,409 had not been reported to the police (Hindlegang and Davis 1977: 97–9). How many were not reported to the interviewers either (*ibid.* 89) cannot be known. Other papers in the same collection as the above cite estimates that 10 per cent (Griffin 1977: 48) or between 5 and 35 per cent (Peters 1977: 339) are reported to the police; another study (Macnamara and Sagarin 1977: 228 n. 20) even cites the same LEAA/Census Bureau survey as indicating that only one case in three was reported. Recent small-scale surveys in Britain claim to show that a substantial proportion of rape allegations are false, made typically by teenagers excusing lateness, wives concealing infidelity and prostitutes cheated by clients. However, many genuine victims are dropping charges, rather than make an appearance in court (report in *The Times*, April 29, 1985).

12. Macnamara and Sagarin (1977) 38–9. Procedure under English law since the Sexual Offences (Amendment) Act of 1976 protects the woman even after trial and appeal (if any) of the offender by preserving her anonymity; the man's anonymity is preserved only until conviction (Honoré 1978: 64–5).

13. C. 9.9.20.

14. Honoré (1978) 77–9; Criminal Law Revision Committee (1980), paragraph 17.

15. D. 25.7.1.1. In English law, restrictions on the questioning of alleged rape victims in court about their sexual experience were introduced only as recently as

1976, and such facts as being a prostitute might still be deemed relevant by a judge (Honoré 1978: 64). What the attitude of a Roman judge might have been to a rape charge brought by a prostitute (or rather on her behalf, since as *infamis* she could not do it herself) is a matter for speculation. Sexual relations with married prostitutes or women (e.g., barmaids) in work associated with prostitution were not held to constitute adultery (Quint. *Inst.* 7.3.6; Paul. *Sent.* 2.26.11), but rape involved the extra factor of force (*vis*).

16. D. 48.5.6.1, 34.1; 50.16.101; Mommsen (1899) 694. Boys: D. 47.11.1.2.

17. Val. Max. 6.1.3 and 6.

18. Pliny *N.H.* 14.14.89–90; Watson (1967) 69–70. The connection with divorce is more explicit in Gell. *N.A.* 10.23.4.

19. Livy 8.22.3 (329 B.C.), and see also Val. Max. 8.1.7, where the charge is not stated; 10.3.9 (295 B.C.); 25.2.9 (213 B.C.).

20. Broughton (1951–2) 1.178.

21. Mommsen (1899) 690 ff.; Kunkel (1962) 123.

22. Since they were married, their *stuprum* was adultery, but *adulterium* is not found with that meaning in Livy.

23. Anna Perenna: Ovid, *Fasti* 5.523 ff.; temple of Venus Obsequens: Livy 10.31.9; Scullard (1981) 90, 106 ff., 177.

24. Livy 25.1.6 ff.

25. *Coll.* 4.2.2.

26. Thomas (1961) 65. The *quaestio* is almost totally absent from the sources. Cases involving senatorial or equestrian families are reported as being held before the senate or the emperor. The *quaestio* probably heard cases involving the lower classes in society and was superseded, probably by the end of the second century, by the jurisdiction of the urban prefect or provincial official: Garnsey (1967) 56–60, (1970b) 21–4.

27. D. 23.2.24; 25.7.1; 3 pr., 1; 48.5.14(13).2; 48.5.35(34) pr. See also the remarks of Williams (1968) 526–42 and Syme (1978) 200–3 on the mistresses of Roman poets.

28. D. 47.10.25; 48.19.38.3. Attempted seduction of those of age meant deportation; if successful, it was a capital charge: D. 47.11.1.2.

29. Honoré (1978) 81–2.

30. Mommsen (1899) 682–8; Guarino (1943) and references in Chapter 3 above, nn. 23–5.

31. Fox (1967) 54–5 protests strongly against confusion of the two.

32. Honoré (1978) 71.

33. Guarino (1943) 178.

34. So Guarino (1943) 179 ff. Mommsen (1899) 684 n. 2 cites D. 48.18.4 to the contrary, but the actual response of Papinian referred to there (D. 48.5.40.(39) 8) says only that the slaves of an owner accused of incest should be tortured only if adultery also is involved. The main legal texts relating to incest are G. I. 58–64; Ulp. *Reg.* 5.6–7; Paul. *Sent.* 2.19.3–5; *Coll.* 6.6; D. 48.5.39.(38).1–7. See also D. 23.2.57a.

35. The distinction between incest by 'the law of nations' and by 'our law' (D. 48.5.39.(38). 2) may be post-classical (Guarino 1943: 248).

36. D. 48.5.39(38). 4. By the second century A.D., *cognitio extra ordinem*, special consideration by the emperor, became regular in such cases; see also D. 23.2.57a.

37. On the *lex Julia de adulteriis*, see Corbett (1930) 133–46; Csillag (1976); Raditsa (1980); Richlin (1981).

38. *Pace* Herrmann (1964) 100 ff.

39. Dio 55.5.4; *Coll.* 4.11; D. 48.4.28(27). 6; 48.18.17 pr.; C. 9.9.6; Buckland (1908) 86–91; Garnsey (1970b) 215; Brunt (1980) 256–9; Raditsa (1980) 311. The owner was forbidden to manumit the slaves before the trial (D. 40.9.12–14), and the prosecutor had to furnish a bond of indemnity in case the slaves should die or lose value, and the woman not be convicted (C. 9.9.3). Torture of slaves for this purpose

was allowed, besides this offence, only for cases of *maiestas* and falsifying census returns.

40. D. 48.5.11.11; 16.(15) 9; 17.(16); C. 9.9.8.
41. Paul. *Sent.* 2.26.14;Garnsey (1970b) 104.
42. Ulp. *Reg.* 13.2. From Ulpian's discussion in D. 23.2.43.13, it seems that the law said merely 'a woman *taken* in adultery'; one condemned, he argues, is liable under the heading of those condemned in a criminal court.
43. Martial 10.52; Juv. 2.68 ff; other references to prostitutes' clothing in RE XV. 1. 1025–6; Marquardt (1886) 42 n. 7. This is further discussed in Chapter 11 below.
44. D. 22.5.18.
45. Astolfi (1965).
46. Gell. *N.A.* 10.23.5; Paul. *Sent.* 2.26.4; *Coll.* 4.10, 12.3; D. 48.5.25.(24) pr; Corbett (1930) 136 ff.; Watson (1967) 28.
47. Paul. *Sent.* 2.26.4, 5; *Coll.* 4.3.1–4; D. 48.5.39(38).8; 48.8.3.5; Corbett (1930) 135–7; Csillag (1976) 187.
48. Paul. *Sent.* 2.26.1–2; *Coll.* 4.2.3–7, 8, 12.1–2; D. 48.5.23(22).4; 24(23); Corbett (1930) 137–9; Raditsa (1980) 313.
49. Paul. *Sent.* 2.26.11; D. 25.7.1.2; 48.5.11(10).2; C. 9.9.22. Constantine in A.D. 326 drew a distinction (C. 9.9.28(29)) between the proprietress of a *taberna* and the barmaids. The former, if she did not personally serve the customers, was 'respectable', and therefore subject to the application of the adultery law. See also Tac. *Ann.* 2.85; Suet. *Tib.* 35; AE 1978. 145; Levick (1983).
50. Garnsey (1967) 56 ff, (1970b) 21–4.
51. Dio 77.16.
52. D. 48.5.2.2–7; 9(8); C. 9.9.10; RE XII. 2.1942–3.
53. D. 48.5.27(26). pr.
54. Tracy (1976).
55. D. 48.5.11(10).1, 30(29).2. Daube (1972: 374) oddly supposes that a man was penalised if he took a bribe to refrain from prosecution, but not if he merely took one to keep silence, whereas a woman, who would not be bribed not to prosecute (since she could not, anyway) was penalised simply for keeping her mouth shut. This is a strained interpretation of the texts and is in itself a strange notion. What was penalised was not the inaction (since there was no obligation on outsiders to act) but the taking of bribes with the intention of hindering the course of justice.
56. D. 48.5.34(33).2.
57. Greenidge (1894) 173 ff.
58. D. 23.2.43.1–5, 9; RE XV. 1.1020.
59. Livy 39.19.5; Watson (1967) 33 ff.; references in note 42 above.
60. Quint. *Inst. Or.* 8.5.19; Suet. *Dom.* 8; D. 29.1.41; 37.12.3 pr.; 34.9.14; Astolfi (1965) 41 ff.
61. Paul. *Sent.* 2.26.11; D. 48.5.14(13).2.
62. D. 5.3.27.1.
63. D.12.5.4.3.

8 Children

Roman family law was originally created for a society in which marriage was almost always accompanied by the entry of the wife into *manus*, divorce was very rare, and women had little or no control over the testamentary disposal of their property. In consequence, the law had little to say about the mother–child relationship. It was concerned rather with the child in relation to the *familia* to which, through the *pater*, it belonged. The legitimate child was in the *potestas* of its father, and in no circumstances could the mother have *potestas* over her child, legitimate or illegitimate (and, indeed, unless married with *manus*, she did not even belong to the same *familia*), nor could she adopt a child, nor even be a tutor. If married with *manus*, she was her child's agnate for inheritance purposes; otherwise, she was only a cognate. The illegitimate child took its civic status from its mother (in default of a *pater*), but this gave her no rights over the child.

Despite the changes in Roman society itself, the law remained in essentials unchanged right through the classical period, such changes as there were being minor. Those relating to the status of illegitimate children were made to serve interests other than those of the mother as parent; though they could have important legal consequences for the child, and social consequences for both, the only legal rights of the mother over the child that were affected (indeed, the only ones she had) were those of cognate inheritance. On tutorship and *potestas* the law stood firm at least to the end of our period. Although in practice a mother might have physical charge of her child, she could act independently in none of the matters falling within the responsibility of a tutor. If, say, a dying *pater* wished his wife to administer their child's property, it could be arranged only through some legal device such as a fideicommissary legacy. Only in the law of inheritance was there any significant change, and this did not affect mother and child symmetrically. In the early second century A.D. mothers were given preference over remoter agnates in succession to their children — but only after *sui heredes* and the child's father and siblings, and only if the mothers already had the *ius liberorum*; the children, on the other hand, half a century or so later, were given priority in intestate succession to their mothers. Since women by this time already had freedom of testamentary disposal, this concession did little to damage the rights of the agnates in the mother's family, while those in the child's were, in comparison, carefully preserved. (These changes in the law of succession will be disussed more fully in the chapter on inheritance.)

The law, then, was primarily concerned with preserving the integrity of the *familia* and its property; and, as usual, the law would become important only when, for some reason or other, what we regard as normal family affections either could not or would not find expression.

Status

A child born of a *iustum matrimonium* (that is, where there was *conubium* between the parents) was legitimate, took the father's status and was in his *potestas*. If there was no *conubium* between the parents, then in law they were not married, and the child took its mother's status. So, the offspring of a Roman man and a woman who was Latin or peregrine (without *conubium*) or a slave was Latin or peregrine or servile in status.

The rule was modified, possibly as early as the beginning of the first century B.C., before the Social War, by the *lex Minicia*, according to which, where one parent was Roman and the other peregrine, without *conubium*, the child's status was to follow that of the 'worse', i.e., non-citizen, parent. As Gaius (I. 78) noticed, the law was superfluous where the father was a citizen; what the Roman lawmakers were guarding against was the admission to the Roman citizen body of the offspring of a Roman woman and a peregrine. The law apparently did not apply to the child of a citizen woman and a slave; until the passing of the *senatusconsultum Claudianum* (see below), such a child was apparently treated in the same way as one *incerto patre* (of unknown father) and had the mother's status.[1]

Some confusion was caused by the legislation on manumission, the *lex Aelia Sentia* and *lex Junia*, which gave Latinity to slaves manumitted under the age of 30, but also apparently allowed them *conubium* with citizens. One opinion, therefore, was that the children of a marriage between a Junian Latin and a Roman woman should take the father's status, as would happen also with the child of a

Roman woman and a 'peregrine' Latin (i.e., one without *conubium*). However, this was anomalous, since the *lex Aelia Sentia*, or the *lex Junia*, had also provided that Junian Latins, even if married to wives of the same status, could gain citizenship for themselves and their child, by having a child who reached the age of one year. So, irregularly manumitted slave couples, who showed themselves stable and responsible members of society by marrying and starting a family, were admitted to the citizen body. Hadrian resolved the matter by a *senatusconsultum* stating that in all cases the child of a Latin father and a Roman mother was a Roman citizen.[2]

The child of a slave woman was a slave, and belonged to her owner at the time of birth.[3] In general, it was held that the status of a child conceived in wedlock was determined at the moment of conception (so covering the case of the posthumous child or the child born after divorce), and that of the child conceived outside marriage was determined at the time of birth. Nevertheless, by the time of Paul, the law was liberally interpreted to mean that if a slave woman was free, even if only temporarily, at any time from conception to birth, the child was born free (this application could benefit also the Roman woman temporarily in captivity or penal slavery); this applied also if, through mischance or the deliberate delay of others, her manumission was delayed.[4]

The owner of the slave woman and her child could dispose of them as he or she wished. Natural families could be, and were, broken up by sale or bequest. A typical will from Oxyrhynchus, dated A.D. 127, contained the bequest of a slave woman together with any progeny she might have. They at any rate (though not perhaps the natural father) had a chance of staying together, but only as long as the inheritor saw fit. Less fortunate was a woman manumitted in a will dated between A.D. 161 and 169. Her twins, ten months old at the time of the will, were not freed, but were bequeathed to the testator's daughter. Their mother could keep them with her until six months after they were weaned, then she must hand them over to the new owner. There may have been in the missing portion of the text a *paramone* clause (the testator has a Greek name), requiring the mother to stay on for some time in the service of the beneficiary. Livia Culicina, freedwoman of the wife of Augustus, mother of a chief centurion and married twice, to high-level *apparitores* in the freedman civil service, was the child of a broken slave family, her parents having been manumitted at the death of their previous owner, while she passed to the emperor and thence to his wife (perhaps as a gift 'for manumission').[5]

Even when the slave woman's child was fathered by her owner, this was no guarantee that they would be allowed to stay together, let alone that they would be freed. Two examples must suffice.

First, there is the family of the veteran C. Julius Diogenes, living in Egypt. His freedwoman Julia Primilla bore him illegitimate twins, C. Julius Sp. f. Diogenes and Julia Isarus. He left them a legacy in his will, but nominated as his heirs two slave women, both aged over thirty, whom he manumitted. It looks rather as though these two were his natural daughters. They were evidently older than the children of Julia Primilla. We do not know what happened to their mother. Perhaps they were born to Julia Primilla before her manumission; her twins were born free, in the year of her manumission. As Diogenes' natural daughters, the older women could have been manumitted with citizen status without waiting until the age of 30; Diogenes apparently preferred to keep them in his personal service until well after the age at which they would normally have been married and bringing up families of their own.[6]

The second is Petronia Justa, whose efforts to prove her freeborn status are preserved in a dossier, mainly of sworn statements, from Herculaneum. She was the child of Petronia Vitalis, freedwoman of Petronius Stephanus. Petronius and his wife, Calatoria Themis, seem to have claimed that Petronia Justa was Stephanus' freedwoman and, according to one witness, had rebuffed her mother's claim to have the girl, saying that they were treating her 'like a daughter'. She may in fact have been Petronius' natural daughter. Other witnesses, including Petronius' freedman C. Petronius Telesphorus (who, incidentally, was Calatoria's tutor), said that Vitalis had been freed before the girl was born and that the latter was therefore freeborn. The girl herself underlined her claim to be freeborn, *incerto patre*, by including *Sp(urii) f(ilia)* in her name; as a freed slave she would, in the eyes of the law, have had no parents. We do not know the outcome of Petronia's case, but one thing is clear — she and her mother had been separated.[7]

Julia Primilla's twins had better luck, not being separated from their mother, but then, they were born after she obtained her freedom; what is more, she could prove it. In A.D. 148, when she testified before the prefect of Egypt that her son Isarus had reached his twenty-first year (the *epikrisis*), she produced a copy of the certification of Diogenes' reaching that age in A.D. 104–5 (so establishing that he had been old enough to manumit her legally), her own manumission certificate dated A.D. 127–8, and a copy of her sworn declaration of the birth of Isarus later that year, so establishing his freeborn citizen status. Clearly, the bureaucracy which pervaded life in Egypt had its beneficial aspects.[8]

Until A.D. 52, if a Roman woman had sexual relations with a slave, whatever social or legal repercussions there might be for her, any offspring born of the union were free and citizen. In that year, a *senatusconsultum* (the *sctum. Claudianum*) was passed, ordering that, if the slave's master did not consent to the association, the woman became his slave; if he did consent she was nevertheless, if freeborn, reduced to freedwoman status, with the master as her patron, and the children might 'by agreement' (though, as the master had the whip-hand, this was likely to be the condition for his consent) be his slaves.

There were exceptions. For example, if the slave had belonged to the woman's own freedman or to her son, she was not enslaved. In the latter instance, says Paul, it would not be seemly, because of the reverence due a mother, and he cites the former case as the model (i.e., because of the reverence due to a patron from a freedman). If the woman was the master's own freedwoman, she was not enslaved because, says Paul, 'she appeared not to have wished to desert the household'. Until Hadrian, it will be remembered, her patron could make sure at least of her inheritance, even if she had freeborn children, so long as they were less than four in number. If, however, she had relations with another owner's slave without her patron's knowledge, she was re-enslaved to her patron and was not to have any chance of ever attaining citizenship. A daughter *in potestate* was not enslaved if she had not acted with her father's consent; if he had consented, she was enslaved. This may seem odd; but the reasoning was that a daughter had no power to make her father's situation worse (by the loss of a daughter) but a *pater* could, if he wished, worsen the situation of his children. These exceptions apart, in general the consequence was that, whether the master had consented to the union or not, the children would be born slaves.[9]

Given that, by the first century A.D., Roman society was no longer dependent for its supply of highly trained, educated slaves on prisoners taken in campaigns in the eastern Mediterranean, but on domestic breeding, Roman masters would be reluctant to see the sexual energies of their male slaves expended on women outside the household.[10] This would seem likely to happen, however, in view of the relatively low proportion of female to male slaves in large urban *familiae* (precisely those in which skilled slaves were most in demand). In practice, though, as we have seen, only a small proportion of the wives of freedmen and consorts of slave men at Rome were freeborn women. Even this small proportion may have been enough to concern the *domini* in general and so ensure senatorial support for the measure. It may however have had a more specific aim, that of controlling the status of 'wives' and especially of children in the imperial slave household (*familia Caesaris*); the originator of the idea was Claudius' freedman Pallas. Imperial slaves were apparently highly desirable catches in the eys of freeborn women, who make up about two-thirds of the known consorts. The emperor's financial secretary may, in his master's interests, have had designs on the estates of the women who thus became freedwomen, or even slaves, of Caesar; even more probably, he wanted to have a continued supply of home-bred slaves, *vernae*, for training in the imperial administrative service.

Hadrian changed the rule. Agreements were no longer to be made rendering the children slaves. Where the woman remained free (although as a freedwoman) the child also was to be free; otherwise, both were slaves. This remained the situation until Justinian repealed the *senatusconsultum*.[11]

Legitimacy

Children born in *iustum matrimonium* were legitimate. They were in the *potestas* of their father and were his heirs on intestacy. This status could, however, be denied a child, in the opinion of some lawyers, if it were known, for example, that the husband was impotent, or that illness had prevented his sleeping with his wife for some length of time, or if, adds Julian, he had, say, been away for ten years and found in his house on his return a year-old baby (*anniculum*). Even though the neighbours might bear witness that the child had been born in the house, that would not be enough to establish its legitimacy.[12]

The procedures, initiated by a *senatusconsultum* under Vespasian and established in the reign of Hadrian, for determining the legitimacy of children born after a divorce, have been outlined in Chapter 3 above. Before they were systematised, an appeal to the praetor would be required to settle disputes. For children born after a woman was widowed, it was important to have their legitimacy established because of their inheritance rights; as we saw from the case of Petronilla (p. 53, above), these could be challenged. The question of *potestas* did not arise, but there would be a *tutor legitimus* or one assigned by the father's will.[13]

Children not conceived in lawful marriage were illegitimate. In law, they were fatherless and *sui iuris*; their mothers could not have *potestas* over them, and they had no inheritance rights from their fathers. Children born in slavery and subsequently freed had, in law, neither mother nor father.[14]

Illegitimate children, many of them born of stable unions which did not constitute marriage, were common in the Roman world. All slaveborn freedmen and freedwomen were illegitimate. So were the children of concubines; indeed, desire to avoid prejudicing the patrimony of existing legitimate heirs may have been a motive for some men to take a concubine rather than remarry.

In the provinces, where, before the *constitutio Antoniniana* of A.D. 212, there was a mixed free population, unions between peregrine and Roman were common. There is copious evidence from Egypt in the Roman period; Roman women seem to have been 'married' to peregrine men more frequently than peregrine women to Roman men. Under the *lex Minicia*, the children were peregrine, and this consideration would be of more significance for a Roman man, as potential head of a *familia*, than for a woman. If mistake about the spouse's status could be proved, the children could acquire citizen status and be in the father's *potestas*, if the latter was Roman, but mistake might be rather harder to prove if the partner was a foreigner than if, say, he was a Latin. The nomenclature would surely have given the game away.[15]

As serving soldiers were not permitted marriage, the offspring of their unions were illegitimate, although Hadrian, as we have seen, did intervene to protect their children against hardship by allowing them inheritance rights as cognates.[16]

Illegitimate children, or *liberae naturales* as they were sometimes called, were not, in classical law, legitimated by the subsequent marriage of their parents. This first became possible only under Constantine, who was anxious on moral grounds to suppress concubinage, but he does not seem to have made the law prospective, and he limited it to children of freeborn mothers and of fathers who had no children by a previous marriage and who were not still married to someone else. It was not until Justinian that legitimation by marriage (or by imperial decree in circumstances, e.g., after the death of a parent, when marriage was not possible) became a permanent option.[17]

The father, if free or freed, could adopt a male child by *adrogatio*, so acquiring *potestas* over him and giving him legitimacy. For much of the classical period, it would not have been possible to adopt female children in this way (or children of either sex away from Rome); from the Antonines onwards, female as well as male children could be adrogated by imperial rescript. One may doubt whether many humble people, such as ex-slaves, attempted this, although there is some evidence from Rome, discussed in Flory (1984), indicating that slave couples sometimes gave priority to securing the woman's manumission, so that their children could at least have citizen status.[18]

Women could not adopt children, because they did not have *potestas*. However, Ulpian mentions in passing that women could not adopt 'without the emperor's authorisation', implying that by that time adoption by women was allowed by imperial rescript, although only one instance is known, from the end of the third century A.D. Diocletian and Maximian allowed a woman to adopt her stepson as consolation for the loss of her own sons. Justinian's *Institutes* reiterate the ban, and cite this as the exceptional circumstance in which adoption might be allowed; clearly, women never acquired a general power to adopt.[19]

Adoption by a woman would give the child the inheritance rights already available since A.D. 178, under the *senatusconsultum Orphitianum*, to the woman's own freeborn children, legitimate or otherwise. It could give the woman the right of cognate succession to the child (if not actually her natural child), but none of the rights deriving from *potestas*, since women could not exercise *potestas*.[20]

Birth Certificate

It was not compulsory at Rome to register the birth of a child. However, the Augustan *lex Aelia Sentia* and *lex Papia Poppaea* established a procedure for the registration of legitimate children of citizen status, to be carried out within 30 days of the child's birth. It need not be made by the father; the mother or grandfather could do it.[21]

The declaration (*professio*) was made before a magistrate. The particulars were entered in the official record (*tabula professionum*) and the form is known to us from copies preserved on diptych tablets from Egypt containing a copy of the extract from the records. No independent check was made of the truth of the declarations, so the register provided only prima facie evidence. (The same is true of declarations of birth in modern England, although failure to declare is an offence.) The diptych copies start with the date, then a statement that this is a copy from the official register. The text of the entry follows, with reference by *tabula* and page number for the year in question. The details supplied were the father's name, tribe and filiation, the child's name, that of the mother, and the date.[22]

Several provisions of Augustan legislation made it important to be able to provide evidence of age and citizen-status, either for oneself or one's children, and also of the fact of having had legitimate children. The existence of one or more children increased their parents' capacity to receive inheritances from outsiders; the 'privilege of children' (*ius liberorum*) freed women from *tutela*, and after the *senatusconsultum Tertullianum*, of Hadrianic date, it also gave them some rights of inheritance from their children (described in more detail in Chapter 9). Manumitters, under the *lex Aelia Sentia*, had to be over 20 years of age. Obviously, once birth registration became customary, it could be used for other purposes, e.g., to establish that one had reached marriageable age.

Registration of illegitimate children was forbidden under these laws; Augustus had been interested in encouraging procreation within lawful wedlock. Nevertheless, some illegitimate children had citizen status, and it could be important for them to be able to prove this in later life. The practice developed, therefore, of making private sworn declarations (*testationes*) before seven witnesses. One already cited, from Herculaneum, was made by a Junian Latin freedman, L. Venidius Ennychus. He declared the birth of a daughter and then, a year later, he attested that she was one year old, so that he and his wife could claim citizenship. In an example from Egypt, dated A.D. 131, a soldier attested the birth of a daughter, so staking her claim, under Hadrian's ruling, to inherit from him. In A.D. 145 a woman, Sempronia Gemella, recorded the birth of twin sons (clearly, twins ran in her family) 'of unknown father', *incerto patre*, with the filiation therefore given as *Spurii f.* According to Ulpian, one more child would get her the *ius liberorum*, though according to Paul three *separate* births were necessary, an alarming prospect, given her genetic inheritance — and they had to be live births. By this time, on the evidence of the *senatusconsultum Tertullianum*, illegitimate children possibly counted for the *ius liberorum*.[23]

Marcus Aurelius removed the ban on official registration of illegitimate children. By this time, as we have seen, there were so many circumstances in which couples, with the best will in the world, could not marry, and consequently so many children of citizen status born out of wedlock, that it was pointless to retain it. One of the few references to registration in the legal texts, however, actually concerns a false registration of a child as illegitimate. A woman was divorced by her husband while she was pregnant. When her son was born, in her husband's absence she registered the child as *spurius*, illegitimate. She died intestate, and the husband then had to try to prove the child's legitimacy and his own paternity so that he could establish his *potestas* and claim the inheritance on his son's behalf.[24]

Guardianship, Custody and Control

The *potestas* of a father over his legitimate children included the right to custody of the child and, as well as those powers of discipline and punishment already noted and the ownership of all property acquired by the child, it also included powers which might be classed as 'care and control'. The father would have the final say on such matters as the child's education and marriage, where the child would live, and so on. The extent to which mothers had any say in these matters would depend not on any legal right but on the nature of the personal relationships between them and their husbands, and no doubt they did normally play an active part in the upbringing of their children, especially in the early years. Cornelia, mother of the Gracchi, is an example often cited. Although the husband of Corellia Hispulla, Pliny's friend, is apparently still alive, it is to her that Pliny writes (*Ep.* 3.3) to give advice on the choice of a rhetoric teacher for her young son. 'Until now', he writes, 'he has been too young to be away from you, and has been taught at home.' If there were disagreements, however, the mother's wishes carried no legal weight at all.

After divorce, the father retained *potestas*, and with it the right to keep the children with him. There are indications, though, that it was sometimes recognised that it was in children's best interests to stay with their mother rather than their father. From the time of Antoninus Pius at least, appeal could be made to a magistrate, who might rule that a child should continue to live with its mother, on account of the father's bad character; the mother could also claim basic maintenance for the child.[25] Even in these circumstances, however, although the mother had physical custody of the child, the father's *potestas* was otherwise untouched. Clearly, a view such as that which eventually prevailed in English law, that the welfare of the child was the prime consideration, had made very little progress in the Roman world. As between the *familia* and the individual, the former prevailed.

Widows and unmarried mothers might have their children living with them, but they had no *potestas* over them. The children were *sui iuris* and required a tutor. Women could not be tutors; classical law was quite clear on this point, and the principle was maintained throughout the classical period. Again, there is a contrast with modern English law, according to which all rights and powers are vested in the mother of an illegitimate child, even when the father is known, and the latter has to bring proceedings, in order to claim custody; also, although a father can appoint a guardian for a legitimate child in his will, since 1886 it has been the law that the mother is to act jointly with any such guardian.[26]

In Roman law, the mother had no such powers. If a guardian had not already been appointed by the father's will and there was no *tutor legitimus*, the widow had to apply to the magistrate for one to be appointed, as we saw Petronilla doing, and similarly for an illegitimate child. The powers of the Roman mother were more restricted than those of her Greek or Egyptian counterpart in Egypt appear to have been. The latter could, by virtue of the terms of her husband's will or of her marriage contract, or by application to a magistrate, acquire the capacity to do such things as giving a daughter in marriage, putting a child to apprenticeship or even prostitution, and, with her mother-in-law's consent, exposing an infant. Papyri from Roman Egypt, some falling within our period, have been cited as showing Roman women in Egypt apparently exercising similarly extensive powers.[27] It may indeed have been found impracticable to impose Roman ways universally after the *constitutio Antoniniana*. However, allowance must also be made for a certain confusion, already noted, in the minds of ordinary people not themselves expert in either Roman or Greek law, about what the rules were, what forms of expression should be used, or even the legal significance, if any, of their actions. Analysis is not helped by the incompleteness of many texts. Space does not permit a detailed consideration even of the texts cited in Taubenschlag (1955: 152–5), but to mention two examples may be instructive.

P. Oxy. 1273 (A.D. 260) is called by the editors 'a marriage-contract', and the resemblance between the *tabulae nuptiales* and the Greek marriage contract has already been noted. The bride's mother says that she has given her daughter in marriage; otherwise, her part in the document as preserved amounts to no more than a specification of the dowry she is giving the groom and an undertaking on the latter's part that it is to be returned to her or to the bride if the marriage should break down. The dowry agreement, apparently, was in the form of a *stipulatio*. The mention of having given the girl in marriage stems originally from Greek models: Roman fathers usually added that they did so in accordance with the *lex Julia de maritandis ordinibus*. However, a daughter old enough to marry would no longer be a minor. If her father was dead, she would be *sui iuris*, and if she was not herself constituting a dowry from her own property, not even tutor's consent to her marriage would be necessary. There need be no question here of 'maternal *potestas*', so-called, replacing that of a deceased father.

In *P. Oxy.* 1274 a mother is described by Taubenschlag (1955: 154 n. 28) as 'manager of her children's estate without designation'. In this document the mother, apparently free from the necessity of having a tutor herself but acting with an 'adviser' (*synestos*) has recently been widowed. She is appointing someone to go to the appropriate official office and register the value of her late husband's property on behalf of her son, who has been instituted heir. At the same time, she wants to make a declaration about what she is owed from the estate as dowry. Clearly, the husband's death has only just occurred. It was apparently sudden, and while he was carrying out his duties as *basilicogrammateus*. The mother is not actually managing the property, merely recording its value and staking her own claim to part of it. The surviving portion of the text does not indicate that she is actually going on to make a *cretio*, formal acceptance of the estate, on the child's behalf, which was a step which would normally require a tutor's authorisation. However, it could be held that her registering the value of the estate was tantamount to acting as heir (*pro herede gestio*) on the child's behalf and therefore amounted to accepting the estate. There is no reason to suppose that she is not going to ask for a tutor to be appointed. Technically, she should already have done so; and for all we know this may subsequently have been pointed out to her.

The tutor to a minor was expected not merely to give assent and authorisation, but actually to administer the ward's property. Although the legal powers of a mother in regard to property were very restricted, in practice we do find mothers administering their children's property. They are sometimes referred to, especially in the papyri, as acting jointly with a guardian (as *epakolouthetria* or similar title), though the guardian's function may be merely to give the legally necessary assent to the woman's arrangements; women did, after all, customarily manage their own property in this way. So we find, for example, a mother, Marcia Athenais, accepting her late husband's estate on behalf of their child, Herennia Helene, whom he instituted as heir, with the authority of a tutor, L. Valerius Onnos.[28] Ulpian finds it necessary to point out that even when a mother is administering her son's business affairs in accordance with the wishes of her late husband, nevertheless her transactions are not legally valid and enforceable. Cervidius Scaevola was more disposed to the view that their validity should be accepted on grounds of equity, where to do otherwise would be unjust, e.g., to debtors acting in good faith. A mother could be barred from the intestate succession to her child afforded her by the *sctum. Tertullianum*, if she had not taken steps to have tutors appointed. This suggests that it was not uncommon for mothers to handle the property affairs of their children without actually bothering to acquire tutors for them; for many, occasions may seldom or never have arisen when the validity of a transaction came into question and the lack of tutorial authorisation became important.[29]

It is not until well after the end of the classical period of Roman law, until A.D. 390, that we have clear evidence for women being allowed to act as tutors.[30] A constitution issued that year by Theodosius and his colleagues states:

Mothers who after the loss of their husbands claim tutorship of their children for the administration of their property must, before they can rightfully be confirmed in such an office, give an undertaking that they are not entering a second marriage. No one, of course, is forced to do this. They should submit to the conditions we lay down of their own free will; for if they prefer to opt for another marriage, they ought not to administer the guardianship of their children. But to prevent their being easily taken over (*ne sit facilis in eas inruptio*) after acquiring the tutorship, we have ordered that the goods of anyone seeking to marry a woman who exercises *tutela* should be pledged and held as security for the financial administration of the little ones' affairs, so that there may be no losses either through neglect or fraud. To this we add that a woman, provided she is of advanced age (*aetate maior*), may apply to be a tutor if and only if there is no *tutor legitimus*, or the latter has been excused on claim of privilege or removed as suspect or is found unfit, for reasons of mental or physical health, to manage even his own affairs.

They add that if the woman does not want the *tutela* and prefers remarriage, and there is no *tutor legitimus*, then the *praefectus urbi* or the provincial magistrates shall take steps to have guardians appointed.

It used to be held that women had no capacity at all to be tutors until this constitution; it is now thought, on the contrary, that they had a limited capacity previously, and that Theodosius' constitution merely added some more stringent conditions. The new contribution is probably the requirement of an undertaking not to remarry or, failing that, of the provision of security by the new husband. The dangers being guarded against are the birth of children of a second marriage who might be favoured at the expense of those of the first (the qualification about the woman's age is also relevant here) and the exercise of undue influence on the wife by her second husband. If the second husband was himself the child's tutor, he would in any case, as a tutor, by this period have been required to give security. A tutor was not allowed to marry his ward, but it was perfectly legal for him to be married to his ward's mother.[31]

It seems, then, that prior to this constitution women had for some time past been allowed, in certain narrowly specified circumstances, to take on the guardianship of their children. What the circumstances were can be inferred. The deceased father had left no testamentary instructions for the appointment of a tutor, and there either was no one eligible as *tutor legitimus*, or those eligible were, for one reason or another, not available. Whether the qualification about the woman's age is new, or taken over from earlier practice, is uncertain.

How long, and by what means, this possibility of being appointed tutors to their children had been available to women before A.D. 390 is not known. Only two texts are apparently significant, one of Gaius and one of Neratius (the latter's legal writings belong mainly to the reign of Hadrian, though he was already known as a jurist under Trajan). Gaius remarks: '*Tutela* is usually (*plerumque*) a man's duty.' Neratius says: 'Women cannot be appointed tutors, since that is an office belonging to men, unless they specially ask the emperor for the guardianship of their children.' However, in A.D. 224 the emperor Alexander Severus bluntly informed one woman, 'Administration of *tutela* is a man's function, and such a task is beyond feminine weakness', and seventy years later Diocletian and Maximian told another, 'To take up the defence of another is a man's task and beyond the female sex; so, if your son is a minor, get a tutor for him.' In neither case is there any hint of a possible exception to the rule.[32]

Various attempts have been made to resolve this discrepancy, the most drastic being simply to assume that the texts of Gaius and Neratius were interpolated. Recently, Masiello (1979: especially 9 ff., 79) has denied interpolation, and argued that policies changed from one reign to another, the rules being slackened under the earlier Antonines and reaffirmed under the Severi. Perhaps most satisfactory is an explanation along the general lines of that suggested by Crifo (1964), that *tutela* had been opened to women in the classical period, but only to individual cases, on direct appeal to the emperor, and only in certain narrowly specified circumstances. The general principle that women were excluded from *tutela* remained unaltered and could be restated where these circumstances were not fulfilled.

Given the absence of *tutores legitimi*, the only persons who could, after the passing of the *sctum. Tertullianum*, have a prior or equal claim to that of a mother (with the *ius liberorum*) to succeed to her child's inheritance were the child's siblings. Her practical administration of her child's property, it could be held, did not always need the safeguard of a tutor's authorisation, since she would be damaging no one else's expectations from the property. The personal tie between mother and child is recognised as having some weight — but not at the expense of the *familia*.

The constitution of A.D. 390 relates specifically to married mothers of legitimate children: but is there any reason why the concessions reported by Gaius and Neratius (if the texts are accepted as they stand) should not have been made equally, or perhaps especially, to mothers of illegitimate children, who may have wanted personally to administer their children's property? There may not have been many who applied, but some illegitimate children, even though owning nothing at birth, may soon have acquired property by gift or bequest. An illegitimate child, other than a freed slave, could have no *tutor legitimus* and no agnates. There is another text of Neratius (D. 26.3.2) which may also relate to the situation of the unmarried mother and her child:

> It is not correct for a woman to assign a tutor to her child in her will; but if she does so, the appointment will be confirmed, after due inquiry, by decree of the praetor or proconsul, and he (the tutor) will not be required to give the ward a guarantee of good management.

The exemption in the last clause is not, *pace* Masiello (1979: 21 ff.), an appreciation of the good sense of the mother's choice, but simply the normal practice (G. I. 198–9) where the tutor was appointed either by the testator himself or by a magistrate, and so approved by one or the other. A man could appoint a tutor in his will; if a woman did so, the nomination had to have the magistrate's approval. Children who were *impuberes* at the time of their mother's death would require to be assigned tutors only if her death itself effectively deprived them of a tutor, that is, if she herself, as a widow or an unmarried mother, had either been fulfilling that function with official approval, or had previously neglected to obtain a tutor.

A woman acting as tutor would inevitably have to undertake obligations on behalf of someone else (her ward), which was against the provisions of the *sctum. Velleianum* of A.D. 46, but she could get round this by renouncing the protection of the *sctum.* afforded her. We have no text concerning this provision before A.D. 350 (*Nov.* 118.5); how early it was first applied to women acting as tutors cannot be determined.

Whatever the law might say, some Roman fathers evidently thought that the best person to have in charge of the interests of their children was the children's mother, and they would try to appoint their wives as tutors in their wills. Papinian was quite definite that this was impermissible:

> Under our law, a provision in a father's will that the *tutela* of their common children is to be assigned to their mother is of no effect; and if a provincial official should have fallen into error through inexperience and ruled that the father's intentions are to be honoured, his successor will not be correct in following a policy which our laws do not permit.

Elsewhere, however, referring to a situation in which tutors had indeed been appointed, but expressly released by the father from all responsibility, because he wanted the mother to be in charge of the child, Papinian points out that this also is of no effect, but remarks that good men ought to take heed of beneficial advice (*salubre consilium*) from the mother.[33]

One way of getting round the law was to disinherit the child and make the mother heir, subject to a *fideicommissum* to hand over the estate to the child when he or she reached a specified age. Ulpian says 'many' did this. Then the estate became the mother's property, to be administered as she wished, until the child grew up.[34]

Things could go wrong, of course, in the chances and changes of human life. Paul cites such a case. A certain Fabius Antoninus disinherited his daughter Honorata and his son Antoninus, a minor, making his wife Junia Valeriana the heir, subject to a *fideicommissum* to hand over the whole estate to her son on completion of his twentieth year; if the son died before reaching that age, the estate was to be handed over to the daughter Honorata. Unfortunately, the mother died before that time arrived and could not fulfil the trust. Both children were her heirs at law. Then the son died, in the course of his twentieth year, leaving a daughter, whose tutors went to law to recover from her aunt the *fideicommissum* and the portion of the inheritance due her from her father's will, and succeeded. What appears to have happened was that on the mother's death the two children had shared equally what she left, as heirs on intestacy, and the *fideicommissum* had been ignored as not yet due for fulfilment. Young Antoninus had made a will leaving his portion to his daughter, but his sister had claimed the lot, under the terms of her father's will, on the grounds that her brother had died before reaching the required age. The *praeses* (apparently all this took place in one of the provinces) seems to have decided, on grounds of equity rather than of strict law, not only that the son should be deemed to have completed his twentieth year (the tutors cited a constitution of Hadrian to the effect that a year begun should be counted as completed), but that the non-fulfilment of the *fideicommissum* by the mother should also be disregarded.[35]

If a mother was given a *fideicommissum* in this way, omission to seek tutors for the children was perhaps pardonable, since the children inherited no property of their own. Another method was to make the children heirs, but to bequeath their mother the usufruct of the estate for a specified period, e.g., for five years, or until the children reached puberty, or a daughter reached the age of 18, etc. The property belonged to the children, but during that time the mother had the management and control of it, and received the profits. She was not prevented from remarrying, but the estate was preserved for the children. In effect she was being paid to look after the children. This could be done more directly, without a legacy of usufruct; but in at least one example the usufruct is limited in such a way that it amounts to a payment to the mother for her services in managing the estate. The father's will gave the wife usufruct until the fifteenth year but asked her to retain only 40,000 sesterces a year and pay the rest of the income over to the heir or heirs. This method had its dangers, too. If the mother died before the specified time had expired, the children might have to wait until the time limit was reached before they could receive their inheritance, while their mother's estate benefited from the usufruct.[36]

Without giving his widow any control over the estate, the father might provide for the care and rearing of the children by instructing the heir to make the widow regular payments, conditional on the child still being with her. (If the heir *was* the child, these would be made by the tutor.) The intent was not so much to discourage her from remarrying (conditions of that sort were, in any case, held to be contrary to the *lex Julia et Papia*) as to guard against the possibility of the children being neglected after a second marriage.[37]

In Greco-Egyptian law, mothers not only had rights over their children, but also duties. During marriage, or after divorce, maintenance of the child was the father's duty. After the father's death, it was an obligation on the mother.[38] In Roman law, there could be no such obligations; the child was *sui iuris*. The mother's natural feelings could, perhaps, usually be relied upon to secure the child's maintenance, but Roman fathers, as we have seen, sometimes took steps to secure by testament what the law could not compel. However, by the time of Ulpian there are indications that it was felt that the blood relationship, even between mothers and illegitimate children, gave some claim in equity to maintenance, and magistrates did occasionally make rulings accordingly (D. 25.3.5.4, 5).

Unwanted Children

For various reasons, children might not be wanted. Their birth could be prevented, by contraception or (perhaps more efficaciously) abortion, or once born they could be disposed of. Obviously, the former alternative was more directly under the control of the woman. The latter, in the eyes of the law at any rate, was the prerogative of men.

Infanticide and Exposure

Whether infants, other than the diseased or monstrous, were often directly murdered is uncertain; it is a subject about which the Romans kept rather quiet. Philo, the Jewish–Hellenistic philosopher, alleged that the newborn were sometimes strangled or drowned, and regarded exposure as tantamount to murder: 'Others expose them in some desert place, hoping, or so they assert, that the infants may be rescued, but in reality leaving them to suffer the most terrible fate' — such as being devoured by beasts or birds of prey, unless they have the luck to be picked up by passing strangers, showing more kindness than their own parents. Roman sources, however, talk mostly about the exposure of children, i.e., their abandonment.[39]

The *pater* had the right to decide whether to acknowledge and rear the child or to expose it. This right was grounded in the *ius vitae necisque*. In practice, the power of life and death, at least so far as grown children were concerned, had become obsolete by the early empire. If it was necessary to punish them, they should be referred to the magistrate for this; Hadrian punished a father who killed his son for adultery with his stepmother.[40] In law, nevertheless, the right continued to exist not merely, where infants were concerned, in theory, but in force. Paul indicates as much (D. 28.2.11). The claims of children to inherit from their father are not removed, he says, by their being omitted from his will. It is no obstacle that the father has the right (*licet*) to disinherit them; he also had the right (*licebat*) to kill them. The difference in tenses is surely significant. By the time of the Severi, exposure was beginning to be regarded among jurists as tantamount to murder, but it was not actually prohibited until A.D. 374.[41]

There was one set of circumstances in which the *pater* was deprived of his right to decide the fate of the infant. By the *sctum. Plancianum* (no later than Trajan) and another of Hadrianic date it was established that, if a divorced wife had given notice of pregnancy within 30 days of divorce, the husband must specifically deny paternity, or else, even if he did not acknowledge the child, he must rear it. Whichever he chose to do, he lost the right to decide to expose the child.[42] The father of an illegitimate child, of course, had no *potestas*, and so no right to expose the infant. Exposed children were sometimes brought up as slaves of the finders, although, if they should subsequently be able to prove their freeborn status, they must be released. In Egypt, from which most of our evidence for slave-foundlings comes, anyone adopting a foundling as his own child was liable to forfeiture of one-quarter of his estate at death.[43]

Exposure was the right of the *pater*, and only his. It is to be hoped that in most cases, where a family could not or would not bring up another child, the father secured his wife's consent. In one famous instance, however, the foundling C. Melissus of Spoletum, who ended up as a librarian in Augustus' service, had been exposed as the result of a quarrel between his parents.

If a mother had exposed a child without her husband's consent, the latter would presumably have grounds for an action against her, since she had made away with something that was his. If a mother exposed an illegitimate freeborn child, on the other hand, what was the situation? She had not actually killed the child, and as it had no *pater*, there was no one to claim that it be produced or surrendered to him. Should it become known that the child had been enslaved, or died, or come to some harm, it would presumably be open to a third party to bring the appropriate action, against the owner in the first instance, the mother in the latter two. In practice, this possibility was likely to remain academic, since proof might not be easy to come by, nor, indeed, would the child's fate be of immediate practical concern to many outsiders. The same applied if she killed the child. Technically, this was murder, as it is in modern law, but there might be no one with an interest in prosecuting and, in a society in which infant mortality ran high, proof of murder would be difficult.

One might expect female children to be exposed more often than male. Whether this was so, and to what extent, the evidence does not allow us to determine. The so-called 'law of Romulus' enjoining that all free males and the firstborn daughters were to be reared cannot be taken as evidence for historical practice. Dio remarked that there were fewer females than males in the freeborn population in 18 B.C., which is demographically rather surprising if infant-disposal is excluded. The plots of Roman comedy in which true love prevails when the girl is discovered to be a foundling of citizen birth can be seen as evidence for Greek rather than Roman practice. In any case, the story had to be that way round; Roman audiences would not have warmed to the predicament of a Lady Chatterley, even unmarried.[44]

In Roman Egypt, children rescued 'from the dung-heap' to be reared as slaves were commonly put out to wetnurses by their owners. The surviving contracts of employment of nurses mention only a few female children. Does this mean that more male than female children were exposed, or that people preferred to pick up the males, and left the females? In fact, many of the texts have no indication of the child's sex, and so relative proportions cannot be gauged, even supposing we knew, as we do not, that the surviving texts constitute a representative sample, not only of foundling, but of all exposed children. Moreover, there are some grounds for supposing that economic conditions specific to Egypt resulted in an unusually high proportion of slaves being bred within the country itself, and not imported. One wet-nurse (*P. Grenf.* 2.75: A.D. 305) was employed to nurse 'the fourth part of the slaves'. Her employer may have been a slave-dealer, specialising in foundlings. A substantial proportion of the nursing contracts come from Alexandria.[45]

Treggiari (1975a and 1979b), considering attitudes to females as workers, rather than family members, examined the tomb-records of two large households at Rome, the Statilii and Volusii, and noted the relatively low number of female slave children commemorated, three girls to seven boys among the Volusii, not more than three girls to 17 boys among the Statilii. She conjectured that slave women were normally sent to country estates for their confinement, though what then happened to the girl babies remains a puzzle. Her supposition, endorsed in the subsequent discussion by Biezunska-Malowist (Treggiari 1979b: 201), that they were kept in large numbers on the country estates simply as breeders (there being little other employment for them there, and only limited employment in town households) seems implausible. This would be a very expensive way of procuring a supply of hands for unskilled labouring work. Other outlets she suggests (1979b: 201) for girl children were sale to brothel-keepers or to poorer people looking for maids-of-all-work. However, her sample is, she admits (1979b: 189) too small to give more than a rough indication that the percentage of girls was lower, and some allowance must be made for other factors leading to the under-representation of females in tomb inscriptions.[46]

It seems likely that abandonment of unwanted children of both sexes was common in the Greco-Roman world.[47] Demographers, anthropologists and historians concur in the belief that, in other societies practising infanticide, more females than males were disposed of, and Roman society may have been no exception. If girls were abandoned more frequently than boys, to an extent causing an imbalance between the sexes in the free population, this might be a factor in encouraging marriage at an early age, but it need not be the only factor. The economic situation of families, and the lack of alternatives to marriage, because of limited opportunities of employment and education for women, could also be relevant.[48]

Abortion[49]

The other way of limiting family size, especially since current contraceptive practice was unreliable, was abortion. In classical Roman law, abortion was not illegal, and even when it does find a mention in the *Digest*, it is not the act itself, but the circumstances, which make it illegal.

Whatever medical or philosophical opinion might be as to whether the foetus was or was not a human being, in the eyes of the law, the foetus was not a person. Until a child was actually born, it had no status, and could be neither *in potestate* nor *sui iuris*, but some protection was afforded to its rights. Julian says, with some exaggeration, 'The child in the womb, in almost the whole of civil law, is regarded as existing in the world (*in rerum natura esse*).' Paul was more accurate. 'The child in the womb is protected, as if it were part of human society, when any question arises of the advantage of the child when born, though before it is born this is of no advantage to anyone else.'[50]

There were two areas of legal importance. The mother's circumstances during pregnancy might have a bearing on the child's status and, secondly, a prospective claim to an estate could be lodged on behalf of an expected legitimate heir.[51] Until born, however, the foetus was not legally a person, and so abortion did not constitute a crime.

There is a good deal of literary evidence from the early empire about the practice of abortion, and even some practical advice and recipes in Soranus and the elder Pliny,[52] but no suggestion that abortion was a criminal offence, although it might serve as a reason for divorce. Tacitus (*Annals* 14.16) cites it among the allegations that Nero heaped up concerning Octavia's behaviour, in his attempts to justify himself in public opinion for divorcing her — sterility, adultery, treason and conspiracy with the commander of the fleet and, finally (forgetting the earlier charge of sterility), abortion. The first item in the list is clearly not a crime, and the adultery (if true) with or without the addition of treason could have sufficed to incur her banishment to Pandateria. The abortion was no doubt supposedly that of the embryo consequential upon the equally imaginary adultery, rather than any offspring of Nero himself, and so this sorry tale has nothing to tell us about any supposed rights of the husband in marriage. There may, however, be something in the suggestion of Brunt (1971: 147) that abortion against the husband's wishes was one of the lesser matrimonial offences for which he could retain an eighth of the dowry on divorce.

Cicero, in the *pro Cluentio* (32–4), expresses moral disapprobation of abortion, not so much on behalf of a 'disappointed father' (Brunt, 1971), since the children expected are posthumous, but on the grounds that such an action is likely to lead to the dying out of families, and to decline in the citizen population. Both the women he mentions, the Milesian, given capital punishment, presumably under Greek law, for her abortion, and the widow of Magius, who, far from being punished, was married a few months later to the man who had bribed her to have an abortion, were carrying posthumous children and accepted a bribe from people who had an interest in there being no direct heir.

It is not in fact until fairly late in the period of classical law, under the Severi, that abortion appears as a punishable offence. Severus and Antoninus in a rescript declared that a woman who had an abortion should be sent into temporary exile since, according to Marcianus, it could 'appear unfitting that she should have cheated her husband of children'. The same rescript is cited by Tryphoninus, who refers more specifically to a situation in which a divorced woman was determined not to bear a son to her ex-husband. Ulpian's brief statement, that a woman who laid violent hands on herself to procure an abortion was to be exiled probably refers to the same ruling. The implication is that abortion with the husband's consent still did not constitute a crime, and neither, one must assume, did abortion by unmarried women.[53]

The other relevant references in the *Digest* concern those who administered abortifacient drugs, love potions, or drugs to cause conception. They suffered the extreme penalty if the recipient, male or female, died, but even if they did not the giver was punished, *quia malo exemplo est*. The 'bad example' is the administering of dangerous drugs, even with good intent. Clearly, abortion as such is not what is being punished.[54]

Notes

1. G. I. 76 ff.; Ulp. *Reg.* 5.8–10; D. 50.1.1; Buckland (1966) 99 ff.; Crook (1967a) 40; Kaser (1971) 280. On the dating of the *lex Minicia*, see Watson (1967) 27 n. 4.

2. *Tab. Herc.* LXXXIX (L. Venidius Ennychus); G. I. 29; Ulp. *Reg.* 3.3; Buckland (1966) 95.

3. Ulp. *Reg.* 5.9–10; Paul *Sent.* 2.24.1; D. 13.7.18.2; Taubenschlag (1955) 76 n. 41.

4. G. I. 89–91; Paul *Sent.* 2.24.2–4; D. 1.5.5, 2; 22; 26; 18; 48.23.4; Buckland (1908) 399–401.

5. *P. Oxy.* 496.6, 9, 15; *P. Strassb.* 122; C. 6.1815 (= ILS 1926); Montevecchi (1935) 96–7; Biezunska-Malowist (1977) 95. The child could be sold even before birth: D. 18.1.8 pr.; 19.1.21 pr.

6. *P. Lugd. Bat.* XIII. 14; Amelotti (1966) 41.

7. *Tab. Herc.* XIII–XXX; Crook (1967a) 48–9.

8. FIRA III no. 6.

9. Tac. *Ann.* 12. 53; Paul *Sent.* 2.21; Weaver (1964 and 1965); Crook (1967a) 62–3, (1967b); Buckland (1908) 412–8.

10. Biezunska-Malowist (1962); Harris (1980).

11. G. I. 84; Paul *Sent.* 4.10.2; C. 5.18.3.

12. D. 1.6.6.

13. D. 25.3; 40.4.29; Watson (1967) 81; Kaser (1971) 346.

14. G. I. 64; Ulp. *Reg.* 5.2; D. 38.17.2.2.

15. G. I. 67–8; *P. Gnomon* 46–52; Taubenschlag (1955) 106–8 and notes.

16. FIRA I no.78 (= BGU 140).

17. *Lib. nat.* could also be used of the biological relationship, and include legitimate children: Meyer (1895) 36–7, 39 ff.; Niziolek (1975); van de Wiel (1978).

18. G. I. 100; D. 1.7.21, 26; D. 8.48.2.1, 6; Thomas (1967) esp. 414 ff., 423 ff.; Kaser (1971) 348.

19. G. I. 104; Ulp. *Reg.* 8.8a; D. 5.2.29.3; *Inst.* I.11.10; C. 8.48.5.

20. D. 5.2.29.1; Buckland (1966) 373.

21. D. 22.3.16; Schulz (1942–43).

22. FIRA III nos. 1–3; *P. Mich.* III 166 (Cavenaile 151); *P. Cairo* 29.807 (Cavenaile 156).

23. *Tab. Herc.* V, LXXXIX; FIRA III nos. 4 and 5 (*P. Mich.* III 169; BGU VII 1690); Paul *Sent.* 4.9.1–2; D. 50.16.129; *Inst.* III.3.2 and 6; Kaser (1971) 232–3.

24. *SHA Marcus* 9; D. 22.3.29.1. As the *Digest* text cites immediately before, apparently with reference to this case, a rescript of Marcus Aurelius and Verus, the child's claim to inherit will not be under the *sctum. Orphitianum* (A.D. 178), but under the provincial edict, failing other heirs, as a cognate (D. 38.8.2).

25. D. 25.3.5.14; 43.30.1.3, 3.5–6; C. 5.25.3.

26. Bromley (1981) 285. However, recent developments in the law (1973 and 1975) recognise co-equal rights and authority of both parents in marriage, and allow either to act without the other, a convenient, but also potentially unjust, situation (Bromley, *l.c.* 281).

27. Préaux (1959) 143–5; Taubenschlag (1929), (1955) 149–56. Prostitution: BGU 1024; Taubenschlag (1929) 117–8.

28. The terminology resembles that of Greek practice, but in Roman law there would be no question of the mother having *authority* jointly with the tutor. For Marcia, see FIRA III no. 59 (= PSI 1027), A.D. 151; there is no reason to suppose that Valerius was the mother's tutor.

29. D. 3.5.30.6 (Ulpian); 38.17.2.23 ff.; 46.3.88 (Scaevola).

30. C. Th. 3.17.4; Crifo (1964) especially 113–4, 123–6.

31. *Frag. Vat.* 109; on the care taken to protect the patrimony of children against

their mother's second marriage see Humbert (1972) 182 ff., 295 ff. Testamentary clauses banning remarriage were held to be of no effect: D. 35.1.62.2.

32. D. 26.1.16 (Gaius); 18 (Neratius); C. 2.12.18; 5.35.1.

33. D. 26.2.26 pr.; 36.1.76.1.

34. D. 28.2.18; see also the will of Antonius Silvanus (FIRA III no.47: A.D. 142).

35. D. 36.1.76(74).1; see also 38.17.2.25.

36. D. 7.8.4.1; 33.1.21.5; 33.2.37; 35.1, 72 pr.; Humbert (1972) 234.

37. D. 32.30.5; 35.1.8, 62.2.

38. Taubenschlag (1929) 122–3.

39. Philo, *de spec. leg.* 3.114–5; see also Lact. *Inst.* 5.9; D. 25.3.4; Boswell (1984) 13–16 tries to make a case that exposure was regarded as an alternative to infanticide. For a brief historical survey of infanticide, see Langer (1973–4); for comparisons with other societies see, e.g., Hufton (1974) 318–51 on eighteenth-century France and Sauer (1978) on nineteenth-century England. For the treatment of diseased and monstrous infants see, e.g., T. XII. 4.1 (Cic. *de leg.* 3.19); Livy 27.37; Sen. *de ira* 1.15; Soranus *Gynaec.* 2.9–10.

40. D. 1.16.9.3; 48.9.5; C. 8.46.3 (A.D. 227); Selb (1966).

41. D. 25.3.4; C. 9.16.7.(8).

42. D. 25.3.1.4; C. 8.46.9; Lemosse (1975) 260.

43. Pliny *Ep.* 10.72–3; Suet. *de Gramm.* 7, 21; *Gnomon* 41 and 107; Buckland (1908) 402; Wenger (1953) 152–8; Taubenschlag (1955) 74, 135; Crook (1967a) 58; Watson (1967) 171. On 'exposure' as a cover for illegal sale, Engels (1984: 391).

44. Dion. Hal. 2.15; Dio 54.16.2; Watson (1967) 98 ff.; Brunt (1971) 151.

45. Biezunska-Malowist (1971a and 1974); Harris (1980) 121 ff.; for details of the nursing contracts, see Herrmann (1959); Adams (1964); Hengstl (1972); Van Lith (1974); Bradley (1980).

46. Durand (1959–60); Hopkins (1966).

47. See Golden (1981) and Harris (1982) against the arguments of Engels (1980).

48. Dixon (1978) 449–50 and the literature cited there. Brunt (1971) 136 ff. argues against early marriage for the poor, but accepts it, and suggests female infanticide as a likely reason, for the rich (151–2).

49. For texts relating to abortion, see Hähnel (1937) 238–47 and Nardi (1971); there appears to have been some confusion as to which medicaments were contraceptive and which abortifacient in effect: Hopkins (1965a) 136 ff.

50. D. 1.5.7 (Paul); 26 (Julian); see also D. 25.4.1.1 (Ulpian) — the foetus is part of the mother's body. A modern discussion of the same legal point, Glantz (1983), reaches similar conclusions (116): 'A foetus is not a person under the law. However, this does not mean that we may not offer it certain protections or rights.' In Roman law, execution of sentence on a condemned woman who was pregnant, or torture of her, was deferred until after her confinement: D. 48.19.3.

51. Mother's status during pregnancy: see texts cited in n. 4 above. Claim to estate on behalf of the *venter*: D. 25.5; 25.6; 37.9. A posthumous child could be appointed heir in a will: D. 28.2.27, 28.

52. Hopkins (1965a) 131 n. 19, 133 ff.

53. D. 47.11.4 (Marcianus); 48.8.8 (Ulpian); 48.19.39 (Tryphoninus); Watts (1973) 92.

54. D. 48.8.3.2; 48.19.38.5; Brunt (1971) 147–8; on the contrast with the views of philosophers, Étienne (1973) 20–3.

9 Inheritance and Bequest

The law of inheritance is one of the most elaborate and complicated areas of Roman law. This chapter will aim to do little more than set out the main principles on which the system operated, with the most important changes that occurred during the classical period of Roman law, and to indicate how they affected women.

From an early period women had extensive rights as heirs on intestacy. Their power of bequest, however, was severely restricted initially, the aim being to ensure the return of a family's property to the agnates after the death of an heiress. In general, women acquired progressively greater control over the disposal of their property, while their inheritance rights were, from time to time, enhanced or decreased in certain respects, though still remaining substantial. Much of this change, however, was incidental to their sex and arose out of the needs of a changing and developing Roman society. While the agnate system of succession lost considerable ground to the cognate, the structure of the Roman family and of Roman property-holding remained essentially patriarchal throughout the classical period.[1]

In any discussion of 'rights' however, it is as well to bear certain things in mind. First, rights were mainly rights of inheritance on intestacy; those of heirs-at-law (of either sex) against a will were relatively limited and consisted essentially in the right, in certain specified circumstances, to make a claim which the praetor might or might not grant. Secondly, while rights on intestacy were initially established with reference to the agnatic *familia* (though weakened progressively in favour of the cognates) the actual testamentary habits of *patres* may have followed quite different principles. So, for example, a wife (if not *in manu*) ranked very low in the praetorian rules of intestate succession and had no claim at all in civil law; but in practice Roman men seem to have liked to leave their widows suitably provided for and capable of maintaining their standard of living. The interests of children might be safeguarded by leaving their mother only the usufruct of the property, but it was not uncommon for the mother to be made an heir.[2] A daughter, on the other hand, ranked very high among heirs on intestacy, but might sometimes receive a relatively small share of her father's patrimony by will, specially if she had brothers, in consideration of her having received a dowry. A son, though, was likely to be the chief heir. Sometimes, the will made a son heir, while the daughter figured merely as recipient of a legacy, which might be specified as intended for her dowry. In one late Republican will (D. 33.1.22) an heir was instructed to pay the testator's daughter a fixed sum every year, while she was unmarried. Several examples are cited in the *Digest* of wills in which male testators institute possible posthumous children as heirs; in each case the expected child is to receive a substantially larger proportion of the estate if it turns out to be a son than if a daughter is born. Two common patterns of bequest are attested from Roman Egypt. In one, the children, irrespective of sex, receive equal shares; in the other, some preference is shown to the oldest son.[3]

It will be convenient to look first at some of the rules governing testamentary disposal of property, and then at succession on intestacy.

Forms of Will

The little that is known about the early history of testamentary disposition in Roman law suggests that originally the making of a will was exceptional, confined to men and undertaken only when there were no *sui heredes* (immediate heirs on intestacy). Of the two earliest forms of will (both out of use by the later Republic) one, made at a special meeting of the *comitia calata*, an assembly of the Roman people, held for that purpose twice a year, amounted to the adoption by *adrogatio* of a named heir, to take effect at the testator's death. The other, *in procinctu*, was essentially an emergency form of the same procedure, being executed before the mobilised army on the point of battle. Obviously, civilian emergencies were not adequately covered by these, and so, Gaius tells us (II. 102), a third form was developed, *testamentum per aes et libram*, by which, originally, the estate of someone threatened with sudden death was mancipated by formal sale to a *familiae emptor* (buyer of the *familia*), who was both heir and executor.[4]

All these procedures were designed to supply the lack of *sui heredes*; if no will was made, the estate would revert to the agnates.

The first two procedures were available only to men, since women had no standing in the *comitia* and were not part of a citizen army. In any case, women had no *sui heredes* and, unlike men, did not become heads of *familiae*. It seems likely, then, that they had no means of testamentary bestowal before the institution of the *testamentum per aes et libram*.

This, originally an emergency procedure, became the regular and customary form of Roman will. The *familiae emptor* became a formal figure, distinct from the heir. The heir or heirs designated need not be the *sui heredes*, but a rule was applied, possibly from the first century B.C. onwards, that if the *sui heredes* were passed over without being specifically excluded, the will could be made void, and even if they were excluded, it might be challenged. Even without the formality of the mancipation, a written testamentary disposition sealed by seven witnesses could be accepted by the praetor, who could award 'possession according to the terms of the will' (*bonorum possessio secundum tabulas*), with the technical consequences, whose detailed effects need not be examined here, that the beneficiaries were not *heredes*.[5]

Although women could be witnesses in courts of law, they were excluded from being witnesses to wills — along with minors, slaves, deaf-mutes, lunatics, prodigals and convicted adulterers.[6]

The Right to Make a Will

A man *sui iuris* was a *pater* and, from as far back in the classical period as our knowledge extends, had the right to make a will. Women, however, acquired freedom to dispose of their own property after death only gradually. The reasons for this difference have already been indicated. The *pater* was the sole owner of the property of his *familia* in his lifetime and had absolute control over its disposal. If he made no testamentary provision, the *sui heredes* had first claim, and after them the agnates. Women headed no *familia*, and the agnates' claim was primary. No doubt it would have been much simpler for the Romans to control the devolution of property and the maintenance of family status by confining succession entirely to the male line. They chose not to do this, and instead developed a system of property transmission in which important features were inheritance through both sons and daughters, dowries, arranged marriages, monogamy and agnate inheritance. This may have been a 'strategy of heirship' for a society which found it difficult to ensure the existence of male heirs.[7]

Whatever the reason, in the classical period women *sui iuris* could inherit, by will or otherwise, and could receive legacies. Their right to dispose of their property, however, was partially controlled by *tutela*. Gradually, women acquired increasing control over the disposal of their property, not only in their lifetimes but after death as well; at the same time, the succession rights of the agnates were progressively reduced. Most of the steps in the process have already been mentioned: appointment of a testamentary tutor; the availablity of *coemptio* (with tutor's consent) for the purpose of making a will; the *ius liberorum*; the abolition of agnatic tutelage; the possibility of compelling the consent of tutors (save *legitimi);* the abolition of *coemptio*. The admission of a woman's children, under the *senatus-consultum Orphitianum*, to her intestate succession further weakened the position of agnates.

However, the weakening of the rights of the agnates was not solely attributable to the increase in women's control of property disposal; they lost ground also to the cognates, in a long historical process of movement away from the early collection of territorially based, exclusive agnatic *familiae* to the relatively fluid, interconnected urban society. Within this society, claims to family succession based on 'family' relationships in a wider sense, including blood ties through females, were also important as a means of maintaining social equilibrium by keeping wealth moving, especially between persons of the same or similar social status.[8]

Freedom of testamentary disposal had always been the prerogative of the Roman *pater*. Bequests to persons outside the family played, particularly in the late Republic and early empire, a very important role, both socially and politically, among the upper classes. The slackening of restrictions upon women's rights of property disposal can be seen, not so much as a recognition of female 'rights', as something necessitated by the importance of maintaining this mobility of wealth. At the same time, since the structure of society remained essentially patriarchal, this freedom was *not* accorded to women in certain precise and closely defined circumstances. The nature of these circumstances is significant; they were, essentially, those in which the woman's nearest heir on intestacy was, not a cognate, not even an agnate, but a *tutor legitimus*, a (quasi) *pater* — that is, after Claudius, only a *parens manumissor* or a patron — whose consent to the making of a will could not be compelled. The *ius liberorum* interfered with this to some extent, but the principle remained in force for women without the *ius* (and, as we shall see, even for some freedwomen with it). We have already observed changes in some of the other features of the system: weakening in the authority of the *pater* over the marriage, maintenance of monogamy, but through easily dissoluble serial marriages, and changes in the concept and function of dowry.

It would not be particularly appropriate, then, to regard these changes as representing progressive stages in a deliberate process of female 'emancipation'. The most important steps had already been taken, before the start of our detailed historical knowledge, by allowing women to be *sui iuris* and capable of owning property, and to be *sui heredes*.

No will was valid unless made by someone possessing testamentary capacity (*testamenti factio*). For this, certain conditions had to be fulfilled. Some affected both sexes equally: e.g., the testator must be free, of citizen status and capable of 'attesting' (*testabilis*) — so slaves, captives, lunatics, congenital deaf-mutes and those punished with *infamia* could not make wills.[9]

Some conditions, however, affected the sexes differently. Firstly, testators must be *sui iuris*. Not only men and women with a *pater* still living, but women married with *manus* would be excluded by this requirement. Secondly, they must have reached puberty. Here women had the advantage, being deemed to be of age at twelve years, men at 14.

However, the most important difference was the requirement of tutorial consent for a woman to make a will. This has already been discussed to some extent in Chapter 2, where the function of the *tutela* in maintaining some control over the woman's property in the interests of the *familia* was described. Tutorial consent operated in two stages. First, until Hadrian abolished the requirement, it was compulsory for a freeborn woman to cut her links with her *familia* of origin by going through a *coemptio*, a change of status (*capitis deminutio*) involving a notional sale, before she could make a will. This cut the agnatic connection. On *coemptio*, she could be assigned to a tutor of her choice. Freedwomen were not required to make a *coemptio*, since they had already undergone a change of status (and had no agnates anyway), nor did daughters emancipated by a *pater* who was still living. If the woman was not exempt and had not made *coemptio*, the will was void.[10]

Secondly, all women had to obtain tutor's consent to the actual making of the will, otherwise it was invalid. The only women exempted from this requirement were, under the Augustan legislation, those who had acquired the *ius liberorum*.[11]

By the time of Gaius at the latest, as we have seen, the consent of tutors, except *tutores legitimi*, could be compelled; thus, many, and probably most, freeborn women had virtually free capacity of testamentary disposal. Two categories of women (three, until the Claudian abolition of the agnate *tutela legitima*) did not. One was the emancipated daughter, whose *pater* was her *tutor legitimus*; the praetorian rules maintained his right to intestate inheritance from his daughter, though a common motive for emancipation was, probably, to allow a daughter to make a will in her children's favour. This right was not inherited by his heirs. In the other case, however, that of the freedwoman, not only her patron but the children as well (of a male patron), should he predecease her, had the right to secure intestate succession. A female patron, however, could not be a tutor, and the tutor assigned by the praetor was not a *tutor legitimus*. For women not in *tutela legitima*, obtaining tutor's consent to a will became in effect a formality.

Even if the woman had neglected to obtain her tutor's consent, the heirs named in the will could still succeed to the property by applying to the praetor for possession under the terms of the will. Gaius (II. 118) tells us that this would be granted so long as the will was properly sealed and witnessed and so long as there were no heirs under the civil law on intestate succession (i.e., agnates or patron).

The consent seems to have been required only to the making of the will; the tutor does not seem to have had any control over its contents. So, Gaius remarks (III. 43) that if a patron had given his consent and then found that his freedwoman had not made him her heir, then he had only himself to blame. This presumably means that, so long as the actual heir could prove that the patron had consented to the making of the will, the latter could not break it by appealing to the praetor, on the grounds of his rights as patron, for possession against the terms of the will (*bonorum possessio contra tabulas*). Since the patron had had the power to take everything, by preventing his freedwoman from making a will, his exclusion under a will could only be the result of his own act. In contrast, the praetor might grant possession, notwithstanding a will, to a patron of one-half of the estate of a freedman, against any heirs other than *sui heredes*.[12] In this connection, the *ius liberorum* was not an unmixed blessing for freedwomen; see further on this point below, in the discussion of patronal rights of succession.

The Institution of Heirs

A will had to provide for the disposal of an estate in its entirety; it was not possible to make bequests of part of it and leave the rest to be assigned by the rules of intestate succession. An heir or heirs must be nominated, among whom the whole estate was divided, in proportions designated by the testators. If a male testator did not want the *sui heredes* to be his heirs, he must expressly exclude them. Males must be disinherited individually and by name; for females, a general clause of disinherison was enough. (This was the praetorian ruling; the civil law insisted only on the naming of sons; grandsons could be passed over in a general clause). This indicates the relative importance in the eyes of the law of male heirs, who could head, and transmit property to, a *familia*, and females, who could not. If there was no exclusion clause, the *sui* passed over could appeal to the praetor for *bonorum possessio* against the will. Specific legacies, to heirs or others, were either 'prior', i.e., deducted before the division of the estate, or were a charge on the estate, for which the heirs were liable in proportion to their shares. If the will lapsed through refusal of the heir or heirs, these legacies were protected by the praetor's granting an action to the beneficiaries against the heirs on intestacy.[13]

Heirs were also responsible for maintenance of the family *sacra* (if any — they could not be transmitted by women) and for the debts — in their entirety — of the deceased. The latter requirement sometimes resulted in heirs refusing the inheritance. *Sui heredes* could not, strictly speaking, refuse, since they were automatically heirs on intestacy. However, they were allowed the 'privilege of abstaining'. This would mean that the debt liability of the estate would be limited to the actual assets, which would be sold. A dutiful son or daughter might not want to bring the disgrace of bankruptcy on a dead father's name in this way. The younger Pliny wrote (*Ep.* 2.4) to reassure one such daughter, his relative Calvina (to whose dowry, it will be remembered, he had contributed). We learn that Calvina's father had died heavily in debt. Pliny, however, had paid off the other creditors so that he himself should be left as sole creditor, and he informed Calvina that he had given instructions for the debt to be written off. The intention was to encourage Calvina 'to defend your father's honour and reputation' by accepting the inheritance; that is, her father's bankruptcy was being hushed up. Pliny remarked: 'If your father had been in debt to several people, or indeed to anyone other than me, you might have hesitated to accept an inheritance which even a man would have found a burden.'

Why 'even a man'? *Sui heredes* of either sex would have been *in potestate* until the father's death and unable to acquire property of their own. Extraneous heirs could be of either sex. Pliny probably had in mind certain sources of wealth for people of his class, for example, public service, especially provincial commands, and forensic activity, which were available to men and not to women.

The Voconian Law

More than once under the Republic it was found desirable to legislate in order to limit the proportion of estates which might be apportioned in legacies. The two most important laws were the *lex Voconia* of 169 B.C. and the *lex Falcidia* of 40 B.C.[14] The *lex Voconia* provided that no legatee of either sex was to receive more than the heir or heirs taken together. That meant that it was possible to leave a single legacy, of almost half the estate. A device of this sort, known as the *legatum partitionis*, by which the heir was instructed to share the estate with a named legatee, giving the latter just under half the total value, was known at least as early as 133 B.C. and may even have predated the *lex Voconia*.[15] One use was to enable someone to be effectively heir to half the estate without liability for *sacra*; it could also be used as a way of evading, partially at least, another restriction imposed by the *lex Voconia*, which forbade the institution of women as heirs. Murdia (FIRA III no. 70) made provision in her will for her daughter in this way, but made all her sons heirs.

This latter provision of the *lex Voconia* apparently applied only to citizens registered at the last census in the highest property class. The irregularity of the holding of the census in the late Republic will have impaired the effectiveness of the law and, although Gaius (II. 274) speaks of it in the present tense, it probably ceased to be applicable once the census itself became obsolete in Italy after the time of the Flavians. In any case, its provision on legacies was superseded by the *lex Falcidia* of 40 B.C., which provided that a maximum of three-quarters of the net estate could be taken up in legacies. Dowry, amongst other items, must be deducted from a man's estate before the calculation was made.

There may also have been another provision in the *lex Voconia* applying specifically to women. Paul (*Sent*. 4.8.20) remarks, on a provision of civil law restricting agnate succession by women to full sisters of the deceased, that this was done *Voconiana ratione*. If this is taken to mean 'on the principle of the Voconian law', the remark becomes evidence for Paul's belief about the intention of the enactors of the law, but not for the date of this particular enactment. On the other hand, the meaning may be that this provision also was included in the *lex Voconia*. Its effect would be substantially to diminish the possibility of dispersal of property on intestacy outside the male line, and so into other *familae*.

However, the most notorious and controversial provision of the *lex Voconia* was that which forbade testators in the first census class to nominate women as heirs. Controversy is mainly concerned with the reasons for the passing of the law. A favourite explanation in modern writers is that the law was primarily aimed against the possession of large amounts of wealth by women; it is even called 'anti-feminist'.[16] This interpretation rests largely on the surviving fragment of Cato's speech in support of the bill (quoted in Chapter 4 above), which is taken as evidence of male resentment of wealthy women. It may be evidence of Cato's attitude, but not necessarily of that of the proposers or other supporters of the bill. Another version of this interpretation sees the law as essentially sumptuary, like the earlier *lex Oppia*, and designed to check the extravagance of women; it is not obvious how its provisions could have achieved that end.[17]

The 'anti-feminist' explanation also appears, in superficially more sophisticated dress, in Hallett (1984: 92 ff.). She suggests that the law was passed because wealthy heiresses were regarded as 'a threat to the Roman patriarchal social structure'.[18]

The nature and content of this threat is unclear. Hallett says that such heiresses were 'in a strong position to make decisions regarding their families' private, and even public, expenditures — and thus to influence their families' interactions with and image in Roman society.' Her idea seems to be either that Roman heiresses were the sole source from which their kinsmen might hope to borrow, or that Roman upper-class men funded their personal life-style and political careers not from their own property and/or personal loans, but from some hypothetical common family kitty, on the disposal of which the largest contributors (here, the wealthy heiresses) had the chief say.

Consortium, or the joint ownership of estates, was not unknown to classical law, but it existed in two forms, neither of which is apposite to the *lex Voconia*. One was the consensual partnership in property, of a type which could exist between other persons than joint heirs, which could be set up by a process before the praetor. This, according to Gaius (III. 154a–b), was modelled on the other, an ancient community of property, which he speaks of as obsolete, known as *ercto non cito* and existing between *sui heredes*. It came into existence automatically on intestacy of the *pater* and existed until the heirs took steps for the division of the estate. Clearly, it originated in an early period before methods of testamentary disposal were introduced. There is no evidence for its being common practice in the classical period; the *actio familiae erciscundae* was commonly used for the division of the estate. In any case, it applied on intestacy, and so is irrelevant to a law limiting rights of testamentary disposal.[19]

The maintenance of joint families seems never to have been usual at Rome. If it had been, it would itself have threatened the patriarchal structure of Roman society, since the stability of the joint family would have depended upon acceptance of the headship of the eldest brother. In practice, brothers and sisters were equal heirs on intestacy. As many *familiae* were created as there were siblings (those of the sisters were end-stopped). Each brother, on the death of the *pater*, became *pater* of his own *familia*, with absolute control, independent of his kin of either sex, of his own property and of the finances of those in his *potestas*. 'The Roman family system is uncompromisingly patriarchal' (Zulueta 1953: II. 177). The joint ownership of property within a family is a voluntary association. It might originally have been created by bequest, but its maintenance was voluntary. In classical law, it is treated on a par with other types of voluntary partnership, and agreements on joint ownership, such as those arising from bequests of shares in specific items of property, are not relevant to this discussion.

The idea of a wealthy heiress directly controlling the purse-strings of her brothers and kinsmen is patently absurd. She could not do so in law. At most she might threaten their expectations by her will (that is, if she had a complaisant tutor) and so possibly reduce their borrowing power elsewhere — but that is a long way short of making decisions on their private and public expenditure. However, if a woman were the preferred heir, there would be less of an estate available for distribution among men.

Did married women, then, control their husbands' public expenditure and so their careers? Borrowing by husband from wife could and did occur (see, e.g., Cato's speech, mentioned above, and Sallust, *Cat.* 35, where Catiline expresses confidence in his wife's willingness to help pay his debts), and a large dowry could be useful to a husband, as it was to Caesennia's, but it is difficult to see any threat to the patriarchal structure in such purely personal and individual arrangements. The dowry, in any case, of a wife married while still *in potestate* would not have come out of her own property; and so long as the marriage lasted, it was the husband's property.

Cicero's Terentia was very rich in her own right, but though he consults her on details of domestic finances, such as the selling of plate to raise cash for Tullia's dowry, and sometimes asks her to arrange various matters for him while he is away from Rome (and suspects her of cheating him), there is no indication that Cicero, from time to time hard-pressed for money, either regarded his wife as a natural source of funds, or allowed her to determine his activities.

What could happen, as Hallett notes (1984: 95) was that wealthy women may have used their own money to help their husbands and kinsmen in their careers; but this is not the same as controlling them, nor does it seem much of a reason for wanting to keep wealth out of the hands of such women, as a class.

Unfortunately, no explicit statements about the purpose of the *lex Voconia* have survived. The earliest, and most direct, comment is in Cicero's *de republica* (3.17), where he says that the law was passed *utilitatis virorum gratia*, for the practical advantage of men, but was full of injustice to women. However, he himself goes on to observe, in the same passage, that the law set no limit to the actual amount of wealth that an individual woman might actually come to possess. His feeling that the law was unfair appeared earlier in the second Verrine oration (2.1.104 and 112); he expected that any father who felt a natural affection for his daughter would, like himself, be outraged at Verres' attempt to use the *lex Voconia* to overthrow the will made by a father exempt from the law (since he was not registered in the census) in favour of his only daughter. The notion of *utilitas* is repeated by Gellius (*N.A.* 20.1), who, it is worth noting, distinguishes this law from various sumptuary laws.

Augustine (*C.D.* 3.21) links the law with the curbing of extravagance but, with an obvious reminiscence of Cicero, goes on to say: 'The *lex Voconia* was passed, forbidding anyone to appoint as heir a woman, not even his only daughter. I know of nothing that can be spoken or thought of more unjust than this law.' Gaius (II. 226) comments only on the provision, applying to both sexes, which restricted the proportion of the estate to be given in legacies, for the protection of the heir — in which aim, he says, it failed.

Let us return to Cicero's statement. 'The law was passed for the sake of the practical advantage of men, but it is full of injustice to women.' The injustice which chiefly concerns him is apparently that involved in the extreme case of the daughter and only child, who cannot be made her father's heir by will if he has been registered in the first census class. It was perhaps excessive concentration on this type of case which led some modern scholars (references in Vigneron 1983: 144, notes 20–3) to the supposition that the intention was to strengthen the agnatic *tutela*. The effect of the law, it was pointed out, could be evaded by intestacy, but the heiress would then automatically come under agnatic *tutela*. As Vigneron observes, this hypothesis is altogether too tortuous, and in any case applies only to a proportion of testators. It takes no account of various other possibilities. A testator might wish to make his heir a woman who was not in his *potestas* — for example, his wife, married without *manus*, or his sister, already *sui iuris*. He would have no control over the designation of her tutor. Moreover, some testators would themselves be women. A daughter might not be the only child. Even if she were, it would still be perfectly legal for the father to appoint outsiders as heirs and leave the daughter a legacy of up to half the property. Daughters in a large family stood to lose relatively little, since each individually could receive as much as the heir or heirs together in legacies; on intestacy, they would each get only a fraction of the heir's portion, if the latter were not *sui*, and might even get less themselves, if there were several heirs, who were *sui* also.

If the intention of the proposer of the law, Q. Voconius Saxa, had been to prevent large patrimonies falling into the hands of women, he would presumably also have forbidden women's right to be *sui heredes*;[20] intestacy could come about in other ways than by the intention of the deceased person. Women's right of agnate inheritance was partially restricted but, as we have seen, this may not have been under the law itself but at some later date.

The 'practical advantage' for men of which Cicero speaks surely refers to the importance of wealth for social and political status in the increasingly competitive society of the period in which the law was passed. In order to participate in the competition, men must have wealth available to them. Wealth in the hands of women was, in a sense, out of circulation for such purposes, and might, indeed, remain so, if women, in turn, made other women their heirs. Moreover, the new wealth coming in from foreign wars and conquest probably consisted mainly, in the first instance, of *res nec mancipi*, i.e., not land or buildings, though possibly some livestock, very probably some slaves, but mostly money (Shatzman 1975: 63 ff. gives some examples of the fortunes made). Some of this wealth might be converted fairly quickly into land, but there would be much in the form of liquid assets. Once in female hands, these would not be subject to tutorial control and would be particularly vulnerable to dispersal.

There is little evidence from which to determine whether upper-class Romans at the period of the passing of this law tended, where there were heirs of both sexes, to leave land to the males and property other than *res mancipi* to the females. L. Aemilius Paullus Macedonicus, for example, had two sons, and one or two daughters, married to Q. Aelius Tubero and a son of Cato. What provision he made for his daughter(s) in his will is not known; but it is perhaps significant that at his death his sons had to sell *res mancipi*, land and slaves, to raise cash towards repayment of the dowry of 25 talents to his widow.[21]

Later, and at a lower level in society, wills from Roman Egypt reveal, according to Hobson (1983: 320–1) 'a tendency to leave real estate to male children and household furnishings to females', though this is not universal. However, in the absence of male children the desire to keep property in the immediate family, so far as possible, must sometimes have resulted in females inheriting. Hobson also observes that a wife was not usually bequeathed her husband's real property, perhaps because she had property of her own, from her dowry or from her own family.

The evidence of the *Digest* indicates that children of both sexes were often left as legacies land and real estate, i.e., houses with their furnishings, farms with their equipment, business premises and so on. These, of course, would have to be specified separately as legacies, since they could not be arithmetically divided. Dowry was certainly sometimes left as cash. Boyer (1965: 358–9) has collected a number of instances in the *Digest* in which a daughter was not made heir, but was left a cash sum, chargeable upon the heir, as dowry. *Mancipia* (slaves) are included in one instance, but it is specified that these are due only if the girl marries within the *familia*. Obviously, for practical reasons, it would be more convenient to make provision for eventual payment of dowry for a daughter, unmarried at the time of the testator's death, in cash. This does not exclude the possibility of other bequests to the daughter, for her immediate possession and use, and daughters married without *manus* could, of course, also be beneficiaries.

There is at least a fair possibility that upper-class Romans in Cato's time tended, where there were children of both sexes, to leave their 'old' wealth, the *res mancipi*, to the males as heirs and the *res nec mancipi*, the more liquid assets, to the females, who had already formed, or were likely to, marriage ties with other *familiae*. Where sons were lacking, the estate was quite likely to go to the daughters, either in entirety, as heirs, or in bulk, as legatees, with a remoter male relative as nominal heir, to preserve the *sacra*. It might even go to the widow: Aemilia, wife of Scipio Africanus, benefited greatly in this way.[22] Voconius' law may have been meant to ensure that at least a sizeable portion of large patrimonies would always pass directly into male hands and be available for the purposes of male public life, though it did not, apparently, go so far as to prescribe the nature of the bequests which might be made to women.

We do not know enough about fertility and mortality and their effects in the first half of the second century B.C. to determine the extent, if any, to which the maintenance of social and political status by marginally upper-class males was felt to be imperilled.[23] However, the desire to ensure an adequate financial backing for these male activities, rather than absolute hostility to women's ownership of wealth *per se*, seems a plausible motive for the law. The opportunities for women to acquire wealth were still substantial. Women could not be heirs of men in the top census class; but they could receive up to half the value of an estate in legacies, the restriction on legacies affected both sexes, and the (possibly later) restriction on agnate inheritance left the rights on intestacy of daughters, wives *in manu* and sisters unaffected. Incidentally, the prevalence or otherwise of *manus*-marriage by the time the law was passed is unlikely to have made much difference overall to women's independence, given that daughters and wives were the most likely heirs. With *manus*, the effects would be that wives and unmarried daughters became *sui iuris*, but were in the *tutela* of the deceased man's family or of a tutor designated by him, while married daughters would be in the *manus* of their husbands. Without *manus*, the wife would either be *in potestate* or already *sui iuris* in the *tutela* of her own family or as designated by her *pater*, while daughters, married or unmarried, would be in *tutela* as determined by the deceased, or agnate *tutela*. In both situations, it was open to the *pater* to determine, in two out of three cases, the nature of the tutelary control he wished to impose.[24] As for the disposal of property in their possession, except for the ban on appointing other women as heirs, and the restriction (applying to men also) on legacies, women's rights were the same after the passing of the law as before it.

It was not too difficult to find ways around the law. The curious story of the 'dowry' which, as mentioned in Chapter 4 above, Scipio Aemilianus, as heir, was required to pay to his adoptive aunts on their mother's death may have concealed legacies which amounted to more than his share. More definite examples are found in Cicero. Someone who (whether deliberately or not) had not been registered in the census was not liable to the law. So, he says, 'no law forbade' P. Annius Asellus to follow the dictates of nature and make his daughter his heir, and, indeed, legal equity, praetors' edicts and current legal practice all tended the same way. However, Verres, the corrupt praetor in Sicily, declared that under the terms of his own edict the law did apply, and, Cicero says, he took a bribe from the man designated heir in second place. Later, however, says Cicero, many such wills, of persons not in the census, were successful. He mentions particularly a wealthy woman, Annaea, who made another woman her heir.[25]

Less successful was an attempt, also related by Cicero (*de fin.* 2.55), by a certain Q. Fadius Gallus to bind his heir P. Sextilius Rufus by a *fideicommissum* to pass the entire inheritance over to his, Fadius', daughter. *Fideicommissa* were not legally enforceable during the Republic; they became so under the Principate, with gradually increasing protection for the heirs against external claims on the estate, and the use of the *fideicommissum*, according to Gaius, seems to have become the routine way of avoiding this restriction.[26] Sextilius, however, was not bound by the *fideicommissum*, and he accepted the inheritance and denied the trust. Many eminent persons, says Cicero, thought the daughter should be given no more than she was entitled to under the *lex Voconia* (he may mean one-half, as a legacy, rather than nothing); but if right-thinking men had had their way, Sextilius would not have touched a penny.

Augustan Legislation on Inheritance

As part of his programme to encourage marriage and the procreation of legitimate children, Augustus, by the *leges Juliae et Papiae*, imposed certain limitations on the ability of the unmarried (*caelibes*) and childless (*orbi*) to receive under a will.[27] These rules did not apply to persons who had a right of intestate inheritance at civil law, that is, to relatives up to the sixth degree. Some relatives by marriage were also empowered to receive bequests — not only husbands and wives, but parents-, sons- and daughters-in-law, step-children and step-parents. We have already seen that divorcées and widows could receive under the wills of others only within the 'period of grace' after the end of their marriages.

The rules applied more or less equally to both sexes. They applied only within certain age-limits, namely 20–50 for women and 25–60 for men, related to the capacity for reproduction. They did not affect the majority of bequests, which were between relatives. The leaving of bequests to friends outside the family was conventional mainly among the wealthier classes.

Although husband and wife could receive bequests from each other, these were limited to one-tenth of the estate, unless they were outside the prescribed age-limits, or related within six degrees, or had the *ius liberorum*, or the husband had been away on public service. One living child of the marriage, or one that had survived to puberty, sufficed to give capacity to inherit. They also received some 'credit' on account of children of other marriages.

The rules were complicated and inevitably produced anomalies and contained loopholes, some of which were removed by later emperors. A series of *senatusconsulta* tried to cope with the problem of the person who did not marry or have children at all within the age-limit and who, it was felt, should not automatically regain capacity after reaching it. If a husband aged over 60 married a wife under 50, then they benefited. Apparently, however, some women over 50 (and so very unlikely to bear children) had been marrying themselves to men under 60, and hoping to become eligible to inherit. Claudius closed that loophole. Nero took action against fraudulent adoptions.[28]

Domitian banned women of immoral life (*probrosae*) from receiving legacies; previously, even if married, they had had a limited capacity, being allowed to receive only one-quarter.[29] (He also forbade them the use of litters — a more direct and frequent inconvenience.) So, convicted adulteresses, prostitutes, actresses and the like would not benefit, regardless of how many children they had. Nor, presumably, would concubines, not because they were regarded as immoral, but because they were unmarried and their children were illegitimate.

The rules on intestate inheritance by female patrons were also affected; these will be described below.

Some people attempted to evade the ban on receipt of legacies by passing on money in other ways. Under Vespasian, gifts under *fideicommissa* were brought under the same rules as legacies, and by the time of Hadrian gifts *mortis causa*, including those between husband and wife, were allowed only in so far as the recipient had capacity to receive legacies.[30]

Wills and Social History

As well as the exhaustive, and exhausting, discussion of the minutiae of testamentary law in legal sources, a certain amount of literary and epigraphic evidence of actual wills survives. Cicero and the younger Pliny[31] are notable among literary sources. Egyptian papyri have been the subject of special studies, notably those of Montevecchi (1935) and Hobson (1983), and epigraphic records of charitable foundations and other bequests by wealthy men and women feature prominently among the evidence drawn upon for the masterly study of the economic context and social application of wealth in the Roman world by Duncan-Jones (1982). There is also a useful collection of wills from various sources by Amelotti (1966).

Several wills have already been mentioned in the course of this book. Cicero and Pliny give us glimpses of the arrangements made in upper-class Roman society, in which legacies to one's friends and social equals were clearly a normal and, indeed, expected provision. Pliny (*Ep.* 10.94) specifically mentions, in support of his request for the *ius liberorum* for his childless friend Suetonius, that this would enable the latter's friends to express their consciousness of his merit (i.e., by making legacies which he would then be qualified to receive).

A wealthy banker from Puteoli left an estate to Cicero and at the same time a legacy of 50,000 sesterces to Terentia, which, Cicero noted with satisfaction, was to be deducted from someone else's share of the estate, not from his own (*ad Att.* 13.46). In 50 B.C. a certain Livia made Dolabella heir to one-ninth of her estate, on condition of changing his name (i.e., having himself adopted into her *gens*). In Cicero's view (*ad Att.* 7.8), there are two main considerations to be balanced by Dolabella in deciding whether or not to accept. One is the possible effect on a young nobleman's political career of his changing his name because of a woman's will. The other is the value of the bequest. That there is any hesitation suggests that Livia must have been very wealthy.

There is considerable evidence under the empire of wealthy testators choosing to perpetuate their memories by setting up alimentary foundations in towns in which they were interested, or by providing towns, *collegia* or other bodies with which they were associated, usually as patrons, with endowments for such things as regular distribution of wine and oil, or annual banquets. Several women figure among these benefactors.[32]

The commonest recipients of specific legacies, however, at all levels of society, were members of the testator's immediate family and household. Sons and daughters were quite likely to receive the family house, or a part-share in it (shared houses appear frequently in papyri), with its furniture, and perhaps farms and shops, with all their stock and appurtenances (*instructa*), as a going concern. This could also be a way of providing a 'pension' for the old family retainers, i.e., freedmen and freedwomen. Like the children, they might individually be left houses or estates, or a share in them; the death of a patron or owner could mean loss of their living-accommodation. For instance, a third-century will from Egypt (FIRA III no. 10) manumitted a thirteen-year-old girl, freeing her from all patronal obligations, and making her a gift of her *peculium*. As it was apparently not contemplated that she should live with the testator's son, she was also bequeathed the fourth-part of a dwelling-house, with a few sticks of furniture, and the proviso that she should sublet to no one other than her own brother. Provision might also be made, individually or collectively, for them to receive food and clothing (*cibaria* and *vestiaria*), either out of the revenue of a sum of money, or as usufruct of an estate. Pliny actually gave a small farm during his own lifetime to his old nurse, to provide for her support, but was obliged to arrange for someone to work it on her behalf, and presumably give her an income from the proceeds (*Ep.* 6.3). A whole title of the *Digest* (34.1) is devoted to bequests of this sort. Sometimes a tract of land was left to the freedmen and freedwomen collectively, with the specification that it remain in perpetuity in the possession of them and their descendants. One of the best-known examples is the bequest by Junia Libertas at Ostia of an enclosed area, including houses, gardens (i.e., produce-gardens) and shops, left for the use of her freedmen and freedwomen and their descendants inalienably; if the *familia* should die out, the property was to revert to the community of Ostia.[33]

As we have already seen, widows commonly received, not only personal effects provided for them by their husbands, but also legacies of maintenance, either directly (*penus*) or as the usufruct of part of the estate, either for life or for a specified period, and the details of such bequests afford us glimpses of the style and standard of living of the parties involved.

Wills are potentially a useful source of evidence for the study of social and economic history. Taken in isolation, they may be misleading or relatively uninformative. Montevecchi (1935: 73) is pessimistic about the value for statistical studies or as social documents of the wills in the papyri and indicates some of their drawbacks. For instance, even if the document itself is complete, we cannot always be certain that all members of a family have been specified; or the bequest of an estate *in toto* to one person may leave us uninformed about the number of slaves, the real estate and other property included, etc. Hobson (1983), however, shows that it is possible to some extent, by combining wills with other kinds of evidence, such as census declarations, tax lists and receipts of sale, to draw some tentative conclusions about the types of property mainly owned by women in Egypt and its sources, and about the nature and level of their economic activity. Making a special study of Socnopaiou Nesos, a commercial rather than an agricultural centre, she concluded that women's involvement in the economic life of the community consisted mainly (though not entirely) in the acquisition of land and houses by inheritance, and also partly by way of dowry, from their families, and its disposal by sale or by will. Her conclusions are not necessarily valid for the whole of Egypt, let alone for the Roman world, and her sample is a small one; nevertheless the approach has value.

Breaking a Will

A man's will, as we have seen, could be challenged if he had failed either to institute or expressly to disinherit his *sui heredes*. The praetor's rules also allowed other *liberi* to make a claim on this account, which would allow not only other emancipated children, but perhaps also former Vestals, to claim. Whether the latter, or *flamines*, could claim while still in office is uncertain; the relevant text (D. 37.4.1.6) says only that *liberi*, whether they have been emancipated or passed out of *potestas* in some other way, are admitted to succession by the praetor. Omission of a son, without his being specifically disinherited, made the will void. A daughter omitted had merely the right of accretion, i.e., she could share equally with other *sui* but she could not exclude extraneous heirs; against them she had a right only to half. While it was for much of the classical period possible for *liberi* in fact to exclude extraneous heirs entirely, since the praetor might grant the latter possession only *sine re* (in title only, without effect against civil law heirs), Antoninus Pius issued a rescript allowing women heirs to receive no more than they would by the rule of accretion.[34]

A woman's will could be challenged by her *parens manumissor* or her patron, if the necessary consent had not been obtained.

Provision for Posthumous Children

A man's will could also be broken if no provision was made for *postumi*, born within ten months of the father's death. An expectant mother could make a claim to the estate on behalf of the *venter*, the child in the womb, both in these circumstances and on intestacy. She was allowed maintenance from the estate; this was not reclaimable if she had a miscarriage. Customarily she asked for one or more *curatores* to be appointed, both for the child and the property — usually from the relatives and friends of the deceased. Since the curator of the property was personally responsible to any creditors, he must be solvent.[35]

If there were other heirs standing in the same grade of priority as the expected child there might be problems about determining the proportion of the estate due to each of them in the meantime, since there was the possibility of multiple births. Paul, though sceptical, cites some remarkable examples — seven at one birth (to 'many' women in Egypt). One woman was brought specially from Alexandria to be shown to Hadrian. She had quintuplets, of whom four were born together, and a fifth 40 days later. Paul himself recommends that the praetor strike a happy medium and make an interim award on the basis of possible triplets, since that could happen; the Horatii were a famous example.[36]

Once possession had been granted to the *venter*, Hadrian advised in a rescript, any accusation of adultery against the woman should be postponed, to avoid prejudice to the child's interests. The possibility of fraud by women was recognised, whether by feigning pregnancy, or arranging to transfer the property to another, and the praetor's edict specified what actions could be brought (D. 25.5 and 6). The woman could be punished with *infamia*.[37] Rules were introduced, as we have seen, under Hadrian requiring the expectant mother to notify interested parties and to allow her pregnancy to be monitored. Poor Petronilla suffered under this edict. However, it did allow the widow some protection against harassment. If the family had not taken advantage of the procedure, then presumably they would be unable subsequently to challenge the child's claim to the estate.

A child, posthumous or otherwise, who was challenged as being supposititious or illegitimate could be allowed possession by the decree of the praetor, under the Carbonian edict.[38] The mother could demand a decision from the praetor. The edict was available only to children under the age of puberty, and the claim must be made within a year. Unless the praetor was satisfied that the allegations were proved, he was expected, in the interests of the child, to award possession and defer a final decision until the child reached puberty. Petronilla's in-laws may have been trying to oust not only the expected baby but also her existing son from the succession, by such a challenge.

'Unduteous' Will

These rules did no more, essentially, than protect the *liberi*, if their father had failed to provide for them. Of much wider scope was the procedure, existing in some form at least by the middle of the first century B.C., known in classical law as the *querela inofficiosi testamenti* ('complaint of unduteous will').[39] This was available against the wills both of men and of women, and was limited to certain heirs on intestacy. The persons with a claim were the close relatives of the deceased — children, parents, brothers and sisters. Ulpian commented that it was a waste of time for cognates remoter than brothers to claim, and Diocletian gave a similar response.[40]

The grounds for breaking the will were not technical, such as failure expressly to disinherit *sui heredes*, but moral. A claim could be made on the grounds that the will was unjust, by *sui* who had received less than the 'Falcidian fourth'. If the petition was accepted (details of the procedure are controversial and need not be discussed here), by a legal fiction it was deemed that the testator must have been insane (*color insaniae*).

Complaints by *sui heredes* of either sex could be made against the wills of fathers. The elder Seneca quotes[41] from the maiden speech before the centumviral court of the prolix orator of Tiberius' reign, Votienus Montanus. The case concerned Galla Numisia, who had been made heir to only one-twelfth of her father's estate. She was being accused of poisoning him. Votienus had at least four attempts at making the same point:

> A twelfth is the due neither of a daughter nor of a poisoner.
>
> In a father's will a daughter should either have her own place or no place.
>
> You are leaving her too much if she is guilty, too little if she is innocent.
>
> A daughter cannot fit such a narrow place in her father's will; she ought either to have it all or lose it all.

Votienus' verbosity notwithstanding, some details can be made out. First, Galla was the only *suus heres*, otherwise Votienus could not talk about her entitlement to all the estate. Secondly, she was not the only heir, otherwise, while her father would have violated the *lex Falcidia*,which required at least one-quarter of the estate to remain with the heir or heirs, this could have been rectified without voiding the will by a simple calculation: by reducing the amounts of the legacies, she could have been given one quarter, which sufficed to exclude the *querela*, and there would have been no one with a reason for alleging poisoning. It looks rather as though Galla was proceeding under the *q.i.t.*, hoping to oust the extraneous heirs entirely. They for their part were making allegations of poisoning, probably in an attempt to argue that her father's treatment of her was justified. They may also have been offering her the 'Falcidian fourth' to settle, but Votienus on her behalf was holding out for the full amount.

A case that was the talk of the town, according to the younger Pliny (*Ep.* 6.33), was brought by Attia Viriola, wife of an ex-praetor, against the will in which her father had disinherited her in favour of the bride he had wooed, won, wed and widowed in the space of a week or two. The case was held before the united panels of the centumviral court, meeting in full strength, and the court was packed. Fathers, daughters and stepmothers all had an interest in the outcome. Gaius remarked, some time later (D. 5.2.4), that second marriages were apt to have such results, as testators were turned against their offspring by 'the blandishments of stepmothers' (*novercalibus delenimentis*). The jury split evenly; nevertheless, Attia won.

Consanguineous brothers and sisters were agnates, and so might quite often be each other's nearest heirs on intestacy. It would not be surprising if the *querela* was available, and used, against the wills of siblings from an early date. A mother, however, was related to her children only as a cognate. They ranked very low in the order of heirs on intestacy, even under the praetorian rules. How early the *querela* was first used against a mother's will is not known — possibly not until after the establishment of the praetorian rules of succession.

The earliest reference to a child claiming possession against a mother's will appears to be the case pleaded by Asinius Pollio on behalf of the heirs of Urbinia against her son Clusinius Figulus or, as Pollio insisted he should be called, Sosipater. However, this seems unlikely to be an instance of the *querela*. Clusinius' statement was that he had fled after defeat on the field of battle and after many adventures, including being detained by a king, had returned to Italy to his people, the Marrucini, and been recognised. His case may have been that his mother had made her will, appointing external heirs, in the mistaken belief that he was dead; this would be a parallel to a case decided by Hadrian in favour of the son but, as Paul explicitly says, not on the grounds of unduteousness. If Clusinius had merely been a prisoner of war, he could regain his rights, under the rule of *postliminium*. The heirs, on the other hand, argued that he was not Urbinia's son but a slave, who had had two masters at Pisaurum in Umbria, had actually been manumitted and voluntarily gone into slavery again.[42]

Augustus gave a decision by decree in favour of the sons of Septicia, whom she had disinherited in favour of the elderly second husband whom she married when she was already past the age of childbearing. Valerius Maximus, who tells the story (7.7.4), exclaims at length against the mother's unnatural behaviour. However, it seems likely that Augustus' decision was influenced partly, if not principally, by the belief that she and her elderly husband had merely been trying to escape the penalties of the Augustan inheritance laws; he refused to allow the husband to retain the dowry, on the grounds that the marriage had obviously not been contracted for the purpose of procreation.

Valerius also tells (7.8.2) of a certain Aebutia, possibly someone of his own acquaintance, wife of L. Menenius Agrippa. She had apparently married three times, having daughters called Pletonia and Afronia. She favoured Pletonia and made her her heir, leaving the other daughter's children a relatively trifling amount. Afronia, however, did not want to contend in a lawsuit with her sister, but preferred to put up with her mother's will, 'showing herself the more undeserving of the injury done her, the greater the patience with which she bore it'.

Valerius tells this story among a group of examples of wills that could or should have been voided on grounds of insanity. The references, moreover, to the possibility of a lawsuit and to Afronia's being unjustly treated, make it likely that Valerius thought she could have used the *querela* against her mother's will.

Pliny had been made one of the heirs under the will of a certain Pomponia Galla, who had, justly, according to Pliny (*Ep.* 5.1), disinherited her son, Asudius Curianus. The latter tried to do a deal with Pliny, asking him to give up his share and promising to restore the capital eventually (i.e., when he died). Pliny, along with two distinguished friends, held a kind of informal court in private, at which Curianus put his case, and they decided that he had been justly disinherited. Curianus then challenged the other heirs in the centumviral court, but they (for reasons which suggest blackmail by Curianus) wanted to settle out of court and asked Pliny to be their intermediary. He persuaded Curianus to settle for the 'Falcidian fourth', which would have excluded his claim, had his mother left him that much in her will, and Pliny offered to contribute his own portion, even though, as he says, two years having elapsed, Curianus no longer had a claim against him. (In due course, Curianus honoured his promise, and Pliny got his legacy back.) Pliny is rather pleased with his own conduct in the business, and would have us understand that he acted purely out of consideration for his friends. Nevertheless, Pomponia's will was broken, not because her son received a judgment in his favour, but simply because some of the heirs refused the inheritance.[43]

Claims by a woman's children against extraneous heirs had probably more chance of success than those against the mother's own
agnates, before the passing of the *senatusconsultum Orphitianum*
(see below, page 198) which gave the children priority in intestate
inheritance. Though there are a few juristic texts from the Hadrianic
period relating to the *querela*, most fall under the Severi, and those
concerning children's claims against the wills of their mothers belong
to the period after the passing of the *sctum*. From a case cited by
Scaevola, it seems that the court might sometimes award the decision
to a daughter nominated as her mother's heir, against a son. Papinian, some time later, mentions an instance of a son winning against
his maternal uncle. Eventually, illegitimate children had a claim,
and so, according to Ulpian, did posthumous children (including
those delivered by Caesarean section). Fathers could apply on behalf
of children still *in potestate*.[44]

Postumi of a mother did constitute something of a problem. A
rescript issued by Septimius Severus in A.D. 197 (C. 3.2.8.3) established the principles for such cases. If a woman had, say, instituted
her two children as heirs, and then had a third child but neglected
to make a new will, the third child (assuming that it had not been
justly disinherited) could make a *querela* in the ordinary way. But
what about the case of a woman who died in childbirth (and so
would have no opportunity to make a new will, nor, indeed, any
certainty that she had produced a child)? 'The unfairness of this
sudden misfortune must be made good by a conjecture of maternal
affection. Therefore our decision', writes Severus, 'is that your son,
against whom no blame can be laid save that of causing his mother's
fate, shall be awarded the appropriate portion of the estate, just as
if she had instituted all her children heirs. But', he adds, laying
down a principle to apply beyond this case, 'if external heirs had
been appointed, then there is no bar to bringing a complaint of
unduteous will.'

The emperor's decision is not entirely logical. If it was 'unduteous'
not to make provision for her expected child in a will nominating
strangers, then why not also when the nominated heirs were her
other children? The reason for the distinction may be to avoid
causing further upset within a bereaved family. In any case, the
principle was established that a woman's will, like a man's, could
be challenged if it failed to make provision for anticipated offspring.

Mothers, both before and after the passing of the *senatusconsultum
Tertullianum* (see below, p. 196) had some rights of intestate suc-

cession to their children, but ranked very low in the order of priority, and so would be unlikely to be able to bring a claim based on the *q.i.t.* — unless, that is, they had been married with *manus*, in which case they would rank as sisters of the deceased. There are two instances from the Republic in which orators assume the existence of some claim by a mother to her dead son's estate, but in both the circumstances are ambiguous.

According to Quintilian, Asinius Pollio spoke on behalf of Liburnia, who had been left nothing under her son's will; the latter had made a certain Novanius his heir, with expressions of appreciation and gratitude for his past friendship. Asinius parodied these expressions in an imaginary disinheritance clause which the son might have employed: 'My mother, dearest and sweetest to me, who devoted her life to me, who gave birth twice on the same day', and so on and so forth, 'is hereby disinherited'. A few chapters earlier, Quintilian cites Asinius again (in discussing questions intended to embarrass the opposition and prevent feigned misunderstanding): 'Do you hear? I am talking about an insane will, not an unduteous one.' These two citations are usually regarded as belonging to the same speech, and, taken together, certainly give the impression that a complaint was being brought on the grounds of unduteous will. If the *Voconiana ratio* was in force at that time, then Liburnia would have a claim, as an heir on intestacy, only if she had been married with *manus*, and not if she had merely ranked as a cognate.[45] Asinius' rhetoric has moral, but not of itself any legal, force: the blood relationship was subordinate to the legal one.

The same may be said of the notorious Sassia, mother of A. Cluentius Habitus. Cicero (*pro Cluentio* 45) says that the reason for her son's having not yet made a will was that 'he could bring himself neither to bequeath anything to such a mother, nor to omit entirely from his will the name of a parent'. Omission of his mother from the will, even if she had been married with *manus*, could not have invalidated it, since she would rank as an agnate, not a *suus heres*. We cannot even say for certain that Cicero was alluding here to the idea of an unduteous will, in the technical sense. Like Asinius, he is appealing to the customary moral values of his audience, by which, despite his mother's behaviour, Cluentius felt himself still to some extent bound.

The section of the *Digest* devoted to the *querela* (5.2) contains several references to the right of a *pater* to claim a dead child's inheritance, but none to that of a mother. Such claims were possible, so long as the mother had given her child no just cause of offence, and Constantine in A.D. 321 instructs the governor of Dacia accordingly (C. 3.28.28), but her claim as a cognate was so remote that probably few occasions for a successful claim under the *querela* would arise.

The *Codex Justinianus* lists 25 imperial responses on the subject of the *querela* between the years A.D. 193 and 304. Nine are Diocletianic,[46] of which six involve women either as testators or claimants, and some are of particular interest for their revelations about possible motives for disinheritance.

Twice (C. 3.28.18, 20) we find a parent trying to use the threat of disinheritance as a sanction against refusal by a daughter to get a divorce. In A.D. 286, Diocletian and Maximian reassure Faustina, whose father had actually gone so far as to disinherit her, that she will be able to use the *q.i.t.* In A.D. 294 they answer a man, possibly the disinherited woman's husband. Her father was already dead. She had married with her mother's approval, but then the latter had changed her mind. The daughter has given no just cause for offence, they say, nor is she obliged by law to be married or unmarried (*vidua*) according to the momentary whims of her mother. Though this particular type of pressure may have been applied quite often, these are the only two attestations of its use. Under Marcus Aurelius, fathers had lost the power to compel divorce; mothers had never possessed it.

There is a stepmother who had been made heir, to the total exclusion of her stepdaughter. There is no comfort for her; the daughter can use the *querela* and claim the lot; the widow can have only what was owing to her at the time her husband died (C. 3.28.22).

Another woman's children had tried to prevent her making a will. She did, in spite of them. A daughter who enquires is told that by their own admission they had given their mother just cause of offence (C. 3.28.23).

An anxious father asks for reassurance that his scapegrace daughter would not be able to overturn his will (C. 3.28.19). He is told:

If your daughter has been living a thoroughly scandalous and immoral life, so that you think she should be disinherited, then you are free to make your final dispositions as you wish, if you are not acting in the heat of unreflecting passion but have been justifiably alienated by her behaviour.

We have already seen how a mother, such as the wife of Regulus (Pliny, *Ep.* 4.2), might institute a child as heir, on condition of emancipation by its father. Before the *sctum. Orphitianum*, it was relatively difficult for the father to inherit simply by refusing the condition, since the child ranked low among the heirs on intestacy, whereas after the *sctum.* the children had first claim. A mother, if she were wise, would take the precaution of adding a substitute, to whom the estate would fall if the father refused to fulfil the condition. One father seems to have enquired whether, in that case, he might claim possession on the children's behalf under the *querela* (C. 3.28.25). The answer is a firm negative. If a mother had imposed the condition because she was mistrustful of the character of the children's father, then, far from having done them an injury, she had been looking after their interests, and the will should stand.

Intestate Succession under Civil Law

In early Roman society, intestate succession was the norm; the claims of the *familia* were paramount. The earliest known rules of intestate succession are those of the Twelve Tables. These were gradually superseded, first by various additions to the praetorian edict, and then from Hadrian onwards by pieces of legislation. The general trend was to give less weight to the claims of agnates and more to those of natural blood relations. For most of the Republic, however, the civil law rules operated.

These rules were framed primarily with reference to a deceased *paterfamilias*. The order of priority of claim was (i) *sui heredes*, (ii) agnates, and (iii) *gentiles*.[47]

Sui heredes were all persons in the *potestas* of the deceased who became *sui iuris* by his death, that is, his children of both sexes, including adopted children; his son's children, if the son was dead already; and his wife *in manu*. Obviously, women could have no *sui heredes*. They could be *sui heredes*, most commonly as daughters, but also as granddaughters or wives *in manu*.

Agnates, in Roman law, meant all those persons who, together with the deceased, were descended from the same male ancestor and who would be in the latter's *patria potestas*, were he still alive.

Among these, only the nearest in degree were offered the inheritance; if it was refused, it was not offered to the remaining agnates. Both male and female agnates counted, but succession between generations went through the male line only (since a woman's children would not be in the *potestas* of her *pater*). This originally meant, for example, that a woman might succeed as agnate to the brother of her late father, but a man could not succeed to his mother's brother. This explains decisions like that made, in about A.D. 41, by the centurion of the legion III Cyrenaica between claimants to the estate of a deceased cavalryman (FIRA III no. 64). The claimants were his brother and his sister's sons, and the decision was, quite properly, given in favour of the former.

At some unknown date, the eligibility of women for agnate succession was severely restricted; only the sister of the deceased (*consanguinea*) was permitted succession. This rule was well established by the time of Gaius; Paul apparently believed that it was instituted either by the *lex Voconia* itself or by subsequent juristic interpretation of the law.[48] The effect, as noted above, would be to limit the possibility of dispersal of the property outside the male line and into other *familiae*. A woman could share with her other brothers and sisters the estate of her childless brother. If she was his only surviving sibling, she could take the lot. This circumstance, one may suspect, would be unlikely to arise unless the male line through the brothers had died out (i.e., unless there were no nephews) and then only if the deceased had neglected to make a will.

A freedwoman had not only no *sui heredes*, but no agnates either. Her estate therefore fell to her patron or his heirs. The same applied to an emancipated daughter; her father, if alive, inherited from her as *parens manumissor*; however, this right was not transmitted to his other children.

Failing inheritors in the first two categories, the Twelve Tables assigned the estate outside the family, to the members of the *gens*. This part of the law of succession had fallen into disuse by Gaius' time, though it was evidently still flourishing in the first half, at least, of the first century B.C. Watson (1971: 181) observed that the apparent vigour of the institution is accounted for by the fact that, if refused by the nearest agnate, the estate was not offered to successive agnates. The latter would presumably be able to claim among the *gentiles*, although our evidence does not reveal whether *gentiles* claimed as a group or individually.

The last certain references to the inheritance rights of *gentiles* belong to the first quarter of the first century B.C., and it may be at that period that they were effectively superseded by the introduction to the praetorian edict of succession by the cognates. The attempt made by certain persons to impose on 'Turia', about the middle of the century, a *tutela* of the *gens* was fraudulent (see Chapter 1, note 41).

A passage of Catullus (68.119–124), written probably about 60 B.C., appears to allude to some claim by the *gentiles*. In a simile he draws comparison with the joy felt by an aged father whose only daughter is now nursing his late-born grandchild (*una caput seri nata nepotis alit*), spoken of as male. At long last this child has appeared, who can be named in a will as heir to his grandfather's fortunes, so putting to scorn the claimant from the *gens* and destroying his wicked joy, and driving away the vulture from the old man's snowy head. The old man was unable to make his daughter heir, under the *lex Voconia*, but was apparently unwilling to die intestate (so depriving himself of the opportunity to 'remember' friends, reward slaves by manumission, etc.). At most, he could have left his daughter half his estate under a will, but the rest would have had to go to an heir not descended from him by blood. If Catullus fully understood the legal situation, then he does not mean that the *gentilis* is deprived of the inheritance; that would have gone on intestacy to the daughter. He may mean the *tutela*, which would have gone to the *gentilis* too, in default of closer relatives, and could have been used to prevent the daughter making a will.

The Praetorian Scheme of Succession

The rules of intestate succession under civil law were modified by a series of additions to the praetorian edict, probably starting in the lifetime of the jurist Trebatius, that is, at the very end of the Republic. Their development is obscure; the rules as we have them are as codified under Hadrian.[49]

The praetor did not designate heirs; he merely assigned *bonorum possessio*, 'possession of property'. This did not convey actual possession of the property, but merely entitled the recipient of the grant to take legal steps to acquire the property. Possession could be assigned both where there was no will (*ab intestato*) and where cause had been shown for setting aside an existing will (*contra tabulas*).

The edict ranked in order of priority the principal categories of persons to whom the praetor would be willing to assign possession. These were (i) *liberi*; (ii) *legitimi*; (iii) cognates; (iv) patron's family; (v) husband or wife. Successive time-limits were set for applications to be made in each category.[50]

Liberi (children) included not only the *sui heredes* but emancipated children, grandchildren (through sons only) and adopted children (but not children adopted into another family). Emancipated children had lost their agnatic relationship, but clearly it was felt that some recognition was owing to the blood relationship. The commonest reasons for emancipation of a daughter are likely to have been to allow her to receive a legacy or otherwise acquire property in her own name, or to make a will benefiting her children. As we have already seen, the competing claims of *sui* and emancipated children could cause family problems, and daughters were expected to 'bring in' their dowry, along with their other property, in laying claim to part of a paternal estate.

There could be no claim to a woman's estate under this heading. Her children could appeal, before the *senatusconsultum Orphitianum*, only as cognates and, after it, as *legitimi*.

Legitimi ('legitimate heirs') were those with a statutory claim. These included the agnates and a number of other categories besides. A father who had emancipated his child had a claim. So had the patron, and his children, of a freedman or freedwoman. The freedman's children, as *sui* or *liberi*, excluded the patron's rights both in the praetorian rules and in civil law. A freedwoman, on the other hand, had neither *sui* nor agnates, and so her patron was entitled to succeed to her estate, whether she had children or not. Succession to freedwomen will be more fully discussed below. The *senatusconsultum Tertullianum* gave mothers with the *ius liberorum* a right of succession to their children in the category of *legitimi*, ahead of agnates.

Cognates were, broadly, any blood relations within six degrees, regardless of whether or not there had been emancipation, and including relations through females. Gaius (D. 38.8.2), commenting on the provincial edict, says that the tie was recognised, on grounds of equity though not of civil law, between a mother and her illegitimate children. Posthumous children, born by Caesarean section, were also admitted.

Husbands and wives could claim the estates of their partners, but only in the absence of claimants in all the previous categories, and subject to the limitations of the *lex Julia et Papia*. A childless widow under fifty years of age would not qualify; but her succession prospects were improved if she had had children, and proportionately more, the longer the children had survived after birth. Husbands and wives ranked low in the order of succession. The praetorian rules recognised the claims of affection only after those of kinship and of property (patrons).

Succession to Freedwomen[51]

A patron was *tutor legitimus* to his freedwoman and could, unless she had the *ius liberorum*, ensure that she died intestate. Under civil law, patrons succeeded on intestacy next after *sui heredes*. That is, they had first claim on the estates of their freedwomen, since women had no *sui*; the patron's *sui* had the next claim. The position was similar under praetorian rules; the patron and his family claimed as *legitimi*, and still had first claim, since freedwomen had no agnates and their children ranked only as cognates.

If the patron had allowed his freedwoman to make a will, then, at least until the *lex Papia*, he could not break her will on the grounds of unduteousness, since it was held that he could have been excluded only by his own act. On the other hand, he could claim up to half the estate of an 'ungrateful' freedman, against any heirs other than *sui*, since the freedman had not required his patron's consent to the making of the will. If the woman's patron was also her husband, the matter of a will might be of less importance, since it was quite likely that she would wish their children to benefit anyway, and without his consent she could not divorce and contract another marriage.

In order to encourage the more wealthy freedmen to produce legitimate children, the Augustan *lex Papia* actually worsened the situation for their heirs, the fewer there were. Regardless of the existence or otherwise of a will, patrons could claim a proportion, related inversely to the number of surviving children, of the estates of freedmen leaving more than 100,000 sesterces. It took three children to exclude the patron entirely.

In contrast, some freedwomen at least might seem at first sight to be better off than freedmen under the *lex Papia*. The *ius liberorum*, granted in respect of four children, allowed them to make a will without the patron's consent. However, since this meant that the patron could be excluded by extraneous heirs, it was provided that, notwithstanding any will, the patron should receive a share of the estate, the *virilis pars*, calculated on the supposition of an equal division between him and the surviving children; on intestacy, of course, he could still take the lot, and exclude the children. 'So', says Gaius (III. 44), 'if she leaves all four children surviving her, a fifth is owed to the patron; but if she outlives them all, the whole inheritance goes to the patron'. He does not say what would happen if there were more than four surviving children, i.e., whether the patron's portion would still continue to decrease. If no children survived her, then the will was effectively set aside in the patron's favour.[52]

After the *lex Papia*, as before, therefore, freedwomen continued to have less control over the disposal of their property than freedmen. The latter could bequeath up to half their estates as they wished; freedwomen's wills could, in some circumstances, be entirely set aside.

The descendants of patrons for up to three generations in the male line (a female stopped the descent) also had a claim. Female patrons and patronal descendants, however, were less privileged than male.[53]

Under the civil law, female patrons, and the daughters, or sons' daughters or sons' sons' daughters of male patrons had the same succession rights as male patrons. Under the praetorian scheme, however, only male patrons and the male *liberi* of patrons had a claim. The reasoning may have been that, with a female patronal descendant, the *familia* effectively stopped; and besides, by the time the praetorian rules became established, families of freed origin were a significant enough portion of the population for their rights to be given some consideration.

The *lex Papia* in many cases limited female patronal rights to those who had had children. Succession of a patroness to her own intestate freedwoman followed civil law, irrespective of the *ius liberorum* — that is, the patroness took the whole estate; but if either she or the freedwoman had undergone *capitis deminutio*, the patronal tie was broken, and the freedwoman's children succeeded. If the freedwoman left a will, the patroness could claim the same rights as a male patron against a freedman, i.e., up to half the estate against any heirs other than *liberi* — but only if the patroness herself had the *ius liberorum*. Her son (though not her daughter) could in his turn exercise patron's rights, so long as he had had at least one child.

To succeed to their own freedmen, under the *lex Papia*, the patronesses had to have had children, but fewer than required for the *ius liberorum* — two for a freeborn woman, three for a freedwoman — but only a freeborn patroness with the *ius lib.* could claim the same rights of succession to wealthier freedmen as male patrons. The reason for this limitation may have been that only such a patroness would have both the full control of the testamentary disposal of her own property and heirs on intestacy (agnates or cognates) who could retain the whole estate.

Under the *lex Papia*, women had rights of inheritance from their male ascendants' freedmen and freedwomen only if they themselves had the *ius lib.* A patron's daughter, granddaughter or great-granddaughter, in the male line, with the *ius lib.*, could succeed to the estate of an intestate freedwoman, taking a share proportional to the number of the latter's surviving children. The position if the *liberta* had left a will was unclear. Some thought that the patron's daughter had no claim, even if she had the *ius lib.*, while others thought that the *ius lib.* gave her the same claim against the will as male patronal descendants. This appears to have been Gaius' own view, and he comments (III. 47) that this section of the law was carelessly drafted, implying that doubt arose only because of some ambiguity in its wording.

To sum up, the *lex Papia* considerably increased the freedwoman's powers of testamentary disposal, as against her patron, so long as she bore children. However, it was almost two centuries before, with the application of the *senatusconsultum Orphitianum* to the children of freedwomen, the latter were able entirely to exclude patrons from the intestate succession.

The Senatusconsultum Tertullianum[54]

Under civil law, a mother had originally no claim at all to succeed her children. Under praetorian law, she ranked only as a cognate, whereas a manumitting father ranked among *legitimi*. The *senatusconsultum Tertullianum*, of Hadrianic date, gave her a right of succession under civil law. The order was: *sui heredes* and *liberi*; father; consanguineous brothers and sisters; mother, sharing with sisters. *Infamia* did not bar her from inheriting. The effect, for a mother of legitimate children, was that she succeeded ahead of cognates. Illegitimate children had no father and no *consanguinei*, so their mother was excluded only by *sui heredes* of a son, and by no other heirs, in the case of a daughter. However, only women with the *ius liberorum* benefited under the *sctum*.

The purpose of the restriction to women with the *ius liberorum* may emerge from examination of its effects. It need not mean that the law was intended 'for the encouragement of marriage' (Buckland 1966: 374), or even necessarily to encourage the production of children, since the *ius liberorum* was sometimes awarded by imperial favour to the unqualified. For most women, however, the *ius* was acquired only by the requisite number of live births; the children need not survive to any specified age, nor need they all have been by the same marriage. Children born of the same marriage would be *consanguinei* of the deceased, and would in fact exclude the mother totally (if male) or partially (if female) from inheriting; children of another marriage would not exclude her, since they belonged to their father's family.

Women with the *ius liberorum* had no tutors and did not require tutorial consent to make a will. Restriction of the succession to mothers with the *ius lib.* could mean, for example, that a freedwoman mother was at liberty, in due course, to will at least some of her children's property back to her late husband's family and her surviving children; otherwise, the latter would have had to put up with the ultimate prospect of seeing all their relative's property pass to an outsider, the woman's patron. A freeborn mother without the *ius lib.* would have a tutor, possibly a relative from her own family. Both in theory and in law a tutor could refuse his consent to a will. Compelling his consent could, it seems, be done by appeal to a magistrate, but the woman herself might not feel warmly enough towards her in-laws to want to take the trouble, against pressure from her own family. Besides, she might have married more than once, and have links of affection with still other families. Restriction to mothers with the *ius lib.* would considerably shorten the odds in favour of the children's family of origin. Mothers who had acquired the *ius lib.* through the children of one marriage *and* outlived all that husband's children, either her own or any other mother's (since consanguinity was reckoned through the father), were likely to be relatively few; even if the mother acquired the *ius lib.* through more than one marriage, the restriction shortened the odds in favour of the deceased child's relatives. In restricting, therefore, the right of inheritance to mothers with the *ius lib.* the legislators, while giving some recognition to the mother–child relationship, showed themselves still concerned to maintain some restraint on the dispersal of a family's property.

Meinhart (1967: 32 ff.) argues that mothers of illegitimate children were not originally included in the *sctum*. By the end of the second century A.D., jurists state that they do benefit.[55] This is consistent with developments ameliorating the position of the illegitimate child. The ideological bias of Augustus' legislation in favour of marriage was to some extent superseded. The lifting, under Marcus Aurelius, of the ban on entering the birth of illegitimate children in the public register is significant. Admission to the public records indicates official acceptance and recognition of what was presumably by then a fairly common situation. It may very probably have become accepted some considerable time before that illegitimate children could be admitted to count for the *ius lib.* The children themselves already had some rights of succession under the praetorian edict, and Hadrian expressly allowed soldiers' children some rights to inherit from their fathers. So long as a woman had taken the trouble to make sworn declarations, she would have had no difficulty in proving that she had borne the requisite number of children. Of course, only children born in freedom counted (hence the exception made, by a rescript of Severus and Antoninus, of a child born in captivity and restored, with its mother, to freedom).[56] From the point of view of the relatives, it would make no difference whether the other children, outside the family of the deceased, qualifying the mother for the *ius lib.* had been born in marriage or not. If the deceased was himself illegitimate, of course, there were no agnates or cognates to claim the inheritance, and there might not seem to be much reason to restrict the right of inheritance to mothers with the *ius lib.* Nevertheless, the rule was maintained.

It was recognised that the interests of a fatherless minor might be in need of protection. Ulpian notes (D. 38.17.2.23) that a mother was not allowed succession under the *sctum.* if she had failed to have suitable tutors appointed for her dead child.

The Senatusconsultum Orphitianum

As we have already seen, women had no *sui heredes* under civil law, and no *liberi* under the praetorian rules; their children, therefore, could rank only as cognates. The primary claim on intestacy was that of the agnates (or, in the case of a freedwoman, the patron).

In A.D. 178 the *senatusconsultum Orphitianum* gave children the first claim in succession to the mother. They were in the category of *legitimi*, and were apparently given priority in that category. Illegitimate children were allowed to succeed, just as the mothers of illegitimate children were allowed to benefit under the *sctum. Tertullianum*. Posthumous children (i.e., in this context, those removed by Caesarean section) were also allowed to benefit. Only freeborn children counted. It did not matter if there had been *capitis deminutio* since mother and child were in different *familiae* anyway.[57]

When *manus*-marriage was usual, mother and child had been agnates, with appropriate succession rights. With free marriage they were merely cognates, under praetorian rules, and had no standing at all under the civil law of the Twelve Tables. The idea that the children, by virtue of the blood connection, ought to be allowed some share in a mother's property, even although this meant its passing out of the mother's family, had found expression in the rules for retention of part of a dowry at the end of a marriage and in the gradual relaxation of *tutela*, allowing a mother greater freedom of testamentary disposal. Meinhart (1967: 22) suggests that the increasing instability of marriage and the decreasing importance of dowry in a woman's total property made dowry a less reliable way of ensuring provision for children from their mother's estate; Saller (1984: 200 ff.) also draws a connection between divorce and a decline in the size of dowries. To some extent, wills could offset this. The son of Murdia (FIRA III, no. 70) records with gratitude that, far from favouring her children by a later marriage at his expense, she had made a point of making all her sons equal heirs, and had in addition bequeathed to him intact the property she had had from his father.

However, situations could still arise in which a mother, for one reason or another, either had not made a will at all, or had not made an effective will. She might have a recalcitrant tutor, either an agnate himself, or one with the interests of the agnates at heart, or the will itself might be invalidated for some reason. We have seen that the *sctum. Tertullianum*, in giving mothers some rights of inheritance, had not done so at the expense of the father or agnates.

Moreover, there were by this time two large groups whom the options of cognate succession or testamentary succession still left relatively disadvantaged: that is, the children of freedwomen and illegitimate children. The latter had no right to maintenance from a *pater* and could not benefit from a dowry, and the former ranked after the patron in order of succession. Those who were both were particularly badly placed, since it was less likely that a freedwoman would, in addition to illegitimate children, who did not originally count for the *ius lib.*, also have enough legitimate children to qualify her and so enable her to make a will.

The *senatusconsultum Orphitianum*, giving illegitimate children the same rights of intestate succession as legitimate ahead of the agnates, can be seen as part of a process of increasing recognition of their rights as blood relations of their mothers and even, in some circumstances (e.g., the children of soldiers, mentioned above), of their fathers.[58]

The other group, the children of freedwomen, were a harder case. To give them rights as *legitimi* would conflict with the patron's inheritance rights in that category. Meinhart (1967: 69–89) argues that the *sctum.* did not mention freedwomen, and so did not of itself exclude the patron in favour of his freedwoman's children, but that this practice developed through jurists' interpretations, at least from Ulpian onwards, being finally incorporated into law by Justinian; the matter remains controversial.[59] Jurists might well have based their interpretation on the comparable situation, under the *sctum.*, of the children of emancipated *ingenuae* in respect to the claim of the patron's analogue, the *parens manumissor*.

The children took priority over agnates. Whether they also took priority over the emancipating *pater* (or patron) is less certain but may perhaps be deduced from the explanatory comment ascribed to Ulpian, *ad Sabinum* 12 (D. 38.17.1.9). 'If none of the sons or of those to whom along with them (*simul*) the inheritance falls wishes to claim it for himself, then the old law is to apply.' ('Son' is to be taken as covering daughters as well.)[60] That is, the estate would be offered to the nearest agnate, the *parens manumissor*, or patron. He continues that if even one son claims, the rules on intestacy do not apply. So, if one of two sons claims and the other rejects the inheritance, the latter's portion accrues to the former; and if there is a son and a patron then (my italics) — *if the son declines the inheritance, it falls to the patron*. The clear implication is that, within the category of the *legitimi*, children do not only exclude agnates, but they are regarded as having priority over patrons.

The effect of the *sctum.* Orphitianum was to give children, legitimate or illegitimate, the same priority in intestate inheritance to (initially) freeborn women as *liberi* had to men. *Liberi* already excluded the patron of a freedman (if the latter was not too wealthy); in due course, the children of a freedwoman were also allowed to exclude him.

Notes

1. So we find, for example, a concern on the one hand to establish the legitimacy of posthumous *sui heredes* and *sui* born after divorce, as evinced in the *senatusconsultum Plancianum* (D. 25.3.1) and the edict *de inspiciendo ventre* (D. 25.4), so protecting the interests of the agnates, while the *edictum Carbonianum* (D. 37.10) protected those of the *suus*; and, on the other hand, the opening up of intestate succession under the praetorian rules, first by the institution of the rules themselves, and later, by the admission of illegitimate children and of mothers and their children, among the categories of heirs.

2. Humbert (1972) 233 ff., 245. In *P. Oxy.* LII, 3692, a will in Latin, C. Julius Diogenes (not the testator of *P. Lugd. Bat.* XIII. 14) makes his three sons and his wife equal heirs. The latest reconstruction of the well-known will of Dasumius (FIRA III no. 48; Amelotti (1966) 17–19; Eck (1978)) has four heirs in the first rank; the daughter gets half, a man described as 'most rare friend' a third, and Dasumius' wife and a woman called Dasumia one-twelfth each.

3. Legacies: Boyer (1965) 358–9; Posthumous children: von Woess, (1911) 97; Egypt: Hobson (1983) 319–20. On the differential treatment of sons and daughters generally, von Woess, *op. cit.*, especially 94–106.

4. Kaser (1971) 105–9.

5. Schulz (1951) 268 ff.; Buckland (1966) 282–6; Watson (1971) 41 ff. For a grant of *b.p. secundum tabulas* see *PSI* 1101: Amelotti (1966) 60.

6. Ulp. *Reg.* 20.7; D. 28.1.18 pr., 1; 20 pr., 4; 26; *Inst.* 2.10.6; Buckland (1966) 293–4.

7. Goody (1973 and 1976b); Hopkins (1983) 69–78.

8. We may note that extension of praetorian succession to cognates at the end of the Republic (Watson 1971: 84) marks an important stage in the decline of the concept of the agnatic family; Thomas (1980: 370) argues that this change went *pari passu* with the extension of the definition of 'incestuous' marriage.

9. Buckland (1966) 288 ff.

10. G. I. 15a; Buckland (1966) 134–41, 288; Watson (1971) 22–3. Volterra (1941) believes that women did not originally become *sui iuris* at the death of a *pater*, but remained *in potestate* under *tutela* and had to be made *sui iuris* by the tutor in order to make a will.

11. Cic. *Top.* 4.18; Chapter 2, note 67 (above).

12. G. III. 40; D. 37.1.6 pr.; Watson (1967) 231 ff.

13. Disinherison: G. II. 127–9. Lapsed will: D. 29.4.

14. There is a voluminous literature on both laws, particularly on the *lex Voconia*. For the *lex Falcidia* see, e.g., Wesel (1964) and Ankum (1984). For the *lex Voconia*, Re XII. 2.2418 ff; Wesel (1964); Crook (1967c); Watson (1971) 29 ff.; Kaser (1971) 683 ff. and (1977) 50–3; Wieling (1972) 22–3, 26–7; Astin (1978) 113–8; Vigneron (1983).

15. Metro (1963); Watson (1971) 128 ff.

16. By, for example, Watson, Astin and Vigneron.

17. Crook (1967c) 121–2; Kaser (1971) 684; Pomeroy (1975) 162–3, 181. Astin (1978) 116 is doubtful.

18. Few examples of wealthy women of senatorial rank are known from the period down to the Gracchi: Shatzman (1975) 241–63.

19. On *consortium* and *societas*, see Zulueta (1953) II. 174–78. The brothers Domitii (Pliny *Ep.* 8.18) are sometimes thought to have been maintaining an old-fashioned *consortium* of their inheritance, but see now Tellegen (1982) 55–9.

20. Whether or not Roman men may have been reluctant to die intestate is a matter for debate: Crook (1973) argues against Daube (1965). If a woman was *suus heres*, she could acquire the estate by 'doing nothing', i.e., by not accepting it as

testamentary heir, so long as no substitute heir had been appointed. As Kaser (1977: 51) notes, there is no trace of proceedings being taken against women instituted heirs contrary to the law. If a woman was a necessary heir (that is, if the *beneficium abstinendi* had at the date of the law not yet been introduced), it would be unjust to penalise her. The *lex Voconia* may have been a *lex imperfecta*, i.e., one which forbade an action without penalising it (Guarino 1982: 188–91).

21. Polyb. 18.35; Livy *Epit.* 46.

22. Shatzman (1975) 247–50.

23. Hopkins (1983) 74–107.

24. A similar analysis is made by Vigneron (1983: 147–8), who, however, sees the law as a reaction to the weakening of agnate *tutela* by the introduction of *tutores dativi*.

25. Polyb. 31.27; Cic. *Verr.* 2.1.104, 111.

26. G. II. 268–88. On *fideicommissa* as an evasive device, see Besnier (1959) 25–8; Brunt (1971) 561. According to Dio (56.10.2), Augustus exempted certain women from the operation of the *lex Voconia*, probably by the *lex Papia*; von Woess (1911) 80.

27. The rules are too lengthy to quote in detail here; see the references in Chapter 4, notes 33–8.

28. Wallace-Hadrill (1981) 75–6.

29. Astolfi (1965).

30. G. II. 286; D. 39.6.35 pr. (I owe this reference to Mr David Noy); Kaser (1971) 764. See also D. 39.6.9; 22; 36 pr.

31. Pliny mentions various aspects of the law of succession in some 30 letters. Of these, 16 are discussed in great detail in Tellegen (1982).

32. For instance, Junia Libertas (AE 1940.94); FIRA III no. 53, a and d; Duncan-Jones (1982) 27–32; 132 ff.; 227–8. Duncan-Jones notes (p.143) that women in Italian towns benefitted less often than men from cash distributions (*sportulae*) and received smaller amounts.

33. AE 1940.94; D. 31.88.6; 12; 14; Amelotti (1966) 19; Shtaerman and Trofimova (1975) 54–5.

34. G. II. 123–6. Women to whom the *lex Voconia* applied could receive a maximum of one-half under a will in any case.

35. These matters are discussed in D. 37.9, *de ventre in possessionem mittendo et curatore eius*; see also Buckland (1966) 725–6.

36. D. 5.4.3; 5.25.1.

37. D. 3.2.15–19.

38. D. 37.10; Buckland (1966) 398, 726; Kaser (1971) 699.

39. There is an extensive literature on the *querela*. Voci (1963) 670–726 discusses the history and nature of the procedure in detail; see also Buckland (1966) 327–31; Kaser (1971) 709–13 and the references there; Watson (1971) 62–70. It is suggested by von Woess (1911: 84–7) that daughters had less prospect of success than sons with a *q.i.t.*, and he cites from legal and other sources a number of instances of unsuccessful pleas; it would be possible, however, to adduce a comparable number of instances where daughters are explicitly said to have succeeded with their pleas. The operation of *lex Voconia* would not exclude the *q.i.t.*, although it would preclude an appeal to the praetor for *bonorum possessio* on grounds of omission (D. 37.4.3.10).

40. D. 5.2.1; C. 3.28.21.

41. Sen. *Controv.* 9.5.15–16; for Votienus, see RE IX. A. 1.924.

42. Tac. *Dial.* 38; Quint. *Inst. Or.* VII. 2.4 and 26; ORF³ 174.28–34, pp. 522–3.

43. The legal aspects are discussed in detail by Tellegen (1982) 80–94; for the 'Falcidian fourth', D. 5.2.8.8.

44. D. 5.2, especially 6; 8; 13; 16; 19; 29.1.

45. Quint. *Inst. Or.* 9.2.6 and 33; ORF³ 174.26–7, p. 521; Watson (1971) 69–70.

46. Discussed in detail by Tellegen-Couperus (1982) 155–72.
47. Voci (1963) 5–9; Buckland (1966) 367–70; Kaser (1971) 695–6.
48. G. III. 14; Paul. *Sent.* 4.8.20; Watson (1971) 177–8.
49. Voci (1963) 10–17; Buckland (1966) 370–2; Kaser (1971) 697–701.
50. Ulp. *Reg.* 28.7; Buckland (1966) 383 ff.
51. On succession to freedmen and freedwomen, see Voci (1963) 25–35; Buckland (1966) 378–81; Sirks (1980 and 1981).
52. G. III. 39–44.
53. The rules are set out in detail in G. III. 46–53. Watson (1967: 234) thinks the principle of the exclusion under the edict of the patron's female descendants is similar to that of the *lex Voconia*; more relevant, though, is surely the fact that the patron, but not the *patrona*, was in a quasi-paternal relation to the freedman or freedwoman.
54. Ulp. *Reg.* 26.8; Paul. *Sent.* 4.9; D. 38.17; *Inst.* 3.3; Voci (1963) 18–21; Buckland (1966) 372–3; Meinhart (1967).
55. D. 38.17.2.1. Mothers and illegitimate children, and the latter and their brothers and sisters, were by then allowed under the edict to inherit from each other as cognates, in spite of civil law, because of the close blood link; D. 38.8.2.4.
56. FIRA I, no. 78; *SHA Marcus* 9.7; D. 38.17.1.3; C. 8.50.1; Meinhart (1967) 43–5.
57. Ulp. *Reg.* 26.7; Paul. *Sent.* 4.10; D. 38.17; *Inst.* 3.4; Voci (1963) 22–3; Buckland (1966) 373–4; Meinhart (1967).
58. See references in notes 55 and 56 above.
59. *Inst.* 3.4.3; Lavaggi (1946); Meinhart (1967), especially 77 ff.
60. D. 50.16.56.1; 116; 201.

10 Slaves and Freedwomen

Although the Romans are attested as possessing slaves from an early period, slave-ownership on a large scale seems to have developed only with the expansion of Roman power, from about the latter half of the third century B.C. Slaves became an integral part of Roman society, and this is reflected in the range and volume of references to slavery in legal texts.[1] 'Outside the region of procedure, there are few branches of the law in which the slave does not prominently appear' (Buckland 1908: v); this is an inevitable consequence of the slave's being both an item of property and also a person, with human qualities, capable of certain actions, yet lacking full legal capacity.

Most of the law relating to slaves could apply to persons of either sex, and need not be separately discussed here, and in practice female slaves were less likely than men to be employed in certain areas of activity, e.g., as bailiffs or agents (*vilicae*, *actores*) in rural estates. Although male slave bailiffs (*vilici*) and *actores* are frequently attested in inscriptions, many along with their 'wives', the few *vilicae* mentioned are likely to have been the slave-consorts of male bailiffs rather than farm-managers themselves. One was actually a *vicaria*, that is, a 'slave's slave', part of the *peculium* of a *vilicus*. The duties of the *vilica*, as described by Columella, appear to be essentially those of a kind of housekeeper — supervision of the cleaning, the cooking, the sickbay and, to some extent, the activities, such as weaving, of the female slaves. On the other hand, slave *institores*, i.e., managers of branches of a business, are rather harder to trace, since they belong to the category of slaves most likely to achieve freedom, but both Ulpian and Gaius take it for granted that *institores* might be either male or female, and Ulpian says that the sex makes no difference to the question of legal liability, any more than the servile or free status of the *institor*.[2]

Those areas of the law in which the sex of a slave was important concern mostly offspring, blood relationships and sexual relations between slaves or between slave and free, and their consequences.

Slaves as Breeders[3]

As a woman, an *ancilla* (female slave) would normally be capable of procreation, and slave-owners had an interest in the results. The Roman equivalent of a Sale of Goods Act, the aedilician edict, laid on a seller the duty to inform a purchaser of any unsoundness or defect (*morbus vitiumve*) in the merchandise; in regard to slaves, this covered not only physical characteristics, but also mental and moral (e.g., whether a slave had a record of attempted escape, or theft). In Egypt, the most bureaucratic society of the ancient world, sale and transfer of slaves were tightly regulated, and slaves were, it appears, sold, as cars are nowadays, with the equivalent of a log-book, initiated at first sale and attesting successive changes of ownership. One slave girl called Euodia, herself the child of a slave born in Egypt, had, by the time she was 14 years old in A.D. 225, been sold five times. An Egyptian certificate of sale would contain guarantees of absence of defects; some slaves were specifically sold 'without guarantee'. At Rome, according to Gellius, slaves sold without guarantee were marked at the point of sale by the wearing of a felt cap.[4]

Buyers were, to judge by the legal texts, interested in the breeding capacity of female slaves, although this was not the only motive for purchase. If a slave was actually pregnant at the time of sale, this might be held a defect. Vitruvius (*de archit.* 2.9.1), writing about the weakness of a tree's wood in spring, draws a comparison with pregnant women, who, he says, are not judged sound until they have given birth, because the foetus is pre-empting the body's nourishment. For this reason, he says, slaves, when pregnant, are not guaranteed sound. He seems to be thinking of the slave's impaired capacity for work, rather than the possibility of her death in childbirth. According to Ulpian, (D. 5.3.27 pr.) *non temere ancillae eius rei causa comparantur ut pariant*, 'slave-girls are not generally acquired as breeders.'

This remark was made, however, in the context of a discussion of the ownership of offspring; as far as the law of sale was concerned, Ulpian saw no reason to insist on the buyer's being informed if a slave was pregnant. 'Everyone agrees,' he says, 'that she is healthy, for it is the chief and special function of females to conceive and to gestate.' One who had just given birth could also be sold as sound, unless some additional complication had affected her health.[5]

However, even if breeding was not the only consideration, the amount of detailed attention paid to the matter by jurists suggests that buyers did regard a capacity for childbearing as forming at least part of the specifications of a sound and saleable slave. Jurists on the whole seem to have sided with the sellers rather than the buyers, in giving the opinion that barrenness was not a notifiable defect. Labeo thought that a woman found to be barren, like a barren sow or a male slave found to be a eunuch, could be returned to the seller, if the condition had not been made known before sale. In this he went against the general trend. Unless some physical abnormality was present, a woman who was barren, according to Trebatius, or one whose babies were always stillborn, according to Sabinus, was not to be regarded as unsound — presumably because they were still 'of merchandisable quality' for the other purposes for which slaves could be used. This applied, however, only if the woman was congenitally barren, according to Trebatius; if the barrenness arose as a result of some physical ailment she had developed, then she was to be regarded as defective, and declared as such by the seller. A woman 'too narrow to become a woman' was not regarded as sound, nor one whose periods were either too frequent or non-existent (unless, in the latter case, because of her age).[6] Whether the aediles made provision in the market for medical examination or whether, as is more likely, they expected the sellers to provide information is not known.

Sometimes, though, females may have been bought specifically with regard to their breeding potential. If a female slave was sold and the seller had allowed the purchaser mistakenly to believe that she was a virgin, the sale was not void, but the buyer had an action against the vendor. The reason for this ruling is not stated. The supposition was most likely to arise when young girls were sold. The buyer's interest may in some cases have been primarily sexual (e.g., as a *leno* stocking up a brothel), but many buyers may have preferred to acquire a female as near the start of her reproductive life as possible.[7] Unfortunately, little evidence has survived on the age of female slaves at sale. Bradley (1978) examined 29 examples from papyri of female slaves sold in the age range from four to 35 years. Of these, seven were under 14 and only four over 30, while the average age was 22 to 25. On the basis of this evidence, he suggested that the breeding of slaves was a prime consideration in the sale of females in the Roman empire. He did not, indeed, suggest that it was the only consideration; however, the sample is a very small one on which to base conclusions applying to the empire as a whole.[8] In Egypt, it seems that the rearing of slaves from infancy, not merely those born at home but foundlings as well, was a frequent undertaking, and so presumably it was regarded as financially worthwhile. Biezunska-Malowist (1962: 158 ff.) has suggested that, specially for lower-class owners seeking additional money-earners, it was preferable to rear slaves and have them trained in a skill, rather than to buy at greater expense slaves already trained. This spread the cost. In large urban *familiae*, such as are attested at Rome, it made sense to rear home-bred slaves and make use of the training facilities afforded within the household's own ranks of skilled workers. The babies were sometimes sent by wealthy owners to their country estates to be reared in infancy by other slave women, while their mothers presumably continued with their duties in the urban household.[9]

On rural estates (where female slaves were perhaps scarcer than in urban *familiae*), writers such as Varro and Columella recommended that females should be encouraged to have children by the offer of rewards, such as exemption from work for the woman who had had three children, and even manumission for those who exceeded that number.[10] It is suggestive that in the Delphic manumission contracts analysed by Hopkins and Roscoe (Hopkins 1978: 133–71) 80 per cent of the slaves freed as children were freed separately from their mothers, and probably after them. Some manumission contracts for women specified that children born to them (either all or a specified number) during the term of service of their 'conditional release' (*paramone*) must remain the manumitter's property, in order for the woman to secure full release; some relatively generous owners specified in the contract that the children were free, but whether they were the majority is not known.[11] *Paramone* was a Greek practice, not to be confused with the *operae* Roman owners were allowed to require from freed slaves. A closer parallel in Roman law is the situation of the *statuliberae*. These were slaves to whom freedom had been given by the will of their late owner, subject to the fulfilment of a stated condition; until the condition was fulfilled, they remained slaves, and so did any children to whom they gave birth. The latter became the property of the heir.[12] Sometimes, at any rate, the condition of liberty seems actually to have been the production of a specified number of children. Two jurists, Ulpian and Tryphoninus, gave their opinions on the difficult case (possibly a 'textbook' example) of a woman, called Arescusa, given freedom by a will, 'if she gives birth to three children'.

She had, according to Tryphoninus, one child, and then triplets; according to Ulpian two children, then twins. They agree that the last-born, the fourth, child should be free, since the condition was fulfilled before it actually left the mother's body. 'The matter,' says Ulpian, 'is one of fact, not law.' Tryphoninus hypothesises a further complication. The mother's freedom being dependent on the payment of a sum of money, this was paid by a third party just as she was in the process of giving birth. The child, he says, should be deemed free. In some *paramone* contracts these were specified as alternatives — *either* children *or* a specified sum of money as the price of freedom.[13]

Julian took up the question of what should be done where the heir wanted to retain the woman (now called Arethusa), and so tried to prevent her giving birth, either by administering a contraceptive or by making her have an abortion. Julian's opinion (D. 40.7.3.16) was that she should be given her freedom at once, since she *could* have had triplets at one birth. This may be merely an imaginary example, but we should not be justified in assuming that no Roman owner was capable of such physical violence against a slave; and in a case of such a kind there is quite likely to have been a third party, namely the prospective father, interested in securing the woman's freedom.

Women slaves had no automatic right to freedom after the production of a given number of children; that was solely dependent on the generosity of the individual master, and such manumissions may have represented a small proportion of the whole. When a *paramone* contract specified that the woman supply either money or children, in effect, the freed slave was being required to furnish her owner with a replacement. One Delphic contract specifies that a replacement shall be purchased. In one curious example, the manumitter actually saw children as a drawback. His interest was in retaining the slave's services to look after his mother as long as the latter lived. Any child born to the servant during that time was to be free; he did not want to keep it. She could rear it or kill it, as she liked, *but she was not to sell it* (and so, presumably, raise the means to buy her freedom).[14]

Slaves as Livestock — the Offspring

Like other kinds of property, slaves could produce 'fruits' (*fructus*). These might be, in the more abstract sense, 'profits', such as earnings from work; however, those which a female could produce (i.e., children) were more directly comparable with the yield of plants and the natural increase of animals. The latter were 'fruits' under the law of usufruct, and were assigned to the person who held the right of usufruct. Did this apply to the *partus ancillae*, the children of a slave woman? Roman law was, from at least as early as the second century B.C., certain that it did not, though the Romans were less certain *why* it did not.[15]

In the second century B.C., the jurist Brutus stated the view that there was no usufruct of the *partus*, on the grounds that they were human (*homines*) and 'Man cannot be the fruit of man.' Ulpian was puzzled since (a) as Sabinus and Cassius recognised, the offspring of animals could be the 'fruit' of animals and, indeed, had to be used to make good deaths in the herd held by the usufructuary (as — in the case of dotal property — by the husband) and (b) both slaves' children, and the usufruct of such children, could be the subject of legacies. Ulpian's own explanation was that female slaves were not normally purchased for breeding purposes and therefore their offspring were not 'fruit'. Gaius' explanation, which, as Kaser (1958: 158–9) rightly observes, is mere philosophising, was that, as the fruits of the rest of nature were made to serve the interests of man, it was absurd that man himself should be a fruit.[16]

Kaser himself suggests the derivation of the rule, not from any humanitarian principles or 'respect for human dignity' (Buckland 1908: 21), but from the general principle that it was desirable that a slave child should stay with its mother, for the practical reason that she was best able, in the child's early life, to look after it. This explanation, while fitting well enough short-term grants, which would restore the mother to her and her child's owner quickly, does not apply particularly well to usufructs lasting over long periods of time, such as those bequeathed to widows during their lifetime, or until their children came of age. Since the slave mother would not be due to return to her owner until the end of the usufructuary period, she and her child could be separated. In any case, as Kaser himself recognised, mother and child could always be, and not infrequently were, separated by sale.

Whether or not, in law, mother and child remained with the same person depended, in practice, on where the full legal title of ownership rested. Where there was merely usufruct or a conditional title, human offspring were distinguished from those of animals and from crops. A husband's title of ownership of a dotal slave was conditional on the continuance of the marriage. If the dowry fell due for return, any children the slave had had must go back with her — unless, that is, he had held the dowry only 'at valuation', in which case he could, if he wished, hand over only the agreed sum. However, he need return only an equivalent number of animals to those originally received, and could keep any increase.[17]

Matters were more complicated in those situations in which the transfer of ownership was of doubtful validity, e.g., sale of a pledged or stolen slave, or sale in default of creditors. Two elements which jurists appear to have considered important and relevant were the time of conception, and the 'good faith' of the purchaser, i.e., whether at certain material times he had believed the purchase to be lawful and valid.

The offspring of animals were, in effect, treated like other products of the animals, such as wool or milk; so, for example, the offspring of stolen animals belonged to the *bona fide* purchaser, under the title of 'fruits', regardless of when they were conceived.[18] If a slave had been stolen, legal title both to her and to any children subsequently born belonged to the rightful owner, regardless of when they had been conceived. If, however, the thief had sold her, then whether or not the *bona fide* purchaser could claim any children born while she was with him depended on when she had conceived. If she conceived before the theft, or after theft but before sale, the offspring belonged to the original owner; if after sale, she still belonged to her original owner, but the position regarding the child conceived after the sale is less clear. Most jurists seem to have held that the *bona fide* possessor could usucapt the child, providing that he still believed the purchase to have been genuine at the time the child was born.[19]

As we have already seen, the notion that a child had, in some sense, a legal existence from the time of conception, was of some importance in determining matters of status and of inheritance rights, and this was applied not only to the child of a free woman but of one who at some time during her pregnancy was, or should have been, free. It is less obvious that it could be held to have any relevance where what is involved is no question of status but merely of legal ownership, i.e., where the slave is being considered primarily as an item of property. Time of conception was not held material when a slave woman was sold in the ordinary way; children born after the sale belonged to the buyer. The principle was that prenatal existence should be considered only where that was to the expected child's benefit; Buckland (1908: 22) speaks of 'a modification of this in favour of the owner of the *ancilla* at the time of conception'. This will not do; the *bona fide* possessor was not the legal owner of the *ancilla* at any time, yet he might be allowed to usucapt the child.

The time factor *was* important, but surely in a different way from that supposed by Buckland. A slave's child was *partus*, not *fructus*, and belonged to the owner, not the *possessor*. However, one year's uninterrupted *bona fide* possession of movable property gave a right of ownership.[20] If a slave woman could be shown to have conceived after theft and sale, then by the time the child was born the best part of a year would have elapsed. The jurists were probably trying to find ways of ensuring that an innocent purchaser of stolen property should derive some benefit for his expenditure. *Fructus* he could have; that was easy. In allowing usucaption of children in the circumstances specified, they were stretching a point in the interests of equity. The interests of the child were not the issue; all that was being decided was the legal title to ownership.

An explanation is still needed of the distinction between 'fruits' and *partus ancillae*. Buckland's 'respect for human dignity' is not particularly apt. Both humans and animals could be bought, sold, bequeathed and pledged and, where there were no complicating factors, legal title to the offspring of either, born after the transaction was complete, vested in the new owner. The offspring of slaves, as well as the offspring and produce (e.g., wool) of animals, could be bought, sold and pledged in advance. Paul, commenting on the aedilician edict, describes one type of fraud practised (D. 19.1.21 pr.): 'If the *partus* (i.e, prospective offspring) of a woman is sold, and the woman is barren or over fifty years old, and the buyer was not aware of this, he has an action against the seller.'

One might perhaps develop a hint from Ulpian's remark already cited, that since slave women were not normally acquired for breeding purposes, their offspring were not regarded as 'fruits'. Animals *were* bought or their usufruct (effectively, a kind of leasehold) retained for the sake of their bodily produce — meat, wool or hides, milk and young — while slaves were acquired primarily for their services. Animals were essentially consumables, and interchangeable. Slaves were not. Their qualities and abilities were many and various, not always predictable or susceptible of simple numerical quantification. Moreover, slaves were a great deal more durable than most farm animals, even the larger ones. No ancient jurist seems to have developed an argument along these lines, and we have no evidence what reasons, if any, were adduced when the distinction was first drawn. Nevertheless, something like this may be close to the truth. Slaves were simply too valuable to be treated like lambs.

Family Relationships among Slaves

Slaves could not contract legal marriages and have legal children; nevertheless, some, particularly in larger households, could and did form lasting paired relationships, have children and behave, for a time at least, as a family. Since their continuance was entirely dependent upon the slave's owner, who might separate the couple from each other or from their children by sale or bequest, and grant or refuse manumission at will, the stability of these relationships was never to be relied upon. What proportion was stable cannot easily be determined. Different kinds of evidence present different facets of the situation.

In the Delphic manumission records of the last two centuries B.C. the husband–wife relationship is explicitly attested only once, as is that between father and child. The mother–child relationship appears more frequently; there are 29 examples of their joint release. At the same time, as we have seen, mothers might be severed from their children, surrendered in partial fulfilment of conditions for their release. Even allowing for the fact that relatives might sometimes be released together, without the relationship expressly being stated, the overall high ratio of adults to children, together with the preponderance of single over multiple releases, makes it likely that family members were often manumitted separately, and some families may never have succeeded in freeing both parents and children.[21] Not all masters were so generous as the author of the will cited by Scaevola (D. 34.1.20 pr.) who manumitted Stichus, grandson of his old nurse, and bequeathed to him his *contubernalis* and their children (so there were at least four generations in that slave family). Stichus would then be able to free them, and he, and not his patron's son or daughter, would have patronal rights over them.

Similar traces of separate manumission appear in the small number of inscriptions from Rome, noted by Flory (1984), in which the wife had achieved freedom while the husband was still a slave (though some of these were imperial slaves); of the children mentioned, the inscriptions mostly do not give their status at birth, but one-sixth were still slaves.[22] Where, as sometimes happened, specially in larger establishments, freed staff continued work, and possibly residence, in the household, the effects would be less keenly felt. Bequest or sale was more likely to impose actual physical separation.

Some papyri reveal the existence of 'families' stretching over two or three, even four, generations in a single household. Usually, however, the relationship is specified only through the mothers. In bequests of slaves, also, where family relationships are stated, they tend to be between mother and child. Not infrequently the father will have been the woman's owner (or her owner's husband).[23]

The largest single collection of evidence for slave marital couples is the funerary inscriptions from the city of Rome itself. Here, if free husband and wife have the same *gentilicium*, there is at least some presumption of a previous slave (or master–slave) link; the presumption is strengthened if the couple are expressly stated to be freed, and strengthened still further in the relatively small number of instances where some such word as *colliberta* or *contubernalis* is used. There are also some slave couples.[24]

Slave 'marriages' probably had greater chance of stability in very large slave households, or where the 'husband' was living apart from his owner, as *institor*, *vilicus* or the like, and especially if he had slaves in his *peculium*. Parent–child relationships are harder to trace. The children appearing in the inscriptions of freed couples are mostly freeborn; the others may have been left behind, changed owners (and so have different names if manumitted) or lost contact in other ways.[25]

Keeping in touch may have been easier in the large noble and imperial *familiae*, or in the countryside, than it was in towns generally, specially in Rome. We find, for example, a freedwoman of Domitian's wife, Domitia Athenais, associated with her slave brother Januarius in burying their father Phoebus. The funerary *collegia* of the great families probably played an important part in maintaining contact between the freed and their slave relatives.[26]

One mother belonged successively to three households, of the Modii, the Claudii and the Gavii, and left a son in each, before being bought by the Volusii. Freed, she became, as Volusia Justa, the wife of P. Volusius Renatus. Her three sons, all still slaves but now in public service, two with the priestly college of the *septemviri* and one with the *fetiales*, set up her epitaph (*CIL* VI. 2318, with Mommsen's note).

Strictly speaking, these familial relationships between slaves had no existence in the eyes of the law. References in the legal texts to wives and children of slave bailiffs on estates are essentially terms of convenience.[27] The whole concept of the family rested on *conubium* and *potestas*, and slaves had neither. Since, however, slaves on manumission moved into free society, some cognisance had from time to time to be taken of these relationships, at least among the freed.

The rules of dowry did not apply between slaves, since slaves could own no property. However, if a slave woman used her *peculium* as 'dowry', to give to a male slave, and the couple both obtained manumission and continued in the marital relation afterwards, then the law tacitly recognised its conversion into dotal property — always providing, of course, that the former owner had consented to the retention of the *peculium*. Shtaerman and Trofimova (1975: 234) mistakenly take this as amounting to a recognition of slave marriage, and think it an innovation dating to the Antonines or Severi. Buckland (1908: 199) misleadingly talks of 'an effective transfer from one *peculium* to the other'. In fact, there *was* no marriage until both were free and continuing to cohabit; and if either had been freed without the other, the master was under no obligation at all to allow the 'dowry' to remain in the male slave's *peculium*. The point is made even clearer by another reference in the *Digest* to slave 'dowry'. If a slave woman, passing herself off as free, had 'married' a free man, the law was quite clear that the 'dowry' did not become his property but remained that of her owner. (More will be said later about some of the incidental legal consequences of slave–free relationships.)[28]

The laws of inheritance did not apply between slaves. Twice, however, in the *Digest* we find the natural relationship being recognised in judgment of an inheritance case, both times apparently in the absence of any freeborn children. The more complicated case, possibly a textbook example, tells how Pamphilus was manumitted by his mistress's will and left a half-share in a piece of land, with the instruction that the land be transmitted to his children. When he died, his daughter was still a slave, and he instructed his heir to pass on the land to her when she should become free. The question exercising Scaevola was this: under which will, when she became free, had she a claim to the property? If her father's, she had to give the heir the 'Falcidian fourth' of the land's value. Scaevola's response was that the recognition of the natural relationship satisfied the intention of Pamphilus' former owner.[29]

This, however, was a matter of interpretation, rather than of legal right. Labeo thought that the provision of the praetor's edict that the children should not bring suit against their parents should be interpreted as applying to those who had had children while in slavery, as well as to illegitimate children generally. Only mothers, it seems, not fathers, could benefit from this protection. Paul explains: the identity of the mother, even of an illegitimate child, was certain, whereas the *pater* was the person designated by marriage. The basis of this interpretation was the reverence due to all parents.[30]

When it came to marriage by freed persons, however, blood relationships among slaves (*servilis cognatio*) were recognised in law. Marriage between freed persons was banned if, as slaves, they had stood in the prohibited degrees of relationship to each other, since, as Pomponius explains (D. 23.2.8), the ban on 'incestuous' marriages derived originally not from law but from custom (and so, presumably, legally non-existent relationships could be recognised).[31] Nor could a man marry his son's or his father's former slave mistress, since she stood in the relation of daughter-in-law or stepmother, respectively. Her mother was excluded as well. This rule must go back at least as far as the possibility of *conubium* between freeborn and freed.

Paul adds (D. 23.2.14.2–3) that a manumitted father could not marry his manumitted daughter 'even if it is doubted that he is her father'. He is not concerned here with the legal definition of *pater*, in relation to children of lawful marriage and to adopted children, but with actual blood relationships. He must mean that it might be uncertain who had fathered a slave woman's child.

Certain blood relationships were also taken into account in the *lex Aelia Sentia*, which included among the 'good cause' exemptions from the prescribed lower age limits (20 for owner, 30 for slave) that the slave was the natural son or daughter, brother or sister or (according to Ulpian) cognate of the manumitter.[32] Clearly, this could apply not only to natural children of the manumitting patron by his *ancilla* but also to slaves who, having been manumitted themselves, had succeeded in buying, or perhaps had in their *peculium* and were about to manumit, their own relatives.

However, recognition of *servilis cognatio* was accorded in classical law mainly where the interests of free, or freed, persons were concerned. Slaves could always be separated from their relatives by sale or bequest as the owner thought fit. *Ancillae* were sometimes bequeathed along with their children, but legacies of unborn slave children, as of future increase in livestock, or wine as yet unproduced at the time the will was made, were valid, and mother and child would not necessarily be left to the same person.[33]

Paul and Ulpian both tell us that a legacy of an estate 'with its equipment' includes the *contubernales* or 'wives' and children of the male slaves; Paul adds, 'and livestock kept to provide manure, with those who tend them, are included.' This, however, is merely a matter of enumerating the persons and goods actually on the estate (*in eadem villa agentes*). Ulpian, to be sure, adds, 'It is incredible that the testator wished to impose a cruel separation', but mere presumption of intent such as this carried no binding legal force. According to Scaevola, the response was given in one instance that when a business manager (*actor*) living in town was made the object of a legacy, there was no reason to suppose that his wife and daughter were included.[34]

Family groups were sometimes sold together. If the buyer wanted to return one of these as unhealthy, it was 'usual', says Ulpian, for the whole group to be returned, so as not to offend proper feeling (*pietas*); this 'ought' to apply to parents and children, brothers and *contubernales*.[35]

This is not the language of compulsion. Perhaps a little more firmness is detectable when the relationship crosses the barrier between slave and free. When a man's goods are seized and sold up for debt, says Paul, his concubine and natural children are not included. Even by the time of Constantine, recognition has gone no further than the emperor's pronouncement that when an intestate estate is being divided, family groups ought to be kept together: 'For who would bear the separation of children from parent, brothers from sisters, husbands from wives?'[36]

Clearly, by the time of later classical law there was a certain amount of sympathy, in theory at least, though we cannot say to what extent in practice, for the personal ties of slaves; but they had been accorded no legal rights in respect of these relationships against the specific dispositions of an owner.[37]

Slaves sometimes cohabited with free men and women, not their owners. The consequences for the free woman's children and, under the *senatusconsultum Claudianum*, for her own status, have already been discussed. The children of a slave woman belonged to her owner. The free partner might be unaware of the other person's servile status — most likely because he or she was a runaway. The marriage was void, but if genuine mistake could be proved, some of the other consequences might be avoided. In general, however, the law did not go so far in avoiding penalising the innocent victims of mistake as it did in the case of liaisons of citizens with *free* non-Romans (G. I. 67–75). The free woman's child had her status. Until the time of Vespasian, according to Gaius (G. I. 85), there was a law by which the child of a free man and an *ancilla* whom he had believed free was free if male, but if female belonged to the woman's owner; though Gaius does not say so, the son probably had only peregrine status. Vespasian abolished the law; the children of both sexes were to be slaves. This is consistent with the judgment, attested for the second century A.D., that the runaway is a 'thief of herself' and of her offspring, and usucaption is excluded (D. 47.2.61); it is also consistent with the *lex Minicia*.

Money or property might have changed hands as 'dowry'. It did not become the property of the free 'husband' of a slave woman passing herself off as free, but remained that of her owner. On the other hand, if a free woman knowingly 'married' a slave, one would expect the dowry to be irrecoverable. Since there was no legal marriage, there was no dowry, and she had in effect made a gift to the slave of another, which, in law, was a gift to his owner. There were ways round this. Paul cites the curious case of Lucius Titius, who gave his daughter *in potestate*, Seia, in 'marriage' to a slave. The dowry he gave in the form *depositum sub cautione* — that is, not making a transfer of the ownership, but merely entrusting it to the slave's care, subject to return. The father died, and so did the slave husband, without his owner having challenged the arrangement. Paul gave judgement that, as no dowry could have been constituted, Seia as her father's heir was entitled to an action for return of the deposit from the *peculium*. Honest mistake, however, may not have been penalised by loss of the dowry property, especially if there were children. The emperor Antoninus assured Hostilia, who had married Eros in ignorance of his slave status and had children by him, that she could recover the dowry from his *peculium*.[38]

Flight, Abduction and Subversion

It was, it seems, not easy to prevent sexual relations between slaves and outsiders. Relations with male slaves gave concern mostly when they interfered in some way with the well-being of another household or with someone else's property, although the late Republican jurist Alfenus Varus reported that he was approached for advice by an owner whose steward's accounts did not tally because he had been spending his master's money on a 'popsy' (*muliercula*). Varus advised him that he could sue her both for corruption of a slave and for theft of the money. Relations between free women and slaves were punishable as adultery (if the woman was married), but it was not until the *sctum. Claudianum* that any issue, and sometimes the woman herself, were liable to become slaves.[39]

Relations with female slaves (or, indeed, homosexual relations between outsiders and male slaves) were regarded most seriously when they represented a threat to the security of their owner's *familia*. When considering a complaint of corruption of a slave, deflowering of a slave girl or homosexual relations with a male slave, a magistrate should, says Paul, exact very severe punishment 'if the perpetrator is corrupt or such a man that his act seems to go beyond the immediate damage and involve the overthrow of the whole house'. What Paul may be talking about here is alienation of the slave's affections and the danger this might sometimes represent.[40] Sexual relations with an *ancilla* belonging to another man was sometimes called *stuprum*, but Paul remarked that it did not constitute an offence unless it was used as a means of access to her mistress, or unless it made the slave 'worse'. Rape of a slave girl was, as we have seen, punishable as damage to an owner's property, not as an injury to the girl herself.[41]

Runaway slaves, of both sexes, were a perennial headache for the Romans. Possibly the women without the responsibility of children were the more likely to run away, but they could, of course, have children while at liberty, and the law was firm that these belonged to their mother's original owner.[42]

Slaves were valuable property, and slaves of both sexes were liable to be stolen. As we have seen, the law had a good deal to say about the legal position when a slave woman was resold by the thief, and about the legal ownership of any children she might have while away from the owner. Whether female slaves were more likely to be stolen than male is a matter for speculation. Their potential as

breeders, and perhaps in prostitution, makes it a possibility. Iavolenus, a jurist of the time of Domitian, specified a female when
considering the respective rights of action of an owner and a
subsequent purchaser, both of whom had in turn suffered the theft
of the same slave. There are in the *Digest* four references to theft
of a pregnant slave.[43] Male slaves, being stronger and less easy to
handle, might be a more difficult undertaking to steal, though their
possession of specialised skills might sometimes make it worthwhile.

Two texts in the *Digest* mention the payment by a slave to his
master of a stolen *ancilla* as part of the price of his freedom.[44] We
should perhaps think here of an urban context, in which the male
slave was living away from his master and able to amass a *peculium*,
even possibly to acquire slaves of his own, so that he could pass the
woman off as legally bought. She may have been, of course, so far
as he knew.

A slave girl might be abducted for sexual purposes. The law took
this very seriously — unless, indeed, the girl was already a prostitute.
In which case, Ulpian comments, 'it is not theft, for it is not the act
but the motive which is in question and the motive was lust, not
theft . . . nor is he liable under the *lex Fabia* if he concealed a whore
for sexual purposes.'[45]

More about prostitutes later. If the slave girl was not a prostitute,
lawyers advise that her owner might muster the resources of the *lex
Fabia*, the *lex Aquilia* and an action for theft against the man
involved.

The *lex Aquilia* was an action for damages; loss of virginity is
particularly specified. The *lex Fabia*, of uncertain date, but possibly
going back before the beginning of the second century B.C., created
the crime of *plagium*, or 'kidnapping', either of free persons or of
slaves. Anyone who persuaded a slave to flee or concealed, kept
under restraint, or knowingly bought or sold a runaway, was liable
to a penalty which by the time of Ulpian was fifty thousand sesterces.
Later, offenders of lower rank were sentenced to punishment in the
mines, the higher-ranking to the loss of half their property.[46]

What the Romans were worried about was perhaps not only the
possibility of physical harm to their property or a reduction in its
worth but also the subversion of a slave's loyalty to his or her
master (D. 1.18.21). After all, not all sexual activity was necessarily
rape. The slave may have been a consenting party. As for abduction
and concealment, we may suspect that in many cases the slave girl
was not abducted but was a runaway, who may even have eloped

in order to go and live with the man in question. This may be one reason for the distinction drawn by Ulpian. If the girl was a prostitute, the man's intention may have been to detain her only temporarily for his short-term gratification; but if she was an ordinary slave girl, eloping and hoping to set up in conjugal life and pass as free, the absence was intended to be permanent.

Sexual Use of Slaves

Owners could and did have sexual relations with their own female slaves.[47] The latter were scarcely in a position to refuse, but it need not be supposed that they were always unwilling. Literary sources speak, not only of the debauchery of a lord of a harem, like Martial's Quirinalis (I. 84), but of the famous slave or freed mistresses of emperors and nobles, and inscriptions attest not only to the freedwoman concubine, but to the freedwoman wife of her patron. As we have already seen, such liaisons were not necessarily ill-regarded (though marriage was banned, after Augustus, with the senatorial class).

A double standard operated. Women owners could be rather less free in acknowledging slave amours, specially if they themselves were married. Sex with a slave counted, for a married woman, as adultery under the terms of the Julian law.[48] For a man, sex with slave girls did not count.

Many prostitutes were slaves. Their owners suffered the penalty of *infamia* but otherwise were permitted to operate their business undisturbed by the law. A slave *leno*, prostituting the slaves of his *peculium*, would not be affected by *infamia* at all, until he was freed. Severus specified in a rescript that a woman who had given up prostitution on manumission was not liable to *infamia*. It is not until the end of the second century A.D. that we hear of any official intervention to protect the slave whose master compelled her to prostitution. Hadrian forbade the sale of slaves to bawds or gladiatorial schools without cause being shown — that is, he did permit it as a punishment. Under Pius, magistrates were given a duty of enquiring into any complaints of ill-treatment made by slaves who sought sanctuary in temples or at the emperor's statue, and among the grounds was *infamis iniuria*, a rather unspecific term, which may refer to various forms of sexual outrage. Severus laid on the urban prefect the duty of hearing any complaints by slave women who had been forced into prostitution by their masters. Under the Christian empire, the masters were, in addition, severely punished.[49]

However, there seems to have been a feeling that the business of prostitution ought, at least, not to be encouraged. This feeling may partly have underlain Ulpian's view that a lenient view should be taken of someone's abducting or harbouring a slave prostitute. According to Callistratus, also active under the Severi, if a prostitute was manumitted, her patron should not expect to derive any profit from her, since only those services to patrons (*operae*) were considered due which were not morally undesirable.[50]

Some owners at least were opposed to the prostitution of slave women and when they sold them stipulated a penalty, usually a right of seizure, or freedom for the slave, if the new owner did prostitute them. Several emperors, particularly Vespasian and Hadrian, took an interest in the matter, and insisted on the enforceability of these clauses. Even if the woman had been sold several times before the condition was breached, it became effective whenever she was prostituted, and the original seller benefited, either by right of seizure and recovery, or as patron on manumission. Marcus Aurelius may even have allowed the woman her freedom by virtue of a non-prostitution clause, even if liberty was not specified as a penalty on the buyer. Alexander Severus ruled that the device of employing the woman ostensibly as a waitress was a mere evasion, and could not avert the operation of the penalty.[51]

The effectiveness of this protection for the woman would, of course, depend on the thoroughness with which her previous history was known to, or investigated by, subsequent purchasers. As conditions of sale were not uncommon, it would be sensible for any prospective buyer to make careful enquiry.

Manumission

Of the three principal methods of manumission under Roman law, one, inscription in the census list, applied only to men, and was probably little used after the Republic. The common formal method of manumission during the owner's lifetime was *vindicta*, which was modelled on the procedure for allegations of wrongful detention in slavery. Since it was a fictitious lawsuit, the presence of a magistrate was necessary, and the outcome was a foregone conclusion; agreement had already been reached between slave and owner on such matters as payment, services, etc. The other method recognised as legally valid was manumission in an owner's will. The most important feature of both forms was that a slave so freed became a Roman citizen. Any other type of informal manumission left slaves, under the Republic, in practice at liberty, under the protection of the praetor, but legally still slaves, without property or legal capacity.[52]

The situation remained essentially the same under the empire, except for the modifications introduced by the Augustan legislation, the *lex Fufia Caninia* of 2 B.C. and the *lex Aelia Sentia* of A.D. 4.[53] The former limited the number of slaves who could be manumitted under a will; the latter imposed various restrictions, such as minimum age limits. The effect of both was to create new categories of people who were not in fact legally manumitted. Some improvement in their situation was afforded them by the *lex Junia* (or *Junia Norbana*), passed possibly not until the principate of Tiberius (?A.D. 19), which gave them free status, not as citizens but as Latins.[54]

Whether such was the intention of the legislators or not, male slaves achieving 'Junian' latinity were in a better position than female. A male Latin taking a Roman or Latin woman as wife could obtain citizenship for himself, his Latin wife, and his child, by having a child who reached the age of one year (*anniculi probatio*), and he and his wife now also became legally married in Roman law. The treatment of the whole subject by Gaius, the principal legal source, is unsystematic, but it does not appear that this option was available to the Latin woman who wanted to marry a Roman citizen, or to her child. Gaius, discussing *conubium*, says (I.79) that the offspring of a Roman citizen and a Latin woman has Latin status, 'in spite of the fact that the *lex Minicia* does not apply to those who at the present day are called Latins' (it applied originally to peregrines). Earlier, in discussing exceptions to the rules about status of children, in cases of genuine mistake, he says (I. 67) that if a Roman citizen took a Latin or peregrine woman as wife, unless he could prove genuine mistake (i.e., that he thought she was a citizen), the child would be Latin or peregrine according to its mother's status, 'because a child does not take its father's status unless there is *conubium* between father and mother'. Again (I. 71), if a Roman man was mistaken about his own status, thinking himself a Latin, and therefore took a Latin woman as wife, he could, on birth of a child, prove a case of mistake and receive the benefit of the *lex Aelia Sentia*.

The conclusion seems inescapable. A male slave, informally manumitted, could nevertheless achieve citizenship for himself and his child, regardless of whether its mother was Roman or Latin. A female could attain legal marriage, citizenship and citizenship for her child, only by marrying another Latin. If she cohabited with a Roman, she was not legally his wife and her child was not a citizen, nor in its father's *potestas*; nor would she, as a Junian Latin, be able to transmit property by will to her children (G.I. 23). Whether this was in fact the situation of many freedwomen concubines we do not know, and their nomenclature alone would not necessarily tell us. Whether or not the legislator's intention was in part to discourage Roman citizens from taking Latin freedwomen as wives, the law possibly gave owners an actual incentive to manumit informally, in order to secure a slave's intestate inheritance.[55]

Two later measures may have ameliorated the position of at least some Latin freedwomen. According to Suetonius (*Cl.* 19), the emperor Claudius as part of his endeavours to ensure the Roman corn supply offered to those who would build large merchant vessels substantial rewards adapted to the condition of each, 'to a citizen exemption from the *lex Papia Poppaea*, to a Latin the rights of Roman citizenship and to women the privilege of *four* children'. Four was the number of children freedwomen must produce to qualify in the ordinary way for the *ius lib*. The women whose generosity Claudius particularly aimed at tapping may have been wealthy freedwomen (restricted, as we have seen, by having a patron as *tutor legitimus*); if they happened also to be Latins, they could gain Roman citizenship. The other measure was a *senatusconsultum* of unknown date which specified that a Latin woman could gain citizenship by having three illegitimate children. This *sctum.* is unlikely to have been very early; it can scarcely have been passed before illegitimate children were allowed to count for the *ius lib.* generally.[56]

Obviously, it might be important for a woman to be able to demonstrate either that she was freeborn or that she had been properly manumitted. This adds significance to the efforts of Petronia Justa, already mentioned, to prove herself freeborn. If she had in fact been manumitted, it was probably informally, otherwise Calatoria would surely have been able to produce some proof of it. As an informally manumitted *Latina*, Petronia might face considerable difficulty making any match with a Roman citizen, to whom she could offer neither legal marriage, legitimate children, nor an inheritance for the children. She brought her case to try to establish her free birth, possibly because there *was* a Roman in the offing whom she wanted to marry. Given the informality of Roman marriage procedures, some Junian Latin women may have been able, for a time at least, to conceal their true status and find Roman husbands. Discovery was most likely when a child was born and the father attempted to register it as legitimate. His own conscientiousness, or that of the recording magistrate, might require from the woman proof of her own status. All was not yet lost; the child's legitimacy and citizen status could be saved, and the woman could become a citizen, *if* the father could prove 'honest mistake'. But proof that he had not known something might be difficult to establish, and some magistrates might pertinently ask why he had never troubled to enquire.

For slave couples hoping to achieve freedom and marriage the *lex Aelia Sentia* must sometimes have posed problems of strategy. For which was it better to obtain manumission first? The woman was likely to be the younger of the two, and if she was under 30 manumission would not secure citizen status for her (unless she also happened to be her patron's natural child, foster-sister or former nurse), or for any child born before her husband joined her. If the man was over 30, he could become a citizen straight away, but his younger wife would not — at least until *anniculi probatio* — unless he was able to afford to buy and manumit her himself. This, rather than an assertion that the husband had condescended in marriage (as supposed by Kolendo 1981: 291) is probably the significance of the formula *libertae idem coniugi* (both freedwoman and wife) found on some funerary inscriptions. Far from dissimulating his own freedman status, the husband is demonstrating, by the formula, that his wife had been properly manumitted and that consequently she and their children were citizens.

Many slave couples, especially among the less prosperous sections of society, may have had to be content with securing freedom for themselves or their children as and when they could and with the prospect that their children at least, if of Latin status, might go on eventually to secure citizen status through *their* children.

Whether men or women stood a better chance of manumission is hard to determine, and statistics are lacking. Two substantial collections of evidence do seem to show some bias in favour of women, though it may not be justifiable to take these as representative samples. Alföldy (1972) analysed 1,201 recorded ages at death of ex-slaves of private owners from the western provinces. Three-fifths died before the age of thirty (and so, perhaps, tended to be over-represented in commemorations), and of these three-fifths were female. The other set of evidence is the Delphic manumission records, in which women form the majority.[57]

On one hand, male slaves tended to have higher-level jobs, and their value as workers might be an inducement to their owners to retain them as slaves; on the other, the prospect of freedom could serve as incentive to the slave to work harder for the master, while at the same time the more responsible and independent slave had a better chance of raising a *peculium* with which to buy his freedom.[58] With women, a commoner motive for seeking manumission, probably, was to allow marriage and/or the birth of free children. As the specific jobs (if any) on which women were employed tended to be less lucrative for their owners, less value may have been set on retaining them; moreover, there will quite often have been a man, either the patron himself wishing to marry her, or another wishing to buy her freedom, interested in securing her release, and this may have gone some way to offset her own relatively poorer prospects of acquiring a substantial *peculium* and the loss to the owner of any future children.

Marriage and Patrons

A freedwoman did not need her patron's consent to marry, any more than a freeborn woman required the consent of her tutor (unless *manus* or a dowry was involved). This is shown by the fact that from time to time patrons tried to extract from their freedwomen an oath not to marry.[59]

The right to *operae* (services) was lost[60] if the freedwoman married with her patron's consent, since her prime duty was considered to be to her husband. A patroness, however, could always require the *operae*, since her claims were not felt to compete with a wife's duty. Clearly, the burden of proof would be on a patron, trying to exact *operae*, that he had *not* consented to the marriage; the oaths, even if not themselves legally enforceable, may have been meant to try to establish this in advance. If he had not consented to the marriage, it was not void, but he might claim that in opposing his wishes she had failed in the ex-slave's duty of *obsequium* ('respectful compliance'); this was not an offence that normally attracted a very severe penalty.[61]

Under the empire, jurists condemned these oaths as contrary to the *lex Aelia Sentia*; the penalty for the patron was loss of his patronal rights. The practice, however, was probably one that had been going on since the Republic. Patrons had much to lose under the empire, when freedwomen could acquire the *ius liberorum* and so control over their property and at least partial powers of testamentary disposition in favour of their children. The right to services (*operae*) might still be worth having, although these were, after the reforms of the praetor Rutilius Rufus (c. 118 B.C.), limited by law and created only by voluntary agreement; before that, patrons had had an almost limitless right to demand the time and services of their ex-slaves.

Whenever her marriage ended, whether by divorce or widowhood, a freedwoman became liable again for any *operae* that had been agreed. This gave her an incentive to fulfil the intention of the authors of the *lex Julia et Papia* and remarry as soon as possible. Since the marriage-laws applied only within certain age limits, once she reached the age of 50 she was not compelled to render the services; this was probably from an interpretation of the law, rather than one of its original clauses. If a patron had chosen to keep a freedwoman as his concubine rather than marry her, it was agreed that she ought not to be penalised, but should be exempt from any demand for *operae*, just as if she were his wife. Some freedwomen might have gone up in the world. They were not expected to go on rendering services once that became unsuited to the dignity of their position.

Marriage to her own patron placed the freedwoman under a certain restriction. If she divorced him without his consent, she was violating her duty to a patron. The *lex Julia* on marriage recognised the divorce but refused her *conubium* with anyone else, and she could not bring an action for recovery of dowry.[62]

If she had been freed expressly in order to marry her patron, he could compel her to do so, even against her will. Legal opinion sided with the patron; if she married anyone else first, without the patron having renounced his right, the condition of liberty was not fulfilled and she was not free. However, he was not allowed to use this as a device for preventing her marriage to anyone else. If he freed her for the purposes of marriage under the *lex Aelia Sentia* (i.e., when either was under the prescribed minimum age) and did not himself marry her within six months, the manumission was invalid. Julian, indeed, seems to have taken an extreme view, and one not helpful to anyone; even if she was divorced, he said, by her first husband within six months and then her patron married her, she did not get her freedom. The law does not seem to have troubled itself about an alternative possibility — marriage to a complaisant patron followed by a quick divorce with his consent.[63]

None of this applied if the patron had freed her merely in fulfilment of a *fideicommissum*, i.e., a testamentary instruction from a previous owner, since she was held to have been granted her freedom of necessity, and not under a condition of marriage imposed by himself. She was free, whether he married her or not, and she could divorce and marry again at will.[64]

The special position of the patron–husband also explains an apparent anomaly in the law of divorce. As we have seen, a marriage was normally ended by the captivity of the husband, and *postliminium* did not apply. Lawyers differed, however over the patron–husband. Ulpian thought that, if he was captured, the wife was free to marry again, as if he had died. Julian, however, thought that the freedwoman–wife did not have *conubium* with anyone else, 'because of reverence for her patron'. This may mean no more than that Julian found it slightly shocking that a patron could be divorced without his taking the initiative. Nevertheless, Julian may be right, and for good legal reasons.

It has been suggested that the reason that *postliminium* did not normally apply to the marriage of free persons was that it conflicted with the liberty of either to end the marriage at will. Since the freedwoman wife did not have this liberty, *postliminium* could apply, and so, although the marriage itself could not be held to exist while he was in captivity, she was in the same position as one who had divorced her patron–husband without his consent.[65]

Not all patrons, however, married their slave-girl sweethearts, and slave men were, it seems, even less likely to marry up the scale. As we saw in Chapter 3 above, some marriages between patron and ex-slave, or between freeborn and freed, incurred at first social disapproval and later legal prohibition. Augustan legislation banned such marriages to senators. The ban on a freedman marrying his patroness possibly came later (after the extension of the earlier ban to senators' descendants of both sexes). It is understandable from the point of view of a *pater*, especially if the family was rich; part of his patrimony might, as we saw in the previous chapter, end up in the hands of his son-in-law's patron. What was the objection to a freedwoman's manumitting and marrying a slave (*not* her former fellow-slave) whom she had acquired after manumission? The relationship may have begun before she became his owner. As with the *sctum. Claudianum*, the purpose of the ban may have been to try to ensure that a male slave's sexual energies were directed to producing more children in the household of his original owner. An exception was made, if we may trust the relevant text (D. 40.2.14.1) for a freedwoman who managed to acquire and then manumit her own former fellow-slave.

Notes

1. Westermann (1955) 58 ff., 70–84; Watson (1975) 81–97; Morabito (1981).
2. *CIL* XI. 871; D. 14.3.7; 8; Pleket (1969) no. 28; Shtaerman and Trofimova (1975) 47–9, n. 1; Treggiari (1980) 53; Kampen (1981) 123–5.
3. On breeding as a source of slaves, Biezunska-Malowist (1962); Harris (1980); Morabito (1981) 60–5.
4. Gell. *N.A.* 6.4.1–3; D. 14.1.1; *P. Vindob. Bosw.* 7 (Euodia); Taubenschlag (1955) 79, 333; Biezunska-Malowist (1971b) 83–4; (1977) 39.
5. D. 21.1.14.1, 2.
6. Gell. 4.2. 9–10; D. 21.1.14.7, 15.
7. D. 19.1.1.5; Morabito (1981) 60–5, especially 63, n. 184.
8. For objections and Bradley's reply, see Dalby (1979), Bradley (1979).
9. Training of slaves: D. 32.65.3; rearing in the country: D. 32.99.3.
10. Varro *R.R.* 2.1.26; 2.10.6–9; Columella 1.18.19; Harris (1980) 120.
11. Samuel (1965) 262–3; Hopkins (1978) 155–6, 165–6; Tucker (1982) 233–4.
12. Buckland (1908) 286 ff. They were free if manumission had been delayed after fulfilment of the condition: C. 7.4.3.
13. D. 1.5.15; 16; similarly D. 34.5.10(11).1. Samuel (1965) 262–3; Tucker (1982) 234–5.
14. *GDI* 1717, 2171; *P. Strassb.* 122.
15. Kaser (1958); Buckland (1966) 21–9, 221–3.
16. D. 7.1.68 pr.; Cic. *de fin.* 1.4.12; D. 5.3.27 pr., 22.1.28.1. On legacies of offspring, both Julian and Papinian occupied themselves (D. 30.82.4; 31.73) with the possible legal complications of a situation in which an unborn child was bequeathed to someone who then bought the mother, and the child was born before the legacy fell due. He was held not to have purchased the child, but to have an entitlement under the will to the child or a monetary equivalent.
17. Buckland (1908) 21 n. 14 lists relevant legal texts.
18. D. 1.5.26; 22.1.10; 41.1.48.2; 41.3.4.18–19; 33 pr.; 47.2.48.5–6. Jurists' opinions are conflicting on the status of the offspring of slaves sold while under pledge or to defraud creditors: Buckland (1908) 22–4.
19. Buckland (1908) 27; Kaser (1958) 167 ff. A runaway slave was a 'thief of herself', and the same rules applied to her offspring: D. 47.2.61.
20. XII T. 6.3; Cic. *Top.* 4.23; G. II. 42; Ulp. *Reg.* 19.8; Buckland (1966) 241–4; Kaser (1971) 418–25.
21. Samuel (1965) 262–3; Hopkins (1978) 164–6; Tucker (1982). Bradley (1984: 54–9, 64–8) produces some evidence suggesting sale or bequest of slaves in Roman Egypt without regard to family relationships.
22. Treggiari (1981a) 63–9; Weaver (1972) 114.

23. Biezunska-Malowist (1977) 27–8, 113–6.

24. Shtaerman and Trofimova (1975) 82–92 (note 1, pp. 89–92 also gives some examples from other parts of Italy); Treggiari (1981a).

25. And so the small size of freeborn families epigraphically attested need not mean that freedwomen were, as a category, subfertile or particularly given to family limitation: Fabre (1971) 245, on Treggiari (1969) 214.

26. AE 1912.221; Shtaerman and Trofimova (1975) 46–52, 97–104.

27. D. 33.7.12.7, 33; 38.8.1.2; 38.10.10.5.

28. D. 23.3.39; 67.

29. C. 6.59.4; D. 28.8.11, 31.88.12; Buckland (1908) 78–9. Buckland is incorrect in saying that Pamphilus ordered the heirs to manumit his daughter; there is no evidence that she was her father's property.

30. D. 2.4.4, 3; 5; 6.

31. Saturninus makes a similar point (D. 48.2.12.4) in explaining why a slave can be held guilty of parricide.

32. G. I. 19; D. 40.2.11–12.

33. D. 30.62; 63. In the example considered by Julian and Papinian (see note 16 above) it seems to be assumed that the woman is not left as a legacy to the same person as her child.

34. Paul, *Sent.* 6.38; D. 33.7.12.7, 33; 20.4.

35. D. 21.1.35, 39.

36. C. 3.38.11; D. 42.5.38.

37. Polay (1969) attempts to trace the development of attitudes to slave 'marriages' from the early Republic to the late empire, in relation to changing economic and social situations. However, there is very little evidence for the early period, and for the Principate and later he relies almost entirely on literary and legal evidence; more use of documentary material might have made him modify his picture substantially. Though the law largely ignored slave marriage, in practice it was often able to survive and carry through into free life.

38. See note 28 above. Seia: D. 16.3.27. Hostilia: C. 5.18.3.

39. D. 11.3.16. For the *sctum. Claudianum*, see Chapter 8 above (references at note 9).

40. D. 1.18.21.

41. Paul. *Sent.* 2.26.16; Buckland (1908) 76.

42. D. 11.4; Buckland (1908) 267–74; Crook (1967a) 186–7; Biezunska-Malowist (1977) 114. In *P. Berl. Leihg.* 15, a census declaration lists in one household a woman slave with two children, another with her daughter and the latter's two children. Three other female slaves are said to have run away.

43. Iavolenus: D. 47.2.75. Theft of pregnant slave: D. 1.5.26; 41.3.10.2; 47.2.48.5; 50.16.26.

44. D. 41.3.4.16 (Paul); 41.4.9 (Julian). They disagree as to whether the offspring can be usucapted or not.

45. D. 47.2.39.

46. D. 47.1.2.5; 47.2.83.2; 47.10.9.4; 25; 48.5.6.1. On the *lex Fabia* and *plagium*, see D. 48.15; C. 9.20; Buckland (1908) 31–3; Bellen (1971) 44–64; Lambertini (1980).

47. Literary references: Kolendo (1981).

48. D. 48.5.25 pr.

49. *SHA Hadr.* 18; D. 1.6.2., 1.12.1.8, 3.2.4.2–3, 24; Buckland (1908) 37–8, 70–1, 603–4; Morabito (1981) 191–2.

50. D. 38.1.38 pr.

51. C. 4.56.1, 3; D. 18.7.6; 21.2.34; 37.14.7 pr.; 40.8.6; Buckland (1908) 603–4; Morabito (1981) 191.

52. Buckland (1908) 437–551; Watson (1967) 185–200.

53. G. I. 18–46; Buckland (1908) 537–48. Bradley (1984: 87–95) rightly empha-

sises the role of the legislation in encouraging desirable social values and behaviour among slaves.

54. Buckland (1908) 533–7; Crook (1967a) 296 n. 29; Kaser (1971) 296.

55. Sirks (1981) 255 ff.

56. Ulp. *Reg.* 3.1; Buckland (1966) 94, n. 7; Sirks (1980) and (1981) 254.

57. Hopkins (1978) 127, 139–40.

58. Treggiari (1969) 70; (1976) 92.

59. D. 37.14.6.3; 38.16.3.15; 40.9.31, 32 pr.

60. On *operae* in general, see D. 38.1; Treggiari (1969) 69–76; Fabre (1971) 317–30; Shtaerman and Trofimova (1975) 109, 113 ff., 235–6; Morabito (1981) 89–91.

61. D. 1.16.9.3; 37.14.1.

62. D. 24.2.11 pr.; 38.11.1.1.

63. D. 23.2.51; 40.2.13; 40.9.21.

64. D. 23.2.50; 24.2.10; 40.5.52.12.

65. D. 23.2.45.6; 49.15.12.4; 14.1; Chapter 5 (above) note 27; Watson (1961).

11 Women at Work

The extent of women's direct involvement in Roman economic life is hard to determine. Women *sui iuris* could own property and were free to administer it themselves, subject only to tutorial consent for certain transactions, and in fact women appear frequently in papyri and in the Herculaneum tablets engaging in buying, selling, leasing and other activities. Ownership by women of ships and other large-scale business concerns is documented.[1] We do not know, however, to what extent these well-to-do women actively involved themselves in the running of their enterprises, or even in the supervision of the activities of their agents and managers.

There are similar problems with the evidence for what might more properly be called working women, i.e., those attested in connection with particular trades, crafts or lines of work. The range of skilled work is narrower than for men; does this reflect reality, or the accidents of survival? The nature of their active involvement, especially in the case of married women, is unclear. Some are slaves, many freed, few certainly freeborn. Does this reflect a society in which slave girls might be taught a trade and set to work, but free daughters, on the whole, were not, but were destined for marriage?

Women's Legal Capacity in Business

In business life, women who were slaves or *in potestate* had in effect the same legal standing as men. As we have already seen, the law was indifferent to the sex of an *institor*. A slave of either sex, or a man's son or daughter, could manage a business on behalf of the owner or *pater* or work for hire for a third party. Whether many freeborn daughters actually did this is unknown and is perhaps unlikely. Marriage and the assumption of responsibilities in another household followed childhood quickly for many girls.

Although technically these people had neither property of their own nor legal capacity, the necessary transactions were made possible by the provision of *peculium*, a financial 'float' of which they

233

had day-to-day disposal, although it remained the legal property of the owner. Without it, no kind of contract or obligation could have been undertaken; with *peculium*, it immediately became possible for them to act as agents. A third party could sue the master or *pater* up to the extent of the *peculium*, or beyond, to the extent to which the latter had profited.[2]

Women *sui iuris* could conduct business on their own account, although their freedom of action was, to some extent, restricted by the requirement of tutor's authorisation for various transactions. A minor's tutor was responsible for the administration of business, and the legal liability was also his. Women both administered their property and bore legal liability. The tutor's function was essentially a negative one, to restrain the women from action which might diminish the property. How seriously they took their duties depended very much on the individual tutor; in the absence of legal liability, there was no great incentive for a tutor (other than an agnate or a patron) to exert himself. Contracts and the undertaking of obligations generally, as well as the alienation of *res mancipi*, required authorisation, but many property transactions were exempt.[3] Tutor's authority was not necessary for the appointment of a business agent[4] — so Caesennia, for instance, fell prey to a rogue like Aebutius.

By the first century A.D., such tutorial restriction as remained was largely theoretical for freeborn women, though patrons, as *tutores legitimi*, could still maintain a fairly tight control over their freedwomen's handling of financial affairs.

Augustus' institution of the *ius liberorum* changed all this. Some rescue action was felt necessary, in the interest of preservation of property, and this took the form of the *senatusconsultum Velleianum*,[5] which placed a ban on women's giving security or undertaking liability on behalf of others; earlier edicts of Augustus and Claudius had forbidden them to do so on behalf of their husbands. It was suggested in Chapter 4 above that the particular danger against which the two emperors were seeking to guard was that of exploitation of women by their husbands. The *sctum. Velleianum*, however, had a wider application. Women were not to be allowed to take on liability for the debts of other persons.

This ban, if universal, would effectively have excluded women from a whole range of business and commercial activities, since it meant that no creditor would ever have been able to sue a woman guarantor for recovery, and so no one would in future ever have accepted a woman as surety on someone else's behalf. So, this might seem a retrograde step, clawing back some of the economic freedom women already enjoyed. In fact, it was not so severe — nor so foolish — as that. The praetor was given discretionary power to grant *exceptio*; a creditor might be able to recover, if it was established that the woman was fully aware of the consequences of what she was doing. This provision was important for both parties. Creditors were protected against deliberate fraud by women trying to use the *sctum.* in order to evade, or help others to evade, liability; women were protected, not only against undue influence by their menfolk but also perhaps, sometimes, against their own inexperience, which might lead them into taking on open-ended obligations as guarantors. In this aspect, the *sctum.* was seen as a protection to women.[6] So, at least, says Ulpian, though Paul perhaps comes nearer the true motive in remarking that the measure was desirable 'because of the danger to the *res familiaris*'.[7] A further reason that he gives is that women were customarily excluded from the exercise of public functions.

This feeling, that certain functions were properly the province of men, is given also by Callistratus as the reason that women were not allowed to be bankers. Crifo (1964: 151 ff.) is inclined, though with insufficient reason, to place the inception of this ban not long before this comment, i.e., under the Severi. He thinks he finds a banker in one of the freedwomen of a Julio-Claudian Augusta. The woman in question, however, is described as *ab argento* — not a banker, probably not even a silver dealer, but a silver-worker. Another woman mentioned in the *Digest* who might have described herself as an *argentaria* is there called a *negotiatrix*, a dealer. Scaevola ruled that the terms of her bequest to her daughter covered only the silver she had for her own personal use, not the stock of her shop.[8]

The text on which Crifo principally relies to establish the existence of female bankers as late as the mid-second century A.D. is a rescript of Antoninus Pius dated A.D. 155 (C. 2.1.1); he does, however, admit that it is susceptible of other interpretations. A certain Manilius claims that he made a deposit of some money with a woman, and is having difficulty recovering it. The emperor advises him that the judge can issue an order obliging the woman to show her account books. There is no compelling reason to believe that this woman, any more than the grasping Otacilia Laterensis already mentioned (page 73), was professionally engaged in banking. Indeed, the praetor's edict obliged bankers to put their account books into evidence, if required, in any litigation concerning clients for whom they were acting as bookkeepers. The case brought to Pius, however, obviously concerns a private transaction, and the complainant is apparently thinking of bringing one of the actions *bonae fidei*, namely that based on deposit.[9]

Bankers could and did oil the wheels of business by underwriting the debts of their clients, and became responsible themselves for payment under an *actio recepticia*, granted by the praetor.[10] Certainly, such an activity would have been impermissible for women after the passing of the *sctum. Velleianum*, and this limitation may have sufficed to keep them out of banking; previously, there may have been no legal barrier to stop them running a banking business, save the requirement of tutorial consent for any activity likely to diminish the patrimony. A responsible (or impartial) praetor might uphold the tutor's veto against the woman's efforts to compel his consent, and this was an additional safeguard; there was no protection for the patrimony if the tutor was easygoing or indifferent. Though women could not be bankers, they could and did act as moneylenders, whether on a large scale (often, among the upper-class Romans, semi-privately) or on a small, like the pawnbroker Faustilla. It may not even have been necessary to involve their tutors; Otacilia Laterensis would surely never have ventured on a suit against Visellius unless her tutor was superfluous or a party to the fraud and willing to involve himself in the scandal.[11]

Women's exclusion from public functions should have meant that they were unable to participate in the tax-farming companies, *societates publicanorum*. However, in view of its importance to the state's finances, this type of *societas*, unlike others, was not dissolved by the death of a member, and an heiress could find herself involved willy-nilly. There is in the *Digest* one mention of a woman who at her death was a debtor of the *fiscus*, the treasury, and it is specified that this indebtedness arose from tax-farming. No doubt a tutor or other agent would be required to act for a woman partner. Women were also excluded from laying information (*delatio*) with the *fiscus*, as they were from bringing charges before the criminal courts, except on their own behalf. Trajan, we are told, introduced this right of *delatio* to the *fiscus*. It was probably found necessary with the increase in numbers of women who acquired the *ius liberorum* and who therefore had no tutors to act on their behalf; there were many private (not necessarily business) circumstances affecting property which could involve the *fiscus*.[12]

Trades and Crafts

Both slave women and free are attested as working at various crafts, although the status of their employment is not always clear. Slaves in a large urban *familia* might have been producing items for the needs of the household; alternatively, they might have been employed in a workshop, producing for sale. Their employer might be their owner, but trained slaves might also be hired out to work for others. The practice is attested in the *Digest* (7.8.12.61) for house-building and shipbuilding, as well as for wool-working and weaving. However, only the actual owner could hire out his slave's labour in this way. Legal opinion was that a usufructuary must use the slave's labour directly, and could not hire him or her out to a third party. So, for instance, if the person entitled to *usus* had contracted to do some wool-working, he could employ his 'usuary' slave women to do it, and he could use them to work wool for himself — but he could not send them off to work in a *lanificium* and receive payment for their hire.

Apprenticeship contracts for both slaves and free persons (the latter usually male) to be taught weaving survive from Roman Egypt. In small households in the up-country towns, the purpose of having someone taught a craft might be not to produce for the household, but to create an additional wage-earner. Some contracts specify that a wage is to be paid to the owner or parent, during the time (as much as four years) that the pupil is learning. That the learners might come from small households is suggested by one contract in which a slave weaver is hired out by her owner to work for one year for a local weaver, Achillas. She is to have board and lodging with Achillas and eight days' holiday a year, and her owner is to receive a monthly wage for her services. However, it is specified that if he needs her to make bread, she is to come and do so at night, without his forfeiting any of the wage. The poor girl is expected to work all day in the weaving-shop and at night in her master's house. This suggests that he lacked other slaves to do the household baking.[13]

While wool-preparation and spinning on a small scale could be done at home, fabric-weaving was likely, outside very large households such as that of the Statilii, which appears to have had a specialised weaving department, to be entrusted to professional weaving establishments. Women specified in funerary inscriptions as spinners (*quasillariae*) probably worked in such establishments, and not as general household slaves. Eight of the eleven known from Rome come from the monument of the Statilii; one is commemorated by a male wool-dispenser (*lanipendus*), two others by men serving in other departments of the household.[14] Studies of the cloth trade in Pompeii (Moeller 1969 and 1976) and elsewhere in the empire (Jones 1974) indicate that most weaving was done by men, though women *textrices* are attested.[15] On the other hand, clothes-makers and menders (*sarcinatrices*) are predominantly female.[16] Some free women worked in the cloth trade, spinning, weaving or garment-making. Literary references suggest that the reward was meagre and the social status low. Gaius (D. 15.1.27 pr.) brackets the *sarcinatrix* and the *textrix*, both slave and *filiafamilias*, with those practising some other 'vulgar craft', though his reference to the action on the *peculium* may suggest that he had in mind some who did not simply hire out their labour but did independent work.

The work of *sarcinatrices* could be regarded partly as production, partly as service industry, since they did clothes-mending as well. The same is true of the *fullones* (fullers) and dyers, who both finished new cloth and cleaned and rejuvenated old. A few women are attested among the personnel of such establishments at Pompeii, and paintings from one of them include two women (Kampen 1981: 153–4 and fig. 90). As, however, the women are merely sitting examining fabric, they could be customers rather than workers, and the girl standing beside one could be her slave-attendant (*pedisequa*).

Rather better attested is one of the retail trades serving the fabric industries, that of *purpuraria*, seller of the finest dye-stuff, purple (perhaps they sold other colours too). A remarkable group of inscriptions from Rome in the late Republic and early empire reveals a group of freedmen families, men and women, of the Veturii, engaged in the trade, and stemming from more than one patron; with them is associated another family, the Plutii. The precise connections cannot now be traced, but it looks as if some of the women may have begun in the trade as slaves (perhaps even as *institores* or their *contubernales*) and continued after freedom.[17] Whether any of the firms in question were actually in competition with their patrons is not known. Alfenus Varus and Scaevola held different opinions as to whether patrons were entitled to demand that their freedmen should refrain from competition with them; Scaevola held that they were not. This opinion seems to have prevailed, and Papinian says, 'A freedwoman is not considered ungrateful because she practises her trade against the wishes of her patron.'[18]

Firm evidence of women as actual practitioners of crafts is rather scanty. Women are attested in connection with a number of productive crafts, either alone or with their husbands.[19] Whether they were actually engaged themselves in production or merely, like the dealers in beans, vegetables, etc., in retailing the product, cannot now be determined. Where the Latin description actually specifies the activity and not merely the commodity (as, e.g., *sarcinatrix*, 'seamstress') the likelihood is that the woman herself practised the craft. The total number of examples and the range of crafts so attested are both small, and it is not really possible to reach any conclusions as to the extent to which, if at all, freeborn daughters received any training in crafts other than those of the household before they were married. Widows may sometimes have carried on a husband's business but left its actual conduct to managers. The same is possibly true of some of the 21 female *officinatores* leasing clay-yards near Rome. Three are operating jointly with men, probably their husbands. At least one, Nunnidia Sperata, seems to have succeeded her father in the tenancy. We need not suppose that she herself actually took part in making the bricks, tiles or pottery produced.[20]

There was no bar in law to husband and wife forming a business partnership (*societas*), even if she contributed only money and was otherwise a 'sleeping' partner. It was not a gift, since she was entitled to a share of the profits; nor did the partnership violate the *sctum. Velleianum*, since the Roman law of contract did not allow undertakings affecting a third party, and since the partners were liable only to the extent of their contributions to the common fund. If a husband chose to use his wife's dowry for a *societas* (whether with his wife or anyone else), the claims of the dowry took precedence over those of creditors.[21]

As is well known, women are attested as patrons, but not as members, of guilds (*collegia*), other than one or two all-female groups, such as an association of mime-actresses in Rome or nine slave *ornatrices*, not specified as a 'college' but belonging to different owners, at Ostia.[22] There is no positive evidence for their exclusion. The lack of examples may be a result of their relatively smaller numbers and also of their having in many cases given up their work on marriage.

Professions

Women are better attested in certain professional jobs. Commonest are the midwives, of whom there are only a few mentions in papyri but rather more, both slave and freed (or free) in inscriptions. Some may have learned their trade as slaves in large households, others perhaps as apprentices to professionals. The law recognised their professional status; a provincial governor might be called upon to give judgment on their fees, as on those of doctors, scribes and accountants.[23]

Several female scribes and secretaries are known, none certainly freeborn.[24] More striking is the number of female doctors (*iatromeae, medicae*) attested from all over the Roman world. One or two are explicitly attested as freedwomen; most could be. However, Asyllia Polia (*sic*) from first-century A.D. Carthage is *L(uci) f(ilia)*, and a fragmentary inscription from Metz in Belgica seems to attest another freeborn *medica*. Were they apprenticed to professionals, or did they perhaps learn in the family? We do not know. There are some husband-and-wife teams. The wife may sometimes have been essentially a midwife, like Scribonia Attice, wife of M. Ulpius Amerinus; their respective activities are attested in a pair of reliefs from Ostia. The stone commemorating a *medica* in Spain, Julia Saturnina, has on the back a carving of a baby in swaddling-clothes.[25]

Some references, however, suggest a wider competence. Antiochis from Tlos in Lycia is commemorated for her knowledge of the physician's art (*iatrike techne*), and Domnina from Neoclaudiopolis 'warded off diseases'. It may not have been very common for women to receive a general medical training and to practise. One doctor husband, commemorating his wife in Pergama in the second century A.D., wrote, 'Woman though you were, you were not deficient in my art.' Two centuries later, a similar sense of the unusual is detectable in Ausonius' praise of his maternal aunt Aemilia Hilaria, a 'dedicated virgin' (*virgo devota*) who 'occupied herself in the art of healing, like a man'. (Aunt Aemilia, we are also told, was called Hilaria because of her boyish cheerfulness, even in the cradle, and she 'hated the female sex'.) We do not know how she acquired her training; and if she actually practised for gain outside the household, that would be still more unusual in a woman of her class.[26]

Personal Services

Some jobs, such as masseuse (*unctrix*), dresser (*vestiplica*) and attendant (*pedisequa*), seem to have been performed entirely by women working within private households either as slaves or as freedwomen of the household.[27] The latter two, at any rate, may not have required any particular training and by their nature did not give scope for the acquisition of a marketable skill.

Ornatrix (hairdresser) was a skilled job, for which training was required; jurists discussed whether or not trainees should be included when a legacy specified *ornatrices*. There are some examples of freedwomen apparently plying the trade commercially, though no certain examples of freeborn women so engaged. Perhaps the job had servile connotations which made freeborn girls unwilling to train.[28]

On the other hand, freeborn women could and did offer themselves for work for which no qualification, other than that of having borne a child, was required, namely wet-nursing. Here the different nature of the evidence of inscriptions (especially from Rome) and of papyri presents different aspects of the picture.[29]

Those commemorated epigraphically were often the servants of a large household; by the time of their deaths, they may no longer have been so, or at least no longer have been fulfilling that particular function, though gratefully remembered for it. For instance, the freedwoman Birria Cognita, nurse of Publius Birrius Gallus, is unlikely still to have been employed in that capacity when she died at the age of 60 (*AE* 1980: 326).

Strictly speaking, the *nutrix* was a wet-nurse, but some of the women of whom the term is used may also in effect have served as nanny (*educatrix*) in the household once the baby was weaned. This is likely to have been the case of those recorded as having been nurse to several children. With the *educatrix* from Verona who reared four of the commemorator's children we may compare Rasinia Pietas, who set up an honorific inscription to her employer the consul L. Burbulius Optatus Ligarianus, describing herself as 'nurse of his daughters'. Tatia Baucyl(. . .) was nurse to no less than seven of the children of Flavius Clemens and Flavia Domitilla. Rasinia could have been the slave of Burbulius' wife, so accounting for the difference in name. Tatia, Treggiari suggests (1976: 88), might have been a free, paid nurse; this is more likely than that she was a slave whose reward for nursing all those children was not freedom but sale to another master.[30]

The wealthy, Tacitus and Juvenal suggest, employed wet-nurses as a matter of course, while the poor could not afford to. While some writers expressed doubts about the moral desirability of the practice, it was recognised that physical circumstances sometimes made it necessary. In a curious fragment of a letter written in the third century A.D., an interfering mother-in-law (or possibly father-in-law) writes to a certain Rufinus: 'I have heard that you are compelling her to breast-feed. Please let the child have a nurse. I do not permit my daughter to suckle.' The reasons for the objection are not given, but one suspects snobbishness.[31]

While the wealthiest would have an adequate supply of nurses among their own female slaves, those slightly less well-off would hire, as and when need arose. The practice is attested in the *Digest*. Wet-nurses were listed (D. 50.13.1.14) among those jobs for which praetors and provincial magistrates could be asked to adjudicate on the fees; however, it seems that their jurisdiction was limited to actual wet-nursing and not to general child care (*educatio*). Paul (D. 24.1.28.1) refers to a husband paying sums of money *pro capite* to a woman rearing the children of the slave-girls from his wife's dowry. She is apparently not part of his household and may be free. She sounds rather like a child-minder or fosterer, to whom the babies may have been farmed out, leaving the *ancillae* free to get on with their work. One Egyptian document from the very beginning of the fourth century (*P. Grenf*. 2.75) records the receipt of money for food and clothing by a woman who nursed 'the fourth part of the slave children'. She and her employer are both said to be funeral undertakers. It sounds as though both had sidelines, he as dealer in foundling slaves, she as wet-nurse. Whether she carried out her duties on his premises or at home is not stated. In many of the wet-nursing contracts for individual children from Roman Egypt, it is specified that the child is to stay with the nurse at her house, rather than the latter come to the mother or owner's. Sometimes there is a clause providing for regular inspection of the child.

Soranus (*Gynaec*. 2.19) gives detailed instructions for gauging the suitability of a wet-nurse from the appearance of her breasts. Whether free candidates for the job were usually required to submit to physical examination we cannot tell; it is quite likely that slaves were. He gives reasons for avoiding a drunken wet-nurse. The drink will affect the child through the milk; it will also endanger the child, by making the nurse careless and inattentive. He specified, as do several contracts of hire from Roman Egypt, that the nurse should refrain from sexual intercourse. His reasons are partly psychological (diversion of affection from the nursling) and partly physiological — intercourse, he says, is likely either to stimulate menstruation to start again or to cause conception; in both cases the milk will be spoiled or diminished.

Festus (second century A.D.), our sole source on the matter, says that a column in the Roman produce market, the *Forum Holitorium*, was called the *Columna Lactaria*, *quod ibi infantes lacte alendos deferebant*, 'because there they used to *deferre* infants who required feeding with milk'.[32] To how distant a past he referred we do not know, nor what exactly took place, since *deferre* is susceptible of several meanings. It is commonly used to mean 'hand over'. The column may have been a regular hiring place for wet-nurses, but it does not seem altogether plausible to suppose that babies would be brought there on the off-chance, the whole business of examination and determination of suitability of the available women be gone through there and then among the vegetables, and the baby handed over to a stranger; the home either of parent or of nurse would seem a more likely place for the transfer.

Some of the nurses in the Egyptian contracts are slaves, hired out by their owner, but most are free women, some married. Some of the babies are free, but several are foundlings, 'from the dunghill', who will be reared as slaves. The length of hire varies between six months and three years, with two years most common. It is regularly specified that the nurse is not to have intercourse nor get pregnant, nor nurse another child. These conditions, especially the first two, would not be easy to enforce, and it may be doubted whether the free nurses intended to observe them. With effective contraception, they might get away with it. The wages were not high — seven to ten drachmae a month in the first century A.D., 16–20 in the second. A female slave hired out to a weaver (the one required for night-time baking) brought her owner 420 drachmae a year; another was to have wages of 20 drachmae a month in her fourth year of apprenticeship. During the short olive-harvesting season, around A.D. 100, men pickers could earn up to a drachma a day, boys up to 4 obols; the women's wage is not known, but a woman was able to raise a loan of 16 drachmae, to be repaid in instalments out of her daily wages carrying olives at the oil-press, 'at the same rate as the carriers in the village'.[33]

If the child dies, the nurse is to accept another (or, in some instances, possibly provide one — presumably from the dunghill) and work out the contract, or repay the balance of the money.

A family would have to be fairly badly-off for money to undertake a nursing contract on such terms, especially as there were usually heavy penalties for breach of contract (at least another 50 per cent on the balance), and these were enforced. In 4 B.C. at Alexandria M. Julius Felix, a freedman, took back from Eugenia and her *kyrios*, possibly her husband, a slave child to be reared by his own slave. He acknowledges return of the 12 months' maintenance she had already received from him; the claim outstanding is for what was paid in advance, plus the 50 per cent and damages and expenses. The year before, a woman called Apollonia had to return a child to one Harpocration, because her milk was spoiled. She appears to have been looking after the child for some time without any formal contract before an agreement was made; nevertheless, she agrees not only to return the money already received (some eight months' worth) but to pay a penalty as well. If the hirer, on the other hand, withdrew the child, without fault on the nurse's part, she was entitled to the balance of the contracted fee.[34]

The lengths to which a woman might go to avoid forfeiting her fee are revealed in a sad little story of a case that came before the district magistrate at Oxyrhynchus in A.D. 49: Pesuris against the woman Saraeus.[35]

Pesuris' advocate Aristocles states his case:

In the year III of our lord Tiberius Claudius Caesar (i.e., six years previously) Pesuris whom I represent took a male child from the dunghill and called him Heraclas. He handed him over to our adversary and a nursing contract was made in the name of Pesuris' son. She received the nursing fee for the first year. On the due day she received payment for the second year. Here in evidence is her written receipt. When the boy was weaned Pesuris took him back. Then, finding an opportunity, she burst into my client's house, snatched the child and is trying to retain him on the grounds that he is free. I have the initial nursing contract and the receipt for the second instalment.

Saraeus' statement is brief:

I weaned my own boy before the one belonging to these people was handed over to me. I received from them the whole eight staters. Then the boy dies when (number missing) staters were outstanding. Now they are trying to take my own boy from me. A man called Theon adds: 'We have the writings concerning the boy.'

The magistrate gives his decision:

Since from his appearance the boy appears to be Saraeus' child, if Saraeus and her husband give a sworn affidavit that the child handed over to them by Pesuris died, then, in accordance with the prefect's decree I order that she return the money received and keep her son.

The timing is obscure, but what happened is fairly clear. Saraeus did not own up to the child's death, but let Pesuris take her own son, so that she could keep the money. Then, possibly after waiting some considerable time, she managed to snatch him back. The magistrate's decision is fairly lenient. There is no indication that Saraeus has to pay any penalty. True, she had been deprived of her son for some time; but during that time he had been fed and clothed at Pesuris' expense.

Leisure and Pleasure

Purveyors of wine, women and song — that is to say, those engaged in entertainment, catering and prostitution — were in general not highly regarded in Roman society. The praetor's edict declared entertainers and prostitutes subject to *infamia*, and catering tended to be associated with prostitution. Under Augustus, as already mentioned, senators were forbidden marriage with them, and a *senatusconsultum* from the time of Tiberius forbade members of senatorial and equestrian families to perform on stage or as gladiators. It was a black mark against Nero that, amongst his other excesses and enormities, he obliged people of rank to do both.

Entertainment

Some entertainers, nevertheless, could make a good living. An actor on the legitimate stage, such as the celebrated Roscius, might be on friendly terms with leading citizens. Roscius was reputed to earn enormous fees; Cicero, in a speech on his behalf, remarks that even a certain female dancer, Dionysia, could earn 200,000 sesterces — he does not say over what period. In Rome, actors and entertainers seem mainly to have been organised in troupes and to have been slaves or freedmen. Pliny's friend, the lively old lady Ummidia Quadratilla, kept her own private company of entertainers; her strait-laced grandson was encouraged to avoid witnessing their performances. For those not in the service of a great house, making a living was a more precarious business, though, as this was a luxury trade, and the supply of performers perhaps limited, they could ask, and get, more than ordinary workers. A few contracts from Roman Egypt record engagements of small groups of entertainers to perform at local festivals in the countryside. Two in particular, from the third century, in each case for two dancers, offer a fee of 36 drachmae a day for the pair plus, in one instance, food, transport and safe-keeping for the artistes' costumes and jewellery. This is a good deal more than the wage of, say, a weaver, but the employment would be a good deal less regular.[36]

Women singers, dancers and musicians are known, performing both on public occasions and at private functions. They provided a cabaret at the livelier Roman dinner-parties. Pliny (*Ep.* 1.15) twits a friend for turning down his own invitation to a plain meal and such intellectual delights as a literary reading or a singer, in favour of luxurious victuals and Spanish dancing-girls. The dancing-girls from Spain, and specifically those from Cadiz, were famous. Their act seems, from the descriptions of Martial, to have been a designedly erotic kind of belly-dance, 'enough to make Hippolytus himself masturbate'.[37]

Women did not appear on the 'legitimate' stage, but only as mime-actresses. Horace brackets them with prostitutes, in discussing men's various sexual preferences. They seem, like prostitutes, to have had little protection or chance of redress against sexual molestation. When Cn. Plancius was prosecuted for electoral bribery in 54 B.C., part of the routine character-assassination by the prosecution was the allegation that as a young man he had been involved in a gang assault on a mime-actress at Atina. Cicero, speaking for the defence, does not deny this; he merely brushes it aside, as happening *vetere quodam in scaenicos iure, maximeque oppidano*. 'It is an old tradition to allow such treatment of stage-players, specially in the country towns.' Already for the late Republic it was customary for the audiences at mime performances, at any rate at the *ludi Florales*, to make loud demands for the *mimae* to 'take them off', and for the women to comply and strip.[38]

Those performers known to us by name were slaves or freed-women, with names usually of Greek origin. Some of these seem to have been more or less appropriate stage names, such as Eucharis, 'charm', Paizusa, 'playful'. Eucharis, already a freedwoman when she died at the age of 14 in the late Republic, was commemorated by her (unnamed) father who praises her education and training 'as if at the Muses' hand' and represents her as saying: 'I graced the games of the nobles with my dancing and first appeared before the common people in a Greek play.' The claim is not that she was the first mime actress to appear in Rome; mimes had been performed since the third century B.C., and there is an epigram from the second century B.C. on the departure of a Greek actress for Italy. The innovation, possibly dating to the time of Eucharis' own brief career, may have been the introduction of certain mime plots from Alexandria. Eucharis' skill as a dancer is eulogised, and the whole tenor of the epitaph is to emphasise the high-class nature of her accomplishments and of the milieu in which she exercised them. It is particularly stated that she appeared in 'the games of the nobles', which probably means not the regular public games in honour of various gods given by aediles and urban praetor, but privately sponsored games, either votive (as on the occasion of the celebration of a triumph or the dedication of a public building from the spoils of campaigning) or funerary. Her owner was a woman, Licinia, but from which of the contemporary great families of that name is not known.[39]

Some women fought as gladiators; Domitian encouraged this. An inscription from Ostia refers to games given there, probably during the reign of Septimius Severus, by the local *duumvir*, Hostilianus, and his wife. These included women sword-fighters. In some respect, Hostilianus claims a 'first' with these games; in regard to the women gladiators, they may have been among the last. Septimius issued an edict banning single combat by women in the arena. In the early empire, performing in the arena or on the stage held an attraction for some upper-class men and women. In A.D. 19, Tiberius banned them from doing so, and part of the text of the *senatusconsultum* passed at the time has been found at Larinum. From this it appears that some people had actually deliberately contrived to incur *infamia*, either from a criminal conviction or in some other way, so as to forfeit the status of their rank and be able to pursue their passion. (One is reminded of the women who registered as prostitutes in an attempt to evade the adultery law.) Since *infamia* was not enough, additional penalties are prescribed, such as denial of a funeral — however, this will not be inflicted on the sons or daughters of those who are actors, trainers, gladiators or bawds. The text also refers to an earlier *senatusconsultum*, passed under Augustus in A.D. 11, which laid down that, unless under compulsion (apparently as a punishment) by the emperor, freeborn women under the age of 20 and men under 25 were not to offer their services for the arena, the stage or any other 'filthy source of gain' (*spurcos quaestus*). Nevertheless, there were those who persisted. Juvenal satirises the unfeminine (and, he suggests, unfaithful) wife who cannot resist at least training as a gladiator; and Nero, as already indicated, flouted the prescriptions of his predecessors. A recrudescence among some upper-class women, and the raillery this provoked among the audience was, according to Dio, what provoked Septimius to ban all women from taking part in such displays.[40]

Enthusiasm for less bloody forms of exercise, however, did not attract the same moral opprobrium. Sabinus and Cassius, jurists of the time of Tiberius, gave it as their opinion that the stigma inflicted by the praetor's edict on actors and gladiators should not be held to apply to athletes. Women athletes are known from the Greek part of the empire. An inscription of A.D. 45 honours several women, citizens of Tralles, who have won victories at Greek games, mostly for foot-racing, but including apparently a chariot-race in armour(?).[41]

Catering

The social life of the Roman upper classes was conducted for the most part in their own homes, with entertainment provided by domestic or hired performers and food and drink catered for by the household staff. Hence, no doubt, much of the distaste evinced in literature for the public bars, taverns and eating houses (*tabernae, cauponae, popinae*). They were regarded as rather shady and seamy places, like Catullus' *salax taberna* (37.1), not only centres and meeting places for those interested in promoting and arranging commercial sex, but also, in the eyes of the authorities, potentially dangerous as meeting places for disruptive social elements.[42]

Successive emperors tried to reduce their attractiveness. Tiberius instructed aediles to put restrictions on cookshops and eating-houses (*popinas ganeasque*); not even fancy pastries, says Suetonius (*Tib.* 34) were to be shown for sale. Claudius pursued a rather erratic course. Despite his affectionate memories of the *tabernae* where he went to drink wine in his younger days, he issued an edict abolishing them, and forbidding the sale of cooked meats and hot water in eating-houses. However, he is said to have banished a senator who fined tenants on Claudius' own estates for violating this ban, and also took the *popinae* out of the jurisdiction of the aediles. By the time of Nero, *popinae* were again offering a wide menu; he forbade the sale of cooked foods other than pulse and vegetables. Vespasian issued a similar ruling. Clearly, none of these measures was effective; the social life of the bars and restaurants continued.[43]

It was taken for granted that in many of these establishments, particularly the *cauponae*, which also had accommodation available, the women waitresses were also working as prostitutes. Alexander Severus, as already mentioned, ruled that a buyer could not evade a ban on prostitution of a female slave he had purchased by claiming that she was working as a waitress; the two were regarded as synonymous.[44]

The women attested epigraphically, either directly in such establishments, as at Pompeii, or in occasional funerary inscriptions, mostly are referred to by one name only, and could be either slaves or freedwomen; one or two are freedwomen, and married. Some were proprietors, some *institores*, some (probably slaves) were waitresses.[45]

An interesting inscription was found near the Via Latina, between Aquinum and Casinum, at the location of an ancient sanctuary of Venus:[46]

> Flacceia Lais, freedwoman of Aulus, Orbia Lais, freedwoman of Orbia, Cominia Philocaris, freedwoman of Marcus, Centuria Thais, freedwoman of Quintus, set up a kitchen (*culina*) for Venus, at their own cost; concession revocable.

The four freedwomen have apparently been granted what nowadays would be called a concession or franchise to run an eating house for the benefit of visitors to the sanctuary. As the most recent editor observes (*AE* 1980.216) their *cognomina* are typical of prostitutes, and the likelihood is that they 'did business with their bodies as with their table'.

There are some intriguing features about the arrangement. The women specify that they set up the establishment *de suo*, 'at their own expense'. In other words, they are not *institores* but proprietors. How did the four, formerly slaves of four different owners, meet and form close enough links to wish to set up in business together? They may have met after gaining their freedom; or perhaps their owners had hired them out, to a brothel-keeper or (in view of the catering connection) the proprietor of a *caupona*. Ulpian more than once in the *Digest* recognises that some people maintained an appearance of respectability while deriving income indirectly from prostitution. 'Brothels', he says, 'are operated (by tenants) on properties belonging to many men of rank.' Elsewhere, he remarks that a woman may be classed as a bawd, not only if she personally runs prostitutes but if she does so through the agency of a third party.[47]

However they met, the four women, once freed, set up in business together — possibly one of the world's earliest examples of a women's co-operative!

Prostitution

Some aspects of the law affecting the prostitute's personal life have already been mentioned — e.g., they and their pimps were subject to *infamia* under the praetor's edict. They were exempt from Augustus' adultery law, but unable to marry freeborn citizens or receive inheritances in full. Domitian forbade them the use of litters, and they had less protection than respectable women against sexual harassment.

They were apparently required to register with the aedile, the magistrate responsible for public order. This emerges not only from the references already cited to women registering as prostitutes in an attempt to evade the adultery law, but also from a story cited by Gellius on the authority of the late Republican historian Ateius Capito.[48] A curule aedile, Aulus Hostilius Mancinus, brought suit before the people against a *meretrix* called Manilia, on the grounds that he had been struck and wounded by a stone thrown at night from her apartment. Manilia appealed to the tribunes. Her story was that Hostilius had come to her house at night 'as a reveller' (*commissator*), and so presumably somewhat the worse the wear for drink. She thought it against her interest to let him in. He tried to break in, and was driven off with stones. The tribunes refused to allow Hostilius to proceed with his case, on the grounds that he had quite rightly been driven off from 'that place to which it had not been seemly for him to come wearing a garland'.

The implication is that it was quite proper for an aedile to visit the premises of known prostitutes in the course of his duties, and that he had on such occasions a right of entry. The purpose of registration of prostitutes was presumably so that those premises could be identified on which it was desirable, in the interests of public order, for the aedile to keep a watchful eye. In other words, it was a police operation. There seems to have been no other particular purpose. The activities of prostitutes were not banned by the law, there was no compulsory health inspection, as in some modern states, and, at the time of the story, taxes on prostitution do not yet seem to have been imposed.

Those expected to register as prostitutes were presumably all those, whether operating from fixed premises or not, whose sole or principal source of income came from offering themselves for sale to any paying member of the public. Later, as we have seen, whether a woman was or was not categorised as a prostitute had financial and social consequences for her. Women working in *tabernae*, it is plain from Ulpian's comment (D. 23.2.43), were not registered as prostitutes; nevertheless, he thought, for the purposes of implementation of the *lex Julia et Papia*, both they and their employers ought to be regarded as coming under its terms, just as much as those working in brothels. From the point of view of the aedile and the problems of keeping public order (and also for proof in lawsuits alleging assault), it could be important to be able to establish that what was going on under an archway or in a dark alley was merely a prostitute servicing her client.

Dress could be an indicator of whether a woman was a prostitute. An offence under the edict prohibiting sexual harassment was considered considerably less severe if the women had been dressed, not in the customary long robe of a respectable woman but in the more showy garb favoured by prostitutes, and aped, according to Martial and Juvenal, by loose-living society ladies — typically, bright colours, a tunic showing part of their legs, diaphanous fabrics and a toga instead of the customary cloak. Elaborate hairdressing and make-up were part of the self-presentation for the better-class whores.[49]

It is often repeated that prostitutes were *obliged* to wear this style of dress. The source for most of the statements is probably either scholiasts on Horace, or Marquardt (1886). Marquardt cites a treatise of Heineccius, *ad legem Juliam et Papiam*.[50] In fact, most of the literary references merely state that particular styles were worn by prostitutes. The inference that they were obliged to wear them may have been drawn from one or two passages in the poets. Martial (10.52) wrotes: 'Numa saw the eunuch Thelys wearing a toga, and remarked that he was a condemned adulteress.'

Again, Juvenal (2.68): 'Fabulla is an adulteress; suppose Carfinia were to be convicted as well; even if she were, she would not take on the toga.'

From these texts the conclusion drawn, and repeated even in recent commentaries,[51] is that women convicted of adultery, like prostitutes, were compelled to adopt this garb. In fact, Juvenal envisages the possibility that one woman at least could get away with not doing so. In another epigram (2.39) Martial remarks on the expensive presents that an acquaintance is sending to a notorious adulteress. 'If you want to give her what she really deserves, send her a toga.' (In other words, tell her that you think she is a whore.) Convicted adulteresses were forbidden marriage with freeborn citizens, under the Augustan law. In these circumstances, some women, especially among the upper classes, may have preferred to remain unmarried and either become full-time prostitutes or at least advertise their availability by dressing immodestly.

It would hardly seem necessary to compel prostitutes to adopt a style of dress different from that of other women. After all, it pays to advertise. There is no firm evidence that they were prevented from wearing the modest, concealing garments usually associated with Roman matrons, and one possible hint that some of them sometimes did. One line survives of a play by the writer of mimes T. Quinctius Atta, who flourished about 100 B.C.[52] The title, *Aquae Caldae* ('Hot Springs') indicates that the setting is one of the fashionable resorts around the Bay of Naples. A character remarks, *cum nostro ornatu per vias meretricie lupantur*: 'They are hunting harlot-fashion through the streets in our attire.'

Unfortunately, this is ambiguous. Who is speaking? It could be a Roman husband, complaining that in the lax atmosphere of the resort married women are parading around dressed like whores, *nostro ornatu*, wearing the toga. Or it could be a Roman matron, complaining that the tarts are giving themselves airs and dressing like respectable women. Either offers scope for comic complications.

High-class courtesans and kept women might receive large sums of money and lavish presents in kind, but ordinary prostitutes would charge by the bout. Prices quoted in Pompeii range from two asses (most common) to 16 asses.[53] Caligula was the first to levy a tax. The rate was a prostitute's fee from one encounter, and a rider made it retrospective on former prostitutes and their pimps. The incidence of the tax is not stated in Suetonius (*Gaius* 40), but it may have been monthly.

At Socnopaiou Nesos, in the Fayum, collection of the tax was farmed out in A.D. 46 for the sum of 288 drachmae and two jars of wine. An inscription from Palmyra, dated A.D. 137, sets out the scale of levy. Prostitutes charging six asses a time pay six asses, those charging eight asses pay eight, those charging a denarius or more pay one denarius. In Egypt, in A.D. 142, a Roman official signed a licence issued to a prostitute by the *tel(onai) hetairikou* (collectors of prostitute tax).[54] Egypt was notoriously bureaucratic, but the existence of this text suggests the obvious point that at Rome, from Gaius' time at least, it may have been found desirable to enquire more closely into the activities of women of no other obvious source of income, who might be registered and become liable to the tax — but that no doubt depended on the zealousness of those responsible.

At Rome, Gaius took the collection of that and his other new taxes out of the hands of the publicans and had them collected directly by the centurions and tribunes of the praetorian guard. As we have seen, that was not the system used in Egypt, and at Palmyra collection seems to have been in the hands of a tax-farmer. However, in the Crimean Chersonese in A.D. 185/6 soldiers from the Roman garrison were collecting the tax from the local town. The townspeople complained to the emperor about harassment by the troops doing the collection. The tax may have been used, in that area at least, directly to meet the expenses of the local garrison. In the second quarter of the third century, Alexander Severus decided to devote the proceeds to repair of various public buildings at Rome.[55]

Notes

1. *ESAR* V. 272; D. 3.5.31 acknowledges women's right to transact business.
2. Buckland (1966) 533–5; Crook (1967a) 188–9. See especially *Inst*. IV.6.8–10; IV.7.4.

3. G. I. 192; Ulp. *Reg.* 1.27; Schulz (1951) 190; Taubenschlag (1955) 177–8; Buckland (1966) 167.

4. *Frag. Vat.* 325, 327.

5. Solazzi (1953); Buckland (1966) 448; Kaser (1971) 667.

6. These points were cogently made in Crook (1982). I am grateful to Professor Crook for his making available to me a copy of this unpublished paper. Similarly, children *in potestate* would in theory have been excluded from commercial life by the *sctum. Macedonianum*, which denied action to those who lent them money; in practice, *exceptio* was allowed: Buckland (1966) 465; Kaser (1971) 532.

7. Paul: D. 16.1.1.1. Ulpian: D. 16.1.2.1; he cites (*ibid.* 2–3) rescripts of Pius and Severus denying the protection of the *sctum.* in case of fraud, with the comment, 'For it was the weakness (*infirmitas*) of women, not their cunning, that deserved protection.'

8. D. 2.13.12; 34.2.32.4; *CIL* VI. 5184; Treggiari (1975b) 68, n.91.

9. D. 2.13.4; 10; Buckland (1966) 703. Action on deposit: G. IV. 64. On private lending in the late Republic, see Shatzman (1975) 75–83. Loans, both with and without interest, are mentioned several times in Pliny: *Ep.* 2.4; 3.11; 3.19; 6.8.

10. *Inst.* IV.6.8; RE I A. 372 ff. This was distinct from the *actio de pecunia constituta* covering payment only of existing debts, which was available against women (D. 13.5.1.1).

11. Shatzman (1975) 416–20 finds two women to whom Cicero owed money and one who owed him some. The emperor Antoninus was approached for advice in A.D. 212 by a soldier who was having trouble with a female creditor — possibly a pawnbroker — who had refused to accept his repayment and return the pledge (C. 4.32.6). For Faustilla, see Chapter 2, note 56, above; for Otacilia, Chapter 4, note 22.

12. D. 17.2.59 pr.; 48.2.1 and 2; 49.14.16; 18 pr.; 47 pr.; Klingenberg (1983) 146 ff. Severus and Antoninus made a similar exception on the grounds of 'public good' for accusations relating to the state-controlled food supplies (*annona*): D. 48.2.13.

13. *P. Wisc.* 5; Biezunska-Malowist (1977) 88–9.

14. The Statilii: Treggiari (1976) 82 ff.; elsewhere (1979a: 69) she suggests that they were involved also in commercial production.

15. The evidence used by Moeller (1976) to identify the supposed commercial purposes of buildings is sometimes slight and should be treated with caution; a 'minimising' study is forthcoming (Finley 1985: 194 and 257 n. 73).

Of 13 weaving contracts from Egypt studied by Zambon (1935), ten were for male pupils, of whom at least eight were free; the three females were all slaves. The terms vary, depending, e.g., on whether the trainee lives with the weaver or not. Wages are sometimes payable on a graduated scale as the apprenticeship progresses; again there is great individual variation in the terms. See also *ESAR* II. 389–91; Hengstl (1972) 87 ff.; Straus (1977) 76–7.

16. Treggiari (1976) 85. Few are attested outside Rome: e.g. *CIL* V. 2542 (Cisalpine Gaul); VIII. 10938 (Mauretania Caesariensis).

17. Treggiari (1979a) 71–2.

18. D. 37.15.11; 38.1.26 pr.; 45.

19. E.g., *CIL* III. 2117 (lead-work); V. 7023 (nails); VI. 6939, 9211 (gold-leaf work); cf. Treggiari (1979a) 66, 70 ff.; Kampen (1981) 125 ff.

20. Helen (1975) 112, 123.

21. G. III. 148–54; D. 17.2, especially 5.1; 27; 65.10; 66; 82; C. 4.37.1; Buckland (1966) 426, 506 ff.; Kaser (1971) 572 ff.

22. *Ornatrices*: *CIL* XIV. 5306; *Mimae*: *CIL* VI. 10109; Waltzing (1895) I. 348.

23. Midwives in papyri: commentary on *P. Oxy.* LI. 3620; in inscriptions: Kampen (1981) 116–7 and notes; *AE* 1980. 936 (Africa). Fees: D. 50.13.1.1–3, 6.

According to Paul, *Sent.* 2.24.9, it was a capital offence for a midwife to introduce a supposititious child.

24. Scribes and secretaries: Treggiari (1976) 78; Kampen (1981) 118 and notes 49–50; *AE* 1982.46.

25. *CIL* II. 497, VIII. 24679, XIII. 4334; Pleket (1969) nos. 20, 27; Kampen (1981) 70, 116, 140 (Cat. I. 6), 143 (Cat. II. 16).

26. Pleket (1969) nos. 12, 20, 26; Ausonius, *Parentalia* 6. Domnina also apparently shunned marriage: Pleket no. 26.

27. Kampen (1981) 120–1.

28. D. 32.65.3; Treggiari (1976) 101 n. 13.

29. RE XVII. 2.1497–8; Treggiari (1976) 88 ff.; Kampen (1981) 109–10. For wet-nursing contracts from Egypt, see *ESAR* II. 286–90; Herrmann (1959); Adams (1964) 146–65; Hengstl (1972) 61–9; van Lith (1974); Biezunska-Malowist (1977) 105 and n. 138; Bradley (1980).

30. *Educatrix: CIL* V. 3519; VI. 9792; Rasinia: *CIL* X. 6006; Tatia: *CIL* VI. 8942.

31. Juv. *Sat.* VI 592–3; Tac. *Germ.* 19; Gell. *N.A.* 12.1 (the philosopher Favorinus lecturing a senator's wife); *P. Lond.* III 951 *verso* (the mother-in-law).

32. Paul *ex. Fest.* 88.

33. Weavers' wages: *P. Wisc.* 5; *P. Oxy.* 1647. Olive-gatherers: *P. Fay.* 91 and 102.

34. BGU 1110, 1112.

35. *FIRA* III no. 170 (= *P. Oxy.* 37).

36. Cic. *pro Rosc. Com.* 23 with Gell. *N.A.* 1.5.3; Pliny, *Ep.* 7.24; *Cornell Pap. Inv.* 26; *P. Grenf.* II. 67; Westermann (1924); Adams (1964) 166–92.

37. Mart. 14.203; see also 5.78, 6.71, 11.16.

38. Hor. *Sat.* 1.2.58; Cic. *pro Plancio* 30; Val. Max. 2.10.8; Lact. *Div. Inst.* 1.20.10 (who remarks that at that time prostitutes fulfilled the role of actresses); Wiseman (1985) 11–12.

39. Beare (1964) 152, 166; Garton (1964); Wiseman (1985) 32–4. Eucharis: *CIL* I². 1214 = VI. 10096.

40. Juvenal 6.111, 246 ff.; Suet. *Dom.* 4.2; Tac. *Ann.* 15.32; Dio 76.16; *AE* 1978. 145; Cebeillac-Gervasoni and Zevi (1976); Levick (1983).

41. D.3.2.4 pr.; Pleket (1969) no. 9.

42. For detailed studies of these establishments, see Kleberg (1957); Hermansen (1981) 185–206.

43. Suetonius *Cl.* 38, 40, *Nero* 16; Dio 60.6.6–7; 62.14.2; 65.10.3.

44. C. 4.56.3.

45. Kleberg (1957) 74–6; D'Avino (1967) 14–21, 30–2.

46. *AE* 1975.197; 1980.216. That they were concessionary tenants is shown by the phrase *loco precario*; on *precarium*, see D. 43.26; Buckland (1966) 524–5; Kaser (1971) 388–9.

47. D. 5.3.27.1; 23.2.43.7–8.

48. Tac. *Ann.* 2.85; Suet. *Tib.* 35; Gell. *N.A.* 4.14. Hostilius was probably aedile in 151 B.C.: Broughton (1951–2) I. 455.

49. Details and literary references are given in RE XV. 1025–6.

50. Scholiasts on Horace, *Sat.* 1.2.63; Marquardt (1886) 42 n. 7.

51. Those of Courtney (1980) on Juvenal and Norcio (1980) on Martial.

52. *CRF*². 160; RE XXIV. 1009–10.

53. Duncan-Jones (1982) 246.

54. *P. Grenf.* 2.41 pp. 67–8; *C.I.S.* II. 3, Inv. 3913; Dessau (1884) 517–8; *ESAR* IV. 183; SB VI. 9545, 33.

55. *CIL* III. 13570; *SHA Alex. Sev.* 24; Lopuszanski (1951) 10–12.

12 The Emancipation of Roman Women

The title of this chapter is ambiguous. The question with which it will mainly be concerned is whether Roman women were 'emancipated' in the sense of possessing a notably high degree of economic and social independence and self-determination. A distinct but related question is whether this could be said to have been achieved during the classical period through any deliberate, traceable process.

The trouble with attempting to answer such questions is that the definition of an 'emancipated' woman varies in relation to the personal historical experience and expectations of the observer. For Cornelius Nepos, at the very end of the Republic, the salient contrast was with Greek women, who customarily stayed secluded at home, while Roman women actually accompanied their husbands to dinner parties at the homes of other men, and joined in when they entertained guests at home (Nepos, *Lives*, Preface). For an English writer at the end of the last century, Roman women in the time of Juvenal were 'entirely independent, they could do as they pleased, go where they liked without comment, and were mistresses of their fortune and estates', and, what was more, they could divorce their husbands 'at pleasure' (Dale 1894: 492, 495).

In 1894, freedom from the obligation to cohabit, financial autonomy, power to divorce — all were recently won gains for married English women. Only three years before the publication of that article, in 1891, an English civil court for the first time intervened to prevent a husband from compelling his wife, by restraint, to remain in his house against her will.[1] An Act of 1857 had made it possible for a civil court to grant divorce, but the only ground was adultery, and that of a husband must be 'aggravated' — i.e., combined with incest, bigamy, rape, sodomy, bestiality, cruelty or desertion. It was nearly 70 years more (until 1923) before women, like men, could sue for divorce on grounds of simple adultery.[2] Until 1857, all a wife's property passed into the ownership of her husband at marriage, and she had no legal right to acquire or own property while married. In 1857, a separated wife gained the right to keep property and earnings; those still with their husbands did not. In 1870, married women were given ownership of earnings and investment income only; in 1882, the Married Women's Property Act allowed them to retain ownership and control of earnings, property, inheritance and gifts; by 1935, remaining restrictions had been removed.[3]

Against such a background, it is no wonder that to a late-Victorian writer Roman women seemed unrestrained to the point of licence. The author, however, contrasts Roman women unfavourably with those of contemporary England. The former, lacking any intellectual or public interest, had, it is claimed, fallen prey to the worst lures of pleasure and depravity. In contrast, contemporary English women of the upper classes were notable for their interest in intellectual pursuits and good works. The author attributes this to the availability for them of higher education, a phenomenon at that time barely one generation old.[4] No notice is taken of the fact that in neither society were women able to vote or to hold public office.

As late as 1971, the Act of 1882 was seen as a major step on the road towards equality for women. A (female) barrister wrote (Puxon 1971: 260–1) 'By a stroke of the pen the emancipation of women was made inevitable.' She wondered what the monarch who assented to the Act (Queen Victoria) would have thought,

> if she had foreseen the direct and indirect results of this legislation — women in every trade and profession, even invading the House of Lords itself, doing as they wished with their lives and their possessions, their husbands powerless to stop them after the sanction of financial control had been torn from their hands!

Social attitudes have undergone striking changes in the last 25 years. Expectations have risen, and there has been a corresponding re-evaluation of the degree of independence already achieved by women in modern society. There have been fresh analyses — not always objective — of the purposes allegedly served in history by marriage, the family and family law.[5] The 'independence' of Roman women may well seem less striking now, especially since there is more awareness of the situation of women outside the wealthy upper classes. The Act of 1882, it has been said (Sachs and Wilson 1978: 137)

> did little more than save wealthy women from the irksome restraints of holding property through trustees. In fact, men

continued to control the property of women, even if only in the capacity of advisors rather than husbands or trustees, since women were precluded from acquiring the skills thought to be needed for the proper administration of their property, such skills being locked within the male professions. Since few married women were able to earn sufficiently to acquire their own property, the effects of the Act were necessarily limited.

Similar points have arisen more than once in foregoing chapters, in relation to Roman women. It is not necessary to repeat here all that has already been said on the functions and authority of tutors, or the actual or expected consequences of feminine inexperience in business matters. According to Callistratus (D. 49. 14.2.7), several emperors issued rescripts (concerning the rights of the *fiscus*) to prevent people from damaging their own interests by inadvisable admissions. Those categories thought to be specially at risk from inexperience and ignorance of their rights were rustics and women.

A century ago married women in England achieved in essence (though the process was not complete until the Matrimonial Causes Act of 1937) what Roman women *sui iuris* and in free marriage had had as far back as our historical knowledge extends — separate property in marriage. The disadvantages of this have subsequently become apparent, and legislation beginning in England in 1969–70, and paralleled in other countries, has made some steps towards implementing the idea of community of property in marriage or, alternatively, maintaining a wife's standard of living after divorce. It was realised that separation of property in marriage leaves many women at an economic disadvantage when the marriage ends. The demands of motherhood and the home give most women less scope to earn money on their own account. Husbands' earned income, and often most of the property, is in their names. The effect is the *de facto* economic dependency of women in marriage unless they are independently wealthy or have a full-time career.[6]

The same (except the 'full-time career', which was not a commonly available option) was true for Roman women. Moreover, the range of employment open to Roman women appears to have been limited and the rewards low. In addition, as tradesmen in a pre-industrial society in general operated small-scale family businesses, it is likely that women of the family who participated, whether in producing or in selling, merely provided their labour, while ownership and financial gains remained with the husband. At the end of a marriage, a wife was entitled to her dowry; at the humbler levels of society, that would not amount to much, probably not to a subsistence. On widowhood, she was dependent on her husband's testamentary generosity for any share in his property; on his intestacy, she ranked below cognates, and her situation compares very unfavourably with that of a widow today.[7]

However, to have prescribed community of property by law would have been foreign to the whole way of thinking of the Romans, in which the primary unit for preservation and transmission of property was the *familia*, with descent through the *pater*, and the wife *sine manu* unavoidably was an outsider.

Since both law and literature concentrate on the wealthy upper classes, there is a tendency, in studying Roman women, to attend particularly to that minority. For them, separate property in marriage would often suffice to ensure them substantial economic independence. It is as well, however, to remind ourselves that (ignoring, for the moment, the question of the *tutela*) the only ones who actually had financial autonomy (or, indeed, any other kind) were those who outlived their fathers. Many did not.

Divorce, however it might seem from the viewpoint of England in 1894, is not of much help in gauging the level of female emancipation in ancient Rome. In the first place, neither husband nor wife, if still *in potestate*, could initiate a divorce; that had to be done through the *pater*. Among those *sui iuris*, husbands were perhaps more likely to initiate divorce than wives, having additional motives, such as political relationships, or the desire to secure an heir to the property. Among the poorer classes, economic considerations favoured the husband, though they probably operated to discourage divorce in general — a wife's labour might not be easily replaced.

It is noteworthy that the authors often cited as offering evidence that divorce was rife among the upper classes of Rome itself in the Principate — namely, Seneca, Juvenal and Martial — are actually complaining about the frequency with which, they allege, some women divorce and remarry. It is no more than 'legalised adultery' says Martial (6.7), a sign of immorality and temperamental unchastity. In other words, the double standard is operating. Whatever the legal freedom to divorce might be, moral attitudes in Rome (at least among the male authors — we do not hear from the women) still promoted the ideal of wifely fidelity and chastity in marriage, because of the importance attached to securing the legitimacy of heirs. Since a woman would not be divorcing in order to obtain political advantage, or an heir, through another alliance, sex might seem a likely motive — and that was undesirable, from the male point of view, since it suggested that her interest had already been straying outside her marriage. Until comparatively recent times — less than twenty years ago — a similar stigma attached to divorce in England, as well as other parts of Europe, and even more strongly, since it was reinforced by the sacramental character of church marriages. The strictures of Roman moralists found ready acceptance as representing the actual state of affairs in the society they criticised. Raepsaet-Charlier (1981–2: 167) has noted that the 'received opinion' on the decadence and immorality of ancient Rome was crystallised in the 19th century, precisely when female emancipation was beginning to run ahead of current moral attitudes.[8]

Whether the incidence of divorce in Roman society was particularly high is not easy to determine. Detailed evidence is lacking to provide anything like a representative sample even of the upper classes. Raepsaet-Charlier (1981–2), compiling a prosopography of 562 women of senatorial rank marrying, divorcing or remarrying over a period of about two centuries between 10 B.C. and A.D. 200, found only 27 certain and 24 possible divorces, and of these 20 were in imperial families (15 Julio-Claudian). Five of the grand total of 51 are accounted for by one woman, Vistilia, cited as a natural curiosity by the elder Pliny (*N.H.* 7.5) for having had seven children, mostly born prematurely or after unusually long gestation, by six husbands. The ease of divorce and the essentially contractual and non-sacramental character of Roman marriage, as a shared undertaking dissoluble by either party, might seem to favour a high incidence; however, as we have seen, other factors, social and economic, came into play as well.

Over her children, whether legitimate or illegitimate, the Roman woman had, throughout the classical period, no legal rights at all, except, eventually, a very limited right to intestate succession. This compares badly (at least from the mother's point of view) with the current situation under English law, which gives equal rights to both parents of legitimate children and sole rights to the mothers of illegitimate children (though the father may apply for a court order granting custody or access) and may oblige the father of an illegitimate child to provide maintenance.[9]

This disability and others, such as the *sctum. Velleianum* and those arising from the *tutela* and the powers of the patron, derive from the primacy in Roman law of the *familia* headed by a *pater*. Some legal disabilities derived from women's political incapacity. Although of citizen status and able to produce citizen children, women did not have a vote and could not hold public office. This ban, understandable enough in a society in which, for much of the historical period, citizenship involved an obligation to armed military service, remained in force throughout the classical period, and operated beyond the immediate sphere of politics. Lawyers explained certain legal disabilities of women on the accepted principle that women were excluded from 'citizen functions' (*civilia officia*). So, women could not sit on criminal court juries (presumably since condemnation in such courts could sometimes result in loss or curtailment of the rights of male citizens). They were not allowed to bring suit in such courts either, except in cases in which they had a direct personal interest, such as the murder of a child, parent or patron. Two other exceptions were made, neither involving infringements of the rights of Roman *patres*. The Senate decided that, as patrons' daughters, women could be allowed to bring suit under the *lex Cornelia testamentaria* (of Sullan date) concerning a freedman's will; this decision probably postdates the Augustan legislation on inheritance from freedmen. The emperors Severus and Antoninus stated in a rescript that women should be allowed, in the public interest, to bring charges relating to the *annona* (food supply).[10] Since women had no standing in the comitial assemblies, they presumably did not have the right of *provocatio*, appeal to the people, against the imposition by a magistrate of death and certain corporal punishments (though this right was probably not available at all, away from Rome itself, until the last century of the Republic, and was effectively replaced later by appeal to the emperor).[11] As we have already seen, however, the praetor under the Republic, and later the Senate, sometimes delegated punishment, and even judgment, to the women's own families.

In civil courts, women could not act on behalf of others (as *cognitor* or *procurator*) either on the plaintiff's side or the defendant's.[12] They were entitled to bring suit in their own behalf (with tutorial consent), though the stories told by Valerius Maximus (8.3) suggest that it was rare for them actually to appear in court. He says of those who did that 'their natural condition and the modesty befitting the *stola* (i.e., by metonymy, a Roman lady) did not avail to make them keep silence in the forum and law-courts.' One such woman, Gaia Afrania, wife of a senator, was notoriously litigious and insisted on representing herself in court. Valerius notes the date of her death (48 B.C.), remarking sourly that it was better to record the date of the death of such a monster, rather than its birth.

What was untoward about Afrania's behaviour was her conduct of her own case in court, not the fact that she brought it. There is possibly a garbled memory of this virago in the odd story told by Ulpian, according to whom (D. 3.1.1.5) the ban on women's bringing suit on behalf of others was not original but was introduced into the praetor's edict, 'so that women should not undertake the functions of men, nor involve themselves in the cases of others, contrary to the modesty befitting their sex'. He says that the ban originated from the behaviour of a certain Carfania, a most unconscionable woman, who, by shamelessly bringing suit and pestering the magistrate, gave cause for the edict.

Carfania (or Afrania) may have burned herself into men's memories, but Ulpian cannot be right in making the connection. The ban was not on women's bringing suit but on their taking part, either as plaintiff or defendant, on behalf of others. The reference to the functions of men, found in other texts also, is more relevant. Diocletian and Maximian told an enquirer, Dionysia, 'To undertake the defence of another is a man's function (*virile officium*) and is agreed to be beyond the female sex. So, if your son is a minor, get him a tutor' (C. 2.12.18). A tutor could represent a minor and, as tutor, he had legal liability for his conduct of his ward's affairs. A woman could not be a tutor, nor under the *senatusconsultum Velleianum* could she undertake liability for others. This would also have prevented her being a *cognitor* (representative) in litigation, except in matters concerning her own property, since such transfers of obligation were not permitted by the *sctum*.

It is quite possible that the ban, even if not directly attributable to the *sctum.*, may have been introduced about the same time and for similar reasons. Since women normally needed tutor's authorisation before engaging in litigation likely to affect the property, some alternative control may have been felt necessary once some women were freed altogether from the need to have tutors.

It will have become obvious in the course of this book that the answer to the second of the questions heading this chapter should, in my view, be negative. Women's major personal and financial freedoms had already been conferred upon them by a very early date in Roman history, and for reasons which had more to do with the necessity of maintenance of the social status of the *familia* and co-operation with other *familiae* in a city-based civilisation than with any concern to 'liberate' the female members. Subsequent changes were by no means all in the direction of greater independence for women. When women benefited from them, it was often incidentally, in consequence of the decay of the influence of the *gens*. Greater importance was accorded to blood relationships within the immediate family, but these were never allowed to take precedence over the claims of the *pater*.

Nevertheless, wealthy women, especially from the late Republic onwards, give the appearance at least not only of enjoying a good deal of *de facto* autonomy in their personal lives and the control of their property, but also of playing a role in the public sphere. In the provinces especially, they are epigraphically attested as conferring benefactions, holding priesthoods and honorific magistracies, as 'patrons' and 'mothers' of colleges, and so on. Almost 90 Roman women are attested as accompanying husbands and other male relatives on provincial duty, a practice deplored by Ulpian (D. 1.16.4.2), who reminds governors of a senatorial decision in A.D. 20 (a mistake for 24) that they were to be held responsible for any misdeeds by their wives.[13]

These highly visible activities, however, are more formal than real. The expenditures are essentially liturgical, the offices honorific, the two together serving to buttress and to justify the continuance in power of the ruling élite to which, through their husbands and fathers, they belonged.[14] Provincial women had no say in the actual business of decision-making and no membership of the governing bodies, any more than the governors' wives had authority actually to govern.

From the city of Rome itself, there is a handful of anecdotes, mainly from the Republic, about the wives and other female relatives of Roman politicians, which are from time to time cited as evidence that upper-class women were actively and effectively involved in politics.[15] It would be stretching the evidence, however, to say that they actually determined policy and directed events. Fulvia, wife of Antony, is an exception (and even she was working in her husband's interests). The activities of the others amount to little more than acting as message-bearers for their husbands, providing *salons* at which the men could meet privately, or using their wealth and social connections to help ingratiate their husbands, sons or lovers with their peers and so further their careers. It is probably no accident that there are very few such attestations, outside the imperial household, under the empire. Their influence was exercised on a personal basis, on private occasions in private houses. Their role was essentially vicarious and bears more than a passing resemblance to that of the loyal, involved American 'corporation wife'.

Some may perhaps have grown more assertive with advancing years and confidence, like Sempronia, who hung around on the fringes of the Catilinarian conspiracy, or Brutus' mother Servilia, who undertook in 44 B.C. to cancel her son's unwanted appointment as corn commissioner, and who apparently rudely snubbed Cicero at a meeting at her house at which the matter was discussed.[16] The corn commission was dropped, but we do not actually know that it was Servilia's doing, any more than we know that Sempronia did anything effective to further the conspiracy.

As young, inexperienced brides, many are likely to have followed (and some to have remained in) the pattern of Pliny's hero-worshipping young bride Calpurnia. According to the gratified report he sends her aunt (*Ep.* 4.19), she indulged in unreserved and uncritical admiration of his literary products, memorising passages, setting his verses to music and hiding (in a rather un-Roman way) behind a curtain to hear the commendations at his literary readings. In his law-court activities, similarly, she took a partisan interest — not, apparently, in the actual details of the cases, but in the audience-reaction Pliny evoked.

As for women of the lower classes, lack of the vote may not have troubled them much. The votes of their menfolk were only sporadically important in the Republic and soon ceased to be of any practical importance under the empire.

Notes

1. Puxon (1971) 39.
2. Puxon (1971) 59–62; grounds other than adultery (cruelty, desertion or incurable insanity) were allowed only after 1937: Cretney (1984) 99–101.
3. Puxon (1971) 259–66; Bromley (1981) 415–18; Stetson (1982) 17–20, 54–56, 99.
4. Dale (1894) 498.
5. For example: Sachs and Wilson (1978) 135–46 (on Britain), 147–67 (on the United States); Atkins and Hoggett (1984) 83–123, 147–57; Eekelaar (1984) 15–26.
6. Cretney (1984) 686–92, 723–7, 849–51; Eekelaar (1984) 100–22.
7. Cretney (1984) 698–704.
8. Dale (1894: 491) called divorce 'one of the most significant indications of a vicious and corrupt society'.
9. Puxon (1971) 191–206; Cretney (1984) 287–322, 577–621.

10. D. 5.1.12; 48.2.1; 2; 13; 49.5.1; 50.17.2 pr.
11. D. 5.1.12.2; Jones (1960) 53–65.
12. *Inst*. IV.13.11; Buckland (1966) 708.
13. Tac. *Ann*. 4.20.6; MacMullen (1980); Raepsaet-Charlier (1982); van Bremen (1983).
14. Van Bremen (1983) 236–7.
15. For a recent discussion, see Dixon (1983).
16. Sall. *Cat*. 25; Cic. *Att*. 15.11.

Bibliography

Note: the editors of *l'Année Philologique* have occasionally changed the abbreviation used for a particular periodical. To avoid confusion, in the following list, one form is used throughout in such cases. So, for example, *RHD — Revue de l'Histoire du Droit Français et Étranger; TRG — Tijdschrift voor Rechtsgeschiedenis; ZRG — Zeitschrift der Savigny-Stiftung (römische Abteilung)*. RSA is here used for *Rivista Storica dell'Antichità*.

Adams, B. (1964) *Paramone und verwändte Texte*, Berlin.
Alföldy, G. (1972) 'Die Freilassung von Sklaven und die Struktur der Sklaverei in der römischen Kaiserzeit', *RSA 2*, 97–129.
—— (1981) 'Die Stellung der Ritter in der Führungsschicht des *Imperium Romanum'*, *Chiron 11*, 169–215.
Amelotti, M. (1966) *Il testamento romano attraverso la prassi documentale*, Florence.
Amundsen, D.W. and Diers, C.J. (1969) 'The Age of Menarche in Classical Greece and Rome', *Human Biology 41*, 125–32.
Andreau, J. (1974) *Les Affaires de Monsieur Jucundus*, Rome.
Angel, J.L. (1972) 'Ecology and Population in the Eastern Mediterranean', *World Archaeology 4*, 88–105.
Ankum, H. (1984) 'La Femme mariée et la loi Falcidia', *Labeo 30*, 28–70.
Arangio-Ruiz, V. and Pugliese Carratelli, G. (1955) '*Tabulae Herculanenses*, V', *PP 10*, 448–77.
Astin, A.E. (1978) *Cato the Censor*, Oxford.
Astolfi, R. (1965) '*Femina probrosa, concubina, mater solitaria*', *SDHI 31*, 15–60.
——(1970) *La lex Julia et Papia*, Padua.
——(1973) 'Note per una valutazione storica della *lex Julia et Papia*', *SDHI 39*, 187–238.
Atkins, A. and Hoggett, B. (1984) *Women and the Law*. London.
Balsdon, J.P.V.D. (1962) *Roman Women: Their History and Habits*, London.
Bang, M. (1922) 'Das gewöhnliche Älter der Mädchen bei der Verlobung und Verheiratung' in L. Friedländer, *Darstellungen aus der Sittengeschichte Roms 4*, 133–41.
Beard, M. (1980) 'The Sexual Status of Vestal Virgins', *JRS 70*, 12–27.
Beare, W. (1964) *The Roman Stage*, third edition, New York.
Bellen, H. (1971) *Studien zur Sklavenflucht im römischen Kaiserreich*, Wiesbaden.
Besnier, R. (1949) 'L'Application des lois caducaires d'Auguste d'après le Gnomon de l'Idiologue', *RIDA 2 (= Mélanges Fernand de Visscher I)* 93–118.
——(1959) 'L'Extension des lois caducaires aux fideicommis d'après Gaius, *Institutes* II, 286 et 286a', *Droits de l'antiquité et sociologie juridique: Mélanges H. Lévy-Bruhl*, Paris.
Biezunska-Malowist, I. (1962) 'Les esclaves nés dans la maison du maître en Égypte romaine', *StudClas 3*, 147–62.

——(1971a) 'Die Expositio von Kindern als Quelle der Sklavenbeschaffung im griechisch-römischen Ägypten', *JWG 2*, 129–33.

——(1971b) 'Les Esclaves fugitifs dans l'Egypte greco-romaine', *Studi Volterra 6*, 75–90.

——(1974) 'La traité d'esclaves en Égypte', *Proceedings of the XIVth International Congress of Papyrologists*, pp. 11–18.

——(1977) *L'Esclavage dans l'Égypte greco-romaine: seconde partie: periode romaine*, Wroclaw.

Boswell, J.E. (1984) '*Expositio* and *oblatio*: The Abandonment of Children and the Ancient and Mediaeval Family', *AHR 89*, 10–33.

Boyer, G. (1950) 'Le Droit successoral romain dans les oeuvres de Polybe', *RIDA 4* (= *Mélanges Fernand de Visscher 3*), 169–87.

Boyer, L. (1965) 'La Fonction sociale des legs d'après la jurisprudence classique', *RHD 43*, 333–408.

Bradley, K.R. (1978) 'The Age at Time of Sale of Female Slaves', *Arethusa 11*, 243–52.

——(1979) 'Response', *Arethusa 12*, 259–63.

——(1980) 'Sexual Regulations in Wet-Nursing Contracts from Roman Egypt', *Klio 62*, 321–25.

——(1984) *Slaves and Masters in the Roman Empire: A Study in Social Control*, Brussels.

Bromley, P.M. (1981) *Family Law*, sixth edition, London.

Broughton, T.R.S. (1951–2) *The Magistrates of the Roman Republic*, Cleveland.

Brunt, P.A. (1971) *Italian Manpower 225 B.C. to A.D. 14*, Oxford.

——(1980) 'Evidence Given under Torture in the Principate', *ZRG 97*, 256–65.

Buckland, W.W. (1908) *The Roman Law of Slavery*, Cambridge.

——(1966) *A Text-book of Roman Law from Augustus to Justinian*, third edition, Cambridge.

Calderini, R. (1950) 'Gli *agrammatoi* nell'Egitto greco-romano', *Aegyptus 30*, 14–41.

Campbell, B. (1978) 'The Marriage of Soldiers under the Empire', *JRS 68*, 153–66.

Casavola, F. (1960) *Lex Cincia: contributo alla storia delle origini della donazione romana*, Naples.

Cavenaile, R. (1958) *Corpus Papyrorum Latinarum*, Wiesbaden.

Cebeillac-Gervasoni, M. and Zevi, F. (1976) 'Révisions et nouveautés pour trois inscriptions d'Ostie: des femmes-gladiateurs dans une inscription d'Ostie', *MEFR 88*, 612–20.

Chastagnol, A. (1979) 'Les Femmes dans l'ordre senatorial: titulature et rang social à Rome', *RH 103*, 3–28.

Cockle, H. (1981) 'Pottery Manufacture in Roman Egypt: A New Papyrus', *JRS 71*, 87–97.

Corbett, P.E. (1930) *The Roman Law of Marriage*, Oxford.

Cornell, T. (1978) 'Some Observations on the *crimen incesti*', in M. Torelli (ed.), *Le délit religieux*, pp. 27–37.

Courtney, E. (1980) *A Commentary on the Satires of Juvenal*, London.

Cretney, S.M. (1984) *Principles of Family Law*, fourth edition, London.

Crifo, G. (1964) 'Sul problema della donna tutrice', *BIDR 67*, 87–166.

Criminal Law Revision Committee (1980) *Working Paper on Sexual Offences*, London.

Crook, J.A. (1967a) *The Law and Life of Rome*, London.

——(1967b) 'Gaius Institutes i, 84–86', *CR 81* (n.s. *17*), 7–8.

——(1967c) '*Patria potestas*', *CQ 17*, 113–122.

——(1973) 'Intestacy in Roman Society', *PCPhS 199* (n.s. *19*), 38–44.

——(1982) 'The Position of Roman Women in the First Century A.D. and the

Senatusconsultum Velleianum', text of an unpublished paper delivered to the Ancient History Seminar, Institute of Classical Studies, London.

Csillag, P. (1976) *The Augustan Laws on Family Relations*, Budapest.

Dalby, A. (1979) 'On Female Slaves in Roman Egypt', *Arethusa 12*, 255–9.

Dale, M. (1894) 'The Women of Imperial Rome and the English Women of Today', *The Westminster Review 141*, 490–502.

Dalla, D. (1978) *L'incapacità sessuale in diritto romano*, Milan.

Daube, D. (1965) 'The Preponderance of Intestacy at Rome', *Tulane Law Review 39*, 253–62.

——(1972) 'The *lex Julia* Concerning Adultery', *IJ* n.s. 7, 373–80.

D'Avino, M. (1967) *The Women of Pompeii*, Naples.

Dessau, H. (1884) 'Der Steuertariff von Palmyra', *Hermes 19*, 486–533.

Diósdi, G. (1970) *Ownership in Ancient and Pre-Classical Law*, Budapest.

Dixon, R.B. (1978) 'Late Marriage and Non-marriage as Demographic Responses: Are They Similar?', *Population Studies 32*, 449–66.

Dixon, S. (1983) 'A Family Business: Women's Role in Patronage and Politics at Rome, 80–44 B.C.', *C&M 34*, 91–112.

——(1985) 'Polybius on Roman Women and Property', *AJPh 106* 147–170.

Düll, R. (1953) 'Privatrechtsprobleme im Bereich der Virgo Vestalis', *ZRG 70*, 380–90.

Dumont, F. (1943) 'Les Revenus de la dot en droit romain', *RHD 22*, 1–43.

Duncan-Jones, R. (1982) *The Economy of the Roman Empire: Quantitative Studies*, second edition, Cambridge.

Durand, J.D. (1959–60) 'Mortality Estimates from Roman Tombstone Inscriptions', *American Journal of Sociology 65*, 365–73.

Durry, M. (1950) *Éloge funèbre d'une matrone romaine*, Paris.

——(1970) 'Le Mariage des filles impubères à Rome', *REL 47* bis (*Mélanges Marcel Durry*), 17–24.

Eck, W. (1978) 'Zum neuen Fragment des sogenannten *testamentum Dasumii*', *ZPE 30*, 277–95.

Eekelaar, J. (1984) *Family Law and Social Policy*, second edition, London.

Engels, D. (1980) 'The Problem of Female Infanticide in the Greco-Roman World', *CPh 75*, 112–20.

——(1984) 'The Use of Historical Demography in Ancient History', *CQ 34*, 386–93.

Étienne, R. (1973) 'La Conscience médicale antique et la vie des enfants', *Annales de Démographie Historique 9*, 15–46.

Fabre, G. (1971) 'Remarques sur la vie familiale des affranchis privés aux deux derniers siècles de la republique; problèmes juridiques et sociologiques', in *Annales du Colloque 1971 sur l'Esclavage*, Paris, pp. 239–53.

—— (1981) *Libertus: recherches sur les rapports patron–affranchi à la fin de la république romaine*, Rome.

Fink, R.O. (1941) 'The *Sponsalia* of a *Classiarius*. A reinterpretation of *P. Mich. Inv. 4703*', *TAPhA 72*, 109–24.

——(1966) '*P. Mich.* VII. 422 (Inv. 4703): Betrothal, Marriage or Divorce?', in *Essays in Honor of C. Bradford Welles*, ASPap I, New Haven, 9–17.

Finley, M.I. (1985) *The Ancient Economy*, second edition, London.

Flory, M.B. (1984) 'When Women Precede Men: Factors influencing the Order of Names in Roman Epitaphs', *CJ 79*, 216–24.

Fox, R. (1967) *Kinship and Marriage: an Anthropological Perspective*, Harmondsworth.

Frier, B. (1982) *Roman Life Expectancy: Ulpian's Evidence*, HSPh 86, 213–51.

Gagé, J. (1963) *Matronalia: essai sur les dévotions et les organisations cultuelles des femmes dans l'ancienne Rome*, Brussels.

Garcia Garrido, M. (1957) *'Minor annis xii nupta'*, *Labeo 3*, 76–88.

Gardner, J.F. (1984) 'A Family and an Inheritance: The Problems of the Widow Petronilla', *LCM 9*, 132–3.

Garnsey, P. (1967) 'Adultery Trials and the Survival of the *Quaestiones* in the Severan Age', *JRS 57*, 56–60.

——(1970a) 'Septimius Severus and the Marriage of Soldiers', *CSCA 3*, 45–51.

——(1970b) *Social Status and Legal Privilege in the Roman Empire*, Oxford.

——(1974) 'Aspects of the Decline of the Urban Aristocracy in the Empire', *ANRW II.1*, 229–52.

Garton, C. (1964) 'A Republican Mime-Actress?', *CR 78* (n.s. 14), 238–9.

Gaudemet, J. (1949) *'Justum matrimonium'*, *RIDA 2* (= *Melanges Fernand de Visscher I*), 309–66.

——(1953) 'Observations sur la *manus*', *AHDO-RIDA 2*, 323–53.

Girard, P.F. (1923) *Textes de droit romain*, Paris.

Glantz, L. (1983) 'Is the Fetus a Person? A Lawyer's View', in Bondeson, W.B., Engelhardt, H.T., Spicker, S.F. and Winship, D.H. (eds.), *Abortion and the Status of the Fetus*, Dordrecht, pp. 107–17.

Golden, M. (1981) 'Demography and the Exposure of Girls at Athens', *Phoenix 35*, 316–31.

Gody, J. (1973) 'Strategies of Heirship', *CSSH 15*, 3–20.

——(1976a) *Production and Reproduction: A Comparative Study of the Domestic Domain*, Cambridge.

——(1976b) 'Inheritance, Property and Women, Some Comparative Considerations', in Goody, J., Thirsk, J., Thompson, E.P. (eds), *Family and Inheritance: Rural Society in Western Europe 1200–1800*, Cambridge, pp. 10–36.

——(1983) *The Development of the Family and Marriage in Europe*, Cambridge.

Gordon, H.L. (1932–3) 'The Eternal Triangle, First Century B.C.', *CJ 28*, 574–78.

Gratwick, A.S. (1984) 'Free or Not So Free? Wives and Daughters in the Late Roman Republic', in Craik, E.M. (ed.), *Marriage and Property*, Aberdeen, pp.30–53.

Greenidge, A.J.H. (1894) *Infamia: Its Place in Roman Public and Private Law*, Oxford.

Grenfell, B.P. and Hunt, A.S. (1897) *Greek Papyri, Series II*, Oxford.

Griffin, S. (1977) 'Rape: The All-American Crime', in Chappell, D., Geis, R. and Geis, G. (eds.), *Forcible Rape*, New York, pp. 47–66.

Guarino, A. (1943) 'Studi sull'*incestum*', *ZRG 63*, 175–267.

——(1982) *'Lex Voconia'*, *Labeo 28*, 188–91.

Guizzi, F. (1968) *Aspetti Giuridici del Sacerdozio Romano: il Sacerdozio di Vesta*, Naples.

Hähnel, R. (1937) 'Der künstliche Abortus im Altertum', *Archiv f. Geschichte d. Medizin 29*, 224–55.

Hajnal, J. (1965) 'European Marriage Patterns in Perspective', in Glass, D.V. and Eversley, D.E.C. (eds.), *Population in History*, London, pp. 101–43.

Hallett, J.P. (1984) *Fathers and Daughters in Roman Society*, Princeton.

Harkness, A.G. (1896) 'Age at Marriage and at Death in the Roman Empire', *TAPhA 27*, 35–72.

Harris, W.V. (1980) 'Towards a Study of the Roman Slave Trade', *MAAR 36*, 117–40.

——(1982) 'The Theoretical Possibility of Extensive Infanticide in the Greco-Roman World', *CQ 32*, 114–16.

Helen, T. (1975) *Organisation of Roman Brick Production in the First and Second Centuries A.D.*, Helsinki.

Hengstl, J. (1972) *Private Arbeitsverhältnisse freier Personen in den hellenistischen Papyri bis Diokletian*, Bonn.

Hermansen, G. (1981) *Ostia: Aspects of Roman City Life*, Edmonton.

Herrmann, C. (1964) *Le rôle judiciaire et politique des femmes sous la république romaine*, Brussels.

Herrmann, H. (1959) 'Die Ammenverträge in den gräko-ägyptischen Papyri', *ZRG 76*, 490–9.

Hindlegang, M.J. and Davis, B.L. (1977) 'Forcible Rape in the United States: A Statistical Profile', in Chappell, D., Geis, R. and Geis, G. (eds.) *Forcible Rape*, New York, pp. 87–114

Hobson, D. (1983) 'Women and Property Owners in Roman Egypt', *TAPhA 113*, 311–21.

Holcombe, L. (1983) *Wives and Property*, Oxford.

Holtheide, B. (1980) '*Matrona stolata et femina stolata*', *ZPE 38*, 127–34.

Hombert, M. and Préaux, C. (1952) *Recherches sur le recensement dans l'Égypte romaine*, *Papyrologica Lugduno-Batava 5*, Leiden.

Honoré, T. (1978) *Sex Law*, London.

Hopkins, M.K. (1965a) 'Contraception in the Roman Empire', *CSSH 8*, 124–51.

——(1965b) 'The Age of Roman Girls at Marriage', *Population Studies 19*, 309–27.

——(1966) 'On the Probable Age Structure of the Roman Population', *Population Studies 20*, 245–64.

——(1978) *Conquerors and Slaves*, Cambridge.

——(1980) 'Brother–Sister Marriage in Roman Egypt', *CSSH 22*, 303–54.

——(1983) *Death and Renewal*, Cambridge.

Horsfall, N. (1983) 'Some Problems in the *Laudatio Turiae*', *BICS 30*, 85–99.

Huber, J. (1977) *Der Ehekonsens im römischen Recht*, Rome.

Huchthausen, L. (1974) 'Herkunft und ökonomische Stellung weiblicher Adressaten von Reskripten des *Codex Justinianus*', *Klio 56*, 199–228.

Hufton, O. (1974) *The Poor of Eighteenth-Century France, 1750–1789*, Oxford.

Humbert, M. (1972) *Le Remariage à Rome*, Milan.

Jameson, S. (1980) 'The Lycian League: Some Problems in Its Administration', *ANRW II.7.2*, 832–54.

Jones, A.H.M. (1960) *Studies in Roman Government and Law*, Oxford.

——(1974) *The Roman Economy: Studies in Ancient Economic and Administrative History* (ed. P.A. Brunt), Oxford, pp. 350–64 (= 'The Cloth Industry under the Roman Empire', *EHR 13*, 1960, 83–192).

Jung, J.H. (1982) 'Das Eherecht der römischen Soldaten', *ANRW II.14*, 302–46.

Kaianto, I. (1970) 'On Divorce among the Common People of Rome', *REL 47 bis* (Mélanges Marcel Durry), 99–113.

Kampen, N. (1981) *Image and Status: Roman Working Women in Ostia*, Berlin.

Karabélias, E. (1984) 'La Forme de la *testatio (ekmartyrion)* matrimoniale en droit romain classique et post-classique', *RHD 62*, 599–603

Kaser, M. (1958) '*Partus ancillae*', *ZRG 75*, 156–200.

——(1971) *Das römische Privatrecht*, second edition, Munich.

——(1977) *Über Verbotsgesetze und verbotswidrige Geschäfte im römischen Recht*, Wien.

Kleberg, T. (1957) *Hôtels, restaurants et cabarets dans l'antiquité romaine*, Uppsala.

Klingenberg, G. (1983) 'Die Frau im römischen Abgaben-und Fiskalrecht', *RIDA 30*, 141–50.

Kolendo, J. (1981) 'L'Esclavage et la vie sexuelle des hommes libres à Rome', *Index 10*, 288–97.

Kornhardt, H. (1938) '*Recipere* und *servus recepticius*', *ZRG 58*, 162–4.

Kruger, P. (1870) '*Anecdoton Livianum*' *Hermes 4*, 371–2.

Kunkel, W. (1962) *Untersuchungen zu Entwicklung des römischen Kriminalverfahrens im vorsullanischer Zeit*, Munich.

——(1966) 'Das Konsilium im Hausgericht', *ZRG 83*, 219–57 (= *Kleine Schriften* (1974), Munich, pp. 117–49).

——(1973) *An Introduction to Roman Legal and Constitutional History*, second edition, Oxford.

Lambertini, R. (1980) *Plagium*, Milan.

Landels, J.G. (1979) 'An Ancient Account of Reproduction', *Biology and Human Affairs 44*, 94–113.

Langer, W.L. (1973–4) 'Infanticide: A Historical Survey', *History of Childhood Quarterly 1*, 353–66.

Lattimore, R. (1942) *Themes in Greek and Latin Epitaphs*, Urbana.

Lavaggi, G. (1946) 'La successione della libertà e il sc. Orfiziano', *SDHI 12*, 174–86.

Lemosse, M. (1975) 'L'Enfant sans famille en droit romain', *Recueils de la Société Jean Bodin 35*, 257–70.

Lenel, O. (1956) *Das Edictum Perpetuum*, third edition, Aalen.

Levick, B. (1983) 'The *senatusconsultum* from Larinum', *JRS 73*, 97–115.

Lewis, N. (1970) 'On Paternal Authority in Roman Egypt', *RIDA 17*, 25–8.

——(1983) *Life in Egypt under Roman Rule*, Oxford.

Lienau, C. (1971) 'Die Behandlung und Erwähnung im Superfetation in Antike', *Clio Medica 6*, 275–85.

Lightman, M. and Zeisel, W. (1977) *'Univira:* An Example of Continuity and Change in Roman Society', *Church History 46*, 19–32.

Longo, G. (1977) 'Ancora sul matrimonio romano', *SDHI 43*, 459–80.

Lopuszanski, G. (1951) 'La Police romaine et les chrétiens', *AC 20*, 5–46.

MacCormack, G. (1975) 'Wine-drinking and the Romulan Law of Divorce', *IJ 10*, 70–174.

——(1978) *'Coemptio* and Marriage by Purchase', *BIDR 81*, 179–97.

MacMullen, R. (1980) 'Women in Public in the Roman Empire', *Historia 29*, 208–18.

MacNamara, D.E.J. and Sagarin, E. (1977) *Sex, Crime and the Law*, New York.

Macro, A.D. (1979) 'A Confirmed Asiarch', *AJPh 100*, 94–8.

Magie, D. (1950) *Roman Rule in Asia Minor*, Princeton.

Marquardt, J. (1886) *Das Privatleben der Römer*, Leipzig.

Masiello, T. (1979) *La donna tutrice: modelli culturali e prassi giuridica fra gli Antonini e i Severi*, Naples.

Meinhart, M. (1967) *Die Senatusconsulta Tertullianum und Orfitianum in ihrer Bedeutung für das klassische römische Erbrecht*, Graz.

Merkelbach, R. (1980) 'Der Kult der Hestia im Prytaneion der griechischen Städte', *ZPE 37*, 77–92.

'ro, A. (1963) 'Il *legatum partitionis*', *Labeo 9*, 291–330

1964) 'La datazione dell'editto *de inspiciendo ventre custodiendoque partu*', *Synteleia Vincenzo Arangio Ruiz 2*, 944–57.

——(1975) 'Binas nuptias constituere in D. 3.2.1', *Iura 26*, 101–8.

Meyer, P. (1895) *Der römische Konkubinat*, Leipzig.

Michels, A.K. (1967) *The Calendar of the Roman Republic*, Princeton.

Middleton, R. (1962) 'Brother–Sister and Father–Daughter Marriage in Ancient Egypt', *American Sociological Review 27*, 603–11.

Modrzejewski, J. (1971) 'Á propos de la tutelle dative des femmes dans l'Égypte romaine', *Akten des XIII Internationalen Papyrologencongresses*, pp. 263–92.

Moeller, W.O. (1969) 'The Male Weavers at Pompeii', *Technology and Culture 10*, 561–6.

——(1976) *The Wool Trade of Ancient Pompeii*, Leiden.

Mommsen, Th. (1887) *Römisches Staatsrecht*, Leipzig.

——(1899) *Römisches Strafrecht*, Berlin.

Montevecchi, O. (1935) 'Ricerche di sociologia nei documenti dell'Egitto greco-romano. I: I testamenti', *Aegyptus 13*, 67–121.
——(1979) 'Endogamia e cittadinanza romana in Egitto', *Aegyptus 59*, 137–44.
Morabito, M. (1981) *Les Réalités de l'esclavage d'après le Digeste*, Paris.
Moyle, J.B. (1912) *Imperatoris Iustiniani Institutionum libri quattuor*, Oxford.
Nardi, E. (1971) *Il procurato aborto nel mondo greco-romano*, Milan.
Nicolet, C. (1980) *The World of the Citizen in Republican Rome*, London.
Niziolek, M. (1975) 'The Meaning of the Phrase *liberi naturales* in Roman Law Sources up to Constantine's Reign', *RIDA 22*, 317–44.
Noailles, P. (1948) *Fas et Ius*, Paris.
Noonan, J.T. (1966) *Contraception: A History of Its Treatment by the Catholic Theologians and Canonists*, New York.
Norcio, G. (1980) *Epigrammi di Marco Valerio Marziale*, Turin.
Pearce, T.E.V. (1974) 'The Role of the Wife as *custos* in Ancient Rome', *Eranos 72*, 17–33.
Penta, M. (1980) *La viduitas nella condizione della donna romana, AAN 31*, 341–51.
Peters, J.J. (1977) 'The Philadelphia Rape Victim Project', in Chappell, D., Geis, R. and Geis G. (eds.) *Forcible Rape*, New York, pp. 339–55.
Pleket, H.W. (1969) *Epigraphica, vol. II: Texts on the Social History of the Greek World*, Leiden.
Polay, E. (1969) 'Die Sklavenehe im antiken Rom', *Altertum 15*, 83–91.
Pomeroy, S. (1975) *Goddesses, Whores, Wives and Slaves*, New York.
——(1976) 'The Relationship of the Married Woman to her Blood Relatives in Rome', *AncSoc 7*, 215–27.
Préaux, C. (1959) 'Le Statut de la femme à l'époque hellénistique, principalement en Égypte', *Recueils de la société Jean Bodin 11*, 127–75.
Puxon, M. (1971) *Family Law*, Harmondsworth.
Rabello, A.M. (1979) *Effetti personali della Patria Potestas*, Milan.
Raditsa, L.F. (1980) 'Augustus' Legislation Concerning Marriage, Procreation, Love Affairs and Adultery', *ANRW II.13* 278–339.
Raepsaet-Charlier, M.-Th. (1981–2) 'Ordre sénatorial et divorce sous le Haut-Empire: un chapitre de l'histoire des mentalités', *ACD 17-18*, 161–73.
——(1982) 'Épouses et familles de magistrats dans les ʳrovinces romaines aux deux premiers siècles de l'empire', *Historia 31*, 56–69.
Rantz, B. (1982) 'Les Droits de la femme romaine tels qu'on peut les apercevoir dans le *pro Caecina* de Ciceron', *RIDA 29*, 265–80.
Rawson, B. (1974) 'Roman Concubinage and Other *de facto* Marriages', *TAPhA 104*, 279–305.
Reinach, J. (1956) 'Puberté féminine et mariage romain', *RHD 34*, 268–73.
Rice, M.L.S. (1939) *Working-Class Wives*, Harmondsworth.
Richlin, A. (1981) 'Approaches to the Sources on Adultery at Rome', in H.P. Foley (ed.), *Reflections of Women in Antiquity*, New York, pp. 379–404.
Robleda, O. (1982) 'Il divorzio in Roma prima di Constantino', *ANRW II.14*, 347–90.
Röhle, R. (1977) *'Religare dotem', ZRG 94*, 306–318.
Ruggiero, A. (1981) 'Il matrimonio della impubere in Roma antica', *AAN 92*, 63–71.
Sachs, A. and Wilson, J.H. (1978) *Sexism and the Law: A Study of Male Beliefs and Legal Bias in Britain and the U.S.*, Oxford.
Saller, R.P. (1984) 'Roman dowry and the devolution of property in the Principate', *CQ 34*, 195–205.
Samuel, A.E. (1965) 'The role of *paramone* clauses in ancient documents'. *JJP 15*, 221–311.

Samuel, A.E., Hastings, W.K., Bowman, A.K., Bagnall, R.S. (1971) *Death and Taxes, ASPap X,* Amsterdam and Toronto.
Sanders, H.A. (1938) 'A Latin Marriage Contract', *TAPhA 69,* 104–16.
Sauer, R. (1978) 'Infanticide and Abortion in Nineteenth-Century Britain', *Population Studies 32,* 81–93.
Schaps, D.M. (1979) *Economic Rights of Women in Ancient Greece,* Edinburgh.
Schulz, F. (1936) *Principles of Roman Law,* Oxford.
——(1942–3) 'Roman Registers of Birth and Birth-Certificates',
(i) *JRS 32,* 79–91, (ii) *JRS 33,* 155–164.
——(1951) *Classical Roman Law,* Oxford.
Scullard, H.H. (1981) *Festivals and Ceremonies of the Roman Republic,* London.
Selb, W. (1966) 'Vom *ius vitae necisque* zum beschränkten Züchtigungsrecht und zur magistratischen Züchtigungshilfe', *IJ 1,* 136–50.
Setälä, P. (1977) *Private Domini in Roman Brick Stamps of the Empire,* Helsinki.
Shatzman, I. (1975) *Senatorial Wealth and Roman Politics,* Brussels.
Shtaerman, E.M. and Trofimova, M.K. (1975) *La schiavitú nell'Italia imperiale,* Rome.
Sijpestein, P.J. (1982) *Michigan Papyri XV,* Zutphen.
Sirks, A.J.B. (1980) 'A Favour to Rich Freedwomen (*libertinae*) in A.D. 51', *RIDA 27,* 283–94.
——(1981) 'Informal Manumission in the *lex Junia*', *RIDA 28,* 247–76.
Solazzi, S. (1939) *'Servus recepticius et dos recepticia', SDHI 5,* 222–5.
——(1953) 'Alla fonti della *exceptio Sc. Velleiani*', *SDHI 19,* 321–6.
Stetson, D.M. (1982) *A Woman's Issue: The Politics of Family Law Reform in England,* Greenwood, Connecticut.
Stone, L. (1979) *The Family, Sex and Marriage in England 1500–1800,* abridged edition, London.
Straus, J.A. (1977) 'Quelques activités exercies par les esclaves d'après les papyrus de l'Égypte romaine', *Historia 26,* 74–88.
Syme, R. (1968) 'The Ummidii', *Historia 17,* 72–105 (= *Roman Papers II,* ed. E. Badian (1979), Oxford, pp. 659–693).
——(1978) *History in Ovid,* Oxford.
Tannahill, R. (1981) *Sex in History,* London.
Taubenschlag, R. (1929) 'Die *materna potestas* im gräko-ägyptischen Recht', *ZRG 49,* 115–28.
——(1955) *The Law of Greco-Roman Egypt in the Light of the Papyri,* second edition, Warsaw.
Tellegen, J.W. (1982) *The Roman Law of Succession in the Letters of Pliny the Younger: I,* Zutphen.
Tellegen-Couperus, O.E. (1982) *Testamentary Succession in the Constitutions of Diocletian,* Zutphen.
Thomas, J.A.C. (1961) *'Accusatio adulterii', Iura 12,* 65–80.
——(1967) 'Some Notes on *adrogatio per rescriptum principis*', *RIDA 14,* 413–27.
Thomas, Y. (1980) 'Mariages endogamiques à Rome. Patrimoine, pouvoir et parenté depuis l'époque archaïque', *RHD 58,* 345–82.
Tracy, V.A. (1976) 'The *leno-maritus*', *CJ 72,* 62–4.
Treggiari, S. (1969) *Roman Freedmen during the Late Republic,* Oxford.
——(1975a) 'Family Life among the Staff of the Volusii', *TAPhA 105,* 393–402.
——(1975b) 'Jobs in the Household of Livia', *PBSR 43,* 48–77.
——(1976) 'Jobs for Women', *AJAH 1.2,* 76–104.
——(1979a) 'Lower Class Women in the Roman Economy', *Florilegium 1,* 65–86.
——(1979b) 'Questions on Women Domestics in the Roman West', in Capozza, M. (ed.) *Schiavitú, manomissione e classe dipendenti nel mondo antico,* Padua, pp. 185–201.

——(1980) 'Urban Labour in Rome: *Mercenarii* and *tabernarii*', in Garnsey, P. (ed.), *Non-Slave Labour in the Greco-Roman World*, Cambridge, pp. 48–64.

——(1981a) '*Contubernales* in *CIL* 6', *Phoenix 35*, 42–69.

——(1981b) '*Concubinae*', *PBSR 49*, 59–81.

Treggiari, S. and Dorken, S. (1981) 'Women with Two Living Husbands in *CIL* 6', *LCM 6*, 269–72.

Tucker, C.W. (1982) 'Women in the Manumission Inscriptions at Delphi', *TAPhA 112*, 225–36.

van Bremen, R. (1983) 'Women and Wealth', in Cameron, A. and Kuhrt, A. (eds.) *Images of Women in Antiquity*, London, pp. 223–42.

van de Wiel, C. (1978) 'La Légitimation par mariage subséquent, de Constantin à Justinien. Sa réception sporadique dans le droit byzantin', *RIDA 25*, 307–50.

van Lith, S.M.E. (1974) 'Lease of Sheep and Goats / Nursing Contract with Accompanying Receipt', *ZPE 14*, 145–64.

Vigneron, R. (1983) 'L'antiféministe loi Voconia et les "Schleichwege des Lebens" ', *Labeo 29*, 140–53.

Villers, R. (1950) 'Á propos de la disparition de l'*usus*', *RHD 28*, 538–47.

——(1969) '*Manus* et mariage', *IJ 4*, 168–179.

——(1982) 'Le mariage envisagé comme institution d'état dans le droit classique de Rome', *ANRW II.14*, 285–301.

Voci, P. (1963) *Diritto Ereditario Romano, II: parte speciale*, Milan.

Volterra, E. (1934) 'Per la storia de bigamia in diritto romano', *Studi Ratti*, Mailand, pp. 387–447.

——(1940) *La Conception du mariage d'après les juristes romains*, Padua.

——(1941) 'Sulla capacità delle donne a far testamento', *BIDR 48*, 74–82.

——(1948) 'Ancora sulla *manus* e sul matrimonio', *Studi in onore di Siro Solazzi*, Naples, pp. 675–88.

——(1972) '*Iniustum matrimonium*, *Studi Scherillo II*, Milan, pp. 441–70.

von Woess, F. (1911) *Das römische Erbrecht und die Erbanwärter*, Berlin.

Walbank, F.W. (1979) *A Historical Commentary on Polybius: III*, Oxford.

Wallace-Hadrill, A. (1981) 'Family and Inheritance in the Augustan Marriage Laws', *PCPhS 27*, 58–80.

Waltzing, J.-P. (1895) *Étude historique sur les corporations professionelles chez les Romains jusqu'à la chute de l'Empire d'occident*, Louvain.

Watson, A. (1961) '*Captivitas* and *matrimonium*', *TRG 29*, 243–59.

——(1965a) *The Law of Obligations in the Later Roman Republic*, Oxford.

——(1965b) 'The Divorce of Carvilius Ruga', *TRG 33*, 38–50.

——(1967) *The Law of Persons in the Later Roman Republic*, Oxford.

——(1968) *The Law of Property in the Later Roman Republic*, Oxford.

——(1971) *The Law of Succession in the Later Roman Republic*, Oxford.

——(1973–4) 'The Rescripts of the Empéror Probus 276–282 A.D.', *Tulane Law Review 48*, 1122–8.

(1974) '*Enuptio Gentis*', in Watson, A. (ed.) *Daube Noster*, Edinburgh, pp. 331–341.

——(1975) *Rome of the Twelve Tables: Persons and Property*, Princeton.

——(1977) *Society and Legal Change*, Edinburgh.

Watts, W.J. (1973) 'Ovid, the Law and Roman Society on Abortion', *AClass 16*, 89–101.

Weaver, P.R.C. (1964) 'Gaius i. 84 and the *Sc. Claudianum*', *CR 14*, 137–9.

——(1965) 'Irregular *nomina* of Imperial Freedmen', *CQ 15*, 323–6.

——(1967) 'Social Mobility in the Early Roman Empire: The Evidence of the Imperial Freedmen and Slaves', *P&P 37*, 3–20 (= Finley, M.I. (ed.) *Studies in Ancient Society* (1974) London, pp. 121–40).

——(1972) *Familia Caesaris: A Social Study of the Emperor's Freedmen and Slaves*, Cambridge.

Wenger, L. (1953) 'Juristische Literaturübersicht (bis 1943)', *APF 15*, 123–222.
Wesel, U. (1964) 'Über den Zusammenhang der *lex Furia, Voconia* und *Falcidia'*, *ZRG 81*, 308–16.
Westermann, W.L. (1924) 'The Castanet Dancers of Arsinoë', *JEA 10*, 134–44.
——(1955) *The Slave Systems of Greek and Roman Antiquity*, Philadelphia.
Wieling, H.J. (1972) *Testamentsauslegung im römischen Recht*, Munich.
Wilcken, U. (1906) 'Zu der genfer Papyri', *APF 3*, 368–79.
Williams, G. (1958) 'Some Aspects of Roman Marriage Ceremonies and Ideals', *JRS 48*, 16–29.
——(1968) *Tradition and Originality in Roman Poetry*, Oxford.
Wiseman, T.P. (1985) *Catullus and His World: A Reappraisal*, Cambridge.
Wolff, H.J. (1939a) *Written and Unwritten Marriages in Hellenistic and Postclassical Roman Law*, Haverford, Pennsylvania.
——(1939b) *'Trinoctium'*, *TRG 16*, 45–183.
Yaron, R. (1960) 'Minutiae on Roman Divorce', *TRG 28*, 1–12.
——(1963) *'Divortium inter absentes'*, *TRG 31*, 54–68.
——(1964) *'De divortio varia' TRG 32*, 533–57.
Zambon, A. (1935) *Didaskalikai'*, *Aegyptus 15*, 3–66.
Zulueta, F. de (1953) *The Institutes of Gaius: Part II, Commentary*, Oxford.

Index

abortion 158–9
actio
   de moribus 89, 122
   familiae erciscundae 108–9, 172
   iniuriarum 76
   rei uxoriae 107, 112
   rerum amotarum 77
actresses 32, 246–7
adoption 8–9, 144
adrogatio 8, 144
adultery 33, 46, 57–8, 123, 127–31
Aemilia, wife of elder Scipio
   (Africanus) 43, 100, 176
Aemilius Paullus, L. 101, 175
agnates 14, 19, 190–1
   tutorship of 14, 19–20; abolished
      by Claudius 20
alieni iuris 6, 9
anniculi probatio 223, 225
   see also Latins, Junian
Apuleius 50, 55
assault
   on slave 119
   on wife 76
   see also lex Aquilia
Atilius 7, 122
Aufidianus, Pontius 7, 121–2

Bacchanalia 6
bankers 235–6
barmaids 32
   see also waitresses
betrothal 45–7
bigamy 91–3
birth-registration 49, 144–6

Caesennia 22, 104
Calvina 97, 169–70
capitis deminutio 12, 17
captivity 25, 87–8, 228
Carvilius Ruga, Sp. 48–9, 83–4
Cato, the elder 72, 171
Cato, the youger (Minor) 41, 82
cautio Muciana 54–5
cessio tutoris 17
children 49, 51–4, 55, 137–61

exposure 155–8
guardianship of 146–54; *see also*
   tutors, women as
illegitimate 137, 143, 183, 197–200
legitimate 137, 142–4
of slaves 139–43, 206–18
paternity of 51–4, 142–3, 146
posthumous 51–4, 182–3, 187; and
   mother's estate 187, 193, 198
status of 138–42
substitution 52, 81
succession to mothers 187, 193,
   198–200; *see also*
      senatusconsultum Orphitianum,
      Tertullianum
   see also adoption, birth-
      registration, infanticide, *ius*
      liberorum
Cicero 41–2, 89–91
coemptio 8, 11–13, 17, 27n30, 167
   change of tutor 17
   fiduciae causa 17
   marriage; *see conventio in manum*
   will-making 12, 18, 167
cognates 193
concubinage 47, 56–60, 227
confarreatio 12, 84
constitutio Antoniniana 36, 143, 147
contracts
   apprenticeship 237
   entertainers' 246
   weavers' 237, 243, 254n15
   wetnurse 243–5
conubium 31–8, 223, 227–8
conventio in manum 13

Demetria 34–5
disinheritance 26, 55, 169
   unjust *see querela inofficiosi*
      testamenti
divorce 11, 52, 81–95, 260–1
   and Augustan legislation 52, 82,
      85–6
   and paternity of children 52, 81,
      142–3, 146
   causes of 81, 83, 88–91

in *manus*-marriage 83–4
moral attitudes to 82, 260–1
notice of 86
see also actio de moribus, adultery,
    captivity, marital fault
doctors, women as 240–1
Dolabella 41, 43, 91, 180
Domitia Lucilla 9, 18
donatio ante nuptias 47, 50
dos, dotis 97–116
    adventicia 105, 106–7, 110
    aestimatio 102–3
    collatio 109–11
    datio 100–1
    dictio 99
    permutatio 109
    profecticia 105–6, 110–11
    promissio 99–100
    see also dowry
dowry 18, 34, 47, 50, 71–2, 77, 97–116
    alienation of 103
    as patrimony 98, 109–11
    constitution of 98–101
    property of husband 97, 100, 102
    return of 71, 101, 103, 105–9, 112–
      14
    see also actio de moribus, actio rei
      uxoriae, dos, maintenance,
      retentio

emancipation from *potestas* 9, 14–15,
    24
    see also dotis collatio, parens
      manumissor, tutor legitimus
entertainers 245–8

familia 5–6, 8, 11, 13–14, 15–16, 76–7
    and property 13–14, 76
    defined 5–6
Fannia 90, 123
filiafamilias 5
    see also patria potestas
flamen Dialis 12, 24, 84
freedmen
    marriage with 32–3, 228–9
    succession to 194–6
    see also Latins, Junian
freedwomen 14, 16, 19–20, 32–3, 57,
    82–3, 86, 124, 167–8, 191–200
    passim, 222–9 *passim*, 238, 240,
    241, 247, 249–50
    as concubines 57, 124
    divorce from patron 86

    marriage 32–3, 226–9; and patrons
      226–9
    operae from 226–7
    succession to 194–6, 200
    see also ius liberorum, Latins,
      Junian, manumission

gens
    succession by 191–2
    tutela of 14, 192
gifts
    between fiancés 46–7
    between husband and wife 10, 47,
      68–9, 74–5
gladiators, women as 274–8

heirs 8, 196–70, 181–2, 190–1, 193

illiteracy 21, 28n68
incest 37–8, 125–7
incestum 23, 37–8
infamia 46, 52, 54, 77, 93, 129, 131,
    133, 221, 245, 247–8
    legal effects of 46
    penalty for adultery 129; bigamy
      93; breach of mourning 52, 54;
      pimping, prostitution 131, 133,
      221, 245, 247–8
infanticide 155, 161n39
institor 205, 238
intestacy and intestate succession 9,
    19, 23, 190–200
    between husband and wife 194
    in civil law 190–2
    praetor's rules on 192–4
    to freedwomen 9, 194–6, 200
    to Vestals 23
    to women 9, 19
    see also legitimi, liberi,
      senatusconsultum Orphitianum,
      Tertullianum
ius liberorum 20–1, 24, 83, 168, 194–
    8, 224, 234
    and freedwomen 83, 194–6, 224
    and *tutela* 20–1
    see also senatusconsultum
      Tertullianum, Velleianum
ius vitae necisque 6–7, 23, 155

Julia Primilla 140–1

Latins, Junian 32, 138–9, 223–4
    see also anniculi probatio

laudatio Turiae
   see 'Turia'
legacies 78, 178–81
   and Augustan legislation 78, 178–9
   see also lex Voconia
legal capacity 118, 233–7, 261–3
   see also senatusconsultum Velleianum
leges Juliae et Titiae 16
legitimi in intestate succession 192–3
lena, leno 86, 131–3, 207, 221
lenocinium 128, 131–3
leno-maritus 132
lex
   Aelia Sentia 32, 138–9, 144–5, 223, 225, 227; *see also anniculi probatio, conubium*
   Aquilia 119, 125, 220
   Atilia 16
   Canuleia 32
   Fabia 220
   Falcidia 170–1, 184
   Fufia Caninia 223
   Julia de adulteriis 7, 33, 37, 57, 93, 119, 127–32; and wife's *pater* 7, 129–30; applied to bigamy 93; *see also lenocinium, l.J. de fundo dotali, stuprum*
   Julia de fundo dotali 103
   Julia de maritandis ordinibus 20, 33, 50, 52, 57; *see also l.J. et Papia, l.Papia*
   Julia de vi publica 118–19
   Julia et Papia 20, 33, 54, 77–8, 86, 103, 133, 178, 194, 251; and marriage of senators 33; penalties under 54, 77–8, 178, 194; *see also probrosae*
   Junia 138–9, 223
   Minicia 138, 143, 223
   Papia Poppaea 20, 52, 144, 194–6, 224; and inheritance rights of patrons 194–6; and *ius liberorum* 20, 224
   Plautia de vi 119
   Voconia 55, 72, 78, 100, 170–7, 191; elder Cato on 72; purpose of 171–7
liberi 192–3
Livia Culicina 139–40

Maenius, P. 7, 122
magistracies, women in 67–8, 264

maintenance 68–71, 102
   and dowry 68
   legacies of 70–1
manumission 222–6
manus 11–14, 15, 18–19, 32, 45–6, 48
   avoidance of 13
   creation of 12, 48
   decline of 13, 15
   tutor's consent to 18, 32
   see also coemptio, confarreatio, usus, capitis deminutio
Marcia, wife of younger Cato 82
marital fault 88–91
marriage 10–11, 12, 31–80
   age of 38–41
   consent to 10, 18, 41–4
   formal procedures of 44–7
   proofs of 47–50
   soldiers' 34–5
   see also conubium
Married Women's Property Act, 1882 98, 113, 258
materfamilias 6
Messalina 63n53, 85
midwives 40
Mucius Scaevola, P. 104
Mucius Scaevola, Q. 71, 73
Murdia 55, 170

noxal surrender
   see pater

Otacilia Laterensis 73, 235–6

parens manumissor 15, 191
pater 5–17 *passim*, 23, 41–3, 45–6, 86
   consent to divorce 86; to marriage 10–11, 41–3; to *usus* 13
   noxal surrender by 7–8
   see also ius vitae necisque, parens manumissor, paterfamilias, patria potestas
paterfamilias 5–6, 24, 32
patria potestas 5–11, 17, 24–5, 42
patron 9, 14–16, 57, 82–3, 86, 194–6, 226–9, 238–9
   inheritance rights of 194–6
   married to freedwoman 57, 82–3, 86, 227–9
   see also freedwomen, *peculium*
peculium 9–10, 24, 226, 233–4
Petronia Justa 140, 224–5
Petronilla 53, 147, 183
Pliny, the younger 43–4, 97, 169–70, 265

postliminium see captivity
potestas see patria potestas
praesumptio Muciana 73
priesthoods 67–8, 264
probrosae 129, 133
probrum 122
    see also stuprum
property, separate 74–7, 83, 259–60
    see also actio rerum amotarum, gift,
        praesumptio Muciana
prostitutes 32, 118, 121, 124, 129–30,
    132–4, 134–5n15, 221–2, 246, 249,
    253
    dress of 129, 251–2
    prices charged 252
    registration of 130, 250–1, 253
    sexual offences and 118, 121, 124,
        246
    slaves as 221–2
    tax on 252–3
    waitresses as 32, 222, 249–50
    see also lena, leno
public life, women in 264
Publilia 89, 101
punishment 6–7, 87

querela inofficiosi testamenti 15, 55,
    183–90
    against father's will 183–5
    against mother's will 185–7
    remoteness of mother's claim 187–
        9

rape 118–21
remarriage
    of adulteress and ex-husband 58
    of widows 51–6; prescribed
        mourning interval 51–2, 53–4
    see also children, paternity of,
        turbatio sanguinis
res mancipi, nec mancipi 18
retentio
    propter impensas 104–5, 107, 113
    propter liberos 90, 112
    propter mores 90, 112
    propter res amotas 113
    propter res donatas 113
    see also dowry

sarcinatrix 10, 238
Sassia 35, 188
Scipio Aemilianus 100–1, 177
Scipio, elder (Africanus) 43, 100, 176

senatusconsultum
    Claudianum 59, 141–2
    Orphitianum 144, 193, 196, 198–200
    Plancianum 155–6
    Tertullianum 145, 146, 149, 151,
        193, 196–8
    see also tutors, women as
    Velleianum 75–6, 152, 234–5
sexual harassment 117–18, 129, 246
    edict on 117–18, 129
sexual offences 117–36
    see adultery, incest, *lenocinium,*
        prostitution, rape, sexual
        harassment, *stuprum*
Silius 63n53, 85
slaves 33, 118, 119, 139–42, 205–31,
    237–8
    abduction of 219–21
    children of 139–41, 206–13
    family relationships of 213–18
    runaway 219–21
    sexual use of 132, 141–2, 219–22
    theft of 219–20
social status of married woman 67–8
societas 236, 239
stuprum 37–8, 41, 58, 121–5
    and concubines 58
    in Republic 121–3
    offence in *lex Julia de adulteriis*
        123–4
    see also rape
sui heredes
    see heirs
sui iuris 5–6, 8, 10
    see also patria potestas

tabulae nuptiales 48, 50
Terentia 22, 41, 89, 101
textile-working trades 237–9
Titinius 90, 123
Tullia 9, 10, 38, 41–3, 89, 91, 101
    divorce 91
    marriage to Dolabella 41–3, 101
turbatio sanguinis 52–4
    see also remarriage
'Turia' 13, 14, 72, 82
    laudatio Turiae 13, 14, 72
tutela
    agnate 14
    impuberis 14
    legitima 15, 168
    mulieris 14–22
    see also ius liberorum, tutor
tutor, woman's 11, 13, 14–22, 24, 33,
    45–6, 166–9, 234

appointed by magistrates 16–17
change of 17
consent to marriage 18, 33
consent to will 18–19, 167–9
dativus 15
duties 17–18, 234
fiduciary 14–15, 17
legitimus 14–15, 17, 19, 21, 166–7,
    234; *see also parens*
    manumissor, patron
testamentary 20–1
see also ius liberorum
tutor, woman as 147–52

univira 23, 51
usus 12, 13–14, 19

Vestals 5, 22–6, 37
vilica 205

Visellius Varro, C. 73, 236

waitresses 32, 222, 249–50
weavers 10, 237–8, 243
wetnurses 157, 241–5
widows 15, 19, 51–7
    see also cautio Muciana,
      maintenance, remarriage
will 9, 11, 13–14, 16, 18–19, 24, 164–
    9, 179–90
breaking 181–90
forms of 164–5
right to make 165–9
tutor's consent to 8–19, 167–9
unduteous *see querela inofficiosi*
    testamenti
Vestal's 24
see also coemptio, heirs, *lex Voconia*